CONNECTING CALIFORNIA

SELECTIONS IN EARLY AMERICAN HISTORY   VOLUME I

First Edition

Edited by George Gastil and Bonnie M. Harris, Ph.D.
Grossmont College

San Diego, CA

Bassim Hamadeh, CEO and Publisher
Michael Simpson, Vice President of Acquisitions
Jamie Giganti, Managing Editor
Jess Busch, Graphic Design Supervisor
Seidy Cruz, Acquisitions Editor
Stephanie Sandler, Licensing Associate
Sarah Wheeler, Senior Project Editor

First published in the United States of America in 2013 by Cognella, Inc.

Trademark Notice: Product or corporate names may be trademarks or registered trademarks, and are used only for identification and explanation without intent to infringe.

15 14 13 12 11   1 2 3 4 5

Printed in the United States of America

ISBN: 978-1-60927-081-0 (ppk)

www.cognella.com 800.200.3908

Contents

Section V: Americanization of California: The Gold Rush Era, 1840–1850   173

Section VII: Connecting California to the Nation: War, Railroads, and Agribusiness, 1860s–1870s

Connecting California

Introduction to the Reader

Volume I of *Connecting California* will introduce you to a variety of topics in California history, from the prehistory era of the indigenous civilizations to California's agricultural revolution of the 1870s. This collection of documents is designed to enhance the study of California as part of a standard course in early American history. While there are many excellent textbooks available on United States history, we have noticed that books written for a national audience tend to neglect California.

Connecting California emphasizes **primary sources**. These are documents created by people who participated in or witnessed the events they are writing about. Notice the particular point of view of the person or persons who left these writings behind. Documents will reflect the time period that the author lived in, as well as biases related to factors such as their nationality or social status. Usually, primary sources were not written for us to read. They were written for some purpose relevant to the time period.

We have also included several **secondary sources**. In these cases, the authors did not participate in the events they write about. Because the writers were not involved in the events, they may be more objective. On the other hand, you may notice that every historian does have a point of view. Historians see the past from the perspective of the world they live in today.

The documents cover a wide range of topics, but essentially they can be understood in terms of three broad themes: culture, economy, and politics. These three themes are at the core of history, whether you are studying California, the United States, or any other society.

Culture refers to how a society views itself, its traditions, and forms of expression passed down through generations. Cultural history may include everything from religion and philosophy to art, music, crafts and cooking.

Economy refers to how people in a society make a living. Economic history includes agriculture, trade, banking, mining, and the development of industry. It also includes the history of workers and their work, from acorn grinding to computer programming.

Politics is all about how decisions are made in a society. Political history includes many of the topics most familiar to us in history books, such as monarchs, wars, treaties, and legislation. Politics includes the opinions of ordinary people as well as social activists and political leaders.

Section I of our reader will give insight into the cultural, economic, and political life of some of California's native peoples. **Section II** will discuss the European exploration of California that began in the 1500s and the interaction between native peoples and Europeans that continued into the early 1800s. **Section III** will cover the Mission Era, when the Spanish government was promoting the building of missions in California. **Section IV** deals with what historians call the Rancho Era in California, from the 1820s to the 1840s. During the Rancho Era, Mexico became an independent country. California became part of the United States in 1848, as part of a treaty ending the U.S. War with Mexico. **Section V** addresses changes that came with the Gold Rush and California's development as a new state in the Union. **Section VI** deals with the expansion of the Anglo American population in California and the decline of native cultures in this era. Finally, **Section VII** addresses the development of a complex modern economy in California in the 1860s and 1870s. In this era, California was connected to the rest of the United States by railway, allowing it to become the nation's most diverse agricultural producer.

The modern society we now call California may seem to be completely different from what we see in the 1870s, but actually, if you look closely, you will see a society not so different from today's. California has certainly changed in 140 years, and this will be the subject of Volume II. However, when you examine the changes that occurred between 1770 and 1870, you will likely see a much more fundamental transformation.

Some historians see the early history of California as laying a foundation for the modern state we know today. Others will tell you that they study topics in early California simply because it is another example of how humans have lived. Either way, we hope you find the history as fascinating as we do.

Section I

California's Native American Cultures

Section I

Introduction to California's Native American Cultures

Sources

The ancestors of today's Native Americans came to this continent in several stages about 30,000 to 12,000 years ago, during the last Ice Age. Various artifacts suggest that people came over a land bridge connecting Siberia and Alaska, in search of large animals such as the woolly mammoth and the giant sloth. Others could have come by boat, traveling from one island to another. As the Ice Age ended, the sea level began to rise, covering the land bridge between Asia and North America.

The evidence suggests that humans were living in North America for several thousand years before they found California. California is surrounded by mountains, deserts, and an ocean. One can only wonder what would motivate nomadic people to make the difficult journey to California. Eventually, California would support several hundred thousand people from a wide variety of indigenous cultures.

Long before the Europeans came, California was one of the most diverse societies on earth. Anthropologists actually see many distinct cultures, with vastly different languages. The languages spoken by California native peoples belong to various language families found in other parts of North America. California was essentially an island with a few thousand villages.

The documents give you a clue as to how these cultures thrived, how they made a living, and how they functioned politically. In truth, the evidence is often sketchy. Much of what we know is not actually from history, strictly speaking, but from anthropology. Anthropologists have observed indigenous cultures in recent times, in California and other parts of the world, and this helps us understand how cultures with similar characteristics would have functioned in earlier times.

Sources

Much of what we know comes from living Native Americans. Historian Malcolm Margolin has collected numerous stories, legends, and personal accounts from members of native cultures in various parts of California. The first three selections in this section are from Margolin's collection, *The Way We Lived: California Indian Stories, Songs, and Reminiscences*. When you are reading these selections, you are reading accounts from people in the twentieth century.

The stories and songs show a living culture, though the recollections do not tell us how that culture may have changed over a period of hundreds of years. We do get a sense of the richness and complexity of the cultures. We also can see how culture was passed down from generation to generation, through personal contact, rather than through written language or large institutions.

Malcolm Margolin collected stories from various cultures, three of which will be represented here. The first selection, "**The Creation**," comes from the Maidu culture of the Sierra Nevada region in northern California. The second, "**Learning to Hunt**," is from a member of the Kumeyaay culture that continues to thrive in the San Diego area and also across the border in Baja California. The third selection, "**A Man without Family**," is from the Pomo people from the northern coastal part of the state. Keep in mind, words like "Maidu," "Pomo" and "Kumeyaay" refer to broad cultural groupings. Many distinct groups exist within these categories.

What do we know about the political life of native Californians? How did they organize themselves and settle disputes? Some remarkable research on this topic has been conducted within the past few years. Randall Milliken studied a variety of documents about life in the San Francisco Bay region from the late 1700s and early 1800s, when tribal villages were in contact with Spanish missionaries or military personnel. In Selection 4, **Native American Societies in the San Francisco Bay Region**, Milliken pieces together a relatively coherent picture from a variety of accounts. Milliken notes that native people in the Bay Area lived in small units, of about 200–400 people. Each one of these groups had its own political system, or polity. Milliken also notes that these small, separate villages were actually connected through a network of intermarriage.

Villages were also connected by trade. Notice the importance of festivals, where one group would share a surplus of crops and the visiting groups would bring gifts of various kinds. Cultural traditions were also shared at the festivals.

More clues about native California cultures come from designs that people made in rock and sand. Gerald A. Smith and Wilson G. Turner explore some of these clues in Selection 5, **Indian Rock Art of Southern California**. Some rock art is ancient and possibly prehistoric, whereas other types are from relatively recent times. Often the designs are interpreted with help from observations of existing cultures that continue to do the art. We do not know if the art has the same meaning to people now that it did centuries ago; such observations can only provide an educated guess.

In Selection 6, **The Culture of the Wintu,** William R. Hildebrandt and Michael J. Darcangelo add a great deal to our understanding of native cultures with their study of one particular culture, the Wintu people of the northern Sacramento River Valley. The selection is from their remarkable study, *Life on the River: The Archaeology of an Ancient Native American Culture*. The Wintu traded with early European settlers, but they were outside of the area settled by Spanish missionaries. The Wintu culture continued to thrive, with minimal interference from outsiders, until the era of the California Gold Rush in the middle of the 1800s.

Hildebrandt and Darcangelo note that there were many triblets within the Wintu culture. Anthropologists use the term "triblet" to describe autonomous groups of native people in California. These groups were small compared to the "tribes" seen in many other parts of North America.

Kent Lightfoot and Otis Parrish approach the topic of hunting and gathering from an ecological perspective. In the Selection 7: **California Indians and their Environment: Harvesting En Masse**, notice how they use information about the land forms and biological diversity of California when they examine the practices of native cultures.

If men in native California were often known for their hunting skills, women in many cultures were perhaps most likely to be known for their basketry. Some of the most prolific basket makers lived among the Mono Paiute people in eastern California, near Mono Lake. In addition to storing food or carrying water, native peoples also used baskets for cooking and for carrying babies. In Selection 8, **The Basketry of the Mono**, C. Hart Merriam describes how the women used baskets in making acorn mush, a staple food of my California peoples. Merriam observed women cooking with baskets in the early twentieth century.

Observations from early European explorers provide much of what we know about the customs of native cultures. In Selection 9, **Early California Native Dress**, we see descriptions of what native people in various parts of California were wearing. The excerpt is based on accounts from Spanish travelers around the time the first missions were established. Accounts of clothing may seem superficial, but actually they contain many clues to help us understand the cultures and their environments.

If you have wondered how important trade was to native California cultures, you will get some great clues in Selection 10, **Trade Routes and Economic Exchange Among the Indians of California**. James Davis studied reports from various anthropologists in order to trace the economic interactions of culture groups in several different parts of California. What may seem like small items to us today must have been especially important to the people who traveled significant distances to get them. For example, the Diegueño, a part of the Kumeyaay culture group named for their proximity to Mission San Diego, supplied acorns to the Yuma and Mohave peoples who lived in desert areas far from any oak trees. The Mohave and Yuma people gave the Diegueño gourd seeds in return.

Davis also notes that many of the highways and major roads that we might take for granted in today's world actually started out as Indian trails. The footpaths of native traders were the starting point for much of today's amazing transportation infrastructure.

What was it like to grow up in one of these societies? In Selection 11, **Puberty and Initiation Rites Among California Native Cultures**, Marcia Herndon gives us a glimpse of ceremonies for boys and girls coming of age in various regions. Each society had a different type of ritual, but you will notice some common themes. Clearly the passage from childhood to adulthood was a major event in each of these cultures; not only for the young people involved but for the entire village.

Readings

1. The Creation

Edited by Malcolm Margolin

Primary Source

The Creation

Different Maidu communities seem to have had widely differing versions of how the world was made. There was no dogmatic orthodoxy, and the idea that war might be waged over matters of belief was simply ridiculous. "This is how we tell it; they tell it differently," is a sentence still heard in many Indian communities.

The version of the creation epic that follows begins with a vision of the world covered with water. A raft with two beings floats out from the north. A feathered rope drops from the sky, and Earth-Initiate climbs down into the raft. Who made the water, the raft, the trinity of Earth-Creators? Like many California creation epics, the Maidu account seems to begin in the middle the story. Mysteriously, elements of the world seem to have always been present, their existence apparently beyond question or speculation.

–Margolin

In the beginning there was no sun, no moon, no stars. All was dark and everywhere there was only water. A raft came floating on the water. It came from the north, and in it were two persons—Turtle and Pehe-ipe. The stream flowed very rapidly. Then from the sky a rope of feathers, called *Pokelma*, was let down, and down it came Earth-Initiate. When he reached the end of the rope, he tied it to the bow of the raft, and stepped in. His face was covered and was never seen, but his body shone like the sun. He sat down, and for a long time said nothing.

At last Turtle said, "Where do you come from?" and Earth Initiate answered, "I come from above." Then Turtle said, "Brother, can you not make for me some good dry land, so that I may sometimes come up out of the water?" Then he asked another

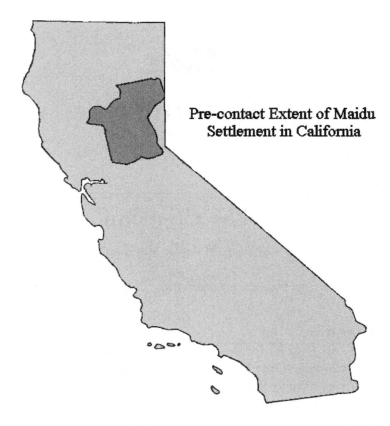

Pre-contact Extent of Maidu Settlement in California

time, "Are there going to be any people in the world?" Earth-Initiate thought awhile, and then said, "Yes." Turtle asked, "How long before you are going to make people?" Earth-Initiate replied, "I don't know. You want to have some dry land: well, how am I going to get any earth to make it of?" Turtle answered, "If you will tie a rock about my left arm, I'll dive for some." Earth-Initiate did as Turtle asked, and then, reaching around, took the end of a rope from somewhere, and tied it to Turtle. When Earth-Initiate came to the raft, there was no rope there: he just reached out and found one. Turtle said, "If the rope is not long enough, I'll jerk it once, and you must haul me up; if it is long enough, I'll give two jerks, and then you must pull me up quickly, as I shall have all the earth that I can carry." Just as Turtle went over the side of the boat, Pehe-ipe began to shout loudly.

Turtle was gone a long time. He was gone six years; and when he came up, he was covered with green slime, he had been down so long. When he reached the top of the water, the only earth he had was a very little under his nails: the rest had all washed away. Earth-Initiate took with his right hand a stone knife from under his left armpit, and carefully scraped the earth out from under Turtle's nails. He put the earth in the palm of his hand, and rolled it about till it was round; it was as large as a small pebble. He laid it on the stern of the raft. By and by he went to look at it: it had not grown at all. The third time that he went to look at it, it had grown so that it could not be spanned by the arms. The fourth time he looked, it was as big as the world, the raft was aground, and all around were mountains as far as he could see. The raft came ashore at Tadoiko, and the place can be seen today.

MAIDU

2. Learning to Hunt

Edited by Malcolm Margolin

Secondary Source

The name Kumeyaay has come to denote the people who have long occupied the desert area of extreme Southern California and the northern portions of Baja California. They are also sometimes known as the Diegueño—so called after Mission San Diego into which many of them were drawn over two centuries ago—or as the Tipai and Ipai, words meaning "person" in the two major dialects of the Kumeyaay language. The variety of names reflects, in part, the fact that while the Kumeyaay share a language and many other cultural characteristics, they are not a "tribe" in any political sense. Historically, they have consisted of some thirty independent, semi-nomadic clans. Some clans were traditional allies, others were enemies. Each clan generally wintered in its own sheltered valley, and as spring unfolded it followed the ripening plants higher and higher into the mountains, migrating back into the valley floors each fall.

While men and boys hunted as a matter of course, carelessness toward the animal world was severely disapproved of everywhere in California, especially among the Kumeyaay. Big game was relatively scarce in their arid environment, and a boy underwent a long and detailed training as a hunter. If he displayed proficiency and luck at hunting rodents, lizards, and other small game he would be taught to hunt rabbits. If successful at that he might eventually be trained to stalk deer and perhaps even mountain sheep. The hunting of big game animals fell under the close supervision of the clan's huntmaster, and was invested with considerable ritual and honor. ...

From his first fumbling efforts as a child to the time he became an accomplished hunter, the Kumeyaay youth was guided closely by tradition. For him—as for all California Indians—hunting was not a direct, primal confrontation between hunter and quarry. Rather the hunter throughout his life moved in a world complexly defined by ritual and custom.

The unmarried Kumeyaay hunter was warned against eating the game he killed lest he get worms and bring bad luck upon himself. But the taboo had broad and important social consequences as well. It meant that as the youth grew in skillfulness he would not become independent; instead he would continue to provide food for his family, while his own meat would be supplied by his father, uncles, and older brothers. In this way family ties were maintained and even strengthened during adolescence. Even after marriage, when the hunter was free to eat what he had killed, he would continue to share his game with family, repaying those who had fed him during *his apprenticeship and providing meat for younger brothers and nephews who were themselves just learning to hunt.*

When a man was in his prime he probably gave more than he received, but when he reached old age, unable to get about easily, his membership in the clan would provide him with the fruits of a nephew's or grandson's first hunting. It was membership in clan and family—rather than individual skills—that provided one with identity and security.
–Margolin

When I was a boy I always hunted with my father's younger brother. I remember when he first took me hunting. I had a small bow and arrows, little better than toys. My uncle told me to poke into a pack rat's nest with a long slick. I asked him instead to let me shoot when the rat sat outside, but he said, "No, you can't wound him." I insisted and shot, but the arrow failed to penetrate for lack of power. I cried and shuffled my feet in chagrin. My uncle told me that it was no use for me to try, anyway, because he would not let me eat it. "If you eat the rat, or anything you kill, you will have worms in your stomach." Up to the time I married I never ate what I killed. Others can eat the game, but a boy cannot eat his kill until he is adult. One who refrains is always lucky. When I was a grown boy, whenever I went to hunt, I killed several rabbits almost immediately.

—Jim McCarthy, Kumeyaay

3. A Man Without Family

Edited by Malcolm Margolin

Primary Source

What is man? A man is nothing. Without family he is of less importance than that bug crossing the trail, of less importance than spit or dung. At least they can be used to help poison a man.

A man must be with his family to amount to anything with us. If he had nobody else to help him, the first trouble he got into he would he killed by his enemies because there would be no relatives to help him fight the poison of the other group. No woman would marry him because her family would not let her marry a man with no family. He would he poorer than a newborn child; he would be poorer than a worm, and the family would not consider him worth anything. He would not bring renown or glory with him. He would not bring support of other relatives either.

The family is important. If a man has a large family and a profession and upbringing by a family that is known to produce good children, then he is somebody, and every family is willing to have him marry a woman of their group. It is the family that is important. …

The family was everything, and no man ever forgot that. Each person was nothing; but as a group, joined by blood, the individual knew that he would get the support of all his relatives if anything happened. He also knew that if he was a bad person the head man of his family would pay another tribe to kill him so that there would be no trouble afterward and so that he would not get the family into trouble all of the time. That is why we were good people.

POMO

CULTURE AREAS

S = Southern
C = Central
NW = Northwestern
NE = Northeastern
GB = Great Basin
CR = Colorado River

Map 1. California Tribal Territories and Culture Areas. Based on maps in Robert F. Heizer, ed., *California*, vol. 8 of William C. Sturtevant, ed., *Handbook of North American Indians*, and Robert F. Heizer and Albert B. Elsasser, *The Natural World of the California Indians*.

4. Native American Societies in the San Francisco Bay Region

By Randall Milliken

Secondary Source

Socio-Political Landscape

The lands around San Francisco Bay and the contiguous Coast Range valleys were occupied by scores of tiny tribes, each of which held territories some eight to twelve miles across. Within each tribal territory lived a number of intermarried families that comprised a small autonomous polity of some two hundred to four hundred people. Members of the local groups hosted dances, pooled their labor during specific short harvest periods, defended their territory, and resolved internal disputes under the leadership of a headman. There were no higher levels of government in the region. The tiny nations were involved with one another in ever-changing alliances and conflicts.

In some areas of California, the families of a tribe shared a single central village location for much of the year; however, Bay Area tribe members lived most of the year in a more dispersed pattern. The Ssalsons of the San Francisco Peninsula, for example, lived contemporaneously at the three villages of Aleitac, Altagmu, and Uturpe. The Huimens of the southern Marin Peninsula also had three key villages, Anamas, Livangeluà, and Naique, on or near Richardson Bay. The Saclan villages of Jussent and Gequigmu were within a few miles of one another in the East Bay hills.

Early Spanish explorers and missionaries occasionally identified male village or tribal group leaders, and bestowed upon them the title of capitan. Evidence is contradictory regarding the amount of power the captains held. Their actions in community coordination and dispute settlement were probably constrained by a myriad of unwritten rules governing action in various specific circumstances. In the partially monetized society of Central California, grievances could be redressed through payment of shell money. Captains seem to have held the role of overseer in dispute settlements:

> No crime is known for which the malefactor cannot atone with money. It seems to be the law however, that in case of murder the avenger of blood has his option between money and the murderer's life. But he does not seem to be allowed to wreak on him a personal and irresponsible vengeance. The chief takes the criminal and ties him to a tree, and then a number of persons shoot arrows into him at their leisure, thus putting him to death by slow torture (Powers 1877: 177).

However, a captain's ability to impose settlements seems to have been limited.

María Estudillo stated that Bay Area natives paid no attention to their captains in carrying out their interfamily feuds:

> In their pagan condition they take up the bow and arrow at the least offence

with one another; committing homicide with the greatest tranquility, without anyone giving the least reprimand, not even their own captains, whom they elect, or should I say retain, as the man they respect as the most valiant… Many of them make use of poisonous herbs to take the lives of those they hate. In this way the desire for vengeance, always the goal of the Indian, is satisfied (Estudillo [1809]).

Unfortunately, the Spaniards neither understood nor cared about the local rules absolving conflicts between the families within tribes, or the specific instances in which the captains would become involved in disputes. Nor is much known about women's power in tribal and intertribal politics. The following statement concerning female leaders on the Marin Peninsula is our only detailed information about this important aspect of social life:

There were two important female leaders. One (*hóypuh kulé(·)yih* or *hóypuh kul(·)éy·ih* 'woman chief') probably was more significant than data indicate. She handled the Acorn Dance, dominated the sünwele Dance, and was deeply involved in the Bird Cult. The second female leader (*máien*) was a genuinely key person: "*máien* bosses everyone, even *hóypuh*." Theoretically, she was head of the women's ceremonial house and *hóypuh* was head of the mixed dance house, "but *máien* did all the work." She bossed construction of a new dance house; had wood hauled for festivals; superintended preparation of fiesta food; sent out invitation sticks for dances and, in some cases, selected the performers (Kelly 1978:419).

Such dances were the key expression of community life, there is no question women wielded considerable influence in the community. Foreign relations between tribes took the form of trade, warfare, and marriage. Territorial disputes and wife-stealing were the most commonly cited reasons for intertribal hostility:

The land also provides them with an abundance of seeds and fruits … although the harvesting of them and their enjoyment is disputed with bow and arrow among these natives and their neighbors, who live almost constantly at war with each other (Fages [1775] 1937:70).

Most fights were individual ambushes or ritualized small group face-offs, but feuds sometimes grew into wholesale attempts to annihilate neighboring groups.

Despite their political divisions, the people of the Bay Area were tied together in a fabric of social and genetic relationships through intertribal marriages. Although most marriages took place between people from contiguous villages within the tribe (i.e., tribal endogamy), approximately ten percent of the adults in most villages had moved there from a neighboring tribe at the time of marriage (tribal exogamy). Such intertribal movement usually occurred between villages of adjacent groups that were only ten or twelve miles apart, although people occasionally moved to villages as far as twenty-five miles from their home.[1]

---

1   The missionaries at Mission San Francisco attempted to record the tribe of birth in the baptismal record entries of new adult neophytes. They were probably not always diligent about it, and therefore not always successful. However, enough newly baptized married couples were noted as being from different tribes for us to establish a

One foreign visitor to Mission San Jose, George von Langsdorff, mistakenly concluded that no intertribal marriages occurred at all:

> These people formerly lived in great enmity with each other … sparks of their ancient enmity still remain alive, and cannot be extinguished. For instance, the fathers never can prevail upon them to intermarry with each other; they will unite themselves only with those of their own tribe, and do not mingle in the society of the other tribes but with a certain kind of reserve (Langsdorff [1806] 1814: 195).

There is abundant evidence of premissionization intertribal marriage in the mission records. There is also evidence that it was used by families as a conflict resolution mechanism, a technique that has been common in the past throughout the world (Boehm 1984). In future chapters I will present evidence involving two specific cases in which conflicts between missionizing tribelets were settled with accompanying intermarriages (Ssalson-Yelamu and Luecha-Tuibun).

Langsdorff's misstatement does underscore an important point: long-distance intermarriage was limited in part because of the commitment people felt to their home territory and to their own way of doing things. The unfamiliar was disturbing and seemed dangerous. Intergroup marriages that did occur certainly gave the linked families enhanced positions in regional affairs.

Neighboring tribes were tied together by bonds of commerce and economic reciprocity as well as by bonds of intermarriage. One mechanism for sharing resources beyond the local tribal territory was the trade feast (Vayda 1967). Groups which found themselves with an over-abundance of some seasonally available resource invited neighboring groups to share in the harvest, and visiting groups reciprocated with gifts of shell beads. In addition to resource-specific trade feasts, tribes invited their neighbors to seasonal ceremonial dances. Trade feasts and regional dances reduced the chance that the people of one local valley might starve, while people just a few Valleys away would have to discard extra food.

Regional dances provided opportunities to visit old friends and relatives from neighboring groups, to share news, and to make new acquaintances. People traded basket materials, obsidian, feathers, shell beads, and other valuable commodities through gift exchanges. Intergroup feuds were supposed to be suspended at the dances, but old animosities sometimes surfaced. All in all, such "big times" strengthened regional economic ties and social bonds.

---

pattern of at least minimal intertribal marriage (Milliken [1983]).

5. Indian Rock Art of Southern California

By Gerald A. Smith and Wilson G. Turner

Secondary Source

Techniques

Four important basic methods of producing rock art have been noted in Southern California. These include petroglyphs, pictographs, rock alignments and ground paintings. Each method is summarized, even though the major portion of this publication relates to petroglyphs.

Petroglyphs include designs made on stone by carving, pecking, scratching, abrading, bruising, or any combination of these techniques. Petroglyphs are probably the most common form of rock art in North America, and certainly the most common form found in Southern California. Most of the petroglyphs appear to have been produced by the pecking technique. The pecking was done by striking the surface of a rock with some hard hammer stone, or for more precise control, by using a hammer stone to drive a stone gouge or chisel into a rock surface. Although many types of rocks bear testimony of having been used as drawing boards, those most frequently selected were sandstone, volcanic basalt, and granitic rocks. In the desert areas of Southern California, these rocks are subject to oxidization, which produces a discoloration on the surface, sometimes referred to as "desert varnish." The surface of the rock exposed to weather becomes much darker than the interior, and perhaps a little softer. It is easily crushed when struck with a hammer stone, which then exposes the lighter color of the rock's interior. In some cases designs engraved into the surface stand out in sharp contrast, giving a negative effect of light on dark. If we assume the rock had not darkened before some of the pecking was done, it is still true that any stone struck with a hammer produces a lighter spot at the point of impact. This is the result of tiny crystals in the rock being shattered by the impact, and this factor increases the negative contrast of light on dark of the petroglyph designs.

Pecking stones of basalt, quartzite, jasper and other hard materials are occasionally found near petroglyph sites. More important than the hammer stone used is the thought, time, patience and perseverance that the maker of the petroglyph used to achieve this type of rock art.

Carving into a rock to create a design was accomplished with any sharp flake of stone, such as obsidian, chalcedony, rhyolite, or jasper. This technique probably required more time than pecking.

More than 250,000 pre-historic rock art petroglyph drawings can be found at the Coso Rock Art National Historic Landmark in the Mojave Desert, located on 36,000 acres at Naval Air Weapons Station China Lake, California.

The grooves in sandstone and the intricate designs found on slabs of slate were apparently made by this technique, or by a combination of scratching and carving. Certain designs exhibit the use of the abrading technique which was accomplished by rubbing the rock with another stone to produce a smooth surface, such as is accomplished by rubbing and grinding the mano on the metate.

The greatest number of known petroglyphs in Southern California are on volcanic, basaltic rocks. Many of these have shiny blue-black surfaces. After the petroglyphs had been made on these rocks by crushing away the dark surface, the patina apparently started forming again, covering the design almost to the same degree as the unaltered surface. In such cases, the design can only be seen when oblique light shadows the engraved lines. Patination will be discussed more in the chapter on dating because the degree of patination may be some indication of the age of the petroglyph.

Different styles of petroglyphs have been categorized by various writers since Garrick Mallery's preliminary paper was published in the Fourth Annual Report (1882–1883) of the Bureau of Ethnology.

Researchers have recognized that some of the petroglyphs are representational (naturalistic), either realistic or conventionalized; some are abstract, either curvilinear or rectilinear, but having little likeness to objects known to us in nature; and some are just referred to as the pit-and-groove style. The same basic techniques of pecking, scratching, carving, abrading, bruising, or any combination of these used by man produced all types of petroglyphs.

Pictographs include any design developed by the use of color. Six basic colors were used in rock paintings found in Southern California. The frequency of use appears to be: first, some shade of red; followed by black, white, yellow; and least frequently, a shade of green or blue. Although most frequently only red designs are found, sometimes as many as four colors, such as red black, yellow and white, have been used at a single site. The red colors were made from iron oxide hematites or magnetites. Both the Paiutes and Cocopahs sometimes heated this ore to enrich the color, and it is probable that this technique was used in prehistoric times as well. The yellow color was obtained from limonite, which is another iron oxide. White pigments were obtained from gypsum, lime, diatomaceous earth, kaolin, talc, or possibly bird droppings. The gypsum may also have been heated to improve the color and usability. Black pigments were made from graphite, charcoal, hydrous oxide of manganese, or from a black earth resembling coal. Roasting or burning graphite reduces it to a fine, sooty, black powder. The green and blue pigments were probably derived from some of the copper ores of the desert area of Southern California. Paint pigments were standard trading items with the Indians of Southern California at the time of Spanish discovery.

The preparation of all pigments for use in rock paintings consisted first of grinding the mineral to a fine powder in a mortar or on a milling slab. Resin or gum, probably from pine trees, was ground also to a powder and added to the pigments. An oil base was obtained by grinding the seeds of the chilicothe plants, or perhaps by extracting grease or oil from animal products. The pigments were moistened and formed into balls for further use or carried in skin containers as a powder. It has already been noted that the Indians made great use of the pigments for body painting and for decorating other objects which they used, such as atlatl shafts, arrow shafts, etc. Water was probably mixed with the pigments for body painting. For more permanent rock paintings, resin, juice of the milkweed, oil from crushed seeds of chilicothe, animal oil, or even birds' eggs made a better binder. Such paint, with water added,

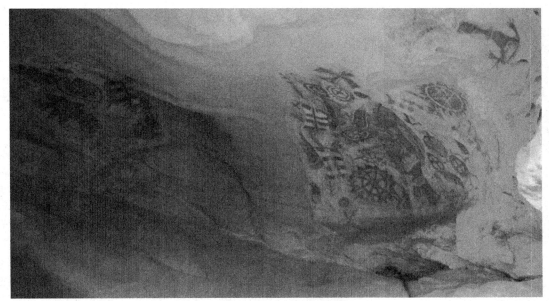

Chumash painted cave art in Santa Barbara, California.

applied to a hot granitic rock, penetrated into the rock with some lasting qualities. When the design was just drawn on a rock with a lump of the pigment, it tended to fade and disappear unless it was protected from the elements of nature. Paints were applied to rock surfaces by fingers or with a brush. The brush was made by shredding the end of a stick or the leaf of a yucca plant, or by using a piece of the hairy skin of some animals.

Like petroglyphs, pictographs vary greatly in artistic quality. Although the artist had a design in mind before he attempted to apply paint, he may or may not have had sufficient skill, patience or self-discipline to accomplish the desired result. Sometimes the rock artist selected the best possible rock surface for his paintings, but on other occasions he must have employed body contortions or climbing feats in order to create the rock art where it is located.

Ceilings and walls of rock shelters, cliff walls, and large conspicuous boulders were frequently selected. Many times, the works of previous rock artists were covered by more recent designs, making it difficult to trace individual designs.

Rock alignments, gravel pictographs, (or *intaglios*) and *grouped cobble-cairns* are placed together as a third method of producing rock art.

Intaglios were made by raking the gravel away, exposing the lighter-colored sand beneath, thus creating a design that stands out in sharp contrast, giving a negative effect of light on dark. A second technique may have been the movement of people in a concerted effort along a definite pattern, such as a circle, on damp desert pavement. The result provided a depressed area on the ground surface. As an example, various investigators have witnessed the Bushmen of the Kalahari Desert dancing in a circle for hours. The result of the dance left a depressed circular outline area several inches deep into the ground surface.

The most famous of the intaglios located in Southern California are the "Giant Figures" at Blythe. The largest anthropomorphic figure is 167 feet in length and can best he observed from the air. Groupings consist of a quadruped and a spiral in addition to the human figure. This site is listed as California Registered Landmark #101, and like all intaglios should be protected from vandalism. (see plates 13, 14, 19)

Coso rock art of bighorn sheep near China Lake, California.

The most expansive gravel-constructed design element reported in North America is the Needles "Mystic Maze" near the Topock bridge at the Colorado River. Controversy regarding the origin of this prehistoric creation has extended over a period of more than eighty years. Today three portions of the total design remain. Part of the "raked gravel" intaglio and the anthropomorphic figures have been destroyed by modern construction of the railroad and highway. (See plates 16, 17.)

Intaglios are found on both the Arizona and the California sides of the Colorado River. Plate #15 on the opposite page illustrates a portion of a design element located in Yuma County, Arizona, near Ripley.

The first written reference to intaglios may have been made by William P. Blake in 1853, while on a geological reconnaissance along the Colorado River.

In plate #18 an anthropomorphic figure can he seen near a well-worn trail on a gravel terrace above the Colorado River. Although the meaning of the intaglios is not now known, historic Indian groups made use of various design elements in sand paintings.

Various circular or elliptical designs are known in Southern California. As these appear much the same as the aboriginal trails of the area, it seems likely that they also were probably made by the feet of Indians as they tramped on desert pavement areas.

The best known intaglios occur on the terraces of the Colorado River. They are the "Giant Desert Figures" near Blythe and the "Mystic Maze" near Needles.

The "Giant Desert Figures" near Blythe, California, are located in Township 4 South, Range 23 East, on typical gravel-covered terraces of the Colorado River.

The surface gravels of the terraces have a dark mahogany-like luster on the exposed upper surface, commonly called "desert varnish." The intaglios, consisting of various designs of which the human, quadruped, and spiral are most easily recognized, have been the subject of considerable interest for the past forty years. Some of the designs are more than 160 feet long and can only be appreciated when viewed from the air.

The intaglios were made by removing the surface gravel to reveal the almost pebble-free sand immediately underlying, thus leaving the design a few inches below the normal ground surface. Some of the figures are outlined by ridges formed by scraping out the surface gravels. The "Mystic Maze" at Topock, near Needles, California, consists of parallel windrows about eight inches in height with an average spacing between ridges of cobble and gravels of about five feet. The whole design covers a land surface of about twenty acres.

Rock alignments occur throughout Southern California, and may be divided into two groups: gravel or rock cairns, and true rock alignments.

Gravel or rock cairns, arranged in groups or single, isolated piles, occur in various locations in Southern California. These are frequently associated with rock alignments as are also the tramped earth circular depressions. The rock cairns may be from two to fifteen feet in diameter and vary from a few inches to three feet or more in height.

True rock alignments were constructed by placing rows of stones in lines to form designs on the ground surface. Some of these designs are nearly 500 feet in length and may extend from flat land surface over hills or ridges. The stones selected to form the design vary greatly in size. Some are only small, fist size: others are so large that they would require the strength of more than one man to carry one of them any distance. Many times it appears that the ground surface has been cleared of all other large stones, so the designs stand out clearly. Other times the terminus of a rock alignment is a rock cairn or a circle of rocks.

The fourth type of rock art includes all ground paintings. This is the most fragile type of rock art. The use of ground paintings has been well documented by early writers of Southern California and the Southwest. The Cocopah Indians practiced ground painting and also employed a technique of raked gravel construction similar to that used in making intaglios. The Yuma, Cahuilla, Fernandeño, Cupeño, Juaneño, Luiseño, Diegueño and the Akiwa ala of Baja, California, all made some use of ground paintings. Many other groups in various parts of North and South America also made ground paintings, using various colors of earth pigments. A few references to the Southern California Indian groups will illustrate how significant this fragile type of rock art may have been approximately 200 years ago.

The Yuma shamans made ground paintings, drew marks on the ground, constructed small mounds of earth, and made circles on the ground to aid in healing a man suffering from wounds.

The Fernandeño made a four-sided ground painting. The shaman stood in the middle of this, holding twelve radiating strings, with twelve assistants each holding the end of one string at the outer edge of the ground painting. When the shaman shook the strings, the earth quaked and the enemy he had in mind became sick.

The Cupeño made circular ground paintings about twelve feet in diameter. Three holes were made in the center of the circle with the middle one representing the heart of the universe. On each side of the circle were the figures of the twin creators, Mukat and Tumaiyowit. It is believed that Mukat was on one side of the circle while Tumaiyowit was on the other side. Each figure had a walking stick and a pipe.

For the boys' initiation ceremony, the Juaneño made a ground painting which included a design of an animal.

The Cahuilla made use of ground paintings for both the boys' and girls' initiation ceremonies. Red, black and white colors were used, and designs depicting the celestial bodies, animals, birds, and the world were all constructed.

The Diegueño made circular ground paintings, fifteen to eighteen feet in diameter, which encompassed celestial bodies, animals, and geographical features. They also made anthropomorphic ground pictographs with cordage made from local plants.

The Luiseño employed ground paintings for both boys' and girls' initiation ceremonies. The circular ground painting for boys was divided into quarters, with a central hole from twelve to fifteen feet in diameter dug into the earth about two feet in depth. The ground paintings for girls

A prehistoric petroglyph near Hemet, Riverside County, California.

employed concentric circles around the exterior, with designs of plants, celestial bodies, animals, and anthropomorphic characters included within the circle. Rock paintings also were an important part of the Luiseño girls' puberty ceremonies.

It is interesting to note that the range of figures reported for ground paintings include anthropomorphic figures, quadrupeds, maltese crosses, circles and spirals. All of these are easily identifiable designs of the intaglios, rock alignments, petroglyphs, and pictographs. Because of their fragile nature, none of the ground paintings are now known to exist.

6. The Culture of the Wintu

By William R. Hildebrandt and Michael J. Darcangelo

Secondary Source

… The Wintu lived in the Upper Sacramento Valley for at least one thousand years before encountering Europeans. At first the contact was sporadic, limited to a few visits by early Spanish explorers, such as Luis Antonio Argüello in 1821. Early diaries associated with these trips provide little detailed information about the local area but they all emphasize the presence of numerous Indian villages in the region.

Wintu Social Organization

Unlike many hunter-gatherer groups, which often have egalitarian social organization, the Wintu were socially stratified, with both rich and poor people living within each tribelet. Items of wealth were clearly recognized, and bows and arrows, elk-skin armor, clamshell disk bead money, and the skins of animals like bear and otters were considered valuable by almost all of the people interviewed by Du Bois. Clam disk money probably originated in Bodega and Tomales Bays, and was considered men's currency (women typically traded in basketry). The value of certain objects was measured using clam disk beads: large fishing nets were 1,000 beads, elk hides 800 beads, large storage baskets 150 beads, bow and arrows 50 beads, and deer hides 20 beads.

Wintu Chiefs

Each tribelet had a chief or headman who lived in one of the largest villages. The chiefs tended to be the wealthiest people in the community, and this prosperity was manifested by their having many wives, along with numerous strings of bead money, elk-skin armor, and other items listed above. This role was usually passed down from father to son, unless the son lacked the skills necessary for the job, in which case some other male relative would be given the position. The duties of the chief were many, including settling disputes, organizing large gatherings, and waging war. He was expected to be democratic and dignified, to have the ability to talk to everybody, and to speak well at large gatherings.

Disputes among members of the group often stemmed from criminal behavior. Murder sometimes demanded blood revenge, but the chief could often negotiate a payment to the grieving family and avoid capital punishment. Problems stemming from thievery could often be solved by returning the stolen item, but the chief was ultimately responsible for assigning a price for the unsanctioned behavior of the guilty party. Finally, habitual troublemakers could be, with the authorization of the chief, soundly beaten by the group. On rare occasions, people were killed if they refused to change their behavior.

Another of the chief's duties was to organize large dances and other social gatherings, an important part of Wintu life. Before a big event, runners were sent to outlying villages to invite the guests and tell them what to bring. The events were often organized around times of food surpluses, like big pine nut harvests and salmon runs. Some people had to travel as many as two days to reach a celebration, and each community did its best to bring plenty of food and a variety of trade goods, both being measures of prestige. Sometimes two to three hundred people would come to these "Big Times," where the feasting, dancing, and gambling would last from three to five days. Gambling contests were a popular activity, with fortunes of shell money and other valuables changing hands on a regular basis.

Shamans

Shamanic doctors were also important members of the social group, and the position was open to both men and women. Initiation ceremonies took place in an earthen lodge, where the initiates would dance through the night until they received the supernatural spiritual power. Every shaman was expected to be a good singer and possess several doctoring songs linked to his or her special spirits. Doctoring often began with the smoking of wild tobacco to help bring on the spirit helper through a trance, after which the sickness was usually sucked out of the body. Equally important to doctoring was shamanistic prophesy, which also took place during a tobacco-induced trance. Prophesies covered a wide range

Image of a Wintu woman pounding acorns, c. 1850, near Lassin's Rancheria, which neighbored Johnson's ranch, 50 miles from Sacramento City, west side of the Sacramento River going up the valley.

of subjects, including predictions about the location of game and the success of hunting trips, the future health of certain individuals, and upcoming weather. Although intended to cure and heal, some shamans were known to have "poisoned," sending sickness to their rivals and enemies.

Marriage

Intervillage gatherings also served as places to meet potential husbands and wives, especially for people from smaller outlying villages. Although there was no formal bride price, sometimes gifts like shell beads, baskets or deer hides were exchanged between families when a match was made.

As long as a man and woman were living together they were expected to be faithful to one another. Divorce was easy and occurred relatively often, as incompatibility and adultery were sufficient grounds for separation. Monogamy was customary but polygamy was permitted, particularly among rich men. Wealthy chiefs could have between two and twelve wives, a factor that helped increase their standing because the women produced food surpluses that could be used as commodities or exchange. Sisters or other related women often formed the multi-wife households.

Post-marriage residence could be either patrilocal or matrilocal (in the village of the husband's or wife's family), but newlyweds were encouraged to establish their own individual households. A mother-in-law taboo was in force, stipulating that a man was not permitted to deal directly with his wife's mother; he was expected to keep his distance and treat her with a great deal of respect. If these restrictions were violated, it was said that the man was liable to be torn apart by a grizzly bear.

7. California Indians and Their Environment

Harvesting En Masse

By Kent G. Lightfoot and Otis Parrish

Secondary Source

A common economic activity of Native Californians was the bulk or mass collection of important resources when seasonally available. We argue that this activity was facilitated by pyrodiverse landscapes. The creation or augmentation of distinctive patches containing dense concentrations of plant and animal resources in the same stages of succession allowed people to bulk-collect food resources, medicinal supplies, and raw materials. This activity might be casually structured among family members and friends, or it might involve a larger, more structured communal organization.

California Indians went to the trouble to gather food and nonfood resources en masse for three primary reasons: to provide fresh food for meals, to support community gatherings, and to stockpile resources for later or winter use. The recent overview of Native Californian culinary practices by Ira Jacknis (2004) provides an ideal source to learn about Indian foods. Some foods were eaten fresh, while others involved considerable processing and cooking. The basic methods for cooking vegetable foods in Native California included parching in baskets, roasting in coals, simmering or boiling in soups and gruels in cooking baskets or steatite/ceramic vessels, and slow-roasting in earth ovens or pit-hearths.

Indian cooks built earth ovens by excavating pits, lining the bottoms with flat rocks that had been fire-heated (providing a critical heat reservoir), and then placing food items on these rocks in layers sandwiched between a protective lining,

such as wild grape leaves. The cooks covered each pit or oven with dirt. They sometimes built a fire over the oven, which they left to burn for several hours or overnight until removal of the succulent food. Earth ovens allowed people to process large quantities of food at one time—enough to feed several families or even an entire community. Pit-baking also provided an essential way of making insulin-rich plants, such as tubers and root crops, digestible and sweet to the taste. Indian chefs also slow-roasted fatty meats in underground ovens, although the more common methods for cooking meats involved broiling on hot coals, seasoning soups and gruels in cooking baskets, or roasting on fire-reddened stones.

A second goal for gathering en masse was to provide vegetables, meats, and craft goods for important community gatherings. Significant quantities of food would be harvested in preparation for multiday feasts, ceremonies, and dances to which people from surrounding communities might be invited. The prestige and social standing of local leaders, leading families, and entire communities were often measured by their generosity during such intercommunity festivals.

The third, and most important, goal for mass harvests was to stockpile food and nonfood resources for later use, especially during winter and early spring months when resource productivity was at its lowest and when inclement weather made it a perfect time for people to stay snugly in warm houses producing and maintaining cordage, baskets, tools, and craft goods. The storage

Rafael, a Chumash who shared California Native American cultural knowledge with anthropologists in the 1800s.

of bulk-harvested foods provided a significant strategy for "overwintering" in Native California.

The bulk harvesting of plant foods typically involved people traveling to specific resource patches to collect large quantities of nut crops, grass seeds, fruits, or roots and tubers when they became ripe. Long poles and climbers knocked nuts to the ground, where harvesters quickly gathered them into burden baskets or woven bags. The gatherers employed seed beaters—fine-mesh baskets shaped like scoops—to knock ripe seeds from plants and into burden baskets on their backs. They picked berries by hand. Fire-hardened, sharpened digging sticks served as ideal implements for exposing roots and tubers. California Indians depended on a variety of sturdy, lightweight baskets to transport and store plant foods in bulk. In some cases, transportation of heavy loads was facilitated by water travel. Local groups employed dugout canoes, tule balsas, and other forms of indigenous watercraft to move across many of the navigable streams,

rivers, and lakes across the state. They used plank canoes (*tomols*) and dugouts to venture into ocean waters in some coastal areas, transporting people, foods raw materials, and cultural objects back and forth between offshore islands and mainland settlement.

Mass collecting of animal foods also took place across Native California. People harvested fishes in rivers and lakes by means of a variety of methods: fish poisons (employed to stupefy prey in fishing holes), hook and line, fish spears, dip nets, and gill nets. But the most effective methods for capturing large numbers of fishes involved seine nets and fish weirs. Long seine nets could be stretched across streams or portions of lakes, often with the help of watercraft, and then men, women, and children could drive hundreds of fishes into the nets, where they would be easily captured in shallow water. Fish weirs or fences built across stream channels yielded many hundreds of kilograms of salmon (*Oncorhynchus* spp.), Pacific Lampreys (*Lampetra tridentate*), Steelheads (O. *mykiss irideus*), and Sacramento Suckers (*Catostomus occidentalis*) during annual spawning. Although the architectural design, materials employed, and size of the weirs varied greatly in Native California, the basic concept was the same. Periodic openings in the fence would allow swarms of fishes to enter basket traps or shallow corrals where they could be easily captured.

In thinking about hunting in Native California, most of us today conjure up images of the lone Indian in an animal disguise stalking a deer (or other large game), hoping to get close enough to let loose a deadly arrow or two. But Native groups probably obtained much of their game from other kinds of mass collecting methods. Ethnohistoric writings and ethnographic observations describe a wide range of traps, snares, nets, and fences for hunting both large and small game. Communal hunts involved deer or antelope drives, where Indians skillfully chased animals past blinds where carefully camouflaged hunters bided their time. Or they would drive Mule Deer (*Odocoileus hemionus*), Pronghorn (*Antilocapra americana*), or other game along fences of cordage, brush, or rocks into dead-end corrals where other hunters waited to greet the animals. Some of these fences were structurally analogous to fish weirs in that they contained periodic openings where deer (or other animals) could escape, only to meet lethal snares. The hunters commonly employed fire in these communal drives—they set fires to force animals over cliffs, or they encircled the beasts with fire on hilltops, forcing the game into confined spaces where they could be easily dispatched using clubs or arrows.

California Indians harvested large numbers of rabbits (Leporidae), quails (Odontophoridae), Band-tailed Pigeons (*Patagioenas fasciata*), and other small game in communal hunts. People beat the bushes to force the animals to follow carefully constructed fences with periodic openings containing snares or traps. Rabbits were also driven into long nets, some stretching a hundred or more meters in length, where hunters waited to dispatch the entangled animals. Indians utilized nets of various sizes and configurations to capture waterfowl from lakes and rivers. Some hunters used fire at night to attract birds that could be caught in nets erected on canoes. In other cases, they strategically placed decoys at the bottom of traps to attract birds that could be entangled in nets. Decoys were also placed near hunters waiting patiently in tule blinds. Some hunters were armed with specially constructed wooden projectile points that allowed the entire arrow to skim across the water, greatly increasing the chances of striking ducks (*Anatidae*) that were taking flight.

California Indians also participated in the mass gathering of insects. After smoking out adult yellow jackets (*Vespula* spp. and *Dolkhovespula* spp.), hunters removed the nests and roasted them over a fire. They ate the cooked larvae or dried them for storage. Indians hunted grasshoppers (*Caelifera*) and crickets (*Anabrus* spp.) en masse with the aid of fire, collecting the scorched insects for immediate consumption or preparing them for storage. Ugan (2005) shows that while the mass collection of small game such as rabbits and quail is rather labor intensive because of the time involved in processing multiple small food items, the return rates for hunting and processing grasshoppers can be quite high, even better than for hunting Mule Deer or Pronghorn (for crickets, see also Sutton 1988).

Coastal areas provided additional opportunities for the bulk harvesting of marine foods. Shellfish could be harvested in large numbers. For example, mussels (*Mytiluss* spp.) could be systematically stripped from intertidal rocks. Smelt (*Osmeridae*) swarms along California beaches during the summer months allowed people to harvest many hundreds of kilograms of fishes using dip nets. Nearshore fishes, such as rockfishes (*Sebastes* spp.) and surfperches (*Embiotocidae*), were taken in large numbers with fishing lines or nets. Ocean-going canoes searched for schooling fishes (anchovies [*Engraulididae*], Chub Mackerel [*Scomber japonicus*], etc.) that could be harvested with nets. The coast, offshore rookeries, and nearby waters offered the promise of hunting immature cormorants (*Phalacrocorax* spp.) and other species of pelagic birds, as well as porpoises (*Delphinidae*), Sea Otters (*Enhydra lutris*), Harbor Seals (*Phoca vintulina*), Northern Fur Seals (*Callorhinus ursinus*), Guadalupe Fur Seals (*Arctocephalus townsendi*), California Sea Lionas (*Zalophus californianus*), Steller Sea Lions (*Eumetopias jubatus*), and beached Gray Whales (*Eschrichtius robustus*). Kelp (*Laminariales*) and seaweeds (*Porphyra* spp.), especially after storms, could also be gathered in large quantities off the beach and dried for storage.

8. The Basketry of the Mono, 1955

By C. Hart Merriam

Primary Source

The Mono Paiute near the ranches now do most of their cooking in frying-pans and tin or iron pails and kettles. At the same time they cook certain things, particularly acorn mush and pine-nut soup, in baskets, and those living farther away appear to do most of their cooking in this aboriginal fashion.

Near the northwest corner of Mono Lake I once watched two squaws cook acorn mush for a band of about twenty Indians. The acorns had been first reduced to meal by hammering with stone pestles in deeply worn mortar pits dug out of the solid rock and had been sifted in the winnowing baskets by an adroit motion which separates the fine from the coarse—a motion the novice can never get. It was then "leached" to take away the bitter taste. This was done by allowing water to filter through it in a primitive but ingenious way. The place selected was a dry sandy knoll. Here a shallow hole a foot deep and four or five feet in diameter was dug and lined with two pieces of cloth, laid over one another at right angles. The meal was placed on the cloth and large basketfuls of water were laboriously brought from a neighboring stream, carried up the hill, and poured over the meal, which was patted by the hands until thoroughly wet. The water sank through into the porous sand and was replaced by fresh basketfuls until, after repeated tastings, the women found the bitterness sufficiently washed out. The meal was then scraped together by the hands and heaped up in irregular masses; part was at once put into a large basket to cook; the remainder was afterwards made into cakes for future use and laid in the sun to dry.

The cooking basket was filled a little more than half full of water and placed near the fire. Then four hot stones, six or eight inches in diameter, were taken out of the fire by means of two sticks and dropped into the basket. Almost immediately the water began to boil and the mush to thicken. During the twenty minutes or half-hour required for the cooking one of the squaws stirred it slowly with a stick, apparently to prevent the stones from resting on one spot long enough to burn the basket. The stuff boiled exactly like porridge, throwing up multitudes of miniature volcanoes and spluttering

Mono Lake Paiute basketmaker Carrie McGowan Bethel, c. 1929.

as if over hot coals. When it was done, the second squaw filled two small bowl-shaped baskets with water to receive and rinse the hot stones, which the first squaw fished out with a flat stick. Quickly and dexterously the old squaw washed off the adhering mush before the water got too hot for her hands and tossed the stones back into the fire. The contents of the small baskets, which had now become thin porridge, were then poured into the thicker mush in the big basket and stirred, giving the whole the desired consistency. This completed the operation.

On cooling, the acorn mush jellies; and if put in a moderately cool place, it keeps for some days. Its color is drab or drab pink, and it has no particular taste when fresh. It always seemed to me that a little salt and a good deal of cream and sugar would improve it mightily. Still, it is eaten without seasoning or sweetening and with evident relish. In summer, if kept too long, it ferments and gives off a sour liquid of a disagreeable odor. Among the Mono Paiute it is not an everyday food but a luxury, for the reason that they have to go so far to obtain the acorns; but it is today the staple food of numerous tribes in northwestern California, of Indians of the west flank of the Sierra, and of many of the Luiseño and other "Mission" tribes in the southern part of the state.

Most of the utensils of the Mono Paiute, including dishes, water bottles, and vessels for cooking, are baskets made by their own hands, as of old. (Cf. pls. 28, *a*, 29, *b*.) These baskets may be classed by forms or uses into a dozen categories: cradles or papoose baskets, large cornucopia-shaped burden baskets, snowshoe-shaped winnowing baskets, scoop-shaped winnowing baskets, spoon-shaped baskets with handles for collecting pine nuts, deep bowl-shaped baskets for cooking; individual mush bowls; ribbed trinket baskets; jugs and bottles for holding and carrying water, deep cylindrical baskets for collecting worms; small flat, oval seed paddles, with a handle, for knocking seeds off standing plants; and small conical baskets worn by

the squaws as hats (cf. pl. 47, *e*), and also used for gathering berries and fruit.

Some of the baskets are plain; others ornamented with intricate, striking, and beautiful designs, woven in black and red. The black is the split root of the brake-fern (*Pteris*), the red the inner bark of the redbud (*Cercis*). Besides these, some of the coarser baskets, particularly the large conical ones for carrying burdens, are ornamented by simply leaving the bark on some of the willow strands of which they are composed.

The best and finest of the Mono Paiute baskets are those made for cooking. They may be large or small, with straight-flaring or rounded sides, but all have flat bottoms and all are of what Professor Mason calls the "three-rod foundation" type. This class includes the ceremonial baskets—the most sacred and precious possessions of the tribe. The designs on these are symbolic, but their meaning is exceedingly difficult to ascertain. At one time I thought the ceremonial baskets should be put in a class by themselves, but the difficulty of discriminating between some of them and some of the ordinary cooking baskets is so great that no hard and fast line can be drawn. The ceremonial baskets are used for cooking acorn meal at certain ceremonial feasts, and are now sometimes used also for cooking the ordinary pine-nut soup—a sign of the waning respect for aboriginal rites.

These water bottles (o-sa, o-sa-ha) are of various shapes and sizes; they hold from half a gallon to twelve or fifteen gallons each. The larger ones are for camp use only, being much too heavy, when full of water, to be carried on horseback. They are always broad and spindle-shaped, a form beautifully adapted for use when lying on the ground. The lower or bottom part is much longer than the upper, which is given off at such an angle that, when one side rests flat on the ground, the mouth is thrown upward so far that the bottle can be filled nearly full without spilling. If the point the bottom is sunk just a little in the sand, it will lie on its side

Baskets created by Carrie McGowan Bethel

quite full without letting any water escape. But this is by no means the only advantage of the spindle shape, for when the basket is full, the weight is delicately adjusted (the broad middle part acting as a fulcrum) that the slightest pressure on the mouth is sufficient to tilt it down enough to let the water flow out—a most convenient arrangement for filling other receptacles and also for drinking when one is reclining on the ground. On the desert at the east end of Mono Lake I have seen a baby crawl to one of these bottles, take the mouth in its mouth, tilt it down and drink its fill, without touching a hand to the bottle. When let go, the bottle immediately tipped back to its former position without the loss of a drop. A more simple, efficient, and ingenious device would be hard to find.

Other kinds of bottles, convenient for use on horseback or for other purposes, are of relatively small size, rarely holding more than two or three gallons. All Paiute water bottles are woven of split willow strands in a thin sheet of diagonal twined weave; they are light, strong, and elastic but will not hold water until coated with the resin or pitch of the piñon pine put on hot, which sinks into the innumerable interspaces and thus adheres on the inside, rendering the bottles continuously

waterproof, even in the arid atmosphere of the desert. They are provided with two small loops or ears of horsehair or plant fiber, firmly woven in on one side, to which the carrying rope is attached. This point of attachment is selected with reference to the center of gravity when the bottle is full and also to the way they are to be supported. In the spindle-shaped bottles they are woven into the swollen middle part; in the tall, jug-shaped bottles they are placed above the middle.

The big camp bottles, when full, are exceedingly heavy. In carrying them the body is inclined forward so as to distribute the weight over the back, and they are kept from slipping down by a broad band which passes over the forehead. I have seen a squaw, who had taken one to a small stream to fill, find herself unable to lift it in position alone; but when assisted, and once the heavy burden was in place, she walked slowly off with it and climbed the hill to her camp, perhaps an eighth of a mile distant. In summer they are usually tucked into the brush at one corner of the wickiup, sheltered from the direct rays of the sun.

The burden baskets (wo-na and ka-wona) are huge conical baskets or cornucopias, three or four feet in length and one and a half or two feet in

"A Lake Mono Native American Woman basket-maker" by Edward Curtis, photographer, circa 1924.

diameter. Like the papoose baskets, they are carried on the back by means of a band which passes over the forehead. They vary in size, diameter, and fineness of weave according to the uses for which they are intended. Those made for carrying fuel, roots, and other light articles are large, coarsely and openly woven, and have broadly open mouths. They are called wo-na, Those intended for grass seeds and other seeds of small size, called ka-wona, are smaller and narrower, are woven closely of fine materials, and are usually somewhat ornamented.

The papoose baskets are of the usual Paiute pattern, of openwork, with flat backs and with arched tops to shade the baby's head. When traveling, the squaws carry them on their backs; when at rest, they stand them up in their wickiups or lean them against a sagebrush bush.

Winnowing baskets (té-ma) are large, flat, broadly subtriangular or showshoe-shaped baskets, more or less concave or scooped and nearly always ornamented by one or more bands, sometimes with rather elaborate designs. They are of two principal types: slightly concave, deepest in the middle or deeply concave, deeply scooped at or near the big end. They have many uses, such as winnowing grain and seeds, sifting meal made from acorns and nuts of the nut pine, separating the fine meal from the coarse, winnowing fly larvae so that the skins are blown away leaving the meat or kernels, and so on. The women become exceedingly skillful in their use and it is interesting to watch them work. The large té-mas, deeply scooped near the broad end, are used for winnowing grain and other heavy seeds, which are tossed up to allow the wind to carry off the chaff.

The shallow winnowing baskets are of two kinds, compactly woven and openly woven. The openly woven ones are used for roasting pine nuts. Coals from the fire and a quantity or the nuts are thrown into the basket and it is adroitly agitated, something after the manner of a popcorn shaker until the nuts are sufficiently roasted. This blackens the interior but does not seem to burn it injuriously. The compactly woven ones are used for separating the fine meal from the coarse after the acorns or pine nuts have been pounded in stone mortars. The movement is graceful and very skillful. …

Plate I: The Indians (Los Indios) 1769–1770

Men:

Skin: Dull, lusterless, reddish-brown or brownish-black; smeared with charcoal, soot, the juice from the black nightshade; yellow from roots of certain plants; red or white; some tattooed; color and tattooing depending on the tribe.

Hair: Black, straight, coarse, thick; sometimes cut or burned irregularly across forehead above level of eyebrows, rest falling to shoulders and sometimes to waist; twisted about the head, where it was kept in place by bands or nets of agave thread, when fighting or hunting; tufts of feathers from eagles, sea-gulls, and other birds stuck in the back or on top of the head, kept in place by coral or bone ornaments and pins; at times packed with clay to make it glossy.

Belt: Woven of agave thread like a net; fastened around waist to hold quiver.

Breech-clout: Deerskin, with the hair left on the outside; fastened about waist with thong and not by the agave thread belt. Breech-clouts were not worn by all tribes.

Shirt: Generally worn by tribes in the north part of the territory; of deerskin, with a hole in the center; slipped over the head, the sides sewn together under the armholes; belted at waist. The deerskin was not cut straight across the bottom, but was left to hang with natural unevenness.

Cape: Universal among the California tribes; worn in winter and as a protection from the weather, being used also as a blanket; of skin of otter, seal, rabbit, fox, or deer, or a combination of these; tanned and sewn with fur outside; sometimes skins cut in strips, twisted like rope, and sewn together; worn like a blanket around the shoulders and fastened in front with shell ornament; fell to the knees. Santa Barbara Indians made capes of sea-gull feathers, carefully designed and sewn on a backing of deerskin or other kind of pelt.

Quiver: Of skin of wildcat, coyote, wolf, or deer; stuck under belt in the back; arrows with stone or shell points.

Bow: Of varying lengths, depending on the tribe. Some were two yards long.

Club: Short, heavy stick with round end; some tribes used a curved throwing stick similar to a boomerang.

Ornaments: Many strings of stone, bone, and shell beads were worn around the neck, some hanging to the waist; some tribes pierced their noses and the lobes of their ears for shell and bone ornaments; bracelets.

Women:

Skin: As above. Women tattooed their faces more than the men, using heavy lines or rows of dots. Markings depended upon the tribe.

Cap: Round, snugly fitting basket; sometimes flat at the top or finished in a peak; reached just to the top edges of the ears.

While traveling with a Russian expedition in 1806, German naturalist Georg Heinrich von Langsdorff sketched a group of Costeño dancers at Mission San José. It is believed this formal dance ceremony was in celebration of having survived a measles epidemic that had decimated the mission's native community.

Hair: As above, except for the feathers. Nets worn while traveling or gathering wood.

Apron: Tanned deerskin with hair taken off; torn into strips and tied in designs with beads and shells; fell in front and behind to the knees like a long fringe, leaving the thighs exposed. Or of otter, seal, or fox skins, with hair outside, hanging from a leather belt about the waist, and falling in front and behind like a narrow apron. Sometimes of agave thread, woven closely in a netted fabric, or even of bark.

Cape: As for men.

10. Trade Routes and Economic Exchange Among the Indians of California

By James T. Davis

Secondary Source

Achomawi

Supplied to:

Atsugewi	Basketry caps, salmon flour, acorns, salmon, dentalia, tule baskets, steatite, rabbit-skin blankets
Modoc	Shell beads, shallow bowl-shaped twined baskets, braided grass skirts, pine nut string skirts
Northeastern Maidu	Green pigment, obsidian, bows, arrows, deer skins, sugar pine nuts, shell beads
Northern Wintun	Salt, furs, bows
Northern Paiute	Sinew-backed bows, arrows, baskets, dried fish, women's basketry caps, clam disc beads, dried salmon flour

Yana	Obsidian
Unspecified tribes	Raw sinew, bows

Received from:

Modoc	Furs, bows, dentalia, horses
Atsugewi	Seed foods, epos roots (*Pteridendia bolanden*), other roots and vegetables, furs, hides, meat
Yana	Buckeye fire drills, deer hides, buckakin, dentalia, salt
Northern Wintun	Salmon flour, clam disc beads, dentalia
Northern Paiute	Sinew, arrowheads, red paint, moccasins, rabbit-akin blankets, various foods, basketry water bottles
Shasta	Dentalia
Northeastern Maidu	Clam disc beads, salt, digger pine nuts
Unspecified tribe	Completed sinew-backed bows, magnesite beads, *Olivella* shells, dentalia

References: Dixon, 1908:211, 215; Curtis, 1924:13:131; Kroeber, 1925:399; Kniffen, 1928:316–17; Spier, 1930:42, 178–90; Kelly, 1932:114, 151; Du Bois, 1935:25; Gifford and Klimek, 1936:83, 91–92, 98; Stewart, O. C. 1941:432; Voegelin, E. W., 1942:179, 191, 194, 196, 199, 201; Sapir and Spier, 1943:258; Garth, 1953:136, 183; de Angulo and Freeland, 1929:320

Diegueño

Supplied to:

Mohave	Acorns
Kamia	Tobacco, acorns, baked mescal roots, yucca fiber, sandals, baskets, carrying nets, eagle feathers
Cocopa	Eagle feathers
Yuma	Acorns

Received from:

Cocopa	Salt
Mohave	Gourd seeds
Kamia	Vegetal foods, salt
"The Desert"[1]	Tule roots, bulbs, cattail sprouts, yucca leaves, mescal, pine nuts, manzanita berries, chokecherries, mesquite beans
Yuma	Gourd seeds

Eastern Mono (Northern Paiute)[1]

Supplied to:

"The West"[2]	Mineral paint, salt, pine nuts, seed food, obsidian, rabbit-skin blankets, tobacco, baskets, buckskins, pottery vessels, clay pipes
Central Miwok	Pine nuts, pandora moth caterpillars, kutsavi, baskets, red paint, white paint, salt, pumice stone, rabbit-skin blankets
Southern Miwok	Rabbit-skin blankets, basketry materials
Tule-Kaweah Yokuts	Sinew-backed bows, piñon nuts, obsidian, moccasins, rock salt, jerked deer meat, hot rock lifters
Kings River Yokuts	Red paint
Washo	Kutsavi
Koso	Shell beads, various goods
Western Mono	Mineral paint, pitch-lined basketry water bottles, acorns, rock salt, piñon nuts, mountain sheep-skins, moccasins, tailored sleeveless buckskin jackets, fox-skin leggings, hot rock lifters, sinew-backed bows, unfinished obsidian arrowheads, red paint
Yokuts (subgroup not specified)	Salt, piñon nuts
Tübatulabal	Salt, pine nuts, baskets, red and white paint, tanned deer skins, kutsavi, pandora moth caterpillars

Received from:

"The West"	Squaw berries,[3] shell beads, glass beads, acorns, baskets, manzanita berries, bear skins, rabbit-skin blankets, elderberries
Central Miwok	Arrows, baskets, clam disc beads, shell beads, glass beads, acorns, squaw berries, elderberries, manzanita berries, a fungus used in paint
Paiute to east	Black paint, yellow paint
Southern Miwok	Clam disc beads
Tule-Kaweah Yokuts	Deer, antelope, and elk skins, steatite, salt grass, salt, baskets, shell beads
Western Mono	Shell beads, acorn meal, fine Yokuts baskets
Koso	Salt
Yokuts (subgroup not specified)	Shell ornaments, buckskins, acorn meal
Tübatulabal	Shell beads, acorns, manzanita berries, elderberries, baskets, rabbit-skin blankets

References: Clark, 1904:45–46; Bunnell, 1911:86; Muir, 1916:228; Gifford, 1932:21, 26; Barrett and Gifford, 1933:193, 224, 255–56; Steward, 1933:250, 257, 266, 277; 1935:8,10, 19–20; Driver, 1937:120; Godfrey, 1941:57; Aginsky, 1943:454; Gayton, 1948a:56; 1948b:146; McIntyre, 1949:5; Latta, 1949:64; Heizer, 1950:39, Merriam, 1955: 76, 112; Steward, 1938:78; Stewart, G. W., 1927:391.

---

[1]   Also called Owens Valley or Mono Lake Paiute.

Western Mono

Supplied to:

Eastern Mono	Clam disc beads, canes for arrows, acorn meal, fine Yokuts' baskets, tubular clam beads, shell beads, acorns, manzanita berries, squaw berries, elderberries, rabbit-skin blankets
Southern Valley Yokuts	Salt, sinew-backed bows, stone mortars and pestles
Kings River Yokuts	Sinew-backed bows
Northern Hill Yokuts	Rabbit-skin blankets, moccasins, rock salt, red and blue paint, piñon nuts

Received from:

Eastern Mono	Unfinished obsidian arrowheads, hot rock lifters of wood, sinew-backed bows, tailored sleeveless buckskin jackets, mountain sheep skins, moccasins, fox skin leggings, rock salt, piñon nuts, baskets, red paint, white paint, tanned deer skins, kutsavi, pandora moth cater pillars, mineral pigments, pitch-lined basketry water bottles
Northern Hill Yokuts	Acorns, willow bark baskets, shell beads
Southern Valley Yokuts	White paint

References: Steward, 1935:8,10, 19–20; Driver, 1937:120; Gifford, 1932: 21, 26; Merriam, 1955:76; Gayton, 1948a:73, 78; 1948b:146, 160, 181, 214–15, 258–59, 265; Latta, 1929:16.

Mainland Chumash

Supplied to:

Kitanemuk	Wooden vessels inlaid with Haliotis shell
Island Chumash	Seeds, acorns, bows, arrows
Southern Valley Yokuts	Shell beads, whole pismo clam shells, *Haliotis* shells, *Olivella* shells, keyhole limpet shells, cowrie shells, sea urchin shells, dried starfish
Yokuts (subgroup not specified)	Shell ornaments
Tübatulabal	Shell beads, shell cylinders, steatite, asphaltum, fish
Salinan	Steatite vessels, columella beads, possibly also steatite and wooden vessels

Received from:

Island Chumash	Chipped stone implements, a dark stone for digging-stick weights, fish bone beads, shell beads, baskets
Southern Valley Yokuts	Fish, obsidian, salt from salt grass, seed foods, steatite beads, various herbs, vegetables
Tübatulabal	Piñon nuts
Yokuts (subgroup not specified)	Clam shells, asphaltum, buckskins, obsidian, abalone

| "The Interior" | Deer skins, acorns, fish, grasshoppers |
| Mohave | Unspecified goods |

References: Mason, 1912:180; Kroeber, 1925:613,630; Voegelin, E.W., 1938:52; Latta, 1949:63, 66, 274–75; Heizer, 1955:151,154; Stewart, G.W., 1927:391; Taylor, 1860–63:vol. 13; Curtis, 1924:14:154; Eisen, 1905:12; Bolton, 1931b:272.

Pomo

Supplied to:

Yuki	Hinnites sp. shell beads, clam disc beads, dentalia, moccasins, sea shells, shell beads, dried *Haliotis*, mussels, seaweed, salt, magnesite beads
Huchnom	Clam disc beads
"The North"	Shell beads
Lake Miwok	Acorns
Wappo	Tule mats, magnesite beads, sinew-backed bows, fish
Patwin	Shell beads, salt, obsidian, fish, clams
Coast Yuki	Clam disc beads, acorns, fire drills of buckeye wood

Received from:

Yuki	Furs, beads, baskets, skins
"The North" (Yuki?)	Iris fiber cord for deer snares, arrows, sinew-backed bows of yew
Patwin	Sinew-backed bows, yellow hammer headbands, woodpecker scalp belts, cordage for making deer nets
Coast Yuki	Surf fish, abalone, giant chiton, seaweed, mussels, dried kelp for salt, shells of *Hinnites giganteus*

Shasta

Supplied to:

Northern Wintun	Deerskins, sugar pine nuts, green pigment, bows, arrowheads, manzanita berries, pelts, meat, dentalia, obsidian
Yahi	Obsidian
Karok	Juniper beads, basketry caps, salt, dentalie, white deer skins, woodpecker scalpa, whole *Olivella* shells, large obsidian blades, obsidian, deer skins, sugar pine nuts, wolf skins, horn for spoons
Rogue River Athabaskan	Acorn flour
Modoc	Bows, dentalia
Klamath	Bows, clam disc beads, conical burden baskets
Yurok	Horn for spoons
Achomawi	Dentalia
Hupa	Horn for spoons

Received from:

Northern Wintun	Woodpecker scalps, acorns, baskets, pine nut beads, clam disc beads, deer hides, dried salmon, clams, shell beads
Karok	*Haliotis* ornaments, *Hallotis* shells, salt, tobacco seeds, baskets, dentalia, seaweed, pepperwood pods for heir dressing, canoes
Rogue River Athabaskan	Dentalia
"Warm Springs Indians"[8]	Buckskin shirts and dresses
Klamath	Otter skins, other skins and skin blankets, buckskin dresses, men's shirts
Yurok	Canoes, acorns, baskets, dentalia, salt
Unspecified tribes	Wooden war clubs with stone or bone insert, grooved stone axes

Southern Valley Yokuts

Supplied to:

Mainland Chumash	Fish, obsidian, salt from salt grass, seed foods, steatite beads, various herbs, vegetables
Tule-Kaweah Yokuts	Tule mats, shell beads
"The East"	Shell money
Western Mono	White paint

Received from:

Mainland Chumash	Shell beads, whole pismo clam shells, key-hole limpet shells, *Haliotis* shells, *Olivella* shells, sea urchin shells, dried starfish, cowrie shells
Buena Vista Yokuts	Asphaltum
Tule-Kaweah Yokuts	Steatite, coiled baskets, burden baskets, pottery vessels
Eastern Mono or Koso	Mineral salt, obsidian
Salinan	Whole shells
Western Mono	Salt, sinew-backed bows, stone mortars and pestles
"The East"	Fire drills, digging sticks, baskets

Western Mono-Yokuts (Entimbitch)[2]

Received from:

Mohave (?)	Pottery

Reference: Latta, 1949:63.

---

2   See Gayton, 1948b:254–55.

Appendix:
Correlation of Indian Trails of
Aboriginal California with Modern Thoroughfares

Modern Roads

- U.S. Hwy. 101 from the Oregon border south to Loleta; from Longvale south to Windsor; from San Jose south to Gilroy; from Salinas south to Paso Robles; from Gaviota south to Ventura.
- State Hwy, 96 along its entire route, from U.S. 99 west and south to Willow Creek.
- U.S. Hwy. 299 from Willow Creek east and north to the Oregon border.
- U.S. Hwy. 99 from the Oregon border south to Los Angeles.
- State Hwy. 1 from Rockport south to Bodega Bay.
- State Hwy. 20 from Fort Bragg east to Willits; from Ukiah east to Colusa.
- State Hwy. 128 from near Albion southeast to Cloverdale; from Harbin Hot Springs east to Sacramento.
- State Hwy. 29 from Lakeport south to Vallejo.
- State Hwy. 16 from Clear Lake Park southeast to Sacramento.
- U.S. Hwy. 40 from Sacramento northeast to Nevada border.
- U.S. Hwy. 50 from Sacramento east to Nevada border; from Oakland east to Manteca.
- State Hwy. 33 from Tracy south to near Los Banos; from Coalinga south to Taft.
- State Hwy. 152 from Gilroy east to Fairmead.
- State Hwy. 25 from Hollister south to Junction with State Hwy. 198, thence east to Coalinga.
- Unnumbered road from Santa Margarita east to McKittrick.
- State Hwy. 166 from near Santa Maria east to Junction with U.S. Hwy. 399.
- U.S. Hwy. 399 from Ventura northward to junction with U.S. Hwy. 99.
- U.S. Hwy. 466 from Bakersfield east to Mohave.
- U.S. Hwy. 6 from Mohave north to junction with U.S. Hwy. 395, thence north to Mono Lake,
- State Hwy. 178 from Bakersfield east to junction with U.S. Hwy. 6.
- U.S. Hwy. 66 from San Bernardino east to Needles
- U.S. Hwy. 60 from Los Angeles east to Blythe.
- State Hwy. 126 from Ventura east to junction with U.S. Hwy. 99.

The preceding list represents only a small fraction of the number of roads which essentially follow Indian trails, but it is sufficient to illustrate the fact that many of the major modern routes of travel in California probably evolved from aboriginal footpaths as suggested previously in this paper.

11. Puberty and Initiation Rites Among California Native Cultures

By Marcia Herndon

Secondary Source

The Tolowa Indians of northern California celebrate a girl's biological puberty with rather elaborate ceremonies (see Dubois, 1932:248–251). This rite of passage is undertaken for the purpose of assuring a long life after a girl is incorporated into Tolowa society as an adult. In order to mark her formal entrance into adulthood, the girl is treated ceremonially on four successive occasions, each lasting ten mornings.

When her first menstruation begins, she is secluded in the common dwelling house under a shelter made of a tule mat. She must remain there, fasting, for four days and sleeping a night on other tule mats. Before dawn she must rise and bathe. In going to and from the river, her head and body are always covered with a tule mat, because it is believed that if she were to see the sun during this period of time, she would later suffer from weakened vision. The tule mats perform two functions—they give magical protection to the girl, as well as signifying her state of transition.

For nine months during the Tolowa girl's period of seclusion, dancing, singing, and feasting take place in an area in front of her tule-mat shelter. In the beginning, only a few singers and dancers are performing. On each successive night, the number of participants increases, until the climax is reached on the ninth night. Dancers are mostly young boys and girls, wearing their best clothing. The ceremony requires that females taking part must have passed puberty, but be neither married nor divorced women. If they have not yet received a facial tattoo, the girls decorate their chins with three fine, black stripes of paint, in imitation of the real tattoo.

At the start of an evening's ceremony, the Tolowa dancers arrange themselves according to height and gender while still outside of the house. They begin dancing as the first men enter the house. They are followed by the women, who move to alternating places in the semi-circle which is formed inside the house. The musicians take their places in two corners behind the dancers and accompany the songs. These songs and dances are no considered to be particularly sacred or special in any way; they may be performed on other occasions as well. Between dances, performers eat dried fish and acorn soup, both of which are believed to make them sing better. Between dances, prayers are said, invoking long life and happiness for the girl.

Early in the evening, dancers are admonished to retire and sleep; especially on the ninth evening, dancing is stopped early so that all may rise and participate in the drawn bathing ceremony.

It is during the dawn bathing ceremony that the Tolowa believe the dancers to be in a state of ritual danger. It is believed that their life will be shortened if they make a mis-step or fall in their descent to the river. As dancers move and twirl about on the path descending to the river, they strip off their clothing, flinging it away from them. They are followed by villagers who recover their garments.

On this tenth morning, the girl is brought forth dressed in a shredded tule skirt, wrapped around with a tule mat, and wears a cap of yellowhammer feathers almost concealing her face. A man who leads her out, places her beside the fire and sings as he shakes her back and forth five times. After this, her tule clothing is removed and replaced by her ordinary dress. Then, a child of six or eight runs down to the river; the girl follows, jumping in, bathing, and then returning to the fire. This ritual bathing is repeated ten times. Afterwards, her seclusion terminated, a big feast is provided by her father and relatives.

The girl's state of transition continues for three more menstrual periods, each observed in the same manner as the first. After the fourth period of seclusion and ceremony, the girl's hair is cut in bangs, and little strips of it are cut below her ears. She is now considered eligible for marriage, and must keep her hair cut in this fashion until after marriage, when she will let it grow again.

In southern California, the Coastal tribes from Los Angeles to the Mexican border are usually referred to as "Mission Indians." More than two centuries ago, Spanish missionaries disrupted their way of life reorganizing them into groups around the closest mission, with little regard for tribal origins, native language, or cultural unity. Although all had been hunters and gatherers, the missionaries forced them to become cultivators and cattle-herders. Under strict mission control, old life-styles were lost within a generation or two; even their own names, for themselves and for each other, were lost in years of mission living so that today, these peoples are known only by the names of the missions wherein they were settled in historic times.

Of the Mission Indians, the Lusieño were the most culturally conservative, perhaps because they lives mostly in the hills instead of the Coastal lowlands. Their ways of life lasted long enough for early ethnographers to record them (see Kroeber, 1926).

For the Lusieño, a girl's puberty ceremony—although supposedly connected with biological puberty—was not usually performed until several girls could undergo the rite at the same time. It is probable that a rich man's daughter celebrated her first menstruation and other girls participated, thus sharing the cost of the event. The sponsoring parents were required to feed any guests attending the ceremony.

At the beginning of the ceremony, the girls swallowed balls of tobacco. Anyone who vomited was thought to exhibit evidence of immoral behavior. After this, the girls were "roasted." They were laid out on a warm bed of sand lined with warm stones in a pit and then covered with more stones. They had to lie perfectly still, fasting, for three days in the pit. During the night, the men danced around them. In the daytime, the women danced.

The girls were let out of the pit once a day for bodily functions while the stones were being reheated. When they emerged, their faces were painted by the village chief's wife; their bodies were decorated and sometimes tattooed.

Exactly one month after the original "roasting," the girls gathered again. There was a solemn admonition, given by the clan chief, for the women to take their places as fruitful, industrious and kind adults. If they failed in such duties, evil monsters would devour them. A sand painting, much simpler than that found among the Navajo or other groups, was executed, and the girls' bodies were touched with balls of meal, which were then placed in their mouths. They then spat the meal into the pit, and the sand painting was destroyed.

For boys, there was also a ground painting and a speech of admonition; however, their ceremonial involved initiation into the Toloache cult. Members of this cult used the narcotic hallucinogen, Jimson Weed (datura plant), and believed in *Chungichnish*, a deity who gave the ritual to them. In addition to weeks of fasting and various ordeals, youths undergoing initiation were expected to have a vision—a rather violent mystical

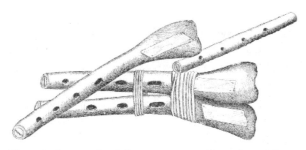

Chumash musical instruments found on San Clemente Island, 1895.

experience induced by ingestion of Jimson Weed. The dreams a boy had at his initiation were to be remembered all his life and determined, to a great extent, his behavior and beliefs.

Songs were an important part of all Luiseño ceremonies. Interestingly, some of the Toloache cult songs were in the Gabrielino language, which may indicate diffusion of the cult from the Gabrielino to the Luiseño.

The Luiseño had only two or three standard dances according to available descriptions. The most spectacular was the Fire Dance, climaxing the Toloache initiation. It began with a huge bonfire; a circle of barefoot men danced around it. They rhythmically closed in on the fire and retreated from its edge, stamping on the hot embers and, by this means, snuffed the fire out.

The Toloache initiation ceremony, like the girls puberty ceremony, was held only once every few years, when there were several boys of the right age to undergo the ceremony at the same time. All the boys, plus any order boys or men not initiated in childhood, or men who had married into the tribe, were brought together and given Jimson Weed to drink. The drug was carefully administered, since an excess could cause fatality. Only the persons being initiated ingested the drug; the Toloache was drunk only once in a lifetime. Those being initiated passed out after they took the drug, and dreamed while the adults danced all night around the fire. A boy usually dreamed about a particular animal, and never again in his lifetime killed that animal.

The usual dance costume was a net shirt decorated with eagle feathers, which swung out as the dancers spun around. Its simplicity, in comparison to the complex dance costumes of Northern and central California, may be the result of the psychology of the Jimson Weed; dancers supposedly had their attention turned inward, recalling their own initiatory visions, rather than outward at any observers.

The Toloache ceremony ran for about six days, with the boys dancing at night and sleeping during the day. Fasting continued for the initiates during the entire ceremony. After the six days of dancing, other rituals went on. The initiation tapered of slowly. For months, the boys ate no meat and took part in occasional night dances. During this time, they acquired the special knowledge and magic of manhood.

After their initial fast, a circular sand painting, twelve to fifteen feet in diameter, was made. In it were representations of serpents, stars, and mountains—a picture representative of the world. At the center of the sand painting was a small depression called the "Hole of the Dead" or the "Navel of the Universe," symbolizing death and burial of cremated remains. After a long lecture on proper behavior, a lump of meal—also found in the girls' adolescent ceremonies—was placed in each boy's mouth, and each spat it into the center pit of the painting. The painting was then swept into the pit so that non-initiates would never see it.

There were several ordeals involved in passing into manhood. One of these was a trial in which the initiates were covered with biting red ants. They had to endure the pain and stings solemnly, without complaint. Another trial involved walking carefully through a trench on stepping stones which had been laid out in the shape of a corpse; stumbling during this trial indicated an early death.

Section II

California's Era of European Exploration, 1500–1821

Section II

Introduction to California's Era of European Exploration, 1542–1821

Sources

In 1521, under the leadership of Hernán Cortez, the Spanish conquered the city of Tenochtitlan, heart of the Aztec Empire. They changed the name of the city to Mexico, and made it the base for the colony of New Spain. In the decades that followed, New Spain continued to expand through conquest and negotiation.

The Spanish were active in North America for about 250 years before they began to settle the area we now call California. In the 1500s, they set up missions and established towns in New Mexico and Florida, but California was still largely unknown to them in that era.

After Cortez established the colony of New Spain, he began a search of the Pacific Ocean near the mainland of Mexico. At the time, many people believed there was an island out there full of gold. In 1535 Cortes personally led an expedition that found the southern part of a peninsula we now call Baja California. The Spanish named it "California" in honor of a mythical island in a novel of the era. The Spanish did not find gold there, but they did find pearls.

A few years later Captain Francisco de Ulloa found where the California peninsula is connected to the mainland of Mexico. The idea of California as an island was slow to die, however, and some maps from as late as the eighteenth century portray California as an island. As the Spanish explored the coastal area north of the peninsula, this area became known as Alta California and the peninsula became known as Baja California. Together, the two areas were called *Las Californias*.

In 1542, the conquistador Juan Rodríguez Cabrillo discovered the area now known as San Diego Bay. He is believed to be the first European to find the coast of today's California. Cabrillo named the bay San Miguel. The Spanish did not pay much attention to this new discovery, nor did any other European power, for about six decades.

Eventually the Spanish became interested in California because of its location along the sea route between Asia and the west coast of Mexico. In the 1560s the Spanish developed a lucrative trade that went through Manila, in the Philippines, using ships known as galleons. In 1601, the viceroy in charge of New Spain appointed Sebastián Vizcaíno, a pearl trader and former soldier, to lead an expedition in search of safe harbors for the galleons in Alta California. Vizcaíno sailed from Mexico up the California coast in 1602 and found two bays that would become harbors, San Diego (what Cabrillo had called San Miguel) and Monterey. Interestingly, Vizcaíno did not discover San Francisco Bay, probably because of the fog.

The Spanish did not actually form permanent settlements along the California coast until the following century. In the mid-1700s, the pace of European settlement in North America was accelerating. Spain became concerned that other European powers were taking an interest in California.

The Spanish continued to explore California during the Mission Era of the late 1700s and early 1800s. The last Spanish expedition took place in 1821, when Luis Antonio Argüello explored the interior of northern California, far from the influence of the missions. That same year, almost exactly three centuries after Spain conquered the Aztecs, the Spanish lost control of California to the newly independent country of Mexico.

Long before any place in the real world had the name, "California" existed in the European imagination. In Selection 1, **The Island of California: A History of the Myth**, Dora Beale Polk explains how California has been a land of dreams for centuries. Mariners of the fifteenth century, even before Columbus, were already thinking about what Polk calls, "the island dream of California." Perhaps it was inevitable that the name would be assigned to an actual place, mistaken for a large island, in the following century.

In Selection 2, **Queen Califia: Labors of the Very Brave Knight Esplandián**, we see the best known representation of mythical California. In 1510 the Spanish writer Garci Ordonez de Montalvo published a novel (part of a series) about the explorations of a mythical knight named Esplandián who travels to the western side of North America. At the time, Europeans knew next to nothing about the area, so it was ripe for fiction. As Ordonez notes in his novel, "… on the right side of the Indies there was an island called California, which was very close to the region of the Earthly Paradise." The knight finds the island inhabited by a tribe of black women led by Queen Califia.

While the Spanish were just beginning to grasp the broad outlines of North America, Cortes and his men traveled to Tenochtitlán, capital of the Aztec Empire, in 1519. Historians estimate the city had about 200,000 people, comparable to the city of Paris in that era. In Selection 3, **The Market in Tenochtitlán**, Bernal Diaz del Castillo, a soldier in the army of Cortes, recalls seeing a huge and well organized marketplace full of gold, silver, gems, and numerous other items, including slaves. Notice that at the time he visited, Diaz and his fellow soldiers were escorted by officers of the emperor Moctezuma. Moctezuma was wise not to trust them.

Around the same time they conquered Mexico, the Spanish developed an interest in a collection of islands near Asia that they later named the

Philippines, in honor of King Phillip II. In the mid-1500s California would become a stopping place between the port of Manila in the Philippines and the port of Acapulco in Mexico. In Selection 4, **The Filipino Role in the Galleon Trade**, Lorraine Jacobs Crouchett notes that Filipinos came to the coast of California long before the Pilgrims came to Plymouth. Crouchett also notes that some of the "Indians" mentioned by European explorers to California may have actually been Filipinos.

Selection 5, **Relation of the Voyage of Juan Rodriguez Cabrillo**, brings us directly to one of the most famous names in California history. While some historians believe he could have been of Portuguese heritage, there is no doubt that Cabrillo worked for Spain. Cabrillo had served under Cortes in the conquest of Mexico and later acquired a reputation as an effective and abusive conquistador in Guatemala. In 1541 he was commissioned by the Governor of Guatemala to lead a voyage up the west coast of the California peninsula and to continue north to explore the coast off the mainland. Cabrillo believed this voyage could make them rich, but they found no cities of gold or lucrative trading opportunities. His crew did name about forty places along the California coast before turning around and heading home. Unfortunately for Cabrillo, he died on the voyage.

Cabrillo's diary discusses various points along the coast of what we now call Baja California and California. When reading the selection, keep in mind that the travelers knew almost nothing about where they were going or who they were likely to meet. When they found a place to port that was "closed and very good" and named it San Miguel, they must have seen some potential for this area that would later be known as San Diego. The diary mentions that the Indians of the area were concerned about other people, who looked similar to the Spanish, who had harmed them. We do not know who those people could have been.

The Spanish were not the only ones interested in California. In Selection 6, **Sir Francis Drake Off the California Coast, 1579**, we get the perspective of a famous English sea captain. The Spanish hated Drake for his acts of piracy against Spanish ships in the Pacific. Drake traveled to California while on a voyage around the world (the second in history). Historians believe he probably landed at what is now called Drake's Bay, a small bay north of the opening of San Francisco Bay. He was knighted upon his return to England in 1581. Notice his observations about native peoples are more detailed than what you saw in the Cabrillo diaries.

While Cabrillo and Drake are well known names in California history, Sebastián Vizcaíno is arguably more important. It was Vizcaíno who found the port at Monterey, which would become especially important to California's early settlement by the Spanish. Vizcaíno had been commissioned by the Viceroy of Mexico, the Count of Monterrey, to locate safe harbors for Spanish ships that were sailing between Manila, in the Philippines, and Acapulco, on the west coast of mainland Mexico. When he found a place he thought particularly suitable he named it Monterey; with a slightly different spelling than the name of the Viceroy.

In Selection 7, **Diary of an Expedition to the Port of Monterey, 1602**, Vizcaíno offers several reasons why Monterey would be a good place for the Spanish to establish a settlement. He undoubtedly got the Viceroy's attention when he compared the area around Monterey Bay to the prosperous region of Castile, in the heart of Spain. In Selection 8, **A Letter from Vizcaíno to King Phillip III of Spain, 1603**, Vizcaíno continues to advocate for the port. Here he emphasizes the value as a stopping place for ships returning to Mexico from the Philippines. His descriptions of the trees and wildlife are also among the most detailed of any early European observations. He describes the native people as "meek, gentle, quiet, and quite amenable to conversion to Catholicism and to becoming subjects of Your Majesty." By the early 1600s, the Spanish had a long track record of converting Indians to Catholicism in many parts of Mexico. Vizcaíno appears to be the first person to actively promote the faith in California.

The office of the Viceroy did begin efforts to colonize Monterey Bay, but these efforts were halted a few years later. The information Vizcaíno gathered would prove useful 167 years later, when the Spanish finally managed to establish a settlement at Monterey Bay.

In our final selection for this section, **The Diary of Captain Luis Antonio Argüello, 1821**, we can see how much has changed since the Vizcaíno expedition. Notice Argüello refers to several permanent settlements, such as San Francisco and San Jose, under the control of the Spanish. Argüello himself had grown up in San Francisco. He also mentions a "neophyte," a native person who had been converted to Christianity. His expedition started in areas of strong Spanish influence but quickly moved to areas where Indians continued to live in their traditional village lifestyle. What Argüello calls the "Jesus and Maria" river is known, in today's world, as the Sacramento River. Argüello visited several villages in the Sacramento River Valley and met many people in the Wintu culture group (see Section I).

Notice on October 24, after traveling for about a week in the interior of California, Argüello's party visited a village that "had never seen people of our kind." Three centuries after the Spanish conquered the Aztecs, they were still largely a mystery to many of the native villages in California!

Readings

1. The Island of California

A History of the Myth

By Dora Beale Polk

Secondary Source

California excites interest, envy, and longing throughout the world. It is a beacon for innumerable refugees, immigrants and tourists from all quarters of the globe, seeking freedom, excitement, or improved economic opportunities.

California is often compared to a loadstone, or a magnet, or the moon drawing the tides. On occasion, California is fancifully described as an enchantress—Circe, or one of the Sirens or the Lorelei. Every utopian name imaginable has been applied at some time—Atlantis, Arcadia, Avalon, the Garden of Eden, El Dorado, the Elysian Fields, the Garden of the Golden Apples, the Happy Valley, the Isle of the Blest, the Land of Milk and Honey, the Land of Prester John, Mecca, the New Jerusalem, the Pleasure Dome of Kublai Khan, the Promised Land, the Terrestrial Paradise, and Treasure Island.

These exotic names may sound like fancy metaphors to people who think the romantic appeal of California is found in the make-believe world of Disneyland, the glamor of Hollywood, the fun-and-sun cult, and the glitter of a highly sophisticated modern state. But many of the above descriptions are far from being mere journalistic hyperbole. They are vestiges of dreams seriously associated with California. These dreams date back to a time long before the lust for gold and the hunger for land attracted newer kinds of dreamers into the state in the middle of the nineteenth century. In fact, they were part of the intellectual and emotional freight brought by Columbus and other explorers to the New World.

Fifteenth-Century Mariners Inherit Medieval Myths

The story of the dream island of California doesn't begin with the Spanish discovery of California some four and a half centuries ago. It begins much further back than that. The ingredients of the dream were already ancient when Europe reawakened to the possibility of a global earth at the end of the Middle Ages.

Bizarre as some of those dream ingredients were, they were revitalized alongside what we now regard as more scientific notions in the period marked by the revival of classical learning. They

Novissima et Accuratissima Totius Americae Descriptio by cartographer Nicholas Visscher, c. 1670. The Visscher family dominated map-making at the height of the Golden Age of Dutch cartography. Visscher died in 1702, leaving the business to his wife, Elizabeth, who continued on until 1726.

formed an integral part of the intellectual cargo of the mariners who set sail to westward in the last decade of the fifteenth century. A close look at that cargo of old dreams and "new" ideas will start us on the road to understanding the California island dream.

What exactly was stowed in the mariners' heads when they embarked on their historic quest? We know they didn't have the slightest suspicion of the existence of the lands that came to be called the New World. Their chief hope was that they would reach the mystery-shrouded regions called "Ind" or "the Indies." These names designated far more than the India and East Indies we know today. The vast, vague area bordered such rumored realms as Cathay, Mangi, Tartary, and the great unknown ocean to their east. The Asian landmass

was then thought of as a much larger area than it turned out to be.

Up to that time, those regions had been approached only by traveling east from Europe. But if the world really was a sphere, and Asia bent around it toward Europe, then Asia should be equally accessible by sailing west. The "Sea of Darkness" was assumed to stretch continuously west from Europe to those rich, exotic shores. The breadth of that ocean was believed to be very much narrower than it ultimately proved.

The mariners' minds were not entirely a blank about those distant unknown regions. Their imaginations were stuffed with various expectations. These came from the common stock of tales transmitted by the culture from generation to generation. This body of received material, called the dreamstock for short, formed the basis of personal aspirations of the mariners.

Our interest in the dreamstock will be primarily with promised places, many of which turned out to be imaginary in the course of events. The shorthand term "dream destinations" provides a useful, neutral way to describe these mythical places. Components of these dream destinations embedded in the dreamstock would one day combine into the island dream of California.

Where and how did the dreamstock originate? We can only guess at this, for it is the very stuff of emerging consciousness. It came into being long before man grew analytical or self-aware enough to take note of his own mental evolution. Perhaps the process of creating legend went somehow like this. From earliest times, sketchy reports by side-tracked travelers or sailors blown off course would have spread from ear to mouth and mouth to ear. As is the way with rumor, these tidbits would have been embellished and distorted into all sorts of outlandish tales about what might lie beyond the then-known world. Gossip being what it is, speculations of the more cautious, tentative sort would certainly have lost out to more wild and passionate fancies. Exciting stories get retold and thus are more likely to endure.

---

2. Queen Califia

Labors of the Very Brave Knight Esplandián

By M.G. de Rodríguez and William T. Little

Primary Source

About the frightening and unheard of succor Queen Calafia brought to the port of Constantinople in order to help the Turks.

Now I wish you to know about the strangest thing ever found anywhere in written texts or in human memory. By means of this dangerous wonder, the next day, when the city was on the verge of being lost, its salvation came from the new danger itself. I tell you that on the right-hand side of the Indies there was an island called California, which was very close to the region of the Earthly Paradise. This island was inhabited by black women, and there were no males among them at all, for their life style was similar to that of the Amazons. The island was made up of the wildest cliffs and the sharpest precipices found anywhere in the world. These women had energetic bodies and courageous, ardent hearts, and they were very strong. Their armor was made entirely out of gold—which was the only metal found on the island—as were the trappings on the fierce beasts that they rode once they were tamed. They lived in very well-designed caves. They had many ships they used to sally forth on their raiding expeditions and in which they carried away the men they seized and whom they killed in a way about which you will soon hear. On occasion, they kept the peace with their male opponents, and the females and the males mixed

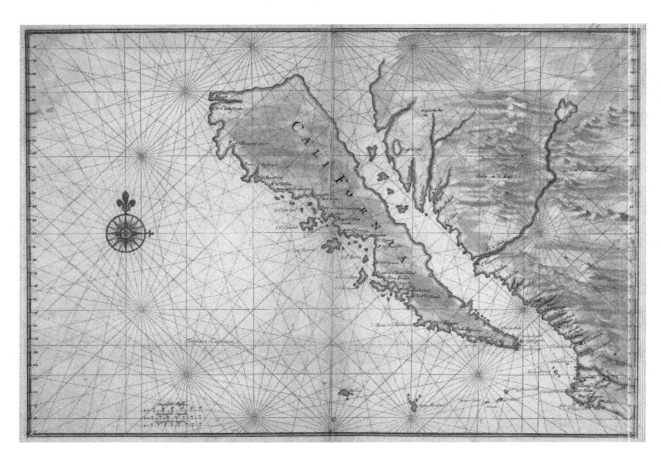

Map of California Shown as an Island, c. 1650 by Dutch cartographer Joan Vinckeboons, who was in the employ of the Dutch West India Company. A half-century would pass before Spanish explorers determined that California was connected to the mainland of North America.

with each other in complete safety, and they had carnal relations, from which unions it follows that many of the women became pregnant. If they bore a female, they kept her, but if they bore a male, he was immediately killed. The reason for this, inasmuch as it is known, is that, according to their thinking, they were set on reducing the number of males to so small a group that the Amazons could easily rule over them and all their lands; therefore, they kept only those few men whom they realized they needed for their race not to die out.

On this island called California, there were many griffins, because these beasts were suited to the ruggedness of the terrain, which was a perfect habitat for the infinite number of wild animals that lived there and that were not found in any other part of the world. When the griffins had offspring, in order to capture the young, these women ingenuously covered themselves in coarse hides; then they took them back to their caves where they raised them. When their plumage was even, they fed them so often and so cleverly with the captured men and the boys they bore that the griffins became well acquainted to the women and never harmed them in any way. Therefore, every man who ventured onto the island was immediately killed and devoured by the griffins; and even though they became stuffed, they never for that reason stopped seizing them, carrying them aloft as they flew through the air, and, when tired of carrying them, dropping them to their certain deaths.

At the time when all of the pagans' grandees left with those very large fleets, as the story has already told you, there reigned on California Island a queen in the flower of her youth who was bigger and more beautiful than the other women on the island, and she conceived a grand design to achieve great deeds. Moreover, of all who ruled that seigniory before her, she had more bold energy and more fire in her brave heart than any of the others. When she heard that most regions of the world were joining together in that expedition against the Christians—regions about which she knew nothing because she was acquainted only with neighboring lands—she conceived a desire to see the world and its various generations, and she thought that her great strength and that of her own people would enable her, by means of force or gratitude, to win the largest share of all the spoils. Therefore, she told all her ladies who were skilled in war that it would be a good idea to join the great fleets and sail in the same direction all those grand princes and mighty men were taking. Then she encouraged them and urged them on by holding up before them the great honor and profit that could redound to them by undertaking such a journey. Above all, she insisted on the very great fame they could achieve by having their glory bruited throughout the whole world;

but, instead, remaining on their island and doing nothing other than what then ancestors did would be tantamount to being buried alive like the living dead and to living out the rest of their days like dumb animals without fame or glory.

That very zealous Queen Calafía said so much to them that she not only moved her people to agree to such a journey, but they themselves were so animated with a deep desire to have their fame divulged throughout the world that they hurriedly put out to sea in order to join those grandees in whatever battles might occur. Seeing her people's will, without delay the queen ordered her huge fleet provisioned with victuals, all their golden arms, and everything else they needed. Then she ordered the largest of her xebecs repaired, which was constructed in the shape of a heavy wooden cage, and in it she put five hundred griffins, which, as you were told earlier, were raised and fed with men. In addition, on board went all the animals they used for mounts, of which there were several kinds, and the most select and best-armed women available. Finally, after leaving orders for the island to be securely guarded, she ordered the other women to board other ships, and they all departed with such speed that they came across the pagan fleets on the same night when the first combat you were told about occurred. Their arrival caused the pagans very great pleasure, and the grandees immediately visited the queen whom they received with full respect.

3. The Market in Tenochtitlán, 1560

By Bernal Díaz del Castillo

Primary Source

On reaching the great marketplace, escorted by the many *caciques* whom Moctezuma had assigned to us, we were astounded at the great number of people and the quantities of merchandise, and at the orderliness and good arrangements that prevailed, for we had never seen such thing before. The chieftains who accompanied us pointed out everything. Every kind of merchandise was kept separate and had its fixed place marked for it.

Let us begin with the dealers in gold, silver, and precious stones, feathers, cloaks, and embroidered goods, and male and female slaves, who are also sold there. They bring as many slaves to be sold in that market as the Portuguese bring blacks from Guinea Some are brought there attached to long poles by means of collars around their necks to prevent them from escaping, but others are left loose. Next there were those who sold coarser cloth and cotton goods and fabrics made of twisted thread, and there were chocolate merchants with their chocolate. In this way you could see every kind of merchandise to be found anywhere in New Spain, laid out in the same way as goods are laid out in my own district in Medina del Campo, a center of fairs, where each line of stalls has its own particular sort. So it was in this great market. There were those who sold sisal cloth and ropes and the sandals they wear on their feet, which are made from the same plant. All these were kept in one part of the market, in the place assigned to them, and in another part were skins of tigers [jaguars] and lions, otters, jackals, and deer, badgers, mountain cats, and other wild animals, some tanned and some untanned, and other classes of merchandise.

There were sellers of kidney beans and sage and other vegetables and herbs in another place, and in yet another they were selling fowl, and birds with great wattles [turkeys], also rabbits, hares, deer, young ducks, little dogs, and other such creatures. Then there were the fruiterers, and the women who sold cooked food, flour and honey cake, and tripe had their part of the market. Then came pottery of all kinds, from big water jars to little jugs, displayed in its own place; also honey, honey-paste, and other sweets, like nougat. Elsewhere they sold timber too, and boards, cradles, beams, blocks, and benches, all in a quarter of their own.

Then there were the sellers of pitch pine for torches, and other things of that kind, and I must also mention, with all apologies, that they sold many canoe-loads of human excrement, which they kept in the creeks near the market. This was for the manufacture of salt and the curing of skins, which they say cannot be done without it. I know that many gentlemen will laugh at this, but I assure them it is true. I may add that on all the roads they have shelters made of reeds or straw or grass so that they can retire when they wish to do so and purge their bowels unseen by passersby and also in order that their excrement shall not be lost.

But why waste so many words on the goods in their great market? If I describe everything in detail I shall never be done. Paper, which in Mexico they call *amatl*, and some reeds that smell of liquid amber and are full of tobacco, and yellow ointments and other such things are sold in a separate part. Much cochineal is for sale too, under the arcades of that market, and there are many sellers of herbs and other such things. They have a building there also in which three judges sit, and there are officials like constables who examine the merchandise. I am forgetting the sellers of salt and the makers of flint knives, and how they split them off the stone itself, and the fisherwomen and the men who sell small cakes made from a sort of weed which they get out of the great lake [Texcoco], which curdles and forms a kind of bread that tastes rather like cheese. They sell axes too, made of bronze and copper and tin, and gourds and brightly painted wooden jars.

We went on to the great *cue* [temple], and as we approached its wide courts before leaving the marketplace itself, we saw many more merchants who, so I was told, brought gold to sell in grains, just as they extract it from the mines. This gold is placed in the thin quills of the large geese of that country, which are so white as to be transparent. They used to reckon their accounts with one another by the length and thickness of these little quills, how much so many cloaks or so many gourds of chocolate or so many slaves were worth, or anything else they were bartering.

Now let us leave the market, having given it a final glance and come to the courts and enclosures in which their great temple stood. Before reaching it, you pass through a series of large courts, bigger I think than the Plaza at Salamanca. ...

Before we mounted the steps of the great temple, Moctezuma, who was sacrificing on the top to his idols, sent six priests and two of his principal officers to conduct Cortés up the steps. There were 114 steps to the summit. ... Indeed, this infernal temple, from its great height, commanded a view of the whole surrounding neighborhood. From this place we could likewise see the three causeways which led into Mexico. ... We also observed the aqueduct which ran from Chapultepec and provided the whole town with sweet water. We could also distinctly see the bridges across the openings by which these causeways were intersected, and through which the waters of the lake ebbed and flowed. The lake itself was crowded with canoes that were bringing provisions, manufacturers, and merchandise to the city. From here we also discovered that the only communication to the houses in this city, and of all the other towns built in the lake, was by means of drawbridges or canoes. In all these towns the beautiful white plastered temples rose above the smaller ones like so many towers and castles in our Spanish towns, and this, it may be imagined, was a splendid sight. ...

Having examined and considered all that we had seen, we turned back to the great market and the swarm of people buying and selling. The mere murmur of their voices talking was loud enough to be heard more than three miles away. Some of our soldiers who had been in many parts of the world, in Constantinople, in Rome, and all over Italy, said that they had never seen a market so well laid out, so large, so orderly, and so full of people.

4. The Filipino Role in the Galleon Trade

By Lorraine Jacobs Crouchett

Secondary Source

From the beginning, the Spaniards took full advantage of the Filipinos' natural affinity for the seas, which dated from the time of their neolithic ancestors who built rugged outrigger sailing boats which carried them from the Southeast Asia mainland and Indonesia to the Philippine Islands. Here they continued to develop their talents as seafaring men. By the tenth century the Filipino people were heavily engaged in maritime commerce with Indonesia, Malaya, China, and Japan. There was also inter-island traffic as Filipino traders from Luzon, Jolo, and Visayas navigated the waters in search of gold and other cargoes.

It is difficult to ascertain how many Filipinos served Spain in the galleon trade with the New World. Several thousand, in one way or another, made up the crews of the galleons. The number of Filipinos ("Indians," as they were called) in the crews varied, but as a rule there was one Filipino to five Spaniards. The Malay seamen who were employed were generally Filipinos, however; and when there was a shortage of these trained seamen, the royal factor usually drafted the natives from the interior of Luzon. To encourage the Spaniards to enter the marine service, private investments of 30 pesos worth of goods were increased to 300 pesos as more Spaniards were needed on the Apaculco route.

The Spaniards were the sailors; the Filipinos were rated as common seamen, serving as navigators, marine officers, and boatmen. The natives of the Tagalog and Camarines served as rowers and pioneers (in construction corps) in expeditions made by the fleet. There was also a difference in pay, not based upon the ability of the seaman. According to Fiscal Leandro Viana, a member of the Council of the Indies, the Filipinos were the best mariners of the Islands. They were the most skilled and dextrous helmsmen in the maneuvers on ship, and could teach the Spanish mariners much about the seas.

In the late eighteenth and early nineteenth century, Americans also recognized the superior skill of the Filipinos in shipboard maneuvers. Thus, Filipinos were generally employed as helmsmen and quartermasters aboard the American sailing ships in the Pacific. Today, even though ships and cargoes have changed, the Filipino's natural affinity for the sea makes him a superior crew member. And as it was in the early days, the Philippines still remain the major source for qualified seamen. This is a unique phenomenon because the Merchant Marine Academy in the Philippines was founded in 1820 and was successively fostered by the Governments of Spain, the United States, Japan, and the Islands themselves.

The Labor Force in the Construction of Galleons

The Spaniards took advantage of the abundant supply of good timber in the Philippines and promptly established a shipbuilding industry in the Islands on a large scale. The galleons were built in shipyards near the city of Manila and, since shipbuilding became the most important industry, the Filipinos developed the trade among their own people. Those who cut the wood and built the ships and galleys were carpenters, called "cagallanes" or "pandais." There were generally 1,400 carpenters required to prepare a fleet. Another 6,000 to 8,000 were employed as woodcutters, the hewers and planers of wood. On these woodcutters fell the strenuous labor of cutting and dragging the wood from the mountains. The masters—those qualified for better trades—laid out, prepared, rounded, and made the masts, yards, and topmasts. Filipino males, ranging in age from 16 to 60, were required to render service to the government ("polo" system, or forced labor). Under this system, they were assigned to work in the shipyards in Albay, Mardinuque, Pangasinan, Masbate, Mindoro, and Cavite, where most of the galleons were built and repaired.

The Filipinos who built the galleons and those who served as seamen suffered many hardships. Because the construction of ships took priority over everything else and because of the polo system, many Filipinos were drafted into shipbuilding during the planting season or harvest time and lost their crops. They worked under severe conditions. Some had not been paid for five years, except in the form of survival aid. Many died in the service of shipbuilding, in the cutting and hauling of wood; the strenuous labor and harsh treatment caused many deaths.

When the chance came to serve as crewmen on the galleons they had helped to build, many Filipinos no doubt saw it as a providential means of escape. And many took advantage of the adventure not only to escape the hardships of shipbuilding in their homeland, but to find a new home in the New World. They deserted ship when the galleons reached port at Acapulco or California rather than return to the Philippines. For instance, of the 75 native "Indians" who served as common seamen on the galleon *Espiritu Santos,* only five returned to the ship. The native seamen who chose to remain on the coast then met other galleons which entered the New World ports and helped other native seamen to escape.

Anonymous early 17th century engraving of a Spanish galleon.

These "New World Filipinos" engaged themselves in finding work among the Spaniards. Many became makers of palm wine, using stills imported from the Philippines. The wine was distilled, and was strong as brandy. No wonder it was preferred by the inhabitants of Nueva España over the wine imported from Spain!

Many of the Filipinos who had been common seamen married among the Spanish women and established households in the New World. As can be expected, this drain of the male population in the Philippines was reflected in a diminished number of families in the Islands. On the island of Panay, for example, when the Spaniards arrived there were more than 50,000 families; in little over half a century this number had dwindled to about 14,000. Could it be possible that some of the

"Indians" that the Americans thought they found in California were indeed Filipino "Indians"?

The Filipinos' First Venture into California

From the very beginning when the Spanish galleons plied the Pacific Ocean and carried on the Manila-Acapulco galleon trade, Filipinos came as crew members, deckhands, and common seamen. And when increased piracy of the annual voyages of the galleons stimulated the exploration of the California coast for a suitable way station, there were also Filipinos who accompanied the priests, soldiers, and explorers. It was here, along the 1,264-mile coastline of California that the Filipino history in the New World began—when the explorers visited the San Luis Obispo coastal regions nearly three quarters of a century before the Pilgrims landed at Plymouth.

As early as 1584, the viceroy of New Spain, aware of all the piracy and dangers of the sea, gave orders to Francisco de Gali, commanding a Philippine ship that same year, to lead further exploration of the California coast, to gain knowledge of possible ports along the coast where vessels coming from Manila could take refuge in case of need, where news of pirate activities could be obtained, and where an escort for the remainder of the voyage to Acapulco could be acquired.

On a return voyage from Macao by way of Japan, Gali encountered a strong oceanic current which carried him to within 200 leagues of the California coast. His narrative contains the first mention of Cape Mendocino on the California coast, and his description of the coast stimulated further explorations of the region after his unexpected death. One of the explorers, Pedro de Unamuno, brought a "few Luzon Indians" (apparently the first Filipinos) to California, and set foot on this soil in 1587.

Unamuno, with two ships, left Manila early in the summer of 1586 and, in spite of his positive instructions, he did go to Macao, where the ships were seized. The Portuguese claimed that Unamuno was planning to turn to privateering of vessels because he had an Englishman, a Frenchman, and great mariners with him. He was arrested by the Portuguese. After his release he was able to retain his command but was forced to buy a small ship, the *Nuestra Señora de Esperanza,* with money probably provided by Fray Martin Ignacio de Loyola. On July 12, 1587, Unamuno, Loyola, two Portuguese Franciscans as passengers, Alonso Gomez as pilot, and a few sailors and Luzon Indians sailed from Macao. On October 18 they entered Morro Bay. Although this area had enjoyed limited contact with other civilized portions of the world, there was substantial evidence that much of the culture found here was indigenous. There were smoke fires at the foot of the hill in some woods near the sea, and many trails leading in different directions. Following the best of the beaten trails, the exploring party found foot prints of many persons, large, medium, and small, up and down the sandy edge along the river. They found an old Indian camp which was made up of seventeen large and small dugouts covered well with branches of trees, each large enough to hold about a dozen people. In another direction was a hut built of stakes covered with earth. It had one small porthole and was large enough for two people. They also found a camp which occupied both sides of the river. Here there were more than thirty dugouts, similar to those found earlier. Inside the camp they found some small cord bags, made like nets with rope fashioned from tree bark. There were some old baskets and a tree trunk hollowed out to form a trough, which was probably used to grind roots or tree bark for making a drink or some dish. There were no signs of grain other than a little seed which resembled wild marjoram.

As Unamuno and the other explorers moved into the interior of the California coast, Filipinos

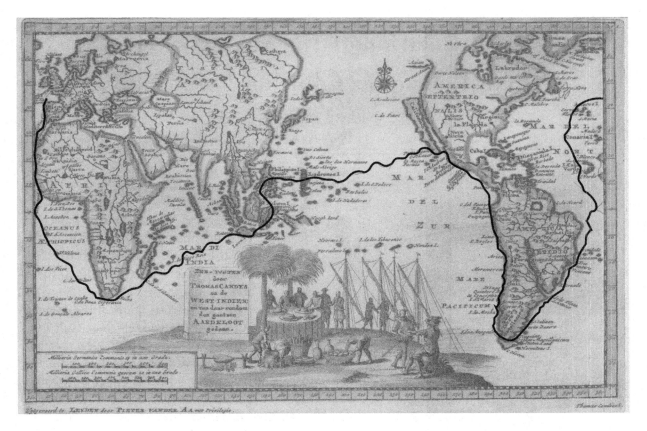

Decorative copper line engraving by Pieter van der Aa, charting Thomas Cavendish's circumnavigation of the world, published 1707, still showing California as an island. Cavendish was an English navigator who became the third circumnavigator of the globe in July 1585 after Ferdinand Magellan (1519–22) and fellow English navigator, Sir Francis Drake (1577–79).

assisted in the undertaking. After sighting Indians on shore, a council was held, and all agreed that Unamuno, accompanied by twelve soldiers, Fray Loyola (carrying a cross), and a number of Luzon Indians (carrying swords and targets), should scout the area and make a survey of the vicinity surrounding the port. Two Luzon Indians, because of their color, were sent ahead as scouts, along with Sergeant Diego Vasquez Mexia and another soldier, to make contact with the local

Indians. On October 18, Saint Luke's Day, they took possession of the port and the land near the ship, which was strewn with oyster shells and the shells of many other crustaceans. On a little hill, the ceremony of possession was performed in the presence of Mexia in due legal form, including the customary cutting of branches from nearby trees, forming across in the sign of the Christian faith, and planting of the cross. They were soon to make their first contact with the Indians.

Oil painting of Juan Rodríguez Cabrillo, artist and date unknown.

While at this Cape of San Martin they went ashore for water and found a small lake of fresh water, where they got a supply. To this watering place came forty Indians with bows and arrows. They could not make each other understood. The Indians were naked; they brought roasted maguey and fish to eat. They are large people. Here they took possession. They were at this cape until the following Monday.

On Monday, the 8th of said month, they left Cape San Martin and sailed some four leagues on a coast running north-northeast–south-southwest, and from there the coast turns northwest. The land is high and bare. Next day they sailed along a coast running from northwest to southeast a matter of six leagues. All this coast is bold and clear. The next day they sailed, with foul winds, a matter of four leagues, still on a coast running from northwest to southeast. On the land there are high broken mountains. On the following Thursday they east anchor about three leagues farther on, under a headland which extends into the sea and forms a cape on both sides. It is called Cabo de Cruz (Cape of the Cross); it is in thirty-three degrees. There is neither water nor wood, nor did they find a sign of Indians.

Having departed from Cabo de la Cruz, because of headwinds they found themselves on the following Saturday two leagues from the same cape on a coast running from north-northwest to south-southeast. At the shore they saw Indians in some very small canoes. The land is very high, bare, and dry. All the land from California to here is sandy near the shore, but here begins land of another sort, the soil being reddish and of better appearance.

On Sunday, the 17th day of the said month, they sailed on in continuation of their voyage, and about six leagues from Cabo de Cruz they found a good and closed port. To reach it they passed a small island which is near the mainland. In this port they took on water from a small lake of rainwater. There are groves of trees like silk-cotton trees, excepting that they are of hard wood. They found thick and tall trees which the sea brings. This port is called San Mateo. The land appears to be good; there are large savannahs, and the grass is like that of Spain. The land is high and broken. They saw some herds of animals like cattle, which went in droves of a hundred or more, and which, from their appearance, from their gait, and the long wool, looked like Peruvian sheep. They have small horns a span in length and as thick as the thumb. The tail is broad and round and a palm long. This place is in thirty-three and one-third degrees. They took possession here. They remained in this port until the following Saturday.

On Saturday, the 23d of said month, they left said port of San Mateo and sailed along the coast until the Monday following, when they must have gone about eighteen leagues. They saw very beautiful valleys and groves, and country both level and rough, but no Indians were seen.

On the following Tuesday and Wednesday they sailed along the coast about eight leagues, passing by some three islands completely denuded of soil. One of them is larger than the others. It is about two leagues in circumference and affords shelter from the west winds. They are three leagues from the mainland, and are in thirty-four degrees. They called them Islas Desiertas (Desert Islands). This day great smokes were seen on the land. The country appears to be good and has large valleys, and in the interior there are high mountains.

On the following Thursday they went about six leagues along a coast running north-northwest, and discovered a port, closed and very good, which they named San Miguel. It is in thirty-four and one-third degrees. Having cast anchor in it, they went ashore where there were people. Three of them waited, but all the rest fled. To these three they gave some presents and they said by signs that in the interior men like the Spaniards had passed. They gave signs of great fear. On the night of this day they went ashore from the ships to fish with a net, and it appears that here there were some Indians, and that they began to shoot at them with arrows and wounded three men.

Locations visited by Cabrillo on his journey.

Next day in the morning they went with the boat farther into the port, which is large, and brought two boys, who understood nothing by signs. They gave them both shirts and sent them away immediately.

Next day in the morning three adult Indians came to the ships and said by signs that in the interior men like us were travelling about, bearded, clothed, and armed like those of the ships. They made signs that they carried crossbows and swords; and they made gestures with the right arm as if they were throwing lances, and ran around aa if they were on horseback. They made signs that they were killing many native Indians, and that for this reason they were afraid. These people are comely and large. They go about covered with skins of animals. While they were in this port a heavy storm occurred, but since the port is good they did not feel it at all. It was a violent storm from the west-southwest and the south-southwest. This is the first storm which they have experienced. They remained in this port until the following Tuesday. The people here called the Christians Guacamal.

On the following Tuesday, the 3d of the month of October, they departed from this port of San Miguel, and on Wednesday, Thursday, and Friday, they held their course a matter of eighteen leagues along the coast, where they saw many valleys and plains, and many smokes, and mountains in the interior. At nightfall they were near some islands which are some seven leagues from the mainland, but because the wind went down they could not reach them that night.

At daybreak on Saturday, the 7th of the month of October, they were at the islands which they named San Salvador and La Vitoria. They anchored at one of them and went ashore with the boat to see if there were people; and when the boat came near, a great number of Indians emerged from the bushes and grass, shouting, dancing, and making signs that they should land. As they saw that the women were fleeing, from the boats they made signs that they should not be afraid. Immediately they were reassured, and laid their bows and arrows on the ground and launched in the water a good canoe which held eight or ten Indians, and came to the ships. They gave them beads and other articles, with which they were pleased, and then they returned. Afterward the Spaniards went ashore, and they, the Indian women, and all felt very secure. Here an old Indian made signs to them that men like the Spaniards, clothed and bearded, were going about on the mainland. They remained on this island only till midday.

On the following Sunday, the 8th of said month, they drew near to the mainland in a large bay which they called Bay of Los Fumos, (Bay of the Smokes), because of the many smokes which they saw on it. Here they held a colloquy with some Indians whom they captured in a canoe, and who made signs that toward the north there were Spaniards like them. This bay is in thirty-five

degrees and is a good port, and the country is good, with many valleys, plains, and groves.

On the following Monday, the 9th of the said month of October, they left the Bay of Los Fuegos (the Fires), and sailed this day some six leagues, anchoring in a large bay. From here they departed the next day, Tuesday, and sailed some eight leagues along a coast running from northwest to southeast. We saw on the land a pueblo of Indians close to the sea, the houses being large like those of New Spain. They anchored in front of a very large valley on the coast. Here they came to the ships many very good canoes* each of which held twelve or thirteen Indians; they told them of Christians who were going about in the interior. The coast runs from northwest to southeast. Here they gave them some presents, with which they were greatly pleased. They indicated by signs that in seven days they could go to where the Spaniards were, and Juan Rodriguez decided to send two Spaniards into the interior. They also indicated that there was a great river. With these Indians they sent a letter at a venture to the Christians. They named this town the Pueblo of Las Canoas. The Indians dress in skins of animals; they are fishermen and eat raw fish; they were eating *maguey* also. This pueblo is in thirty-five and one-third degrees. The interior of the country is a very fine valley ; and they made signs that in that valley there was much maize and abundant food. Behind the valley appear some very high mountains and very broken country. They call the Christians Taquimine. Here they took possession and here they remained until Friday, the 13th day of said month.

On Friday, the 13th of said month of October, they left the pueblo of Las Canoas to continue their voyage, and sailed this day six or seven leagues, passing along the shores of two large islands. Each of them must be four leagues long, and they must be about four leagues from the mainland. They are uninhabited, because they have no water, but they have good ports. The coast of the mainland trends to the west-northwest. It is a country of many savannahs and groves. On the following Saturday they continued on their course, but made no more than two leagues, anchoring in front of a magnificent valley densely populated, with level land, and many groves. Here came canoes with fish to barter; the Indians were very friendly.

On the following Sunday, the 15th day of the said month, they continued on their course along the coast for about ten leagues; all the way there were many canoes, for the whole coast is very densely populated; and many Indiana kept boarding the ships. They pointed out the pueblos and told us their names. They are Xuco, Bis, Sopono, Alloc, Xabaagua, Xocotoc, Potoltuc, Nacbuc, Quelqueme, Misinagua, Misesopano, Elquias Coloc, Mugu, Xagua, Anacbuc, Partocac, Susuquey, Quanmu, Gua, Asimu, Aguin, Casalic, Tucumu, and Incpupu.

All these pueblos are between the first pueblo of Las Canoas, which is called Xucu, and this point. They are in a very good country, with fine plants and many groves and savannahs. The Indians go dressed in skins. They said that in the interior there were many pueblos, and much maize three days' journey from there. They call make Oep. They also said that there were many cows; these they call Cae. They also told us of people bearded and clothed.

6. Sir Francis Drake Off the California Coast, 1579

By Sir Francis Drake

Primary Source

The next day, after our comming to anchor in the aforesaid harbour, the people of the countrey shewed themselves, sending off a man with great expedition to us in a canow. Who being yet but a little from the shoare, and a great way from our ship, spake to us continually as he came rowing on. And at last at a reasonable distance staying himselfe, he began more solemnely a long and tedious oration, after his manner: using in the deliverie thereof many gestures and signes, moving his hands, turning his head and body many wayes; and after his oration ended, with great shew of reverence and submission returned backe to shoare againe. He shortly came againe the second time in like manner, and so the third time, when he brought with him (as a present from the rest) a bunch of feathers, much like the feathers of a blacke crow, very neatly and artificially gathered upon a string, and drawne together into a round bundle; being verie cleane and finely cut, and bearing in length an equall proportion one with another; a speciall cognizance (as wee afterwards observed) which they that guard their kings person weare on their heads. With this also he brought a little basket made of rushes, and filled with an herbe which they called *Tabâh*.[1] Both which being tyed to a short rodde, he cast into our boate. Our Generall intended to have recompenced him immediatly with many good things

he would have bestowed on him; but entring into the boate to deliver the same, he could not be drawne to receive them by any meanes, save one hat, which being cast into the water out of the ship, he tooke up (refusing utterly to meddle with any other thing, though it were upon a board put off unto him) and so presently made his returne. After which time our boate could row no way, but wondring at us as at gods, they would follow the same with admiration.

The 3 day following, viz., the 21, our ship having received a leake at sea, was brought to anchor neerer the shoare, that, her goods being landed, she might be repaired; but for that we were to prevent any danger that might chance against our safety, our Generall first of all landed his men, with all necessary provision, to build tents and make a fort for the defence of our selves and goods: and that wee might under the shelter of it with more safety (what ever should befall) end our businesse; which when the people of the countrey perceived us doing, as men set on fire to war in defence of their countrie, in great hast and companies, with such weapons as they had, they came downe unto us, and yet with no hostile meaning or intent to hurt us: standing, when they drew neere, as men ravished in their mindes, with the sight of such things as they never had seene or heard of before that time: their errand being rather with submission and feare to worship us as Gods, then to have any warre with us as with mortall men. Which thing, as it did partly shew itselfe at that instant, so did it more and more manifest itself afterwards, during the whole time of our abode amongst them. At this time, being

---

1 Possibly tobacco. That Drake and his men should not have recognized it as something known to them is not strange, as tobacco seems not to have been known in England until introduced by Ralph Lane and his colonists on their return from Roanoke Island in 1586.

willed by signes to lay from them their bowes and arrowes, they did as they were directed, and so did all the rest, as they came more and more by companies unto them, growing in a little while to a great number, both of men and women.

To the intent, therefore, that this peace which they themselves so willingly sought might, without any cause, of the breach thereof on our part given, be continued, and that wee might with more safety and expedition end our businesses in quiet, our Generall, with all his company, used all meanes possible gently to intreate them, bestowing upon each of them liberally good and necessary things to cover their nakednesse; withall signifying unto them we were no Gods, but men, and had neede of such things to cover our owne shame; teaching them to use them to the same ends, for which cause also wee did eate and drinke in their presence, giving them to understand that without that wee could not live, and therefore were but men as well as they.

Notwithstanding nothing could perswade them, nor remove that opinion which they had conceived of us, that wee should be Gods.

In recompence of those things which they had received of us, as shirts, linnen cloth, etc., they bestowed upon our Generall, and diverse of our company, diverse tilings, as feathers, cawles of networke, the quivers of their arrowes, made of fawne skins, and the very skins of beasts that their women wore upon their bodies. Having thus had their fill of this times visiting and beholding of us, they departed with joy to their houses, which houses are digged round within the earth, and have from the uppermost brimmes of the circle clefts of wood set up, and joined close together at the top, like our spires on the steeple of a Church; which being covered with earth, suffer no water to enter, and are very warme; the doore in the most part of them performes the office also of a chimney to let out the smoake: its made in bignesse and fashion like to an ordinary scuttle in a ship, and standing slopewise: their beds are the hard ground, onely with rushes strewed upon it, and lying round about the house, have their fire in the middest, which by reason that the house is but low vaulted, round, and close, giveth a marvelous reflexion to their bodies to heate the same.

Their men for the most part goe naked; the women take a kinde of bulrushes, and kembing it after the manner of hemp, make themselves thereof a loose garment, which being knitte about their middles, hanges downe about their hippes, and so affordes to them a covering of that which nature teaches should be hidden; about their shoulders they weare also the skin of a deere, with the haire upon it. They are very obedient to their husbands, and exceeding ready in all services; yet of themselves offring to do nothing, without the consents or being called of the men.

As soone as they were returned to their houses, they began amongst themselves a kind of most lamentable weeping and crying out; which they continued also a great while together, in such sort, that, in the place where they left us (being neere about 3 quarters of an English mile distant from them) we very plainely, with wonder and admiration, did heare the same, the women especially extending their voices in a most miserable and dolefull manner of shreeking.

They are a people of a tractable, free, and loving nature, without guile or treachery; their bowes and arrowes (their only weapons, and almost all their wealth) they use very skillfully, but yet not to do any great harme with them, being by reason of their weaknesse more fit for children then for men, sending the arrowes neither farre off nor with any great force: and yet are the men commonly so strong of body, that that which 2 or 3 of our men could hardly beare, one of them would take upon his backe, and without grudging carrie it easily away, up hill and downe hill an English mile together: they are also exceeding swift in running, and of long continuance, the use whereof is so familiar with them, that they seldome goe, but for the most part runne. One thing we observed in them with admiration, that if at any time they chanced to see a fish so neere the shoare that they might reach the place without swimming, they would never, or very seldome, misse to take it.

After that our necessary businesses were well dispatched, our Generall, with his gentlemen and many of Ins company, made a journy up into the land, to see the manner of their dwelling, and to be the better acquainted with the nature and commodities of the country. There houses were all such as we have formerly described, and being many of them in one place, made severall villages here and there. The inland we found to be farre different from the shoare, a goodly country, and fruitfull soyle, stored with many blessings fit for the use of man: infinite was the company of very large and fat Deere which there we sawe by thousands, as we supposed, in a heard; besides a multitude of a strange kinde of Conies, by farre exceeding them in number: their heads and bodies, in which they resemble other Conies, are but small; his tayle, like the tayle of a Rat, exceeding long; and his feet like the pawes of a Want or moale; under his chinne, on either side, he hath a bagge, into which he gathereth his meate, when he hath filled his belly abroade, that he may with it, either feed his young, or feed himselfe when he lists not to travaile from his burrough ; the people eate their bodies, and make great account of their skinnes, for their kings holidaies coate was made of them.

This country our Generall named *Albion*, and that for two causes; the one in respect of the white bancks and cliffes, which lie toward the sea; the other, that it might have some affinity, even in name also, with our own country, which was sometimes so called.

Before we went from thence, our Generall caused to be set up a monument[2] of our being there, as also of her majesties and successors right and title to that kingdome; namely, a plate of brasse, fast nailed to a great and firme poste; whereon is engraven her graces name, and the day and yeare of our arrivall there, and of the free giving up of the province and kingdome, both by the king and people, into her majesties hands: together with her highnesse picture and armes, in a piece of six-pence currant English monie, shewing itselfe by a hole made of purpose through the plate; underneath was likewise engraven the name of our Generall, etc.

The Spaniards never had any dealing, or so much as set a foote in this country, the utmost of their discoveries reaching onely to many degrees Southward of this place.

And now, as the time of our departure was perceived by them to draw nigh, so did the sorrowes and miseries of this people seeme to themselves to increase upon them, and the more certaine they were of our going away, the more doubtful they shewed themselves what they might doe; so that we might easily judge that that joy (being exceeding great) where with they received us at our first arrivall, was cleane drowned in their excessive sorrow for our departing. For they did not onely loose on a sudden all mirth, joy, glad countenance, pleasant speeches, agility of body, familiar rejoycing one with another, and all pleasure what ever flesh and blood might bee delighted in, but with sighes and sorrowings, with heavy hearts and grieved minds, they powred out wofull complaints and moanes, with bitter tea res and wringing of their hands, tormenting themselves. And as men refusing all comfort, they onely accounted themselves as cast-awayes, and

---

2   In giving a name to the country, and in setting up a monument in token of discovery, Drake laid the foundation of a claim to English sovereignty.

those whom the gods were about to forsake: so that nothing we could say or do, was able to case them of their so heavy a burthen, or to deliver them from so desperate a straite, as our leaving of them did seeme to them that it would cast them into.

Howbeit, seeing they could not still enjoy our presence, they (supposing us to be gods indeed) thought it their duties to intreate us that, being absent, we would yet be mindfull of them, and making signes of their desires that in time to come wee would see them againe, they stole upon us a sacrifice, and set it on fire erre we were aware, burning therein a chaine and a bunch of feathers. We laboured by all meanes possible to withhold or withdraw them, but could not prevaile, till at last we fell to prayers and singing of Psalmes, whereby they were allured immediatly to forget their folly, and leave their sacrifice unconsumed, suffering the fire to go out; and imitating us in all our actions, they fell a lifting of their eyes and hands to heaven, as they saw us do.

The 23 of July they tooke a sorrowfull farewell of us, but being loath to leave us, they presently ranne to the top of the hits to keepe us in their sight as long as they could, making fires before and behind, and on each side of them, burning therein (as is to be supposed) sacrifices at our departure.

The Indians of California Greet Sir Francis Drake, engraving by Theodore de Bry, 1579. De Bry was an engraver, goldsmith and editor who created a large number of engraved illustrations for his books. Although most of his books were based on first-hand accounts by explorers, De Bry himself, acting as a redactor of the information, never visited the Americas.

7. Diary of an Expedition to the Port of Monterrey, 1602

By Sebastián Vizcaíno

Primary Source

We arrived at the port of Monterey on December 16 [1602] at seven in the evening. The next day the General ordered *Alférez* Alarcón to go ashore with the necessary materials to build a shelter where Mass could be celebrated, to see if there was any water, and determine what the land was like. He found freshwater, and near the shore he found a large live-oak tree, where he built the protective shelter to celebrate Mass. Then the General, *Comisario*, Admiral, Captains, *Alférez*, and the rest of the men went ashore. Alter Mass was celebrated and the skies had lifted, for it had been very foggy, we found ourselves in the best port that one could hope for. Besides being sheltered from all winds, it has many pine trees—suitable for masts and lateen yards and many live oaks and white oaks. There is an abundance of water and everything is near the shore. The land is fertile and the climate and soil are like that of Castile. There are many game animals, such as stags that look like young bulls, deer, bison, very large bears, rabbits, hares, and many others. There are also many birds, such as geese, partridges, quail, cranes, ducks, vultures, and many other species of birds that I will not mention so as not to be burdensome.

The land is very populated. An endless number of Indians appeared at different times and many of them came to our camp, They seem to be gentle and peaceful people. Using gestures, they said there are many settlements inland. Besides fish and shellfish, the foods these Indians eat on a daily basis are acorns and another nut that is thicker than a chestnut. This is what we were able to understand from them. …

The weather was extremely cold and the men worked very hard gathering wood and storing water for our voyage to Cape Mendocino. The cold was so intense that when dawn broke on Wednesday, New Year's Day, 1603, all the mountains were covered with snow. They looked like the volcano in Mexico. The well from which we had been taking water was frozen to the thickness of a palm's width. The earthen jugs filled with water had been left outside during the night, and they were so frozen that even if they rolled them around not a drop leaked out. Seeing that we were in a difficult situation, everyone pulled together to help, including; the General, who helped carry the jugs and also did other tasks. Even though he was ill, Captain Peguero came to our aid with the help of *Alférez* Alarcón and the pilots, who worked without stopping to rest. On Friday night, January 3, we were ready.

On this day, the General, accompanied by the *Comisario* and ten archers, headed inland in a southeast direction. They had heard there was a large river that emptied into the ocean, as well as another fine port. They also wanted to get a closer look at the terrain, the animals, and the people.

The General had traveled about three leagues when he discovered another fine port, into which emptied a large river. This river flowed from a range of high, snow-covered mountains with large pine trees, black and white poplars, and willows. There was a large riverbank, along which could be

Sebastián Vizcaíno, a 16th century Spanish explorer of the Americas, Pacific Ocean, and East Asia, portrayed in this facsimile of a 17th century engraving. Artist unknown.

found livestock as large as cows, even though they looked like stags. However, their hide was different; it was wooly and dragged on the ground. Each horn was more than three yards long. They tried to kill one but did not wait long enough. They did not find any people, because they were living in the interior on account of the cold. The General sent *Alférez* Juan Francisco and four soldiers to a *rancheria* to see what was there. They found that it was deserted and returned. As soon as the General and the rest of the men returned to the Admiral's ship at nightfall, we raised the anchor and set sail at midnight, aided by a land breeze.

8. A Letter From Vizcaíno to King Phillip III of Spain, 1603

By Sebastián Vizcaíno

Primary Source

Mexico. May 23, 1603

Among the most important ports that I discovered was one located at 37 degrees latitude, which I named Monterey. I wrote to Your Majesty from there on September 28 of this year, stating that this port is all that one could hope for. It is a convenient stopping place along the coast for ships that are coming from the Philippines. The port is sheltered from all winds, and along the shore there are many pine trees that could be used for ship masts of any size desired. There are also live oaks and white oaks, rosemary, vines, and roses of Alexandria. There are many rabbits, hares, partridges, and other genera and species found in Spain, especially in the Sierra Morena, as well as different types of birds. It is a pleasant place. The area is very populated by people whom I considered to be meek, gentle, quiet, and quite amenable to conversion to Catholicism and to becoming subjects of Your Majesty. The Indians have strong bodies and white faces. The women are somewhat smaller and have nice features.

Their clothing is made from sealskins. They tan and dress the hides better than how it is done in Castile. Seals are found in abundance. They have a large amount of flax and hemp, from which they make fishing lines and nets for catching rabbits and hares. Their boats are made of pine and are very well constructed. They go out into the ocean with fourteen oarsmen and they can sail with ease even during a strong storm.

I traveled more than eight hundred leagues along the coast and kept a record of all the people I encountered. The coast is populated by an endless number of Indians, who said there were large settlements in the interior. They invited me to go there with them. They were very friendly to us, and when I showed them the image of Our Lady they were drawn to it and wanted to join us. They were very attentive during the sacrifice of the Mass. They make use of various idols, as I already have reported to the Viceroy. They are very knowledgeable about silver and gold and said that these metals can be found in the interior.

Map L'Amerique, created by cartographer Nicolas de Fer in 1717.

9. The Diary of Captain Luis Antonio Argüello
The Last Spanish Expedition in California, 1821

By Luis Antonio Argüello

Primary Source

Formed of the Expedition begun 17 October 1821, of the Incidents Occurring on It from the Beginning to the Conclusion, Verified for the Use of Colonel Pablo Vicente de Solá, Governor of Alta California, under the Command of Captain of the Company of Cavalry

17 October

At six in the afternoon today I began to march to the pier of the Port of San Francisco. I was at the head of the troop of Infantry, Artillery, and Cavalry, with the officers of both pickets, Lieutenant of Infantry Francisco de Haro; Brevet of Cavalry José Sánchez; Chaplain the Reverend Father Blas de Ordaz, Apostolic Preacher and Minister of the Mission of San Francisco; interpreter of the English nation, John Anthony Gilroy; the neophyte Rafael of the Mission of San Francisco and the neophyte Marín of the Mission of San Rafael. I was to embark in the launches named *San Rafael* (alias *La Descubridora*) and the one of the Mission of San Francisco named San Antonio. Toward this end they were ready, but the embarkation did not take place because we were going to spend the night before putting ourselves on board. For this reason the entire troop camped on the beach of that pier in order to embark the following day of the eighteenth.

18 October

At eight today I boarded the launches with all the troop of the expedition under my command and setting the sails, I took a northern course for the opposite side of the port where the Mission of San Rafael was. We arrived in the environs of that mission at five in the afternoon at the mouth of the strait. We went toward it where I awaited the high tide in order to continue the navigation with a course to the east. Having achieved this from six in the afternoon until ten at night, we cast anchor on a coast named Ruyutu where we made a stop to give the troop a rest in order to continue the navigation the following day of the nineteenth.

19 October

At eight-thirty today I continued my navigation on the same course to the east to the Strait of Carquínez where I cast anchor at two in the afternoon. Here I found the herd of horses on which we had to continue the march by land with the entire troop that was under my orders. The herd of horses proceeded to this goal from the Presidio of San Francisco to this place, by way of the Missions of Santa Clara and San José, which are found on the coast of the bay of this port. In this regard these horses should join the herd of horses also provided for the same expedition and should conduct themselves with other auxiliaries in order to go to the opposite side of the strait in the launches that the Missions of San Francisco and San Jose gave freely for this purpose. In effect, this operation will begin tomorrow, and meanwhile

I wait in expectation of the launches that are lacking in order to achieve it. For this reason I prepared myself to camp (all the troop having been transported) on the banks of the same strait where I await the morning of the following day of the twentieth.

20 October

During the preceding night and the afternoon of today the two launches *San José* and *San Francisco Solano*, belonging to the missions of those names, were reunited at this place. At nine in the morning [we began] the transport of the herd of horses as there were now four launches. In these, 110 were carried over between three in the afternoon and this time. I considered it prudent to suspend the tiring and painful operation for the repose of the troop and seamen of the launches but remaining always ready to continue on the following day of the twenty-first.

21 October

At nine this morning after the Chaplain had celebrated Mass for this expedition, the transport of the remaining remounts continued in the same four launches, finishing this task with 125 horses at seven at night. With all this work we were in the best condition and ready for the continuation of the march by land on the following day of the twenty-second.

22 October

At nine today after assembly was sounded and the appropriate orders were given for the march, I put myself at the head of the expeditionary troops under my command. We continued the same route to the east, and after having traveled seven hours at a regular pace, I called a halt in the place that is named Suisun (a parched village of the same name). There I determined to spend the night and to await the direction of my march of the following day of the twenty-third.

23 October

At eight-thirty in the morning I continued my route without incident following the course to the north until six in the afternoon when I called a halt at a village that I found named the Libaytos inhabited by heathen of both sexes as was another one I found at noon on the road named the Ululatos that the native guides reached en route to this place where I camped for the night and in order to continue my march on the following day of the twenty-fourth.

24 October

At nine in the morning I continued my march with the same course to the north, without incident, quietly leaving the people of the village the Libaytos from which I took this route. They showed much rejoicing in spite of their having no knowledge of the troop nor of any other people, lending themselves freely to the domestic services of all the troop, even serving as guides in large numbers for the journey to the village named Chila, also inhabited by a large number of natives that I found at two in the afternoon.

This village created a small halt because of the novelty we caused as they had never seen people of our kind. They became agitated for a while, resisting admitting us. They put up a defense with such fury and boldness that they caused some impetuosity that prudence and the goal of our mission successfully repressed. It ended well, with their submission after two hours of confusion and milling around of these natives. I succeeded in pacifying them and leaving them tranquil. They showed their repentance later by presenting themselves to me in great numbers to ask pardon.

They subsequently made available to me guides in order for me to continue my route for the rest of the afternoon. This I accomplished until six when I resolved to camp at a distance of two leagues from this village where I await my march the following day of the twenty-fifth.

25 October

I took my march from this place at eight in the morning following the course between north and east by which I traveled until twelve-thirty when I came upon a village situated on the banks of the river Jesus María named Goroy inhabited by a large number of people who received me with sufficient tranquility and some gifts of their making which they gave me with a show of rejoicing and peace. From these natives I began to receive news of the unknown establishment of foreigners of which I had already been told and which the object of this expedition is to discover. The news was that two men dressed in our style and who also used firearms as we do had come from the next village (to which these natives are to guide us). After two hours of rest, having received this news and having taken the guides that these natives gave me in order to continue my march, which I determined to be in a northern direction, I was led until eight at night. I camped by the bank of the river Jesus María, where, without any other incident, I awaited the morning of the following day of the twenty-sixth.

26 October

At ten in the morning today I continued my march taking the course of the previous day until five in the afternoon. I came to a village named Güillito divided into five fairly large manor lodges inhabited by a large number of people. It could be seen at a distance of a league away. These natives at first sight showed signs of haughtiness by the resistance they made to the offers of peace which I made them according to the particular ends and objects of the expedition. But my offers were in vain and the impulses of their rebellion and inflexibility surpassed [my attempts]. Perhaps [they were] stimulated by such a large crowd. In view of their obstinacy and stubbornness and that they did not want to admit any gentle approaches with which I invited them to peace and tranquility, I proposed to prove to them [my intent]. I ordered the cannon to be loaded. The objective was to intimidate them and make them moderate their pride. For this reason I fired at them, [which was] required by such a [large] group that surrounded us and by their discharging arrows into the troop. This and their obstinacy in resisting caused me to order thus but always with a view not to cause them havoc (for which I ordered that the point be lowered). [I wanted to] frighten them in order to subdue them and also ordered the Infantry and Cavalry to double back to the rear of the cannon and remain in battle formation in order to continue to fire in case the natives should [persist] in their rebelliousness, which in effect they showed in the hurried flight that they made after the discharge of the cannon. But the troop continue in its advance with a short skirmish of fire punishing their indocility, causing the loss of five heathens and some wounded ones who escaped with all the rest of the crowd that favored the river Jesús María that flows between the habitations of these heathens. During this altercation and movements, night fell, which obliged me to camp in the center of these villages with the objective of seeing if they continued in pacification and quiet among them. However, after the troop was camped, [the heathens] let it be known that they were obstinate in their resistance and rebellion with the continuous use of their arms that they discharged into the camp from the opposite side of the river. They continued [during] the night without causing an occurrence other than the one of the day with the untamed ones [causing] the loss of a mule loaded with two thousand cartridges. It threw itself headlong into the river Jesús María and remained submerged in the depths in spite of eight men having searched for it without being able to find it because it was already dark. I thought it more prudent to give rest to the troop and suspend all this fatigue until the following day of the twenty-seventh.

27 October

I considered it convenient to remain all morning of this day camped in this place in order to have a view of the opposite side where the rest of the heathens were who had fled the previous day. At four when they came around the camp [I tried to] make them understand through means of the neophyte interpreter of the Mission of San Francisco called Rafael that it was not my intention to harm them in any way neither before nor after, and that I only wanted them to remain in peace and to guide us in the future march to the next village whence we would get other guides for the continuation. In effect, after repeated innuendoes, it was shown to them with unequivocal proofs that [we wanted] peace on our part, which we had offered before. They were timid and distrustful of humbling themselves, and remained unconvinced, which resulted in their coming to the site of the camp to talk with me. I made them see the reason why I was going through their lands, and they had never met a troop nor seen people of our kind (so they said). Thus I continued parleying with them through the interpreter Rafael until getting word of the new establishment that is sought and what the news showed me was that they knew there were two of them. Both are on the coast of the sea to the north according to the signs and indications and one could arrive at them in three or four days having previously to pass through the Sierra Nevada and some villages that there

are from which they have also this news. With these hopes and having seen that these natives are calmed. I waited until midday passed to continue my march in which I succeeded with the guides that they voluntarily gave me to direct me on the consecutive road to the next villages. With these guides I took the course to the north at two-thirty in the afternoon, which I continued until five, ending at another village named Capa, inhabited by a few heathens, but they received me with much contentment and quiet. I decided to camp in it for the night and to continue my route the following day of the twenty-eighth.

28 October

At ten in the morning today after the Chaplain had celebrated Mass, I again took my march with a course to the northeast which ended in the north at six-thirty at a village named Chac, inhabited by a large number of heathens. I had passed earlier through another one with a lot of heathens, named

Coru in which I made a short stop in order to satisfy them and get some news of the object that is desirable to find. But the news was not as clear as that earlier, which always left us with the same hope and doubt as the first.

These villages although with numerous inhabitants and worthy of attention showed themselves of sufficient peace and quiet and received the troop with much pleasure and celebration, full of confidence and satisfaction according to the demonstrations that their simplicity let be known.

Thus the quiet observed in these heathens as in the rest of the previous villages through which we passed today encouraged me to allow them more civilizing influence between us in order to rid them of the fear that I felt they had. Because of this, I decided to camp in Chac to spend the night here and take my march from this point at dawn the following day of the twenty-ninth.

The Presidio of San Francisco and the Golden Gate. Drawing by Louis Choris, a Russian painter, explorer and writer, during the Rurik Expedition in November 1817.

Section III

California's Spanish Mission Era, 1769–1833

Section III

Introduction to California's Spanish Mission Era, 1769–1833

Sources

1. A Report on the First Plan for Missions in California, 1620
2. Plan for the Erection of Government, c. 1768
3. A Letter to José de Gálvez Reporting on Alta California, 1769
4. A Report on the Abuse of Indians by Soldiers, 1772
5. Report on the Presidio at Monterey, 1773
6. Rules for Pueblos and Missions, 1779
7. Letter of Junípero Serra to the Reverend Father Preacher, Fray Fermin, 1780
8. Life in California: The Journals of la Pérouse, 1786
9. The Los Angeles Census of 1781 Shows a Diverse Ethnic Mix
10. Supply Requisitions for the Mission and Presidio at Santa Barbara, 1802–1810
11. Reminisces of Indian Life at San Luis Rey, 1830s
12. An Old Spanish Woman Remembers the Mission Era, 1877
13. The Potential of Alta California: A Report to the Government in Mexico, 1827

In 1769, the Spanish recognized the territory of Alta California as the northwest corner of their empire. This territory included most of the current state of California, as well as Arizona, Nevada, Utah, and parts of Colorado and Wyoming. In reality, the territory was governed by a variety of native peoples. Alta California was in the province of *Las Californias*, along with the peninsula we now call Baja California, until 1804, when it became a province in its own right.

Very few Europeans had visited Alta California before 1769. In that year, Father Junípero Serra, of the Franciscan Order of the Catholic Church, began founding a series of missions along the California coast. The government of New Spain also sent Gaspar de Portolá, a military leader, to establish various presidios (forts). The military and religious leaders were expected to work together, though they often had conflicting ideas, especially in regard to the treatment of the native peoples.

When people think of California history, they often think of the missions. Many Californians have visited a mission, or built a model mission out of sugar cubes, but few people actually know much about what happened in these buildings.

Between 1769 and 1823, the Spanish established 21 missions along the coast of today's California, from San Diego to Sonoma. About 60 percent of today's Californians live in lands that were once controlled by the missions. In addition to saving souls, the missions focused on agriculture. The missions grew a wide variety of fruits and vegetables and raised livestock. They found an excellent home for many crops they brought over from Spain, such as grapes and oranges. California also became known for cattle, and a thriving trade in leather and tallow.

Though the missions were under the control of Spain, few of the participants in the mission system were actually European. Most of the work at the missions was done by people from the local cultures or by Native Americans from various parts of Mexico who came to California as part of the mission system.

The Spanish missionaries belonged to the Franciscan Order, named for Saint Francis of Assisi, a friar of the thirteenth century known for his simplicity, poverty, and gentle spirit. In many ways, the order had changed little since the Middle Ages. In the eighteenth century, the missionaries sought to bring their brand of Christianity to native Californians. The Franciscans had been active in many parts of New Spain for over two centuries. A native of Spain, Father Serra had served as a missionary in Mexico for twenty years before coming to California.

Earlier, the Society of Jesus (Jesuits), another order of the Roman Catholic Church, had established fifteen missions in the peninsula we now call Baja California. The Jesuits had established a remarkable network of trade and political alliances in many parts of the world. In the mid-1700s, European monarchs tended to see the Jesuits as a threat to their power. In 1767, the Spanish government ordered the Jesuits within the empire to abandon their missionary work.

The Spanish government gave control of the Baja California missions to the Franciscan Order in 1767. The Franciscans were active on the peninsula for just a short time, however, because in 1769 the viceroy told them to focus on establishing missions along the coast of today's California. Acting on behalf of the king, the viceroy transferred control of the Baja California missions to the Dominican Order of the Catholic Church. The Crown approved a boundary line to separate the activities of the two missionary groups, a line that would later become the border between California and Mexico.

Sources

The Spanish had been contemplating the idea of establishing missions long before 1769. As we saw in the previous section, the explorer Sebastian Vizcaino had suggested that the Indians of the Monterey area would be easy to convert based on his observations in 1602–1603.

In Selection 1, **A Report on the First Plan for Missions in California, 1620**, Father Antonio de la Ascension offers his perspective based on his study of nearly a century of Spanish missionary activity. As the Chaplain on the Vizcaino expedition, he was also able to speak based on his direct experience with native peoples in several areas. Ascension emphasizes that the Spanish must work in "a peaceful Christian manner with love and tranquility … " He offers a rather frank assessment of previous Spanish exploits, noting: " … in conquests and attempts to settle new lands, the Lord our God has more often been offended than He has been served."

Notice how specific Ascension is in his instructions. For example, he states that the Carmelites, his own order within the Catholic Church, should be in charge. Perhaps most importantly, he emphasizes that the religious leaders should be able to give direction to the military officials who join them in the expedition. What problems could he be anticipating?

As events proceeded, the missionary activities that Ascension had planned so carefully never happened, at least not in his century. Plans for missionary activity would become more serious in the 1760s as Spanish observers became aware of English and Russian expeditions in their northern territories. In 1765 the Spanish King Charles III appointed Jose de Galvez, a nobleman and attorney, to serve as Visitor General of New Spain. Interestingly, Galvez had studied for the priesthood briefly before changing his mind to study the law. As Visitor General, Galvez was given immense powers to reform the government of New Spain. Upon his appointment, Galvez immediately focused attention on the northern provinces and territories.

In Selection 2, **Plan for the Erection of Government, 1768**, Galvez notes various reports of Russian and English activities and outlines a plan for protecting the "Peninsula of Californias" as well as three provinces in northern Mexico. He is particularly concerned that the "Moscovites" (Russians) might be planning to settle in Monterey Bay. The tone of the report is urgent and lacking in some of the pleasantries and religious references you are likely to notice in other Spanish documents of the era. Galvez concludes with these words: "from now on, the Foundations of Work are going to be laid with Solidity, Integrity, and Zeal."

Galvez focused on both the military and the missionary aspects of settling California. In 1769 he appointed Gaspar de Portola to lead an expedition to Alta California by land. He also appointed Pedro Fages, a young officer who had distinguished himself fighting Indians in the harsh desert areas of Sonora, to sail to San Diego and meet Portola. Supplies ran out long before Fages reached San Diego. After 110 days at sea, his crew was barely alive.

Fages, in selection 3, **A Letter to Jose de Galvez Reporting on Alta California, 1769**, makes several observations about the area and about the native people he encountered. He uses the term *rancherias* to refer to native villages. Notice that fresh water is a key concern of the expedition. The river he mentions is now known as the San Diego River. Perhaps of greatest interest, however, are the items in a box that he sent to Galvez. Notice he is eagerly following instructions from Galvez; but Galvez had never actually been to California. Historians might question if Galvez, who was reading the letter in relative comfort in Mexico City, was really the expert.

Long before the missions were established, priests and scholars such as Father Ascension (Selection 1) had noted how Spanish expeditions had often become abusive toward the native people. Ascension had also emphasized that the religious leaders should guide the military leaders to assure proper behavior and a caring attitude toward the Indians. In Selection 4, A Report on the Abuse of Indians by Soldiers, 1772, Father Luis Jayme shows that some of the fears of Ascension and others had come true. Father Jayme notes that Pedro Fages (who replaced Portola as the military governor in 1770) was extremely stingy in giving food and other supplies to the settlement at San Diego. (When Jayme refers to "Indians from the Californias" he means native people who had traveled to San Diego from Baja California as part of the missionary expedition. "Local Christian natives" are people they have converted. "Gentiles" are people who have not adopted Christianity.) Jayme claims his group has baptized over fifty Indians, but they can make little progress on developing their mission because the Indians have to spend most of their time hunting and foraging for food.

Jayme reports that many native people have been raped by soldiers. He notes that people in native villages often flee when they see him coming, fearing that his party will be like the soldiers. Jayme also notes that in one particular village, "the gentiles … have been on the point of coming here and killing us all … " Three years later Father Jayme was killed by a group of Indians at Mission San Diego.

The next selection, **A Report on the Presidio at Monterey, 1773**, is again from Fages, and here he describes the design of the presidio. We have also included a diagram of the layout from around the time the presidio was built. The presidio was mainly a military fortress, but you will also notice it included a church and living quarters for the priests "who come here to administer to our spiritual life." It also contains a kitchen, a prison, major storage areas, and even a room for selling or giving out clothing to people who live at the presidio. You may be able to tell some of the priorities and concerns of the military officials from how Fages describes each room.

Note that the mission serving Monterey, known as Mission San Carlos, was originally built next to the presidio, but it was moved to an area about three and a half miles away, near the Carmel River in 1771. Fages offers an agricultural reason for the move, but other evidence suggests the move may have been to keep the soldiers away from Indian women who were living in the mission.

Within ten years of arriving in Alta California, Father Serra and his group had built eight missions. 1,749 native people had been converted to Christianity at this point, compared to just a few hundred people of Spanish heritage. Felipe de Neve, who had become the Governor of Las Californias in 1775, saw the potential for pueblos or towns to grow in coordination with some of the missions. The first of these towns, El Pueblo de San José de Guadalupe, was built near Mission Santa Clara in 1777. Today it is known simply as San Jose. Neve is most famous for founding an unruly little town called El Pueblo de Nuestra Señora la Reina de los Ángeles (the Town of Our Lady Queen of the Angels) in 1781. Today we call that place Los Angeles.

In the sixth selection, **Rules for Pueblos and Missions, 1779**, Felipe de Neve lays out his vision for establishing pueblos primarily for "white" (European) people to promote agriculture, raise horses, and take care of other local needs. Essentially, his plan is to make the territory of Alta California more self-sufficient and also to encourage families to grow among the Spanish population. Historians might ask why he gave so much attention to promoting "white" settlements rather than focusing on assimilating and training the converted Indians to make the territory more prosperous. Here we have excerpted some of the specific policies he laid out for the settlements, which provide clues as to how he expected the towns to grow.

In Selection 7, we hear directly from the man who is almost synonymous with the California Missions, Father Junipero Serra. Admirers of Serra see a man who devoted his life to serving God, built the first nine missions from scratch with amazingly weak provisions, argued vehemently with government officials on behalf of the native peoples, and who walked thousands of miles on foot, even when he was in pain. Serra has even been proposed as a candidate for sainthood in the Catholic Church. Some historians, however, blame the mission system he created for widespread misery and death among the native population. The written records indicate that he was better at saving souls and expanding the missions than he was at actually running the missions and caring for the people in them. Perhaps most interestingly, his relationship with the government in Mexico City was terrible, a fact that could be counted against him or perhaps in his favor. If there is one thing historians might all agree on, it is that no other individual has had as much influence on California; and he did it in just fifteen years.

A Letter of Junípero Serra to the Reverend Father Preacher, Fray Fermin, 1780 offers a glimpse into Serra's character. After more than ten years of service in California he did not mind admitting that he could use some rest. The letter also indicates that spiritual concerns are at the heart of every topic. You will also see clues about how he appreciates life, and how common death was in the mission system.

What was life actually like in a California mission? Perhaps the best clues come from a French aristocrat who sailed to Monterey Bay in 1786. Jean-François de la Pérouse visited both the Monterey presidio and Mission San Carlos as part of an expedition to various parts of the world on behalf of King Louis XVI. As part of the project, he kept a journal with detailed observations of the people and places he encountered. In Selection 8, **Life in California, 1786**, we see the impressions of la Pérouse as he visited the mission. Notice his comments on the architecture. The missions of that era looked much different than the structures we can visit today. His perspective on the Indians, and their daily life in and around the missions, is perhaps the most frank and illuminating account available.

The Spanish missionaries were delighted to have la Pérouse and his party visit. France was an ally of Spain in this era, and the two countries were both active in promoting the Catholic faith. La Pérouse was treated very well, a fact that he notes in his journal. Some might expect that he would only say positive things about the mission, but his journal actually includes several sharp criticisms. While la Pérouse had much in common with the missionaries, his outlook was different in some important ways. He was educated in France during the time known as the Enlightenment. He was a strong supporter of individual rights and free thinking.

In the journal, notice how he is sympathetic to the missionary project from a religious standpoint but he is also very critical of their methods. The la Pérouse visit took place two years after Father Serra had passed away; la Pérouse had the opportunity to meet the new President of the Missions, Father Fermín de Lasuén. Notice his high opinion of Lasuén, which would appear to contrast with his criticisms of the missions.

In Selection 9, **The Los Angeles Census of 1781 Shows a Diverse Ethnic Mix**, we see how de Neve's vision for promoting "pueblos of white people" played out in reality (see Selection 6). Los Angeles was a diverse community from the very beginning; purely European people were outnumbered by Indians and people of mixed races. Notice the large presence of people with African heritage. Mulata means European/African whereas Mestizo means European/Native American.

By the early 1800s Alta California had developed significant towns and a thriving system of agriculture. In 1804, the territory was allowed to become its own province. "Nueva California," as it was often called, had grown big enough to have its own governor. Alta California was on the road to becoming self-sufficient, but the people still looked forward to shipments of supplies from the Mexican mainland.

San Blas, on the west coast of Mexico in today's state of Nayarit, was considered the lifeline to the missions. Supply ships typically arrived about once a year in the late 1700s and early 1800s; unless thrown off course by major storms or pirates. Selection 10, **Supply Requisitions for the Mission and Presidio at Santa Barbara, 1802–1810**, shows us lists of items approved by the governor (of Las Californias, and then of Alta California after 1804) for shipment from the Commissariat of San Blas. What do these supply requests tell us about the settlements at Santa Barbara? Why are these products so special that they would make a request to the governor and wait for a long sea voyage to bring them? Why would they order chairs or baskets sent by ship rather than making their own? Also, notice they use words like "good" and "ordinary" to describe some of the products. This would seem to imply that products were not standardized, and the people in Santa Barbara relied on the judgment of the people working at the Commissariat.

In Selection 11, **Reminisces of Indian Life at San Luis Rey, 1830s**, we hear directly from a native person who grew up at Mission San Luis Rey de Francia, north of San Diego. Pablo Tac belonged to a group of Indians known as the Luiseño, because of their association with the mission; they were also called the Payomkowishu, which meant "people of the west." The Friars noticed he was a particularly good student, and they sent him and another boy to study in Rome. Unfortunately, Pablo Tac died at a young age and he left behind only a few writings.

Notice how Tac describes his own culture and their connection to the missions. Also, notice how he describes the divisions between the Friars and the neophytes (converted people). What does Tac say that would indicate he has a lot of pride in his culture and also a strong connection to the mission? Notice how he describes the life of the mission in terms of what various types of people do. Everyone appears to have a well defined place in the mission.

For Selection 12 we turn to another type of document: a transcript of an oral history interview. In the 1870s, a small team of historians went looking for people who could remember life in the Mission Era. They found Eulalia Perez, a remarkably old woman of Spanish heritage who had lived in at least two California missions in the early 1800s, San Diego and San Gabriel (San Gabriel was near the Los Angeles pueblo). In her account, **An Old Spanish Woman Remembers the Mission Era, 1877**, Perez remembers that she grew up in Loreto, in Baja California, and married a soldier serving at the presidio there when she was age 15. (She did not know in what year she was born, but you can make an educated guess from the clues in what she says.) We know she came to San Diego early in the 1800s and she later moved to San Gabriel. She had many children and moved her family as required by her husband's work. She also learned how to deliver babies and became known as an excellent cook. What does her story tell us about the life of a soldier's wife in the mission system? How is her view of life in the missions similar or different from the other perspectives we have seen? Notice how she describes the Fathers and the native people that she worked with at the mission. Her story about the cooking experience might be especially helpful for helping us understand the social dynamics in the mission.

Some might ask, how reliable is the memory of an old woman like Eulalia Perez, who does not actually know when she was born? At the time she was interviewed there were few, if any, people around to verify her stories. What qualities do you see in her stories that make them valuable? Which parts of her account would you say are debatable and which parts are probably solid? You might also consider how written records could be useful in combination with her memory.

In 1823, when the last mission was built, the 21 missions and several related towns were prospering economically. The change from Spanish to Mexican rule (discussed in Section IV) did not appear to slow their progress, at least not immediately. The new government in Mexico was considering how to encourage and direct trade in California, and what role the missions would play. In Selection 13, **The Potential of Alta California: A Report to the Government in Mexico, 1827**, Enrique Virmond, a trader based in Acapulco, discusses the opportunities and challenges in the province in a letter to someone in the government of Mexico. He believes they will have a bright future if they make certain efforts to expand trade. Notice Vermond also suggests that the President slim down the military in the province, believing that most of the *hijos del pais* (native sons) are doing little of value and they are a burden on the government. Notice how he describes the dynamics between soldiers and Indians. At this point, the two groups have actually grown up together, but the power relationship has not changed much from earlier times. Notice also how he describes the Fathers and their relationship to the Indians. Why does he think the mission system needs to be supported? In the next era we will how some of his concerns proved to be valid.

Readings

The duty of recruiting these people should be assigned to one or two Captains who are good Christians and God fearing men as well as persons of merit who have served His Majesty faithfully on other occasions, such as at war *on* land or sea. It should be their responsibility to appoint the officers of their company. They must be satisfied that these men will perform their duties in a careful Christian manner. They also should be experienced men who know how to fulfill the responsibilities entrusted to them, because the order and good discipline of the soldiers depends on these men. This expedition should be entrusted to a courageous and talented person who has had previous experience with similar duties and is accustomed to them. He thus will know how to command with love and authority and will treat each person as an individual. And, be certain that this is a God fearing person, *one* who keeps his own counsel, and someone who is not only zealous in his service to His Majesty but

also in matters relating to the conversion *of* souls. A person with these qualities can be appointed General of the armada. Everyone, from Captains to soldiers, will be under his command and will obey him at all times and follow his orders.

The General, Captains, soldiers, and all others who go on this expedition must be given express orders to hold themselves in strict obedience to and comply with the religious who are accompanying them. Without their orders, counsel, or recommendations, no act of war or any other grievance shall be committed against the heathen Indians, even though they might provoke it. In this way, everything can proceed in a peaceful Christian manner with love and tranquility, which is the method to be used in pacifying this realm and preaching the Holy Gospel. The preparations and expenses are intended for this purpose. If it is not done in this manner, all efforts will fail, and time and money will be wasted. In New Spain, experience has shown many times that in conquests and attempts to settle new lands, the Lord our God has more often been offended than He has been served.

The religious who should go on this expedition are the Discalced Carmelites. They are the ones to whom His Majesty has entrusted the conversion, religious instruction, and teaching of the Indians in this realm of the Californias. On this first expedition there will be a total of six religious, namely, four priests and two lay friars. In the name of His Majesty, the Superiors of this religious order will be asked to identify and appoint people for this voyage. These people must meet the requirements of the enterprise, that is, be holy, loving, learned, and congenial men who not only know how to advise, guide, and direct souls, but can also resolve, with sound Catholic doctrine, any problems that might arise.

By observing the indults and benefits granted by the Supreme Pontiffs in favor of the new conversions in order to increase their numbers, these holy men, with their piety, modesty, simplicity, and religious graciousness, will succeed in winning the affection and hearts of the General, Captains, and all the other soldiers. In this manner they can lead them along the holy path of virtue. They can persuade and admonish *them* in a loving manner to confess their sins and receive the Holy Sacrament of the Eucharist with all possible devotion and resolution and to offer their body and soul in service to His Divine Majesty, asking that He grant them safe passage on their journey. By focusing on this matter with the proper spirit and devotion, these religious will win the hearts and spirit of everyone and they will be able to maintain control to ensure that there is peace, love, and unity among everyone. If by chance there should be some conflict among the men, they could reconcile them with discretion. In this way the grudges, annoyances, and hostilities, as well as mutinies, revolts, and insubordination which usually occur in similar enterprises can be avoided.

The religious will he provided with everything necessary for their journey, such as materials necessary for celebrating Mass and administering the Sacraments, books, vestments, and other items that can be given as gifts to anyone who might be sick. Also, at His Majesty's expense, a number of small items should be placed on board. These items could include Flemish trinkets such as colored glass beads, imitation garnets, small bells, small looking glasses, knives, inexpensive scissors, Parisian Jew's harps, and some articles of clothing. These items should be divided among the religious and the soldiers so that, wherever they land or choose to settle, they can distribute these pleasing gift to the infidels they meet. With signs of love and good will, in the name of His Majesty, the gentile Indians will eventually feel love and affection for the Christians. They will also recognize that the Christians have come to their lands not to take away what the Indians have, but to give them what they have brought, and to save their souls. This is a matter of great importance, for it will enable the Indians to become calm, humane, and peaceful. Then they will obey the Spaniards without opposition or repugnance and receive willingly those who have come to preach the Holy Gospel and the mysteries of our Holy Catholic Faith. Moreover, the Indians will be grateful, and as recompense or payment for what they have been given, they will assist us by sharing what they consider to be of value from their land, namely food, as has happened to us.

With this preparation, the soldiers and religious can set sail on the ships once they have been made ready. However, absolutely no women may board ship or travel with the men, to avoid offending God and to prevent quarrels among them. Even if there are no favorable winds, the ocean currents that head in the direction of the tip of California will enable the ship to land within a month's time, at most, at the Bay of San Bernabé, which is at the Cape of San Lucas, at the tip of

California. This is the most suitable place for the first settlement.

After landing at the Bay of San Bernabé, try at once to set up camp at the most suitable position and place. It should be designed so that the houses protect one another. The first thing to build is a church, so that the priests can celebrate Mass there each day. If the General, Captains, and soldiers go to confession and receive the Sacrament when they arrive in this realm, this will be a very good and sacred way to properly initiate the enterprise. With the help and grace of Our Redeemer Jesus Christ, they will succeed in their endeavors to pacify the realm and convert its inhabitants to our Holy Catholic Faith.

The stronghold that will serve as a castle, watchtower, and defense against adverse situations should be built at a strong, commanding spot at a high elevation. From this place, one can be assured of safe passage to the sea. This would be a very advantageous way of sending for and receiving reinforcements by sea, in case the need should arise. The Portuguese have commonly done this where they have established themselves in India. This strategy or precautionary measure has proven to be very beneficial to them. This castle stronghold should be stocked with artillery that will be brought for this purpose, together with other defenses that usually are constructed at similar fortifications. Weapons and supplies will be kept there. There should be a watchtower above the castle from which a guard can monitor all comings and goings at the camp, because in the land of the infidels, even though the Indians may appear to be friendly and men of peace, one must not trust them too much. First, one must live among the Indians with great circumspection, vigilance, precaution, and astuteness, but also with a kind and loving watchfulness. They should be treated with love and affection and rewarded with gifts that were brought at His Majesty's expense to attract and win them over.

A trading house should be built so that the Indians can gather there in trade and barter with the Spaniards and among themselves. This will greatly facilitate the communication between the Indians and our people, and love and friendship will develop.

From this place they can send the ships, frigate, and other boats to the Christian settlement of Culiacán, to the islands of Mazatlán, or to the *pueblo* of La Navidad to bring back everything that is needed for settling the land, as well as food, cows, sheep, goals, mares, and hogs. The animals can be transported alive from one point to the other in two to four days at the most, because the sea is about fifty leagues wide and the waters are safe and calm. These animals can be raised on this land because it is fertile and suitable for this purpose. They will multiply easily. Wheat and corn can be grown and vineyards and orchards can be planted so that food does not have to be transported from afar. The Indians can be taught how to grow the food and will want to learn when they see how they will benefit.

In addition to what has been said above, the Spaniards will be able to establish fisheries for pearls and other fish because there is an abundance of both here. The pearls and fish can be sent to New Spain so they can be sold in Mexico. Very fine salt works can be established and salt can be extracted from nearby mines. Once these operations have been put into place, with peace, love, and the goodwill of the natives, the religious can focus their attention on their ministry and begin the conversion of these Indians in the manner that seems most appropriate to them. With great prudence and gentleness they will be able to sow the seeds of the new Christian Church that will be planted there. It would be wise to bring Indian musicians from New Spain. With their trumpets and other instruments the divine services can be celebrated with devotion and ceremony. They also can teach the Indians to sing and play the instruments. It would be wise to select some of the brightest Indians. Then, from among this group, the most docile, clever, and talented young men and boys can be chosen. They should be taught the Christian doctrine and how to read from the Spanish primers. By knowing how to read they will also learn the Spanish language. They should also learn how to write, sing, and play all types of musical instruments. A strong building is built on a firm foundation. If care is taken at the very beginning, the end results will be positive.

It is very easy for the children to learn our language in this manner. When they are older they can teach the people they know their children, and their families. Thus, in a few years everyone will know the Spanish language. This will be of great benefit because then there will be no lack of ministers to teach and guide the Indians along the path to heaven and salvation. They then can proceed to establish other Christian settlements and convert the Indians who are scattered in the mountains, drawing them out with love, kindness, and gentleness. Care should be taken not to send the Christian soldiers out in too many directions, so as not to decrease the number of soldiers at the garrison and thus weaken it. For, if the Indians are instigated by the devil to revolt or rebel against the Spaniards, someone must be there to fight them off and keep them at bay. If their actions warrant it, they should be punished for their boldness.

The first recorded baptisms in Alta California were performed in "The Canyon of the Little Christians" in what is now San Diego county, just south of Mission San Juan Capistrano. This is a 1922 sketch by Zephyrin Engelhard for the historical monograph, San Juan Capistrano Mission.

APPENDIX A

Plan for the Erection of a Government and General Commandancy

Which includes the Peninsula of Californias and the Provinces of Sinaloa, Sonora, and Nueva Viscaya

Recently news has come that [the English have gone] as far as the Lake of Bois, from which issues the deep-flowing River of the West, directing its course, as discovered, toward the Sea of that name; and if it empties therein, or reaches the South Sea, or is (as may be the case) the famous Colorado River, which forms the Gulf of Californias, there is no doubt, in whichever of these alternatives, that we already have the English very near to our Settlements in New Mexico, and not very distant from the Western Coast of this Continent of America.

Moreover, the Prime Minister of our Court knows, from the voyages and memoirs that are published in Europe, that the Russians have been gaining an intimate knowledge of the navigation of the Sea of Tartary; and that they are, according to very credible and well-grounded statements, carrying on the Fur Trade on a Continent or Island which, it is estimated, lies at the distance of only eight hundred leagues from the Western Coast of Californias, which runs as far as Capes Mendocino and Blanco.

But, while the attempts of Russia and England need not revive at this time all the suspicions and anxieties that Spain manifested in former days (especially after the Reign of Felipe Second) for discovering and gaining possession, by way of the South Sea, of the alleged passage which the other Nations were seeking by way of the North Sea, it is indubitable that since the year 1749 [*sic*]—in which Admiral Anson came to the Western Coast of this Kingdom, as far as the entrance to the Port of Acapulco—the English and the Dutch (who afterward brought their ships from Eastern India within sight of Cape San Lucas and the Coasts of New Galicia) have acquired a very detailed knowledge of the Ports and Bays which we hold on the South Coast, especially in the Peninsula of Californias. With all this no one can regard it as impossible or even very difficult for one of those two Nations or for the Moscovites to establish, when that is least expected, a Colony at the Port of Monterrey, where they would have all desirable facilities and conveniences; and that thus we should come to see our North America invaded and exploited by way of the South Sea as it has been by that of the North.

In these circumstances, it seems as if worldly prudence may counsel, and even carry into effect, that we should take proper precautions in time, putting into practice whatever measures may be feasible to avert the dangers that threaten us. And, as at present the Peninsula of Californias is free from obstruction, it follows that we should and easily could—its population being increased by the aid of the free Commerce which ought to be carried on between that territory and this Kingdom—transport a Colony to the Port of Monterrey with the same vessels that we now have in the South Sea, which have been built for the use of the Sonora expedition. It only remains to establish in this Province the General Commandancy, which very soon can promote and facilitate the Settlement of Monterrey, and of other points on the Western Coast of the same Californias—where there are good Harbors, and the soil is more fertile and productive than that of the North Shore.

A Chief who is on the ground and energetic will secure considerable extensions to the Frontiers of Sonora and Nueva Viscaya, unless he is insufficiently provided with the funds that are necessary in order that the establishment of his Government may produce the utilities and advantages that ought to be expected. These are set forth at length in the project, already cited, which was presented to the Court in the year 1760, with the aim of securing the erection [of such a Government]. If the decision be reached that it is more expedient to maintain on the Frontiers of Chihuahua an Official, subordinate to the Governor, for the defense of that Mining Centre, a suitable person for that employ is Captain Don Lope de Cuellar, who was appointed by the Viceroy in fulfillment of the instructions addressed to him for the expulsion of the regulars belonging to the Company [of Jesus]. As that measure would do away with the office

of *corregidor* that was established in that Town, which enjoys very considerable imposts, from the fund that they produce can be drawn the Salary of two thousand *pesos*, which of course will be an addition to his pay sufficient to maintain the said Governor. At the same time he ought to look after the affairs of the Royal Treasury, with rank as Deputy of the Intendant of Nueva Viscaya—who must reside in the Capital City of Durango, and be, like the Intendants of Sonora and Californias, directly subordinate to the General Commandant of the three Provinces, since that Chief is responsible for rendering account to the Viceroy of Nueva España of whatever enterprises he may undertake, and of all occurrences worthy of note in the region under his command.

An examination of this plan will make evident at first view that in it are discussed only the principal points and designs of the idea, and that its sole aim, with nothing else in view, is to promote the public Interests of the King and the State in an establishment which, besides the urgent necessity of effecting it, carries the special recommendation that it will be very advantageous in a short time; for, from now on, the Foundations of the Work are going to be laid with Solidity, Integrity, and Zeal.

At Mexico, the twenty-third of January, [in the year] One Thousand, Seven Hundred, and Sixty-Eight.

Don José de Gálvez,
To the Marqués de Croix.

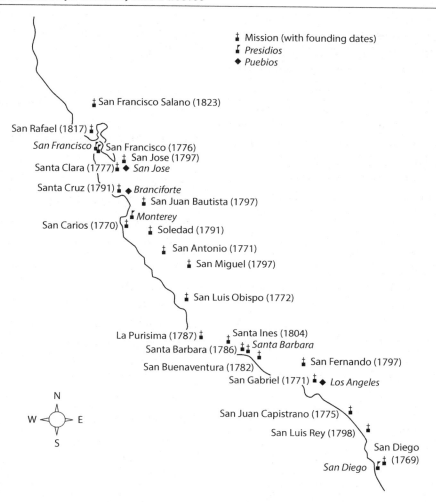

Mission (with founding dates)
Presidios
♦ Pueblos

San Francisco Salano (1823)

San Rafael (1817)

San Francisco — San Francisco (1776)

San Jose (1797)

Santa Clara (1777) — ♦ *San Jose*

Santa Cruz (1791) — ♦ *Branciforte*

San Juan Bautista (1797)

Monterey

San Carlos (1770) — Soledad (1791)

San Antonio (1771)

San Miguel (1797)

San Luis Obispo (1772)

La Purisima (1787) — Santa Ines (1804)

Santa Barbara (1786) — *Santa Barbara*

San Buenaventura (1782)

San Fernando (1797)

San Gabriel (1771) — ♦ *Los Angeles*

San Juan Capistrano (1775)

San Luis Rey (1798)

San Diego (1769)

San Diego

N
W ← ◇ → E
S

3. A Letter to José de Gálvez Reporting on Alta California, 1769

By Pedro Fages

Primary Source

Your Illustrious Lordship—My dear Sir: I am remitting to Your Excellency a box of various little things that I have obtained in trade with the pagan Indians of this vicinity. Here their *rancherías* are many; in fact, in seven leagues around this Port I think there are perhaps eight *rancherías* and some of them are well populated.

We went with Don Miguel Costansó to examine the river which empties into this port. It was somewhat swollen when we arrived. In less than three leagues we found three *rancherías* along the bank. The river has dried up although at a depth of two spans [16 inches], by digging in the sand, very good water comes up. All along the banks there are very good water holes and woods; the land appears to me to be very good.

With regard to the Indians, they appear to be docile and alert. We have made very good friends with them and we are never lacking some little rabbits, hares, and fish that they bring to us. We give them some glass beads, but they value very highly any kind of cloth, no matter how poor it might be, since in exchange for some that I had, I received some furs and nets.

I am enclosing a report of what Box Number 1 contains and I will attempt, in exchange for beads and other items that the *San Carlos* carries for that purpose, to acquire more. Despite the fact that these pagan Indians appear of good character, I am observing precisely that which Your Excellency advised me in Instruction No. 9.[1] I also have very well in mind that which is contained in No. 13,[2] in conformance with which we have covered ourselves in a parapet which is armed with the two small cannon taken off the *Principe* [*San Antonio*] in preparation for whatever attempt they might make by day. By night I maintain two sentinels and they are changed every two hours. Don Fernando Rivera follows his own system for there are never enough precautions in suspicious country.

We have planted some seeds and later will probably plant corn.

I am desirous of additional orders from Your Excellency and can assure my prompt obedience. I ask that Our Lord guard your life many years.

---

1 "9th. The natives are to be impressed with the advantages of peace and salvation and protection from foreign insult offered by the Spaniards."

2 "13th. The natives are never to be fully trusted., but always watched, for the 'common enemy' will surely incite them to mischief."

Port of San Diego, June 26, 1769. Your most devoted servant and subject kisses the hand of Your Excellency.

Pedro Fages

His Illustrious Lordship Don José de Gálvez

Report of What Is Contained in Box No. 1

Large body shields	1
Medium-sized body shields	4
Medium-sized dried gourds	3
Simple straw hats	3
Large otter pelts	6
Small otter pelts	3
Wildcat pelts	3
Double nets for fishing	8
Simple nets for fishing and hunting	7
Feather headdresses of the *Ranchería* chiefs	8
Arrows with which they make war upon each other	18
Mallet painted various colors	1
Piece of red ochre	1
Note	

I exchanged the two medium-sized dried gourds with the sailors of the *Principe* who had brought them from the pagan Indians of the Islands of the Santa Barbara Channel; all the rest I have traded with the pagan Indians of this area. Regarding the red ochre, they have given indications that there is much in the earth; I will not fail to ascertain this and other matters which might be of interest. In this encampment at San Diego, June 26, 1769.

Pedro Fages

Long live Jesus, Mary, and Joseph. The Very Reverend Father Guardian, Raphael Verger: The grace of the Holy Spirit be with Your Reverence and with me. Amen.

On July 30, there arrived at this port of San Diego His Majesty's ship called El Príncipe, and on the 13th day of August there arrived another ship, the San Carlos, both of which came here because they were unable to reach the port of Monterey. On September 16 there arrived from Monterey Father President Junípero Serra and Captain Pedro Fages, and, although the vessels brought eight hundred fanegas of corn, Fages would not give this mission more than one-half of half a cuartillo of corn for the Indians from the Californias, which is just enough for one meal despite the fact they have no other provisions. For the local Christian natives and for the gentiles, he would not give anything. Thus the Californians, granting that they know how to work a little, will have small chance to do so because they will have very little to eat, and there is no place to look for food. We cannot make the natives around here work, and often we cannot teach them the doctrine because they have to go hunting for food every day. Fifty-five have been baptized, counting both children and adults, and, although on the one hand I am happy that we have converted [some of] the heathen, on the other hand it grieves me sorely to see that for lack of food we shall not be able to teach them everything that is necessary.

What grieves me most is that two interpreters, who were among the first that were baptized and already knew something of the Spanish language, now are forgetting what little they did know, and we have no others whom we could use, either to learn the language or to teach the Christians and gentiles. These interpreters can rarely come to the mission because they have to go out and gather their seeds. For about four months now we have not baptized a single one, and I, for one, do not intend to baptize any more unless other measures are taken, for it is better for them to be gentiles than bad Christians.

The captain wants and has requested families from the other side to work for and advance the missions, and I, in reality, do not understand it, for, supposing that there are in the missions some Indians from the Californias, these, and among them most of the new Christians, could work as much or more than the families that can come, yet he will not give them anything to eat, saying that Indians will not be fed, and that no rations whatever shall be given to them. Therefore, if instructions are not issued saying that the Indians shall be fed, and what amount is to be given to each mission, not leaving it to the discretion of this gentleman here, we shall always remain at the beginning and never advance at all. The lands of this mission are so good that a little wheat which was planted yielded very well without irrigation, and some four or five *fanegas* have been harvested. The only thing lacking is corn to support the Indians so that they can work, although it would not be bad if there were some Europeans here so that they could work and teach others to do so.

Last year Captain Pedro Fages gave eight pack mules, two saddle mules, and two horses for the founding of this mission. Father Dumetz brought some mules from the Californias, but the said gentleman is using everything, ordering that everything in the ship be unloaded on these few overburdened mules as if they were his own. Furthermore, if this continues we shall not have any mules in less than two years. We cannot use them to haul wood and plant our crops at least to some extent; so everything is lost. Thus if the mules and horses which he gave, and those which they brought from the Californias are to be used according to the wishes of this man, and if the mission is to use them very little, or none at all, it would be better if the former had never been received and the latter had not been brought from the Californias. Last year after the mules had been given to the missions, he had more than a hundred mules left, and now when he came with the Father President to carry off the provisions, he brought just a few for the escorts, and nearly half of these belonged to the missions. When I told him that he had brought very few mules to haul away the said provisions, he replied that it would be made up of mules belonging to the mission, for they all belonged to the king. So it is that we cannot plow at the missions because the mules are being used for the king's business. Consequently, we cannot do any planting, and likewise, since he did not bring enough mules, they are going hungry at Mission San Gabriel, even after the arrival of two vessels. [...]

With reference to the Indians, I wish to say that great progress would be made if there was anything to eat and the soldiers would set a good example. We cannot give them anything to eat because what Don Pedro has given is not enough to last half a year for the Indians from the Californias who are here. Thus little progress will be made under present conditions. As for the example to be set by the soldiers, no doubt some of them are good exemplars and deserve to be treated accordingly, but very many of them deserve to be hanged on account of the continuous outrages which they are committing in seizing and raping the women. There is not a single mission where all the gentiles have not been scandalized, and even on the roads, so I have been told. Surely, as the gentiles themselves state, they are committing a thousand evils, particularly those of a sexual nature. The fathers have petitioned Don Pedro concerning these points, but he has paid very

little attention to them. He has punished some, but as soon as they promised him that they would work at the presidio, he turned them loose. That is what he did last year, but now he does not even punish them or say anything to them on this point. I suppose that some ministers will write you, each concerning his own mission, and therefore I shall not tell you about the cases which have occurred at other missions. I shall speak only of Mission San Diego.

At one of these Indian villages near this mission of San Diego, which said village is very large, and which is on the road that goes to Monterey, the gentiles therein many times have been on the point of coming here to kill us all, and the reason for this is that some soldiers went there and raped their women, and other soldiers who were carrying the mail to Monterey turned their animals into their fields and they ate up their crops. Three other Indian villages about a league or a league and a half from here have reported the same thing to me several times. For this reason on several occasions when Father Francisco Dumetz or I have gone to see these Indian villages, as soon as they saw us they fled from their villages and fled to the woods or other remote places, and the only ones who remained in the village were some men and some very old women. The Christians here have told me that many of the gentiles of the aforesaid villages leave their huts and the crops which they gather from the lands around their villages, and go to the woods and experience hunger They do this so that the soldiers will not rape their women as they have already done so many times in the past.

No wonder the Indians here were bad when the mission was first founded. To begin with they did not know why they [the Spaniards] had come, unless they intended to take their lands away from them. Now they all want to be Christians because they know that there is a God who created the heavens and earth and all things, that there is a Hell, and Glory, that they have souls, etc., but when the mission was first founded they did not know all

Illustration depicting the death of Father Luís Jayme at Mission San Diego Alcalá, November 4, 1775. The uprising was the first of a dozen similar incidents that took place in Alta California during the Mission Period. Sketched by Francis J. Weber in 1920.

these things; instead, they thought they were like animals, and when the vessels came at first, they saw that most of the crews died; they were very loathe to pray, and they did not want to be Christians at all; instead, they said that it was bad to become a Christian and then they would die immediately. No wonder they said so when they saw how most of the sailors and California Indians died, but now, thanks be to the Lord, God has converted them from Sauls to Pauls. They all know the natural law, which, so I am informed, they have observed as well or better than many Christians elsewhere. They do not have any idols; they do not go on drinking sprees; they do not marry relatives; and they have but one wife. The married men sleep with their wives only. The bachelors sleep together, and apart from the women and married couples. If a man plays with any woman who is not his wife, he is scolded and punished by his captains. Concerning those from the Californias I have heard it said that they are given to sexual vices, but among those here I have

not been able to discover a single fault of that nature. Some of the first adults whom we baptized, when we pointed out to them that it was wrong to have sexual intercourse with a woman to whom they were not married, told me that they already knew that, and that among them it was considered to be very bad, and so they did not do so at all. "The soldiers," they told me, "are Christians and, although they know that God will punish them in Hell, do so, having sexual intercourse with our wives. We," they said, "although we did not know that God would punish us for that in Hell, considered it to be very bad, and we did not do it, and even less now that we know that God will punish us if we do so." When I heard this, I burst into tears to see how these gentiles were setting an example for us Christians. Of the many cases which have occurred in this mission, I shall tell of only two, about which it is very necessary that Your Reverence should know, particularly the last one which I shall relate.

5. A Report on The Presidio at Monterey, 1773

By Pedro Fages

Primary Source

The *presidio* came into existence on June 3, 1770, when it was founded along the shore of the beach of the said port (of Monterey), not very far away from where the packet boats anchor. It commands a view of the roadstead. At its shoulder is an estuary of salt water. On its sides are forests of pine and at its right is Point Pinos.

The *presidio* is about fifty *varas* square. At its center is a base of adobe four *varas* square consisting of four steps half a *vara* in height, on top of which is a cupola in the shape of a half-orange, on which stands the Holy Cross of hewn wood, seven *varas* tall, whose trunk and arms are one-fourth of a *vara* wide. The entire hase is plastered with a mixture of lime and sand.

In the Wing of the *presidio* on the south side facing the base is an adobe church whose foundations are of stone set in mortar. These foundations extend two-quarters above the surface and are a *vara* and a half in width. Upon these foundations rise the (adobe) walls five-fourths in thickness, The church is fifteen *varas* long, seven *varas* wide, and seven *varas* high. Twenty hewn beams, each a palm in width and ten *varas* in length, have an overlay of cane, and upon this rests the roof, which is flat. This has a cover of lime. The roof has four spouts to carry off the rainwater.

Joined to the right of the chapel is a tower six *varas* square, also built of adobe. It is fifteen *varas* high and contains two terraces, in ascending proportion in which to hang bells. The tower is surmounted by a cupola in the shape of a half-orange, and upon this rises an iron cross a *vara* and a half in height which also has a weathervane to show the direction of the wind. This tower has

its foundation of stone mortared with lime and protrudes from the ground for three-fourths of a *vara*. The church and tower are plastered with lime within and without.

To the left of the church is an adobe dwelling for the Reverend Fathers who come here to administer to our spiritual life. This dwelling is about twelve *varas* long and about six *varas* wide. It has its small outside corridor along its length with its pillars and wooden corbels, upon which lies the beam supporting the roof. The roof is flat and is covered with lime. The corridor has fifteen hewn beams ten *varas* in length. This building communicates with the church. It is plastered with lime in its entirely.

Along the east wing of the *presidio* there are six rooms, five of which are eight *varas* square, the other eight by five *varas*. One is used by the mail couriers and the blacksmith, another serves as the carpenter shop, the third contains the gear of the muleteers, the fourth is the dwelling of the servants, and the fifth is for the use of Indians who happen to sleep at the *presidio*. The sixth room is used to store building tools and field implements. All these rooms are built of poles of pine and are plastered, their roofs being of earth. Behind the servants' dwelling is their kitchen, eight *varas* square, with an inside connection. It is built of the same construction.

In the west wing there are two quarters for soldiers, the one fifteen *varas* long and eight *varas* wide, which is used by the volunteers (of Catalonia). The other, twenty *varas* long and eight *varas* wide, is used by the leather-packet soldiers. To the rear of these quarters are two kitchens,

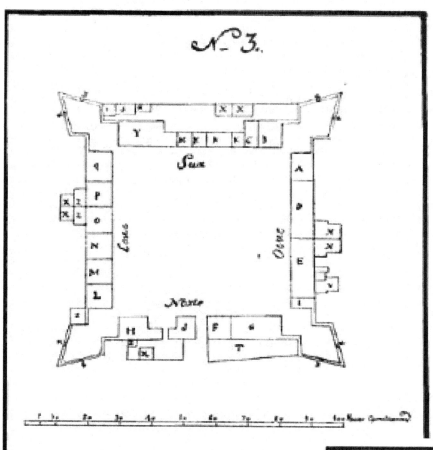

Diagram of the Presidio at Monterey, ca. 1771.

Plano del Real Presidio de
S.ⁿ Carlos de Monterey.
Explicacion.

A. Yglesia actual
B. Yglesia nueva
C. Sacristia
D. Quartel de la Tropa de Cuera
E. Quartel de la Partida de Voluntarios
F. Cuerpo de Guardia
G. Almacen del Pacdis
H. Almacen del Rey
Y. Almacen de los Mision
J. Vivienda del Oficial
K. Vivienda de los P.ᵉˢ Misioneros
L. Herreria, y Fragua
M. Carpinteria
N. Casa del Havio de Regna

O. Casa del Zenzero
P. Enfermeria
Q. Casa y las Señoritas de Mision
R. Aloxmas y los mozos Christianos
S. Casa y las Mugeres Gentiles
T. Corral para las Reses nᵒ
V. Chiqueros de Cerdos
X. Cocinas en General
1. Casa
Z. Lugares Comunes
W. Corral nᵒ

each four *varas* square for the use of the two afore-mentioned groups. There are inside connections between the kitchens and the respective quarters. At the head of the wing of the *presidio* facing the south there is a dwelling place eight *varas* square which serves as a pharmacy, containing the medicine chests. All these constructions are the same as those in the aforementioned wing. The two entrances to the garrisons face the plaza of the *presidio*.

In the north wing there are two storehouses for food and for royal property. Attached to this are two small rooms occupying the space of the width of the wing of the *presidio*, both of which are four *varas* wide and six *varas* long. The first serves as a prison, the second as a guardhouse and as sleeping quarters for soldiers (on guard duty), with a rack for firearms inside and with another outside. Next, one comes to a large main entrance which is four *varas* wide. Next to it is a small room with its display table and shelves with a stock of goods, made of wood. This is the storeroom and salesroom for clothes that are sold and distributed to the dependents of these establishments. There is a door connecting it with the main entrance and an inside connection to the door of the Commander. This room is about six *varas* in length and eight *varas* in width. Along it is a corridor six *varas* in length and three in width, with two pillars and their corbels of cypress supporting the roof beam. Behind this is a kitchen with a chimney to carry off the smoke. It measure four *varas* square.

Then, one comes to the second storeroom, which is ten *varas* long and eight *varas* wide. To one side is a storage bin five *varas* square. Almost all of this wing is of adobe, its foundation being of stone. The walls of the building are five *varas* high and three fourths in thickness. The beams are hewn and are covered with a roof topped with lime, which has its corresponding spout to carry off the rainwater from the *presidio*.

Most of the doors of the dwellings of the *presidio*, which number about thirty, are of pine. Some are of redwood, which is very similar to cedar, while still others are of cypress, sawed and fashioned at the *presidio*. At the four corners of the *presidio* are ravelines with two embrasure each, containing batteries with a bronze campaign cannon placed in each. One of the ravelines is of adobe with a sentry box facing the Point (Pinos), together with three trenches which command the front of the *presidio*. At the front the foundations are of stone, while on the other three sides they are constructed of logs of pine wood. However, stones have already been cut and adobes fashioned which will be used to build walls similar to that in front, because the humidity of the place tends to rot and destroy the wood. Consequently, buildings so constructed have little advantage.

For the east and west wings of the *presidio*, one hundred beams have already been hewn. They are ten *varas* long and a quarter of a *vara* wide. They are roof supports so that these sections of the *presidio* will be the same as the others. The kitchens will be incorporated with them in a corner of the *presidio* leeward to the northwest. There is a very large cesspool, a subterranean outlet going toward the estuary, In another place there are three hogsties for the sows, with the doors facing the open country. And at a distance of forty *varas* there is another large one. The roofs are covered with lime. Outside the Stockade, at a distance of forty *varas* there are two corrals fifty varas in circumference which are for the cows and mules. Next to the first is a hogsty for breeding purposes.

At about a fifteen minute walking distance from the *presidio*, on the other side of the estuary, is the powder magazine, four *varas* square, built of poles plastered inside and out. It has its door and lock. At a distance of four varas there is a stockade of poles four *varas* high. At a musket shot away leeward to the northwest, in which the wind prevails for the greater part of the year, is a small house four *varas* square for the soldiers who stand guard.

For labor service at the *presidio* I had Ordered to be made two *carretas* one for transporting poles, the other being of the ordinary type. Both are now in Service. They have been used to haul all the stone used for the foundations of the structures of the *presidio*. Mules are used for hauling. The *carretas* were built also to haul the goods brought by the ships from the beach to the *presidio*, a musket-shot away and this is over level land. They also transport salt from the salt beds located to the northeast about three leagues away over good land which the *carretas* can negotiate. This year I ordered about two hundred loads of salt to be dug up. This I had piled up and I refined. Lest the rains deteriorate it I intend to build a house with a good roof in which to store it. The salt marshes are located in estuaries which are about nine in number and which, each year in the months of June, July, August, and September, are filled with very good salt that looks like stone. If this were sought each year, one could obtain hundreds of loads. Also, I have appointed six transport teams to conduct the salt hither, with one man incharge each for supplying the establishment.

To the Mission San Carlos by the Carmel River, I will give a *curreta*. I shall do the same for Missions San Antonio and San Luis Obispo when they are made. The terrain is accommodated to their use. I have also constructed launch of eight ribs at its keel with its sail and oars to aid in disembarkment to shore and for the transportation of salt should this be necessary as well as for the transportation of logs. These latter are obtainable along the seashore about six leagues from the *presidio*. The frame and: heel had already come from San Blas. I also had a mast altered which rises from a basket seven *varas* in length and three-fourths in width for use at the *presidio*, should it be needed.

At a distance of half a league from the *presidio* is a garden one hundred and twenty *varas* in length, its width varying from seventy to eighty *varas* in places. It decreases even to forty *varas* at its narrowest. There in have been sown and harvested various vegetables. At present we are gathering many of them by means of irrigation. Next to it is fallow land which I shall order to be sown with two and a half *fanegas* of wheat, all to be under irrigation. On one side of the garden is a house, four *varas* square, for two of the Catalonian volunteers. It has its door and lock and a battery embrasure within for whatever contingency may arise. The roof of the house is of earth. About an eight-minute walk from the *presidio* there are some fallow lands which were sown during the past year with about four *fanegas* of wheat, and I shall see if it can be sown again.

Next to the *presidio* on the side in the direction of the church is where the mission of San Carlos was founded. There it remained until May of 1771, when an order came from. His Excellency the Marquis de Croix, your predecessor, to transfer the mission site to the banks of the Carmel River, since it is only one league away from the *presidio*. Moreover, the site offers better lands for cultivation than those which the port has.

The transfer was soon effected, the change of the mission from one site to the other having been accomplished by the end of December of the said year, although the Reverend Father President with his companion went out to the Carmel River to that mission earlier to administer it. He left at this *presidio* the two missionaries destined for the founding of Mission San Luis Obispo, who were to remain here until that mission would be actually established. So they remained, administering and saying Mass at the *presidio*, until the beginning of June 1777, when they went to found said mission. From that time on, the *presidio* has been without a resident priest, although on Sundays and holy days one of the two missionaries from Mission San Carlos comes over to say Mass.

Now that the Reverend Father President Fray Francisco Palóu has arrived from Lower California with five additional religious to found the other three missions ordered to be established, be offered to me one of the religious to stay at the *presidio*. This I considered very proper, for it has been my experience that in years of heavy rain it is impossible to travel over the roads.

In consideration of the fact that the same original church was destined for the royal *presidio* and for mission purposes, although the order came for their separation, there did not come for the *presidio* church any church goods or other items useful for the church and sacristy. For the *presidio* church there were only those things that belonged to the missions which have been ordered to be founded. Wherefore I beseech Your Excellency to deign to order that the church be furnished with everything necessary to celebrate the Holy Sacrifice, of the Mass and to administer the Sacraments. Meanwhile, those things will serve which belong to the missions as they have supplied up to the present. The same holds true for bells.

Royal *Presidio* of San Carlos de Monterey
September 29, 1773
Pedro Fages

---

6. Rules for Pueblos and Missions, 1779

By Felipe de Neve

Primary Source

Title Fourteen
Political Government and
Instructions for Settlement

1 Since the most important aim for the fulfillment of the pious intentions of our Lord, the King, and to perpetuate His Majesty's dominions over the extensive territory embraced for more than two hundred leagues by the establishment of the presidios and the respective ports of San Diego, Monterey, and San Francisco is to advance the reduction and to make this exceedingly vast country as useful as possible to the State, inhabited as it is by innumerable heathen, excepting the 1749 Christians of both sexes at the eight missions on the road between the first and last presidios; and also to erect pueblos of white people who, being gathered together, shall promote the planting and cultivation of crops, stock raising, and in succession the other branches of industry, so that in the course of a few years their produce may suffice to supply the presidio garrisons with provisions and horses, thus avoiding the long haul, risks, and losses under which these things are brought at the expense of the Royal Exchequer (with which fit idea the pueblos of San José is already founded and settled, and the establishment of another is determined upon, for which settlers and their families must come from the Province of Sonora and Sinaloa, that their progressive increase and that of the families of the troops will provide for the establishment of other settlements and supply recruits for the presidio companies, and thus free the Royal Exchequer

from the inevitable costs which it is now under to gain these ends), since to secure these things it is desirable to establish regulations, the following instructions shall be observed. …

3. To each settler and to the common fund of the pueblo … there shall be given two mares, two cows with one calf, two ewes, and two she goats, all pregnant, one yoke of oxen or bullocks, one ploughshare or tip, one hoe, one spade, one as and one sickle, one field knife, one lance, one shotgun and one shield, two horses, and one pack mule. Likewise, and to the common charge, shall be given sufficient sires for the number of head of stock in each kind in the whole community; one master burro and one common one and three she-burros, one boar and three sows, one forge equipped with an anvil and other corresponding tools, six crowbars, six iron spades, and the tools needed for carpentry and wagon making.

4. The lots granted to the new settlers must be determined by the Government as to location and size according to the extent of land where the new pueblo may be established, so that a plaza and streets shall be left as provided by the laws of the realm; and in the arrangement there shall be marked out sufficient common land for the pueblo, and pasture lands with the suitable arable lands for individuals.

5. … There shall be allotted to each settler two fields of irrigable land and two more of dry. Of the royal lands there shall be set aside such as are deemed proper for the community, and of the remainder, and also of the respective building lots, grants shall be made by the Governor in the name of His Majesty to those who come newly to settle, particularly to soldiers who, by having served the time of their enlistment or because of advanced age, are retired from the service, as also to the families of those who die. These shall carry on their farming with the funds each should have, with out assistance from the Royal Exchequer in salary, rations, or livestock, this privilege being

limited to those who emigrated from their own country with that understanding to colonize this one.

6. The houses erected upon the lots granted and set aside for the new settlers, and the fields embraced in their respective grants, shall be entailed in perpetuity on their sons and their descendants or on daughters who marry useful settlers who have no allotment of fields themselves, all such complying with the conditions which will be set forth in these instructions. And in order that the sons of the possessors of these grants may have the obedience and respect they owe their parents, the latter, if they have two or more sons, shall he free and empowered to choose which one, if secular and lay, shall be heir of their houses and fields. And likewise they shall be free to dispose that the fields be divided among the children, but not that one single field be divided, for these, all and each, must be indivisible and inalienable forever.

7. Neither the settlers nor their heirs shall lease, entail, bond, mortage, nor place other encumbrance whatsoever upon the house and fields granted to them, even though it be for a pious cause. If anyone should do violation of this just prohibition, be shall irredeemably be deprived of the property, and because of that very act hiss endowment shall be given to each other settler as may be useful and obedient.

8. To maintain their livestock, the new settlers shall enjoy the common privileges of water, pasturage, fine wood, and lumber from the public lands, forests, and pastures to be assigned to each pueblo, and each shall also enjoy exclusively the grazing of his own lands. …

11. When the droves of swine and burros shall have multiplied, and the necessary burros adopted for the service of the mares, if the division of each of the two kinds be feasible, said division shall be made by common consent of the settlers among themselves as equitably as possible so that from the first herd each shall have two head, a male and

a female, and one from the second herd. When this is done, the animals should be marked and branded by their owners. ...

15. The maize, beans, garbanzos, and lentils produced by the crops of the pueblos, after the citizens have reserved the amount necessary for their own subsistence and planting, shall be bought for the provision of the pre[] and paid for in cash at the prices established. ...

16. Every settler and resident, head of a family, to whom has been granted or in the future shall be granted building lots or fields, and their [], shall be obliged to keep themselves equipped with two horses, a saddle complete, a shotgun, and the other arms which have been mentioned. These must be furnished them at cost in order that they may defend their respective districts and lend aid without abandoning their first obligations wherever with grave urgency they may be ordered by the Governor. ...

18. And as it is meet for the good and proper government of the *pueblas*, the administration of justice, direction of public works, apportionment of water, and careful watchfulness over whatever has been provided in these Instructions that the pueblos be given, in proportion to the number of inhabitants, ordinary alcaldes and other magistrates yearly. These for the first two years shall be appointed by the Governor, and in following years the settlers shall nominate by and from themselves the public officials that shall have been arranged for. These elections must pass or their confirmation to the Governor, by whom said nominations shall be continued in the three following years if he deems it expedient. [...]

The eight missions already established shall retain the two priests that each now has, but vacancies by death or retirement shall not be filled until they are reduced to one each, excepting the missions close to presidios, in which two priests must be maintained, as one of them, is obliged to serve the presidio as chaplain until such a time as it shall be decided to provide the presidios with secular chaplains. Consequently, if a vacancy occurs in these missions or in those at the Channel, a priest shall come from one of the missions of San Juan Capistrano, San Gabriel, San Antonio, or Santa Clara to fill it or, as aforesaid, one from these shall aid in the founding of new missions.

7. A Letter of Junípero Serra to the Reverend Father Preacher, Fray Fermin, 1780

By Father Junípero Serra

Primary Source

The practice of allowing a friar to enjoy a good rest and relaxation at another mission is one of which I heartily approve. Your arrangement with the padres at San Juan Capistrano is quite acceptable. Beyond that, should there be two successive weeks without a holy day, it is perfectly alright to absent yourself thirteen days even though that would leave the presidio without a Sunday Man. On one occasion when I brought this to the governor's attention, His Excellency acknowledged that the precept of attending Holy Mass does not oblige where none is available. Therefore, Your Reverences can feel free to attend the presidio only when that is physically possible. As they say, "no one need drown in a puddle of water!" Caring for the needs of those who afflict us is exceedingly meritorious and I rejoice at your willingness to do so. Nonetheless, such commendable activities do not preclude us from taking an occasional rest, as long as there be no failing against the virtue of justice.

Regarding the memorial services for the late [Alejo Antonio] González, may he rest in peace. From what you have told me, I think all the Mass stipends for this repose should accrue to your mission. Inasmuch as the deceased was aware of the personnel arrangement there, I and several others will presume to assist you in this obligation on behalf of your mission. Let me know when his estate is settled and what schedule you arrange for offering the hundred Masses. His colts or horses might go to San Juan Capistrano and still serve the needs of the friars at San Diego. Concerning

the query about our friend, Don Raphael de Pedro Gil, the answer is already contained in the letter of Fray Juan [Crespi] to which I have nothing to add. I have seen the annual report for San Diego and among the various favorable aspects mentioned therein, it can surely be said of your mission, in the midst of its poverty. "*Tuvere supergresea as universas.*" Thanks be to God for all things! As soon as the will is liquidated, inform me of all the details so we can begin making the proper provisions. As for the perpetuity of the anniversary Masses, I don't think such a provision is convenient, necessary or expressly ordered by holy obedience in circumstances such as ours. A novena of Masses and some sort of

I am delighted with the good sowings, and I envy the spiritual harvest. Accept my condolences for the deaths of those poor Indians you mentioned as well as that of the poor boy. May God keep them! Should a vessel stop at your port, on route here, do not hesitate to send me all the news, whether it be good or bad. From here there is very little to report. The three of us are enjoying good health, and the wheat and barley are the best. What we sowed amounted to nine *fanegas* along with that which God planted. Though we have given it only taken care, already it is beginning to sprout. We sowed eighteen *fanegas* of wheat. Our lentils, one *fenega*, and God's an additional one. Of horse beans and peas, a fair crop has also been realized. More than half of last year's wheat harvest is in ear, and we don't plan on thrashing it. These have been quite a few deaths here, and

Portrait of Father Junipero Serra, circa 1750, artist unknown.

the *pagara* are keeping their distance. Last year's *okalde* [Baltazer] has not returned from his meandering. Today I planted five fig trees, but already they seem to have dried up and probably will not take root, I am having ever less success with three sarmenta which arrived yesterday from the governor. God repay him for that kindness. He also sent thirteen pomegranates which appear to be thriving along with the other hundred which I earlier planted in the orchard.

From San Francisco and Santo Clara I have heard that the friars are well, and that their plantings are good. Thanks be to God!

Father Manuel Garcia, the Dominican in charge of Santiago de las Coras, died recently, and I would remind you of our obligation to offer three masses for his happy repose. May he rest in peace! With this I will close, sending along the best regards of Fathers Juan [Crespi] and Francisco [Dumétz].

May Almighty God preserve for Your Reverence courage, life, health joy and His holy graces.

From this mission of San Carlos de Monte-Rey, April 17, 1780, I remain your affectionate friend, companion and servant.

Fr. Junípero Serra

The fathers of the mission of San Carlos, at the distance of two leagues from Monterey soon arrived at the presidio.[1] No less obliging than the officers of the two vessels and the fort, they invited us to dine with them and promised to inform us minutely concerning the government of their missions, the manner of living of the Indians, their arts, their newly acquired habits, and in general everything that could rouse the curiosity of travelers. We eagerly accepted this invitation, which we should not have failed to solicit if we had not thus been anticipated. It was agreed that we should set out in two days. Mr. Fages wanted to accompany us and undertook to procure horses.

After crossing a small plain covered with herds of cattle[2] and in which there were only a few trees, which were necessary to shelter these animals against the rain and the sun, we ascended the hills. From there we heard the sound of bells announcing our arrival, of which the missionaries had been previously informed by a horseman from the governor.

We were received like the lords of manors when they first take possession of their estates. The president of the missions, in his ceremonial vestments and with his holy water sprinkle in his hand, awaited us at the gate of the church, which was illuminated in the same manner as on the greatest feast days. He conducted us to the foot of the high altar, where he chanted the *Te Deum* in thanksgiving for the happy outcome of our voyage.

Before we entered the church, we had passed through a square in which the Indians of both sexes were ranged in a line. They exhibited no marks of surprise in their countenance, and left us in doubt whether we should be the subject of their conversation for the rest of the day.

The church is neat though thatched with straw. It is dedicated to Saint Charles, and adorned with some tolerable pictures, copied from originals in Italy. Among them is a picture of hell, in which the painter appears to have borrowed from the imagination of Callot; but as it is absolutely necessary to strike the imagination of these new converts with the most lively impressions, I am persuaded that such a representation was never more useful in any country It would be impossible for the protestant worship, which proscribes images and almost all the ceremonies of our church, to make any progress with this people. I doubt whether the picture of paradise, which sits opposite that of hell, produces so good an effect upon them. The state of tranquility which it represents, and that mild

---

1 Fermín Lasuén, president of the California mission, and Matías Noriega were then serving at Carmel Mission.

2 Cattle prospered when introduced to California. In the 1770s milk saved the mission and presidio from starvation when crops repeatedly failed—although it has been suggested that an inability to digest milk might have brought on some of the illnesses that swept through the Indian community. In later years cattle hides and tallow would be the mainstay of the *rancho* economy, so much so that hides would be popularly known as "California banknotes."

satisfaction of the elect who surround the throne of the Supreme Being, are ideas too sublime for the minds of uncultivated savages. But it was necessary to place rewards by the side of punishment, and it was a point of duty that no change should be permitted in the kind of enjoyments which the Catholic religion promises to man.

On coming out of the church we passed through the same row of Indians, whom the *Te Deum* had not induced to abandon their posto Only the children had removed to a small distance and formed groups near the house of missionaries, which, along with the different storehouses, is opposite the church. The Indian village stands on the right, consisting of about fifty huts which serve for seven hundred and forty persons of both sexes, including their children, who compose the mission of San Carlos, or of Monterey.

These huts are the most wretched anywhere. They are round and about six feet in diameter and four in height.[3] Some stakes, the thickness of a mans arm, stuck in the ground and meeting at the top, compose the framing. Eight or ten bundles of straw, ill arranged over these stakes, are the only defense against the rain or wind; and when the weather is fine, more than half the hut remains uncovered, with the precaution of two or three bundles of straw to each habitation to be used as circumstances may require.

This general architecture of the two Californias has never undergone the smallest change, notwithstanding the exhortations of the missionaries. The Indians say that they love the open air, that it is convenient to set fire to their house when the fleas become troublesome, and that they can build another in less than two hours. The independent tribes, who as hunters so frequently change their residence, have of course an additional motive.[4]

The color of these Indians, which is that of Negroes; the house of the missionaries; their storehouses, which are built of brick and plastered; the appearance of the ground on which the grain is trodden out; the cattle, the horses—everything in short—brought to our recollection a plantation at Santo Domingo or any other West Indian island. The men and women are collected by the sound of a bell; a missionary leads them to work, to the church, and to all their exercises. We observed with concern that the resemblance is so perfect that we have seen both men and women in irons, and others in the stocks. Lastly, the noise of the whip might have struck our ears, this punishment also being administered, though with little severity.

The monks answering our different questions left us ignorant of no part of the government of this religious community, for no other name can be

---

3   If fifty "huts" (*cabanes* in French) indeed served 740 people, it would mean an average of about fifteen people per dwelling—obviously ridiculous for a structure six feet in diameter and four feet high. Even if we assume that most of the women were locked up at night in the *dormitorio*, this would still suggest a level of overcrowding that is physically impossible.

Perhaps part of the explanation lies in the season. Despite the fog, September tends to be the warmest month in the Monterey Bay area, and people may have been sleeping outside, using the tule structures more for storage than as true dwellings. It is also quite possible that the missionaries, hoping to convince the Indians of the virtues of living like Europeans, did not give them time, materials, or encouragement to maintain proper native-style dwellings; the "huts" which la Pérouse describes might have been left over from the previous winter, which would explain their run-down condition.

---

4   The dwellings that la Pérouse describes, made of tule rather than straw, were indeed better adapted to the migratory habits of the Indians than to a permanent settlement. Nevertheless, when the Indians at Carmel were finally forced into European-style houses several years later, terrible epidemics broke out and devastated the Indian community.

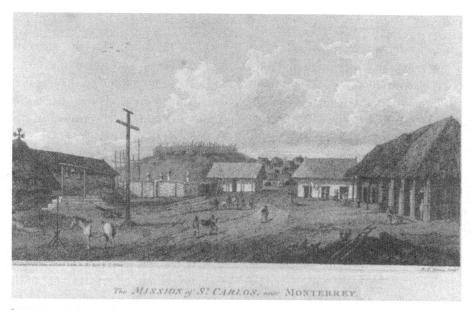

A drawing of Mission San Carlos Borromeo de Carmelo (near Monterey) as prepared by Captain George Vancouver depicts the grounds as they appeared in November, 1792. From *A Voyage of Discovery to the North Pacific Ocean and Round the World*, U.S. National Oceanic and Atmospheric Administration collection.

given to the administration they have established. They are the temporal as well as the spiritual governors, the products of the earth being entrusted to their care. The day consists in general of seven hours labor and two hours prayer, but there are four or five hours of prayer on Sundays and feast days, which are entirely consecrated to rest and divine worship.

Corporal punishment is inflicted on the Indians of both sexes who neglect the exercises of piety, and many sins, which in Europe are left to Divine justice, are here punished by irons and the stocks. And lastly, to complete the similarity between this and other religious communities, it must be observed that the moment an Indian is baptized, the effect is the same as if he had pronounced a vow for life. If he escapes to reside with his relations in the independent villages, he is summoned three times to return; if he refuses, the missionaries apply to the governor, who sends soldiers to seize him in the midst of his family and conduct him to the mission, where he is condemned to receive a certain number of

lashes with the whip. As these people are at war with their neighbors, they can never escape to a distance greater than twenty or thirty leagues. They have so little courage that they never make any resistance to the three or four soldiers who so evidently violate the rights of men in their persons. This custom, against which reason so strongly exclaims, is kept up because theologians have decided that they could not in conscience administer baptism to men so inconstant unless the government would in some measure serve as their sponsor and answer for their perseverance in the faith.

The predecessor of Mr. Fages, Mr. Filipe de Neve, commander of the interior provinces of Mexico, a man replete with humanity and a Christian philosopher who died about four years ago, remonstrated against the practice. He thought that the progress of the faith would be more rapid and the prayers of the Indians more agreeable to the Supreme Being if they were not constrained. He desired a constitution less monastic, affording more civil liberty to the Indians and less despotism in the executive power of the presidios, the government of which might fall into the hands of cruel and avaricious men. He thought likewise that it might perhaps be necessary to moderate their authority by the appointment of a magistrate who might be the tribune, as it were, of the Indians, and possess sufficient authority to defend them from harassments. This upright man had borne arms in service of his country from his infancy, but he was exempt from the prejudices of his profession, and well knew that military government is subject to great improprieties when not moderated by an intermediate power. He might, however, have experienced the difficulty of maintaining the conflict of three authorities in a country so remote from the governor-general of Mexico, since the missionaries, though pious and respectable, are already at open variance with the governor, who appears to me to be a worthy military character.

We were desirous of being present at the distributions made at each meal, and as all the days with this kind of religious community were exactly alike, by recording the proceedings of one, the reader will be acquainted with the history of a whole year.

The Indians as well as the missionaries rise with the sun, and immediately go to prayers and mass, which last for an hour. During this time three large boilers are set on the fire for cooking a kind of soup, made of barley meal, the grain of which has been roasted previous to its being ground. This sort of food, of which the Indians are extremely fond, is called *atole*.[5] They eat it without either butter or salt, and it would certainly to us be a most insipid mess.

Each hut sends for the allowance of all its inhabitants in a vessel made of the bark of a tree. There is neither confusion nor disorder in the distribution, and when the boilers are nearly emptied, the thicker portion at the bottom is distributed to those children who have said their catechism the best.

The time of repast is three quarters of an hour, after which they all go to work, some to till the ground with oxen, some to dig in the garden, while others are employed in domestic occupations, all under the eye of one or two missionaries.

The women have no other employment than their household affairs, the care of their children, and the roasting and grinding of corn. This last operation is both tedious and laborious, because they have no other method of breaking the grain than with a roller upon a stone. Mr. de Langle, who saw this operation, made a present of his mill to the missionaries. It was difficult to have rendered them a greater service, since four women will now do the work of a hundred, thus leaving them time to spin the wool of their sheep and manufacture some coarse cloths.

But the missionaries have hitherto been more attentive to their heavenly than their earthly concerns, and have greatly neglected the introduction of the most common arts. They are so austere as to their own comforts that they have no fireplace in their chambers, though the winter is sometimes severe. The greatest anchorites have never lived a more edifying life. Father Fermín de Lasuén, president of the missions of New California, is one of the most worthy and respectable men I have ever met. His mildness, charity, and affection for the Indians are beyond expression.

At noon the bells give notice of the time of dinner. The Indians then quit their work, and send for their allowance in the same vessel as at breakfast. But this second soup is thicker than the former, and contains a mixture of wheat, maize, peas, and beans; the Indians call it *pozole*.

---

5 The word is not native to California, but is Nahuatl (Aztec), and was adopted and brought north by the Spaniards.

9. The Los Angeles Census of 1781 Shows a Diverse Ethnic Mix

Edited by Iris H.W. Engstrand

Primary Source

Census of the population of the Pueblo of the Queen of the Angeles (Reyna de los Angeles), founded on September 4, 1781, on the bank of the Porciuncula River, distant 45 leagues from the Presidio of San Diego, 27 leagues from the site selected for the establishment of the Presidio of Santa Barbara, and about a league and a half from Mission San Gabriel; including the names and ages of the residents, their wives, sons and daughters, and also showing the number of animals and their kind which have been distributed to them, with a note on those that are to be held in common as sires of the different kinds, the implements for smithing and for field work, for carpentry, and the others that have been received.

That in addition to the cattle, horses, and mules, distributed to the first eleven settlers, as set forth, they were granted building lots on which they have constructed their houses, which for the present are built of palisades, roofed with earth; also two irrigated fields to each settler for the cultivation of two *fanegas* of corn; in addition, a plow share, a hoe, and an axe; and for the community, the necessary tools for making *carretas*, as also the breeding animals as specified, for which the settlers must account to the royal treasury at the prices fixed; with the corresponding charges made against their accounts, as found in the Book of the Population (Población), wherein are also to be found the building lots, planting fields, fanning equipment, and animals belonging to settler Antonio Miranda Rodriguez, who is at the Presidio of Loreto, and which will be granted to him as soon as he presents himself at the said Pueblo.

San Gabriel, November 19, 1781.

Names	Men	Women	Sons	Daughters	Ages
Josef de Lara, Spaniard	*				
Maria Antonia Campos, light-skinned Indian		*			23
Josef Julian			*		4
Juana de Jesus				*	6
Maria Faustina				*	2
Josef Antonio Navarro, mestizo					42
Maria Regina Dorotea, mulata		*			47
Josef Maria			*		10
Josef Clemente			*		2
Maria Josefa				*	4

Names	Men	Women	Sons	Daughters	Ages
Bacilio Rosas, Indian					67
Maria Manuela Calistra, mulata		*			43
Josefa Maximo			*		15
Carlos			*		12
Anto. Rosalino			*		7
Josef Marcelino			*		4
Juan Estevan			*		2
Maria Josefa				*	8
Antonio Mesa, Negro	*				38
Ana Gertudis Lopez, mulata		*			27
Antonio Maria			*		8
Maria Paula				*	10
Antonio Villavicencio, Spaniard	*				30
Maria de los Santos Soberina, Indian		*			26
Maria Antonia Josefa				*	8
Josef Vanegas, Indian					28
Maria Maxima Aguilar, Indian		*			20
Cosme Damien			*		1
Alejandro Rosas, Indian	*				19
Juana Rodriguez, native of the country		*			20
Pablo Rodriguez, Indian	*				25
Maria Rosalia Noriega, Indian		*			26
Maria Antonia				*	1
Manuel Camero, mulato	*				30
Maria Tomasa, mulata		*			24
Luis Quintero, Negro	*				55
Maria Petra Ruvio, mulata		*			40
Josef Clemente			*		3
Maria Gertrudes					16
Maria Concepcion				*	9
Tomasa				*	7
Rafaela				*	6
Josef Moreno, mulato	*				22
Maria Guadalupe Gertrudis, mulata					19
Antonio Miranda Rodriguez, Chino widower	*				50
Juana Maria				*	11
Totals	12	11	11	12	

10. Supply Requisitions for the Mission and Presidio at Santa Barbara, 1802–1810

Edited by Giorgio Perissinotto, Catherine Rudolph, and Elaine Miller

Primary Source

Requisition:
Santa Barbara, January 30, 1802.
Signature: Felipe de Goycoechea

From San Blas for 1803

200 *arrobas* of brown sugar cake

30 *arrobas* of rice

20 *arrobas* of sugar

1 earthenware jar of virgin honey

4 barrels of good quality distilled mezcal

2 saddles with embroidered saddle pads with complete saddletree cover,[1] with their name brand rump covers, also embroidered, and all of their corresponding fittings without stirrups 2 *tercios* of shrimp, packaged so the rats do not damage them. Dried.

1 *tercio* of dried oysters, well-packaged

2 *arrobas* of candlewick

Santa Barbara, January 30, 1802
Felipe de Goycoechea
[signature and rubric]

Approved Arrillaga
[signature and rubric]

Requisition:
Santa Barbara January 14, 1808.

Signature: José Joaquín Maitorena

Royal Presidio of Santa Barbara

Requisition list of the goods and effects which are considered necessary for the maintenance of the Company and military retirees of said Presidio and are requested of the Commissariat of San Blas via the Governor of this Province Don José Joaquin de Arrillaga for the following year of 1809.

25 loads of white sugar cake, well packaged

36 *arrobas* of new rice, and not spoiled like it came last year

30 *arrobas* of good chile

4 crates of assorted ordinary earthen dinnerware including water jars

2 *tercios* of dried banana, well packaged

2 pairs of saddle pads with saddletree cover, complete with rump covers embroidered with pita

2 complete saddles with large leather saddle housing and rump cover heavily embroidered with pita

20 grinding slabs with their two-handed grinding stones

Santa Barbara January 14, 1808
Approved

José Joaquin Maitorena
[signature and rubric]

Arrillaga
[signature and rubric]

---

1 In contrast to modern usage ('backpack'), *mochila* here is in all likelihood a saddletree cover, probably having pouches on either side.

Royal Presidio of Santa Barbara

Requisition list of the provisions and effects which are considered necessary for the maintenance of the Company and military retirees of the referred Presidio and are requested from the Commissariat of San Blas via the Governor of this Province Don José Joaquín de Arrillaga for the coming year of 1811.

30 loads of white sugar cake, well packaged
20 *arrobas* of new rice
25 *arrobas* of chile
8 crates of assorted ordinary earthen dinnerware including water jars, not very large

1 barrel of good mescal, well packaged
100 baskets, half each large and small
24 painted straw chairs which should be medium-large like those which the Indians sell
1 *tercio* of preserved shrimp
1 *arroba* of good tinder
1 earthenware jar of lemon syrup

Santa Barbara February 18,1810

By my instructions

José Joaquín Maitorena
[signature and rubric]

Argüello
[signature and rubric]

Approved
Arrillaga
[signature and rubric]

---

11. Reminisces of Indian Life at San Luis Rey, 1830s

By Pablo Tac

Primary Source

The Fernandino Father remained in our country with the little troop that he brought. A camp was made, and here he lived for many days. In the morning he said Mass, and then he planned how he would baptize them where he would put his house, the church, and as there were five thousand souls (who were all the Indians [Luiseños] there were), how he would sustain them, and seeing how it could be done. Having the captain for he friend, he was afraid of nothing. It was a great mercy that the Indians did not kill the Spanish when they arrived, and very admirable, because they have never wanted another people to live with them, and until those day they were always fighting. But thus willed He who alone can will. I do not know if he baptized them before making the church or after having made it, but I think he baptized them before making it. He was already a good friend of the captain, and also dear to the neophytes. They could understand him somewhat when he, as their father, ordered them to carry stone from the sea (which is not far) for the foundations, to make bricks, roof tiles to cut beams, reeds, and what was necessary. They did it with the masters who were helping them, and within a few years they finished working They made a church with three altars for all the neophytes (the great altar is nearly all gilded), two chapels, two sacristics, two choirs, a flower garden for the church, a high tower with five bells, two small and three large, the cemetery with a crucifix in the middle for all those who die here.

Let us begin with the tower. The tower is placed on the right side of the church with five bells, two small and three large, whose voice or sound is heard from afar, sometimes from Usva, four or five leagues distant from the Mission of San Luis Rey de Francia.

Of the church I have already spoken. After the church comes the place of the masons; here they leave the mortar, lime, etc. After this comes the Storehouse for wine. Within are two hundred casks of wine, brandy and white wine, four hundred barrels, for Mass, to sell to the Spanish and English travelers who often come to the mission to sell cloth, linen, cotton, and whatever they bring from Boston and not for the neophytes, which is prohibited them because they easily get drunk. 5 is the place where the wine is made. 7, the window of the room of the General of California when he comes to the Mission. 8, the door of the Fernandino Father. There are four rooms for travelers. In the middle is the reception room, with three portraits one of the St. Louis King of France, the second of the Good Shepherd, the third of the Virgin of Guadalupe. In one corner is a clock, and beyond, the refectory. 9, glass window of the missionary. 10, a small door for the missionary to get out easily in ease of earthquakes. 11, room of the servant of the missionary. 12, house for travelers. 13, door which called the biggest of all. Through

Pablo Tac penned this drawing from his recollections of life at Mission San Luis Rey in the 1820s and 1830s. The drawing depicts two young men wearing skirts of twine and feathers with feather decorations on their heads, rattles in their hands, and painted decorations on their bodies.

her the neophytes enter and leave for work. 14, 15, 16, 17, 18, 19, houses for the Spanish majordomos of the mission. 20, large room for the neophyte boys with its patio and two gardens. 21, soap house. 22, room for the girls. 23, corral for the stock. 24, mill. 25, enclosure for the lambs. 26, house of the shepherd. 27, corral. 28, granary. 29, granary, 30, place for the horses of the missionary and of the travelers and also for the sacks of fodder, 31, infirmary for the women. 32, infirmary for the men. 33, cemetery. 34, place where *pozole* and *atole* are made. 34, rooms for the majordomos. 35, barracks. 36, *fopanco*. 37, granary. 38, granary. 39, place for the baker. 40, clock. 41, kitchen. 42, chambers for travelers. 43, storehouse. 44, garden. 45, storehouse for blankets, storehouse for flour.

46, mill. 47, small loom. 48, large loom. 49, place where oil is made. 50, blacksmith shop. 51, granary. 52, shoemaker's shop. 53, place of the ass keepers. 54, second biggest door. 55, room of the majordomo of Pala. 56, carpenter shop. 57, place for the presses. 59, place for skins. In a few years, all was done.

Toward the south there is a very big kitchen garden with a pasture to the side. We said that the mission was placed on a hillock. Below this hillock there is an ever flowing fountain from which the neophytes and the missionary bring water to drink. They made two fountains before the gate of the garden, and between them a stairway to go up and down, which made all of bricks. The entering gateway has three thick timbers in the middle. One of them, driven into the earth, reaches high above the wall, the other two are more or less fastened on it, making a cross of all parts, if you would like to see it, and the water carrier, wishing to pass, pushes a timber, and the two turn, and in this way he passes with case, raising the pitcher above his burdened shoulders stronger than those of assses themselves. The stairway is so very high that one cannot ascend by it in the same trip, and it is necessary to rest in the middle. It happens many times that they get tired in vain (as it is said), because when they arrive at the gate and wish to pass through it with haste, the pitcher is broken, and (hey return to the house without water or pitcher, dripping with water.

The timbers were placed in order not to let in the bulls and horses, spirited when there is bullfighting, though they come in often and frighten the old women who wash their clothes here. Beyond the two fountains is the gate of the orchard. The water from the two fountains passes down through a little door, running toward the west as in a ditch, and irrigates another garden almost a league distant from the mission.

The garden is extensive, full of fruit trees, pears, apples, or *perones*, as the Mexicans say, peaches, quinces, pears, sweet pomegranates, figs, watermelons, melons, vegetables, cabbages, lettuces, radishes, mints, parsley, and others which I don't remember. The pears, apples, peaches, quinces, pomegranates, watermelons, and melons are for the neophytes, the others that remain for the missionary. The gardener must bring something each day. None of the neophytes can go to the garden or enter to gather the fruit. But if he wants some he asks the missionary, who immediately will give him what he wants, for the missionary is their father. The neophyte might encounter the gardener walking and cutting the fruits, who then follows him to punish him, until he leaves the walk of the garden, jumping as they know how (like deer in the mountains).

Once a neophyte entered the garden without knowing the gardener was there, and as he was very hungry, he climbed a fig tree. Here he began to eat with all haste a large ripe fig. Not by bits, but whole, he let it go down his throat, and the fig choked him. He then began to be frightened, until he cried out like a crow and swallowed it. The gardener, hearing the voice of the crow, with his Indian eyes then found the crow that from fear was not eating more. He said to him, "I see you, a crow without wings. Now I will wound you with my arrows." Then the neophyte with all haste fled far from the garden.

Toward the west of the garden is the pasture for the horses of the Fernandino Father and for those of the Anglo-American travelers. It is as large as the garden, full of water underneath, and so it has green grass. There are many trees, very many birds. A great many crows arrive in the evening to sleep, and they let themselves fall from the height, turning somersaults until they come to the trees. Here too the workmen found a California lion which is the same as the cat of Europe but more powerful than a tiger, not for its strength, but for its agility. It is very difficult to kill. It kills the horses seizing them with a leap. Then it

Mission San Luis Rey, circa 1890.

beheads them; for this it is feared. The workmen found it, and because they were many, the lion was afraid of them and the cries which they let out following it. It ran leaping here and there around the pasture. The Indians, hidden behind the trees, threw stones at it until one struck the middle of the forehead and soon, weakened, falling, he then died. Here they make bricks and tiles for the mission. Deer are not found. Beyond the garden runs the road to the *presidio* of San Diego, where the General of California is.

What Is Done Each Day

When the sun rises and the stars and the moon go down, then the old man of the house wakens everyone and begins with breakfast, which is to eat *juiuis* heated and meat and tortillas, for we do not have bread. This done, he takes his bow and arrows and leaves the house with vigorous and quick step. (This is if he is going to hunt.) He goes off to the distant woods, which are full of bears and hares, deer and thousands of birds. He is here all day, killing as many as he can, following them,

hiding himself behind trees, climbing them, and then, loaded with hares, he returns home happy. But when he needs wood, then he leaves the house in the morning with this tumpline on his shoulders and his ax, with companions who can help him when the load is very heavy, and in the afternoon he returns home. His old woman, staying at home, makes the meal. The son, if he is a man, works with the men. His daughter stays with the women, making shirts, and if these also have sons and daughters, they stay in the mission, the sons at school to learn the alphabet, and if they already know it, to learn the catechism, and if this also, to the choir of singers, and if he was a singer, to work, because all the musical singers work the day of work, and Sunday to the choir to sing, but without a book, because the teacher teaches them by memory, holding the book. The daughter joins with the single girls, who all spin for blankets for the San Luiseños and for the robe of the Fernandino Father. At twelve o'clock they eat together and leave the old man his share, their cups of clay, their vessels of well-woven fiber which water cannot leak out of, except when it is held before the face of the sun, their frying pans of clay, their grills of wood made for that day, and their pitchers for water, also of clay. Sealed around the fire they are talking and eating. Too bad for them if at that time they close the door. Then, the smoke rising being much, and the opening which serves as a window being small, it turns below, trying to go out by the door, remains in the middle of the house, and they eat then speaking, laughing, and weeping without wishing to. The meal finished, they return to their work. The father leaves his son, the son leaves his sister, the sister the brother, the brother the mother, the mother her husband, with cheer, until the afternoon. Before going to bed again, they eat what the old woman and old man have made in that time, and then they sleep.

12. An Old Spanish Woman Remembers the Mission Era, 1877

By Eulalia Pérez

Primary Source

Whatever may be the real age of Madame Eulalia Pérez, she is certainly a very ancient person. There can be no doubt, from her personal appearance, that she is a centenarian. The accompanying photograph gives a very correct idea of her as I found her when I took from her lips the notes which appear on the annexd. thirty-three pages.

For a person of such an uncommon age, she is not entirely feeble or helpless, inasmuch as she can do some needlework and walk about the house unsupported even by a staff.

She sat by me upon a chair awhile yesterday; but her usual seat is on the floor, and when flies or mosquitoes annoy her, she slaps and kills them with her slipper on the floor. When wishing to rise, she places both palms of her hands on the ground before her and lifts herself first on four feet (so to speak) and then with a jerk puts herself on her two feet—for this she needs no assistance. After that she goes about the house without difficulty. She did it in my presence yesterday, and saying that she felt chilled, walked out and sat on the stoop to sun herself awhile, then came back and resumed her former seat.

I was assured that with support, and occasional rest on a chair taken with her, she walks to their granddaughter's house, a distance if five hundred yards or more.

Her memory is remarkably fresh on some things and much clouded on others, particularly on her age. She is at times flighty, but with patience and by asking her questions only when such matters as she could be conversant with, 1 found no great difficulty in obtaining intelligible answers. I had to resort to Mrs. White's assistance in asking the questions, because the centenarian lady is quite deaf,

EULALIA PEREZ, 139 YEARS OF AGE.
Mother of Rita Guillen de la Osa,

Hubert Bancroft conducted just over 100 interviews with descendants of the original Californios and of those interviews, only 12 were with women. Eulalia Perez's story recounts her life at Rancho San Isidro, near the San Gabriel Mission, where she worked as a manager, cook, and midwife before dying in 1878, at the age of 104. (Contemporary estimates of her age, which ranged as high as 140, were wisely discounted by Bancroft.)

though not to the extent of needing to be addressed in an excessively loud tone.

I discontinued my questions as soon as I discovered that she was fatigued and have not returned to see her, because I had to leave Mission San Gabriel, near which the San Isidro ranch is, and visit this place.

–Thos. Savage, Interviewer and Transcriber
Spadra
December 11, 1877

I, Eulalia Pérez, was born at the presidio of Loreto, in Baja California.

My father's name was Diego Pérez and he worked in the naval department at the presidio.

My mother's name was Antonia Rosalía Cota.[1] They both were white people through and through.

I do not remember the date of my birth, but I do know that I was fifteen years old when I married Miguel Antonio Guillén, a soldier of the presidio company of Loreto. When I was living in Loreto, I had three sons and one daughter. Two of the boys died in Loreto at a young age and another boy, Isidoro, came with us to Alta California. I had one girl, Petra, who was eleven years old, when we moved to San Diego.

I lived in San Diego for eight years with my husband. He continued his service as a soldier at the presidio of San Diego. I assisted the women who were in labor.

I had relatives who lived in the vicinity of Los Angeles and even farther north. I asked my husband many times if he would take me to see them, but he did not want to go with me. The presidio commander would not let me go either, because there was no other woman at the presidio who knew how to deliver babies.

Everyone in San Diego respected me very much. I was treated with much affection in the homes of the important people. Even though I had my own house, those families would have me stay at their homes all the time and they even provided for my children.

In 1812, while I was attending Mass at the church at San Juan Capistrano, there was a huge earthquake that knocked down the tower. I ran through the sacristy and was knocked to the ground in the doorway. I was pregnant and could not move, and people stepped on top of me. Soon after, I returned to San Diego and almost

---

1 Savage's footnote here reads: "Michael White, her son-in-law, says Lucía Valenzuela."

immediately gave birth to my daughter María Antonia, who still lives here in San Gabriel.[2]

After living in San Diego for eight years, we went to Mission San Gabriel, where my husband served in the guard. On October 1, 1814, my daughter María del Rosario was born. She is the wife of Miguel White. I am now living in their house.

About four years later, I returned to San Diego with my husband and family. My husband was sick and wanted permission to be discharged from the military. At first they refused his request, but in the end they granted it. About six months or perhaps one year later, we returned to San Gabriel. My husband was gravely ill and died in Los Angeles soon after. They sent me an escort to take me back to San Diego. Since my oldest son, Isidoro Guillén, was a soldier, they put him in charge of the escort. I returned to San Diego with my entire family and went to spend time at the home of Don Santiago Argüello, the commander of the presidio. Before Argüello became commander, Don Francisco María Ruiz had been the commander for many years. Before him, Don Manuel Rodríguez was commander, and before Rodríguez, some fellow named Don Antonio was the commander.

When I first came to San Diego, there were no other houses at the presidio except for the commander's house and the soldiers' barracks.

There was no church. The missionary who would come from Mission San Diego would say Mass in a shelter made from some old walls covered with branches.

The first adobe house that was built in San Diego belonged to some fellow named Sánchez. He was the father of Don Vicente Sánchez, the *alcalde* of Los Angeles and delegate of the *diputación territorial*. The house was very small

but everybody would go and see it as if it were a palace. That house was built about a year after I arrived in San Diego for the first time.

My last trip to San Diego was probably in 1818. My daughter María del Rosario was about four years old then. Something tells me that I was there when the insurgents came to California. I remember that they captured a foreigner and put shackles on him, but then they took them off.

About three years later I returned to San Gabriel. The reason for my return was that Father José Sánchez, the missionary at San Gabriel, had written to his cousin Father Fernando at San Diego. He asked him to speak with the commander of the San Diego presidio and beg him to give my son Isidoro Guillén an escort to bring me back to San Gabriel with my entire family. The commander granted the request.

When we arrived here, Father José Sánchez provided me and my family with a small house where we could live temporarily until I found work. I lived there with my five young daughters. My son Isidoro Guillén was serving as a soldier in the mission escort.

At that time, Father Sánchez was between sixty and seventy years old. He was a Spaniard and a white man. He was of medium height and heavy set. He was a very good, loving, and charitable man. He, like his colleague Father José María de Zalvidea, treated the Indians very well. Both men were well loved by the *gente de razón* and the neophytes, as well as by the other Indians.

Father Zalvidea was quite old. He was very tall and a bit heavy. He was a white man. I heard it said that Zalvidea was sent to San Juan Capistrano because there was no missionary there. Later I found out that many years later, when Father Antonio Peyri fled San Luis Obispo, it was rumored that the Fathers were going to be killed. Father Zalvidea was very sick and, truth be told, he had not been in his right mind since they took him from San Gabriel. He did not want to

---

2 Footnote by Savage reads, "It must have been María de los Angeles."

leave that mission. I think the Father was scared. Two Indians from San Luis Rey went to San Juan Capistrano and placed him in a *carreta* used for hauling hides. They made him as comfortable as possible and took him to San Luis Rey, where he died soon after, due to the rough ride he had to tolerate.

Father Zalvidea loved his "mission children" very much. This is what he called the Indians whom he personally had converted to Christianity. Sometimes he would go on horseback, and other times on foot, and cross the mountains until he reached the *rancherías* where the gentiles lived, so he could bring them to our religion.

Father Zalvidea introduced many improvements at Mission San Gabriel and helped it move forward in every way. He was not satisfied with feeding only the mission Indians an abundant amount of food. He also wanted the wild Indians to have something to eat. So he planted trees in the mountains and far from the mission so the other Indians would have food when they passed by those places.

The last time I came to San Gabriel, there were only two women in this whole part of California who really knew how to cook. One was María Luisa Cota, the wife of Claudio López, the *mayordomo* at the mission. The other woman was María Ignacia Amador, the wife of Francisco Javier Alvarado. She knew how to cook, sew, read, and write, and she could take care of the sick. She was a fine *curandera*. Her job was to sew and take care of the church garments. In her home, she taught some children how to read and write, but she did not have a formal school.

On important feast days, such as that of the patron saint and Easter, the two women would be called upon to prepare the large meal, the meat dishes, sweets, and other things.

The Fathers wanted to help me because I was a widow supporting a family. They looked for ways to give me work without upsetting the other women. Father Sánchez and Father Zalvidea discussed the matter and decided to see who was the best cook. One woman would cook first, followed by the next one, and I would be the last one to cook. The woman who surpassed the others would be assigned to teach the Indian cooks how to cook. The señores who would be deciding on the quality of the three meals were notified ahead of time. One of the men was Don Ignacio Tenorio, whom they called the "king's judge." He came to live and die in the company of Father Sánchez. Señor Tenorio was a very old man. When he would go out, he would wrap himself up in a little shawl and walk very slowly, aided by his cane. His long walk amounted to going from the Father's house to the church.

In addition to the Fathers, the other judges who were asked to give their expert opinion were Don Ignacio Mancisidor, a merchant; Don Pedro Narváez, a naval officer; Sergeant José Antonio Pico, who later became a lieutenant and was the brother of Governor Pío Pico; Don Domingo Romero, who was my assistant when I was the *llavera* at the mission; and Claudio López, the *mayordomo* at the mission.

Whenever those men were at the mission, they would eat with the Fathers. They were present for the three meals on the designated days. I was not told anything about this until the day Father Sánchez called me over and said, "Look, Eulalia, tomorrow it is your turn to prepare the dinner, because María Ignacia and Luisa have already done so. Let's see what kind of dinner you will give us tomorrow."

The next day, I went to cook. I made several soups, a variety of meat dishes, and anything else that came to mind that I knew how to make. Tomás, the Indian cook, paid close attention to what I was doing, as the Father had told him to do.

The men I mentioned came at dinnertime. After they finished the meal, Father Sánchez asked them what they thought of the food, beginning with the oldest man, Don Ignacio Tenorio. This señor pondered for quite some time. He said that it had been many years since he had eaten as well as he had that day. He doubted that a person would eat better food at the king's table. The other men also praised the meal highly.

The Father then asked Tomás which of the three señoras he liked best and which one knew the most. He said it was me.

Based on this, I was given a job at the mission. First, two Indians were assigned to me so I could teach them how to cook. One was named Tomás and the other was "El Gentil." I taught them so well that I had the pleasure of seeing them turn out to be very fine cooks. They were, perhaps, the best cooks in this whole part of the country.

The Fathers were very happy and this helped me earn more of their respect. I spent about a year teaching those two Indians. I did not have to work; I just supervised them because they now had some basic knowledge of cooking.

The Fathers then talked among themselves and agreed to hand over the mission keys to me. This was in 1821, if I remember correctly. I remember that my daughter María Rosario was seven years old at the time and was gravely ill. Father José Sánchez administered the last rites to her. He attended to her with the greatest care and we were finally able to rejoice because we did not lose her. At that time, I was already the *llavera*.

The *llavera* had various responsibilities. First, she would distribute the daily rations for the *pozolera*. To do this, she had to count the number of single women and men, field workers, and vaqueros—those who rode with saddles and those who rode bareback. Besides that, she had to give daily rations to the people who were married. In short, she was in charge of the distribution of the rations for the Indians and she was also in charge of the Fathers' kitchen. She was in charge of the key to the clothing storehouse, from where material would be taken to make dresses for single and married women, as well as children. She also had to supervise the cutting of clothes for men.

She was also in charge of cutting and making clothes and other items, from head to toe, for the vaqueros who used saddles. Those who rode bareback received nothing more than their shirt, blanket, and loincloth. Those who rode with saddles received the same clothing as the *gente de razón*. They were given a shirt, a vest, pants, a hat, boots, shoes, and spurs. And they were given a saddle, a bridle, and a *reata* for their horse. Each vaquero would also receive a large kerchief made of silk or cotton, and a sash of Chinese silk or red crepe cloth or whatever other material might be in the storehouse.

All work having to do with clothing was done by my daughters under my supervision. I would cut and arrange the pieces of material and my five daughters would do the sewing. When they could not keep up with the workload, I would let the Father know. He would then hire women from the pueblo of Los Angeles and pay them.

In addition, I had to supervise the area where soap was made, which was very large, and also the wine presses. I supervised and worked in the crushing of olives to make olive oil. Domingo Romero would drain off the liquid, but I would supervise him as he did this.

Luis, the soap maker, was in charge of the actual soap production, but I supervised everything.

I supervised the distribution of leather, calfskin, chamois, sheepskin, *tafilete*, red cloth, tacks, thread, silk, etc.—everything related to the making of saddles and shoes, as well as everything that is needed in a saddle workshop and a shoe workshop.

I would distribute rations and supplies to the troops and the *gente de razón* servants every eight days. They would receive beans, corn, garbanzos, lentils, candles, soap, and lard. An Indian servant named Lucio, whom the Fathers trusted completely, was assigned to help me distribute everything.

When necessary, one of my daughters would do whatever I could not find time to complete. My daughter María del Rosario almost always worked by my side.

After all my daughters had married (the last one was Rita, who married in 1832 or 1833), Father Sánchez tried very hard to get me to marry First Lieutenant Juan Mariné, a Spaniard (Catalán) who had served in the artillery. He was a widower with a family. I did not want to get married, but Father Sánchez told me that Marineé

was a very good man, which turned out to be the case. He also had quite a bit of money, but he never handed the box where he kept it over to me. I gave in to the Father's wishes. I did not have the heart to deny Father Sánchez anything because he had been like a father and a mother to me and to my entire family.

I was the *llavera* at the mission for twelve or fourteen years, until about two years after the death of Father José Sánchez. He died at this mission. In spite of his advanced age, Father Sánchez was strong and in good health until shortly before he died.

13. The Potential of Alta California:
A Report to the Government in Mexico, 1827

By Enrique Virmond

Primary Source

The bay of San Pedro could be converted into one of the best ports if its sand bar were removed. If someone were willing to make the effort required, it could become one of the principal harbors in the country.

Agricultural enterprises have been fostered considerably by the missionaries during the last few years, and perhaps they could be increased even more if there were a market for what they grow. Up to now, the Russians have been the only purchasers of wheat. I would estimate that they purchase from twelve to fifteen thousand *fanegas* of wheat at a price of three pesos per *fanega* to send to Sitka, which is the capital of their posses sions along the northwest coast. It is not worth sending the wheat in bulk to Peru, Guayaquil, or any other place in the Pacific. However, if water or windmills

could be built, I believe that California could secure the greater part of the flour business in those countries.

Up to now, English, Anglo-American, and Russian ships, as well as some Mexican ones, have been the only traders in the country. The English bring some goods, and also money, and exchange them for hide and tallow. The Anglo-Americans sail out of Boston with a perfectly supplied storehouse on board, and they take away hide, tallow, and whatever money the country has. This commerce seems to me to be quite harmful, since the outcome is that the country is left almost entirely without money. The retail sales they make in their one and-a-half to two-year treks from port to port along the coast of both Alta and Baja California hinder the *criollo* merchant who wants to purchase these items. As a result, he cannot prosper.

Commerce with the Russians is quite advantageous. They come in search of grain and meat. They bring very few goods. They trade mostly in hard cash.

Recently, a ship arrived looking for horses for the Sandwich Islands. Until recently, the few national [Mexican] ships that have come up generally have brought goods and products of the Republic and some money. However, they have made some miscalculations with respect to their cargo. Assuming that certain items prohibited by the laws would be scarce, they have discovered instead that there is an abundance of these items, since foreigners have been allowed to bring them in.

The national merchants could provide the same items more cheaply with some protection from the Supreme Government and strict observance of the laws. The number of national ships would increase, and a more regular type of commerce beneficial to the country could be established. I, myself, in place of the one ship I now have, would buy more in order to send these products in a national ship all the way to Europe.

To link Alta California to this Republic, it seems to me that the fortification of the port of San Francisco should be a primary focus of Your Excellency. Two strong batteries—one on the side of Point Bonita and the other where the Castillo is presently located—would render the port secure against an attack from the sea, since the entrance is very narrow. In addition, there are three islands within the same port, and if they were well fortified they would provide security to the entire bay.

It seems to me that this port is suitable for a gunnery site that could be established in the northern part of the port, where there are many appropriate locations. The climate there is less harsh and there is also an abundance of timber. I cannot tell Your Excellency with certainty that the timber is adequate for the construction of ships. However,

I should assume that it is, since the spot borders the Bodega River, which is where the Russians have constructed war and merchant brigantines. Also, the launches which go from mission to mission within the port of San Francisco have been built at that river. With such an enterprise in this port it might finally be given its due. People have been avoiding it up to now because of its cool climate, which is also immensely healthy. I dare say to Your Excellency that perhaps nowhere else in the entire Mexican Republic can one find another place that is so useful and that has all essential materials so near at hand as this port.

I should bring another matter to Your Excellency's attention. The majority of the *hijos del país* who are in the military have asked to be discharged, but the Señor Commander General has refused to grant these requests. If these men did retire from the service, it would be a great good for the country in many ways. Their military knowledge does not extend beyond perhaps knowing how to rope a bull. Since almost all of the soldiers are married and their families are growing very rapidly, it is a heavy burden for the state and the missions that have to support them. And they inevitably end up in miserable circumstances. If they were free they would he able to take advantage of the land, work in the fields, and consequently make life much more comfortable for themselves and their families. The unmarried soldiers who would be sent from here to replace them would be trees planted for future settlement. It would be much less burdensome replace them. In case of need, the Government would be able to count on them more, since they would be experienced soldiers. The Indian and the soldier who is an *hijo del país* are enemies who will never become allies. Generally, the soldiers were born at the missions where their father were stationed. They have grown up with the Indian children and have acquired some of their gentile customs as well as their vices. They never forget, however, that they are white and

Bay of San Pedro as Harbor for Los Angeles, circa 1900

they never forget the notion that the Indians were born to be their slaves. Since the soldiers have had and still have power in their hands, at times passion has wielded authority over justice. The Indian, who has no other safeguard than the Father, has had to suffer many times even though he was innocent. He resents this treatment even more because it comes from his childhood companion, the person with whom he played games and got drunk, than if he had received this treatment from a stranger. Believe me, Your Excellency, the unrest that has occurred in California and that can still occur has no other basis than the quarrels an Indian has with a soldier over unjust treatment and from the resentments that inevitably follow.

Because of the great scarcity of missionary Fathers and the advanced age of those who serve, some missions are visibly declining. I cannot recommend to Your Excellency strongly enough that California needs more clergymen. It is not yet possible for the Indians to govern themselves. If there are no Fathers, most of the Indians will return to being gentiles and will abandon the missions and their work. Consequently, the country

will be ruined and without labor, for in California, the Indian is the only one who works.

Finally, if Your Excellency would permit me to say two words in favor of these religious who have spent the greater part of their lives in these remote regions trying to convert some of the unfaithful to Christianity and to render the gentiles useful to the nation. The fact that some of the Fathers have refused to swear allegiance to the constitution of this Republic is a matter of conscience for them. It is not up to me to become involved in this. However, I can assure Your Excellency that I have dealt with most of them for a number of years, and I have found them to be very moral, selfless, and simple men. Their only concern is the preaching of the Gospel and the management of the temporalities of the Indians. On every occasion, they have shown themselves obedient and ready to contribute in any way to the needs of the troops. At times this has meant even depriving themselves and their Indians of what they themselves needed. Even though since 1811 they have been paid basically nothing of the four hundred pesos a year the King of Spain annually allotted to each of them for their work, they have always been content to fulfill their duties.

Your Excellency might be able to find other people of equal virtue and honesty to administer these temporalities, but never any people with more of these qualities. Some people talk about the great riches some missions possess, but believe me, Your Excellency, these are just tales. I have dealt with these Fathers on business matters, and I have seen that everything they have bought from me has been divided among the Indians and the needs of the Church and the missions. This country is currently flourishing, and that is because of the Fathers. They have been tireless in their work and they will continue to be so, if they can rely on the protection of the Supreme Government. They encourage every class of industry and they freely lend their efforts to all public works and to the construction of homes for private individuals. They practice every type of virtue and charity toward their neighbors. They care for and clothe a large number of unclothed people. There is no one, rich or poor, who has not been received in their residences with the greatest generosity and openness while, at the same time and without self-interest, freely supplied with provisions, mules, horses, servants, and whatever else they needed for their journey.

Such has been the conduct of the missionary Fathers of Alta California. It is deeply gratifying for me to have this opportunity to inform Your Excellency of the services they have rendered and provided to the nation every day, which makes them worthy of gratitude and public respect.

Section IV

California's Mexican Rancho Era, 1822–1848

Section Four

Introduction to California's Mexican Rancho Era, 1822–1848

Sources

On September 16, 1810, a revolution broke out in New Spain. After a decade of bloodshed, the independent nation of Mexico was established. Following a brief period as the Mexican Empire, the Mexicans formed a fledgling republic in one of the largest nations on earth. The new government, based in Mexico City, had great difficulty coordinating affairs in the northern part of the country. Mexico officially assumed control of the province of Alta California in 1821, though Californians did not actually get word of this change until a year later, in 1822.

Though the missions had become economically prosperous in the early 1800s, they would gain very little support from the Mexican government. The last of the missions was built in 1823. The Mexicans outlawed slavery and many Mexicans believed the missions were not much different from slave plantations. The question of what to do with the missions became a hot topic of debate in the 1830s.

Catholic leaders had long discussed the idea of turning control of the missions over to the native people who lived there. After running the missions for six decades, however, the Franciscans did not present such a plan. The new government, which professed a strong attachment to the indigenous peoples of Mexico, did not show any interest in turning the missions over to native Californians.

As a result, the missions were secularized in 1834. Essentially, the buildings were transformed into ordinary churches, and the land around them was given to government officials and their friends.

In the 1830s and 1840s, the lifestyle of the Spanish speaking people in California centered on huge ranches. The ranch owners ruled their areas like feudal lords. California only had a few thousand people of European or *mestizo* (European and indigenous) heritage at the time. Roughly 15,000 people from California native culture groups lived in the areas controlled by Spanish speaking people. There were no major cities in Mexican California; the population was scattered in numerous towns and villages. The majority of the people raised cattle and crops for the rancheros. After the missions were closed, the Indians in that system were left on the margins of society, trying to survive as menial laborers and beggars.

Far from major towns, many Indian villages continued to live in their traditional way. Historians estimate that about 100,000 native people lived in Alta California at the end of the Rancho Era, compared to about 300,000 when Father Serra arrived in 1769. Most of the decline was due to disease, or the combination of disease and extreme poverty.

Sources

While historians tend to discuss the significance of Mexican rule in California in broad political and social terms, to many Californians it was actually an emotional event shaped by personal relationships and loaded with cultural symbolism. In our first selection, **Recollections of the Changeover from Spanish to Mexican Rule, 1822**, we see that the people witnessing the event did not completely understand what was happening, but they knew it was important. Notice in this account the crowd yells "long live the Mexican Empire!" For a short time, Mexico was ruled by Agustin de Iturbide, a Mexican army general who seized power and became Emperor following the war for independence. The people in the crowd may not have realized how precarious Iturbide's grip on Mexico was. In 1823 the emperor was overthrown and Mexico became a republic.

During the Mexican Rancho Era, a few prominent families of Spanish heritage dominated Alta California. The most important men were called Don, and their wives or widows Doña. Augustias de la Guerra was born into one these families in 1815. Her father, Jose de la Guerra, popularly known as El Capitan, became captain of the Santa Barbara presidio in 1817, and later Commandant for the province in 1827. In the second selection, **A Leading Santa Barbara Woman Remembers the Rancho Era, 1878**, de la Guerra recalls some of her own experiences as well as many of the social expectations of the time. Notice how frank she is in sharing her perspectives on various leaders. She was a young girl when the Mexican government took control of California; her opinions on this period may have been shaped by accounts from her father or other people she knew.

The interview was conducted when Doña Augustias was an older woman, long after the United States had taken over California. The interviewer, Thomas Savage, is actually the same historian who had interviewed Elulia Perez a year earlier (Section III). If you compare the two interviews, you will notice that both the women are of Spanish heritage, both were connected to the military, and both lived in California in the early 1800s. What differences do you see? Look closely and you may find the differences are as significant as the similarities.

Doña Augustias' comments on the lifestyle and customs of the era might be the most valuable part of the account. She describes interactions between the different social classes in this era; we see her sense of community in Santa Barbara in this time period. Notice also how she views the Indians, and their place in the community.

Next we come to the first written history of the Mexican Rancho Era. Antonio Maria Osio, a former Mexican government official, actually wrote his account in the form of a letter to one of the former mission Fathers, a few years after the United States had taken over the province. In the next excerpt shown here, **A Memoir of Mexican California, 1851**, Osio recounts the time in the 1833 when the Mexican government took control of the missions away from the Franciscan Fathers.

Perhaps most interesting is Osio's account of how the Fathers treated the Indians. Disease often killed off women more than men, leading to a gender imbalance among the native peoples in the mission system. Osio offers perhaps the most lively account of how this imbalance played out in the missions. Keep in mind, Osio never worked in the missions; his recollection could be based on stories he has heard. Whether or not his account is completely accurate, we do know the Fathers played a major role in the personal lives of the Indians living in the missions. Notice what happens in the story when Indians from San Rafael travel by barge to find women among the "gentiles" (Indians who had not joined the missions). Notice also Osio's insights on why illnesses spread so quickly within the mission system. Many people criticized the missions for their poor health conditions, but this account stands out because Osio also notes one particular mission, San Luis Rey, that took steps to improve the health of their people.

Much of what Americans call the "cowboy" lifestyle actually comes from the Spanish culture of the *vaqueros* in California and other parts of the southwest. During the Rancho Era, horses were central to many of the cultural traditions and cattle were a major source of wealth. In **The Cattle Drives of Early California**, historian Siegfried Demke explains what was involved in transporting cattle from the southern part of the state to the buyers in the north. Notice how Demke compares the Mexican *vaqueros* to American cowboys of the post-Civil war era.

While horses and cattle were central to the culture of Mexican California, the architecture of the era is perhaps its most enduring legacy. In **Spanish Colonial or Adobe Architecture of California**, architectural historians Donald R. Hannaford and Revel Edwards point to many different influences that led to a distinct style of adobe buildings in California. The authors point to practical as well as cultural motives for the architectural design; taking into account the Mediterranean climate found in coastal California as well as Spanish and Mexican traditions of hospitality. While hospitality was indeed a hallmark of the ranchos, you might also find features that could reflect a culture of power and privilege. Notice how the adobe buildings reflect much of the history of the Mission Era as well as the Rancho Era.

While the architecture may be known for an open feel, the life of young women inside the buildings was more tightly controlled. Margaret Gilbert Mackey and Louise Pinkney Sooy examined documents related to the rancho lifestyle as well as clothing preserved from the era. In **A Young Lady of the House in Mexican California**, Mackey and Sooy describe the clothing styles of Mexican women. Consider how the clothing could reflect the status of rancho women, and unmarried women in particular. Travelers often commented on the beauty of women in Mexican California. Their outfits were often more colorful and less restrictive than those of women of comparable social status in the United States at the time. In their addendum the authors outline many of the rules of the society, providing a social context to help us understand the clothing styles.

If the women were allowed out of the house, in their beautiful outfits, it was often for parties where they could dance and socialize. In Selection 7, **Dances of Early California Days**, Lucile Czarnowski describes three types of gatherings common in Mexican California: Fandangoes, Bailes, and Fiestas. The authors also describe a social event called a Cascarone ball. Some events were for upper or lower classes, while others allowed for interaction among the classes. Typically events were for all ages, and often involved an entire town.

You would not be invited to a rancho, or any of their social events, without being offered something to eat. In Selection 8, **Recipes of the Ranchos**, Mildred Yorba McArthur shares some recipes collected from actual rancho kitchens. These recipes have been adapted over the years to fit the cooking technology and ingredients available in the modern era.

The legacy of Mexican California is, inevitably, a mixture of fiction and reality. In Selection 9, *Ramona*—**A Novel of Mexican California**, we see an excerpt from one of the best known portrayals of the era in American literature. The novelist, Helen Hunt Jackson, was well known for her efforts to protect the rights of Native Americans in the late 1800s. She wrote *Ramona* in 1884 after visiting Southern California and discussing the state's history with Antonio Coronel (featured in Selection 12) and other people who had witnessed the Rancho era. The novel takes place in Southern California soon after the area was taken over by the United States. In the excerpt we share, Jackson writes about Mexicans facing injustice and trying to keep their land. While Jackson's work may have a political message, it may be her vivid and endearing descriptions of life in Southern California that made the novel such a success. Before she did her research, Jackson, a Protestant minister's daughter from Massachusetts, was about as far away from the rancho experience as any American could be. Perhaps that is one reason why she was able to convey the beauty and essence of the ranchos to a broad audience.

The Mexicans were not the only people interested in settling California. As we saw in Section III, the Russians had shown an interest in the 1760s, a fact that alarmed the Spanish Visitor-General of the New Spain at the time (see Section III, Selection 2). As the Spanish established missions and presidios, the Russians stayed away from areas of Spanish settlement. However, they continued to show an interest in the northern coastal areas of Alta California, outside of the sphere of the missions. While the Spanish connected California to Mexico and the Philippines, the Russians were interested in connecting California with Alaska.

In 1812, a group of Russians established Colony Ross ("Ross" is another name for Russia), in today's Sonoma County. They grew food for the Russian settlements in Alaska, hunted sea otters, and promoted trade with Alta California for three decades. In this colony the Russians, along people from other European or Native American groups who settled with them, constructed the first ships and the first windmills to be built in California. The largest settlement in the colony became known as Fort Ross. In Selection 10, **Colonial Russian America: Fort Ross, c. 1830s**, Kyrill T. Khlebnikov provides a first-hand description of the settlement. Khlebnikov, a manager in the New Arkhangel Office of the Russian American Company, wrote several reports to the directors of the company, outlining problems as well as opportunities for promoting trade in California. The Russian American Company, charted by the Tsar in 1799, held a monopoly on trade in Russian America. Khlebnikov also discusses the natural environment around the settlement. Russians were among the first people to document the plants and animals of coastal California in detail, and here we see one of the most helpful descriptions.

Later in the excerpt he makes suggestions for the development of the colony. Here you can see the troubled relationship between the Russians and the government in Alta California that insisted the area was in their jurisdiction. You will also notice that, in his mind, the Russians have settled in "New Albion," a name Francis Drake gave to an indefinite area of the coast in 1578 (see Section II). In the document you can see reasons Fort Ross could have great potential, as well as some significant problems. The colony would be disbanded in 1842.

While the Mexican government was concerned about Russians from the north, their attention would soon shift to the possible threat posed by Anglo Americans coming from the east. Before gold was discovered in the Sierra Foothills in 1848, relatively few Anglos (white, English speaking people) had settled in California. As long as they met standards of respectability, Anglos were welcomed into the rancho society. Most of the Anglo settlers in this era respected Mexican culture; in fact, many of them married Mexican women. In the 1840s some Mexican officials became concerned that a growing number of people in the United States were heading for California, and that migration on a greater scale could destroy the society they had built.

In Selection 11, **The Arrival of a North American Wagon Train, 1841**, Mariano Guadalupe Vallejo, a prominent rancher and military official in California, warns the government in Mexico City about the threat he sees from Anglo settlers coming to California. He appears particularly alarmed by "a party of thirty-three foreigners from Missouri." He reminds the officials that there are only six thousand Spanish or Mexican people in the province, and 15,000 Indians in the towns and missions of California. (Historians estimate there were over 100,000 Indians in California in the 1840s; most of them were outside of the towns or missions.) Despite the economic success of the missions in their later years, and the vast wealth of the ranchos, Mexican population in California was still rather small and feeble compared to the number of Americans or other foreigners who would be interested in the province. Interestingly, Vallejo would continue to be influential in California long after the United States took over.

Even after the U.S. War with Mexico and the Gold Rush, the rancho lifestyle was slow to

disappear in California. As California was rapidly changing in the late 1800s, many people thought of the Rancho Era as a special time, when life was simpler. Californians were curious about their past, and some of the old rancheros were still alive and eager to share their stories.

We close this section with one of the most succinct and perceptive accounts of the Rancho Era, from a leading citizen in the growing town of Los Angeles. In Selection 12, **Reminisces on Life and Customs of Mexican California**, Antonio Coronel offers the perspective of a man who grew up in Mexico City, came to California in the 1830s, and learned to prosper in his new home. Among his many accomplishments, he was Mayor of Los Angeles and a City Councilman (after being mayor, interestingly) in the 1850s and 1860s. He even served one term as California State Treasurer.

In 1834 Coronel came to Alta California with his parents and siblings as part of group of 239 Mexicans called the Hijar-Padres Colony, an effort supported by the liberal government in Mexico to promote economic development in the province. One of the goals of the colony was to promote the mixing of Spanish and indigenous people as mission lands were secularized. The Hijar-Padres Colony had been planned for the Santa Rosa valley, but the colony dispersed soon after reaching California. Coronel and his family settled in Los Angeles, where his father started one of the first schools in that area. Coronel noticed a sharp contrast between major cultural center he grew up in and the frontier environment he adapted to as a young man.

Coronel looks back on the era with fondness, while also offering a critical perspective. Notice how he sums up two characteristics of the rancho culture, hospitality and paternalism: "A traveler could go up to any house in California, confident he could stay however many days he liked and pay nothing for roof, bed, food, and even horses for his journey. But the mothers took great care of their daughters, and the traveler often met only the men of the family." Coronel's observations of the life of women are among the most interesting. "Women's work was harder, longer, and more important than men's." Thankfully, he offers generous details after making us curious about this and other topics.

Coronel had much in common with Doña Augustias de la Guerra (Selection 2), who experienced the same era just one hundred miles up the coast from Coronel. Both had fathers that had helped build the towns they lived in and both became leaders in those towns, de la Guerra in Santa Barbara and Coronel in Los Angeles. Their viewpoints are different, however, perhaps because their families were different. Jose de la Guerra had come from Spain, and he was part of the culture of the missions and the presidios. Coronel's father, on the other hand, had come from the heart of Mexico, on a voyage sponsored by liberal Mexican leaders, as the mission lands were being dispersed.

As the Rancho Era passed into memory, some people from the era, such as de la Guerra and Coronel, continued to prosper as everything around them changed. Many others, lacking their good fortune and resilience, would suffer terribly or disappear with little trace. In the following sections you will see how the culture that had developed under the Spanish missionaries and the Mexican rancheros, along with the cultures of many native peoples who continued to thrive in the interior of California, were beaten down or transformed by a combination of military defeat, persecution, and economic revolution. Few places have undergone so much change, so rapidly, as California in the third quarter of the nineteenth century. Today we see that while our world is very different, much of the character of our state still reflects developments from before California was part of the United States. These earlier eras, as well as developments in other parts of the world, set the stage for the amazing transformation of California that would follow.

Readings

1. Recollections of the Changeover from Spanish to Mexican Rule, 1822

By Juana Machado Wrightington

Primary Source

The change of flag in 1822 was as follows:
There came from the north (I do not recall whether by sea or land) a prebendary called Don Valentin [Agustín] Fernandez de San Vicente, who brought with him a chaplain or secretary, I do not know what he was. I do not remember ever having seen him dressed as a priest. The prebendary wore a garment of a color resembling red. This gentleman was the agent of the Mexican empire to establish here the new order of things. I well recall that when some woman or girl, excited by the richness and the colors of his dress, which were really very showy and handsome would ask, "Who is this gentleman?" someone would answer, "The prebendary."

Such a person never had been seen before in California. He and his companion stayed above in the house of the comandante. The comandante was Captain Francisco Maria Ruiz, who had been in office for many years.

The troops of infantry, cavalry and some few artillery were ordered to form in the plaza of the presidio; the cannons were put outside the plaza to the door of the guard room, looking toward the ocean. There was as yet no flag. A corporal or soldier had the Spanish flag on a little stick, and another the Mexican flag. When Comandante Ruiz, in the presente of the official, Don José Maria Estudillo, cried out "Long live the Mexican Empire!" the Spanish flag was lowered and the Mexican flag raised in the midst of salvos of artillerymen and musketeers. After this the troops did nothing.

On the following day an order was given to cut off the braids of the soldiers. This produced in everyone, men and women, a very disagreeable reaction. The former were accustomed to wear their hair long and braided with a knot of ribbon or silk at the end; on some it came below the waist; it was somewhat like the manner of the Chinese

Mexico's flag from 1821–1823

with the exception that they did not shave any part of the head.

This order was carried out. I remember that when papa came home with his braid in his hand and gave it to mama his face was very sad and that of mama no less so; she looked at the braid and cried.

The manner in which men dressed during my childhood until Echeandia arrived was as follows:

Undershirt of cotton or other material; waistcoat without facings which came down to the waist; of different colors; but the troops wore blue. Over the waistcoat was the doublet which was a coat with lapels on the sides; with red borders on all the edges; and with a red collar. That is what the troops wore, and the countrymen who were very few and the retired soldiers wore more or less

the same, the color being varied by each according to his likes.

Short trousers of cloth, nankeen.[1] drill,[2] or whatever each one had; the troops wore cloth. These short trousers reached to the knees where they had openings on the outside with flaps which fell on each side and six buttons on each side.

Then came the chamois legging; it was a piece of chamois about three-quartets long, which went around the leg and was tied with ribbons or tapes. This chamois was ornamented with tooling; underneath on the feet were shoes and stockings.

On his head the man wore his hat of fell, straw, [or] vicuna[3] and the fine ones that came from Spain were carefully treated. For common use the men wore hats of palm which the Indians made. …

---

1 A light-colored cotton cloth originally imported from Nankin, China.

2 A course linen or cotton cloth.

3 A soft fur from a South American animal of the camel family used for making hats and coats.

Jefes in Alta California

Don Pablo Vicente de Solá was the last leader under Spanish rule. He was a small man and somewhat of a coward. Don José María Echeandía was a Mexican. He was tall, white, and very well educated. He behaved very well in California. His courage was not tested because there were no revolutions during his tenure.

Don Manuel Victoria was tall, had light-brown skin, and was very brave. During his tenure, the people of Los Angeles revolted and he went there with fifteen or twenty men. Don Romualdo Pacheco was one of those men. As they were approaching Los Angeles, Pacheco saw that they were outnumbered by the opposition and said to Victoria, "Señor, there are many men bearing down on us. We are much fewer in number than they are." The general responded, "Maybe you allow people in skirts to order you around, but I don't." Pacheco then spurred his horse and headed straight into battle, and they immediately killed him. Victoria was mortally wounded and his soldiers took care of him. They took him to San Diego and put him on a ship headed for Mexico. General Victoria wanted to marry me but I did not marry him because he was Mexican and was very anti-Spanish. Ironically, I later ended up marrying a Mexican.

The order to secularize the missions arrived when General José Figueroa was here. This order stripped the friars of their control over the missions and put the missions in the hands of administrators. Some of these administrators were bad and others were good, but most of them did not know how to manage the Indians. The friars treated the Indians as if they were their actual parents.

I got married in 1833, during the time Figueroa was in office. I was seventeen years old. After I got married, I was in Monterey. That is when General Micheltorena came.

When they killed Don Romualdo Pacheco, his wife, Ramona, was at my father's house. That is where Pacheco's son, Romualdo, was born. The year was 1831. I baptized him. Ramona was my cousin and she loved me very much. She was my father's goddaughter. The baby was born in my room. That is the room at my father's house where I would sleep when you were a little girl, Rebeca. Since Pacheco was my godchild, sometimes he would call me "mamá." Several years later, my cousin Ramona married Don Juan Wilson. They had three children—Negra Wilson, Juanito, and Ramoncita. Pacheco had another brother named Mariano. He married Pancha Ortega, the sister of Manuelita Carrillo and Vicente (el Mudo) Ortega.

My Marriage

When I got married, the ceremony took place at the mission. My father would always host a huge feast for the whole pueblo whenever one of his sons or daughters got married. A long table that extended from one end of the corridor to the other would be set up. That is where the pueblo of Santa Bárbara sat to celebrate the wedding of the commander's daughter. My brother-in-law Fray José Jimeno, who was the Franciscan prelate, hosted this feast, not my father. My father later did the same thing at his home. All of the important people of Santa Bárbara ate in the *sala grande*. The rest of the people ate at tables that were set in the interior patio of the house. Later, some good food would be sent to the prisoners.

In the past, the marriage ceremonies here were different. The couple would join hands at night, in the presence of their *padrinos*. The next day there would be a Mass and a nuptial blessing. During Mass, the bride and groom and their *padrinos* would kneel in the sanctuary while holding a lit candle in their hands. The couple would receive Communion and then the priest would perform the nuptial blessing. After this ceremony, there would be a blessing at the tower, which is on the right side as you enter the church. My husband and I also served as *padrinos*. The church is still standing and anybody can see the tower.

The food for the fiestas generally consisted of *olla podrida*, roasted pork, stuffed hens, roasted lamb, and a stew made with lamb chops and wine. The desserts were sweet pumpkin, rice pudding, and bread pudding. We also had olives and raisins.

The missions between Santa Bárbara and Monterey were Santa Inés, La Purísima, San Luis Obispo, San Miguel, San Antonio, and Soledad. Today, in 1881, there are pueblos at almost all of these places.

Marriage

When a poor woman was to get married, her relatives would go with a soldier or with their son to ask the wealthy people to help dress the bride. My father was the commander of the pueblo of Santa Bárbara for a number of years. When the command was taken away from him because of Mexico's independence from Spain, he was still considered a figure of authority. Even up until recently, there were people who would refer to him as "my captain" when they would speak about him. For this reason, many poor people would come to my father's home and would receive courteous attention from him.

Very early in the morning on the day that a girl was to be married, the bride and groom's parents would arrive at my father's home. They would bring "their captain" a gift of small breads and sweets for his breakfast. After the wedding ceremony in the church, the couple would go and visit my father and drink chocolate with him. Then they would invite the family to the wedding banquet.

Soldiers

The soldiers in Santa Bárbara were known as *soldados de cuera* (leatherjacket soldiers). A *cuera* was a jacket made of two thicknesses of sheepskin which was used to keep the Indians' arrows from getting through to the soldiers' bodies. When the soldiers were on horseback, the *cuera* went down as far as their saddle. They also carried a shield made of rawhide. During the Spanish period, the shields bore the coat of arms of the king. The soldiers' wives made the buttons for the men's shirts out of thread. Once, when I was about ten years old, I went to a soldier's house. All the soldiers lived in what was called the presidio quadrangle. There I saw a man making little circles out of gourds. I asked him what he was doing and he told me he was making buttons for his children's clothes. The men had silver buttons on their pants but they only fastened three of the buttons. The largest button was called the *atracador* because it would hold up everything.

Food and Utensils

People had spoons made from horns and those who could also had forks. They would drink water from gourds or in glasses made from horns, but gourds were normally used. They usually ate beef that was roasted. Cattle were the people's mainstay and supplied them with milk, meat, lard, tallow for candles, *reatas*, horns, bones to obtain lime, and hides. They would exchange hides for clothing and other things they needed that were brought on merchant ships.

The *Monjerío* for Indian Women

The place where the young, unmarried Indian women lived was called the *monjerío*. The girls were watched over by older women who had high moral qualities. The *monjerío* was a type of convent. The older women were like mothers to the girls. They would take them out for strolls and would teach them how to do things that would be useful to them, such as sewing. The *monjerío* had three different locks with corresponding keys. The prelate of the convent had one key, the *alcalde* had another, and the corporal of the guard had the third key. That way it was impossible to enter the *monjerío* without the consent of all three people. Whenever the girls needed anything, they would pull on a rope that would ring a bell in the Father's room. When the young Indian girls wanted to get married, they would ask the Father for a husband and then would leave the *monjerío*.

Entertainment

On certain days there would be a general celebration for everybody. The feast day of Santa Bárbara was the most important. The celebration would begin with a sung Mass. Then the Indians would set up what looked like little houses filled with good things to eat. After Mass, the Father would visit the Indians at these little houses. As he passed by, somebody would play a musical instrument and then they would toss out chestnuts, pine nuts, and *islay* (a fruit like coffee). Indians from San Buenaventura, Las Cieneguitas, and Santa Inés would be invited to come. They would arrive dancing and the Indians would toss grains of corn, chestnuts, and other seeds at them.

Sometimes an Indian man would perform the snake dance at fiestas. In this dance, he would call out to the snake and try to make it come close to him. The furious snake would do it, but if it attacked, the Indian would not get hurt because he had put something on his body to counteract the venom from the bite. To keep the snake within a specific area, they would place pieces of cactus around to form a little corral.

Harvests

When the Indians finished their work for the Fathers, they would ask permission to go and gather pine nuts, chestnuts, *islay*, *cacomites* (it has a root like an onion but tastes like a potato), and other things. They would gather this food and save it for the winter.

Land Titles

My husband was the government secretary and for a time he held the position of provisional governor of Alta California. Before the government headquarters were built, a room in my house served as an office. The archives were kept there. Actually, all important papers that needed to be saved were kept at my house. We also had stamped paper that was used for documents, etc. Petitions for the granting of ranchos were made on stamped paper. The petition would be presented and then the commander general would write on the petition, "Have the secretary look into this." Since the secretary had access to the archives, he knew if there would be any problem in granting title to the land. The commander general would determine whether to grant the title, based on the information provided by the secretary. The paper used for the land titles was called "first seal" and was worth eight pesos. The commander general would sign blank sheets of this stamped paper and it would be kept in the office at my home. After the taking of California by the Americans, there were still things in my house that belonged to the government. I found two pieces of "first seal" stamped paper among the items. I gave one sheet to Don Andrés Pico, the brother of Pío Pico, who was the last governor of California during the Mexican period. I gave the other sheet to Don James Forbes. Don Andrés Pico chose the land he wanted and he was granted title to that land on the stamped paper. Señor Forbes was granted title to land that had previously belonged to him, land that he had asked the government to exchange for other land. Since I believed that everything would eventually be lost, I told them, "I am going to give these to you, because in the end the Moor will take what the Christian took."

The Arrival of the French Before the Taking by the Americans, 1842

While I was at my sister's Rancho Alisal, I received a letter from my husband telling me that the French corvette *Danaïde* had arrived with a number of French gentlemen who had come on a pleasure trip. These gentlemen wanted to go to a rancho to see cattle. They arrived at Alisal and the next day a rodeo was put on for them.

We all went on horseback to see the cattle. They were a bit afraid to get too close, but my sister and I went over to the cattle so the men could see that there was no danger. They wanted to see how a bull was roped. I then approached a very brave Californio and told him what a certain gentleman wanted to see. The Californio then picked up a *reata*, lassoed the bull, and threw it down. He got off his horse and tied up the bull. The French gentlemen admitted how quickly and skillfully this was done. One of the men took out a pencil and paper and made a sketch of what he had seen. …

---

3. A Memoir of Mexican California, 1851

By Antonio M. Osio

Primary Source

At the beginning of 1833 the national brigantine Catalina was anchored in the port of Monterey. It carried General Don José Figueroa, who had been appointed commander general and jefe politico of Alta California, some officers, and about thirty infantry soldiers. It also carried a dozen Fathers from the Colegio de Guadalupe de Zacatecas and their Superior, Reverend Father Francisco García Diego, who had the title of Padre Comisario. So as not to interrupt the narrative about the Fathers and the missions, the account about the new jefe will follow later.

The Fathers of the Colegio de San Fernando in Mexico were expecting the newcomers and waiting to be ordered to surrender some or all of the twenty one missions to them. They allegedly wanted to destroy the missions before the newcomers could receive them, as if to say, "I do not want you serving yourself from a table that I have worked so hard to prepare for the members of my community."

It is not my intention to tarnish the conduct of those Reverend Fathers. I am only recounting the deeds. If any proof were needed, their collective discontent would be the first. The second would be that the Prefect sent an order to the Father Administrator of Mission San Luis Obispo instructing him to see how he could destroy the mission interests quickly so that the Indians could take advantage of them. For a number of days the Reverend Father pondered how he could achieve his Prelate's aims. In the end he spent more than twenty thousand pesos purchasing fine woven goods of cotton, wool, and silk and distributed them to his neophytes so that they could dress themselves. The third proof would be that other missions hastened to slaughter cattle only for the hides. When they realized that they did not have enough workers to finish the slaughter quickly, they contracted out half of the work to various people. During the horrible slaughters, the animal fat had to be strewn along the ground and the meal left to rot in the fields. From 1832 to 1834 the traders who received the hides of the Mission San Gabriel steers estimated that more than one hundred thousand hides were taken and loaded onto ships in San Pedro Bay.

Father García Diego had not brought a sufficient number of missionaries administer all of the missions in the territory, so he and Reverend Father Narciso Durán, the superior from the Colegio de San Fernando, agreed that Durán would come down with his subordinates to oversee the southern missions. Father Tomás Estenaga was assigned to Mission San Gabriel. Because Esténaga gave away the possessions of the Fathers, after a short time he was obliged to accept meat and lard as charity. Don Tomás Yorba would send him these items from his Santa Ana Ranch. Yorba also loaned him a cow so that he would have milk, because there were no longer any cattle at the mission. A number of these Fathers suffered the hardships which they had intended for others. However, they were very good religious men and made do when they recognized that all, or at least some, of them were guilty of failing to observe the precept "Do unto others as you would have them do unto you."

To prepare the yearly general financial statement, the territorial government would ask the Father Superior to provide statistics from each of the twenty-one missions. These statistics included an inventory of goods, the number of Indians born and baptized at each mission, the number of infants and adults who by being conquered had been reborn by water and the Holy Spirit, and the number of those who had died. Equally important were the number of bushels of harvested seeds and the number of different types of livestock, although the Fathers never gave an exact number of cattle. In the statistics from Mission San Gabriel, dating from 1824 up to the beginning of its downfall, the number of cattle reported was always the same, forty thousand, However, the numbers were much higher during their years of greatest wealth. By using the approximate calculations made by various interested people along with information acquired from the *mayordomos* charge of the mission fields, and by increasing the number of cattle branded by two-thirds, one can arrive at the following statistics.

San Diego	7,000
San Luis Rey	18,000
Sui Juan Capistrano	60,000
San Gabriel	110,000

San Fernando	25,000	
San Buénaventura	19,000	
Santa Bárbara	12,000	
Santa Ynés	17,000	
La Purísima	20,000	
San Luis Obispo	18,000	
San Miguel	12,000	
San Antonio	16,000	
Soledad	14,000	
San Carlos	6,000	
San Juan Bautista	18,000	
Santa Cruz	12,000	
Santa Clara	13,000	
San José	18,000	
San Francisco de Asís	8,000	
San Rafael	5,000	
San Francisco Solano	7,000	
	435,000	

One should note that this estimate of the number of cattle was made by increasing the number of those branded by two-thirds. The missions' estimates were never done with the enthusiasm or with the accuracy demonstrated by private cattle owners. Consequently, many animals were left unbranded because the missions occupied such large expanses of land.

The experience of many years has demonstrated that the Reverend Fathers were eager to convert the infidels in order to achieve two different objectives. The first was admirable and part of their obligation as true apostles to win souls for Heaven. God, who is as good as He is just, would reward them for their evangelical work. But the Indians cared very little about improving their habits while in reduction. In addition, the lack of workmen to replace those who were dying affected that objective adversely, for once an Indian was baptized and affiliated with a mission, be belonged to that mission alone. So he did not

have the freedom to marry an Indian woman from another mission, since she was obligated to follow her husband, and that would change the total number of Indians at each mission. In the case of an Indian woman, the mission Father would not allow one his flock to be taken from him. In the case of a man, the Father would not want to relinquish a pair of strong arms. As proof I will recount the following incident.

Once, when Reverend Father Tomás Esténaga was the Administrator of Mission San Francisco, there was an illness among his neophytes which affected the women more than the men. According to the statistics, about half the women died. Since a number of young men were left unable to find women to marry, Father Esténaga was continually striving to sustain the marriages. If a wife was unfaithful, he would advise the husband to tolerate the suffering. Meanwhile, the seducer would be flogged as punishment. This had become commonplace, and the Father's advice to the poor husbands was always the same. Finally, one of the many affected Indians decided to break the silence. With desperate gestures he said, "Tell me, Father, if you were married, how many times would you tolerate being a cuckold? It has happened to me so many times that I am ready to explode from your advice. Even if you kill me I cannot take it anymore." The Father was able to contain his laughter and appear serious only because he had a terrible stomachache. He promised the poor soul that he was now going to take more efficient measures to prevent the unmarried men from stealing their women. He would send the men off to work at the mission in Contra Costa.

When he revealed this plan to the guilty parties, they explained the reasons for their conduct to the Father. Some of their reasons were very sensible. They wanted to have a woman, and there were none at the mission except for very young girls. When these girls matured, there still would not be enough of them available for even half of the men. And they could not marry women from another mission because the Fathers there did not want to relinquish them. So they proposed that Esténaga lend them the barge, which was about seven tons, and give them the necessary provisions and some gifts so that they could seek out women wherever possible among the gentiles.

The Father responded to such a reasonable request by providing them with everything they needed for their expedition. They headed in the direction of Point Olompali, which was in the jurisdiction of Mission San Rafael. The estuaries there offer excellent and secure landings for barges. About ten or twelve *vaqueros* had put their horses on board. As soon as they had made the crossing safely, they unloaded the gifts they had brought and headed for the interior. There they found what they were seeking. They joyfully boarded the barge to return quickly to the mission and celebrate their weddings. However, a young Indian from that tribe was bitter because his intended had rejected him by leaving with one of the Indians from San Francisco. In retaliation, he ran to San Rafael to inform Reverend Father José Altimira that the men on the barge and some *vaqueros* from San Francisco were stealing some of the gentile women.

Although these women were not affiliated with Mission San Rafael, because they were not baptized, the Father believed that he had an undeniable right to them. He wanted to act as the judge in his own case and hand down a decision which would serve as an example. To achieve this, he manned a beautiful boat which he had at his disposal with a good, strong crew for rowing. He put a corporal and four armed soldiers from the escort on board and sent them off to confront the barge. Favored by a light breeze from the northeast, the men on the barge were soon sailing past the wall of rock called the Treasure. The boat, meanwhile, had not even cleared the estuary of San Rafael. At that pace the Father believed that

he would not be able to catch up with the barge. Exhibiting his reverend anger, he began to kick violently, without worrying about breaking a plank. He bit his lips and screamed at them to put more energy into each stroke. As soon as they cleared the estuary, the well-experienced Indian chief ordered the crew to stop rowing so he could observe the currents. This, however, irritated the Father. It seemed to him to be a malicious delay, and he hurled insults at the chief, who tolerated them in silence. The Indian who was at the front of the boat could not observe the force of the current, and it was necessary for him to stop rowing for a time. Fortunately he was confident of his skill, so he told the Father to shut his mouth because he did not know what he was saying. The current was about to change, and if they set their course in the direction of the barge, they almost certainly would catch up to it. When the Father heard this, he promised that they would be well compensated if they succeeded, but if not, he would tan their hides. Apparently the Indian slightly changed the boat's heading in order to position it in a favorable current. After sailing a while, he realized that the barge was beginning to slow down because of the counter current. However, his knowledge had enabled him to choose the favorable one. He let out a shout of joy and said, "Now we've got them."

The current shifted on him near the northern point of the strait of Angel Island. By circling around the opposite side of the island from where the barge was heading, he pulled ahead of it and positioned his boat parallel to the barge. They drew closer in order to speak, and the Father ordered the captain of the barge to turn around and head for San Rafael. Seeing that he could not escape because of the boat's superior speed and the soldiers' weapons, the poor soul obeyed immediately. Carried by a northeast wind and a favorable current, they arrived at the mouth of the San Rafael estuary. The tide was beginning to rise, but there was not enough water to allow the barge to pass through, so the Father ordered them all to leap ashore right there. Then he ordered that each Indian from San Francisco be given fifty lashes. After the discipline of the whip, they suffered the greater sorrow of having the women taken away from them. As a crowning indignity, the saddles were taken away from the *vaqueros* as compensation for damages and losses. Finally the Father ordered them all to leave immediately and report everything to Father Esténaga.

When the Indians led the life of wandering savages, they were accustomed to the fresh air of the mountains and valleys where they lived and enjoyed good health. Their subsequent confinement behind infected walls was very harmful to them. Each mission was constructed so as to include two rooms as large as parlors, where the unmarried and widowed people would sleep on the floor, with men and women segregated. The walls were normally a yard thick and there was not adequate ventilation. Imagine the stench that would emanate from those bodies, which generally were not clean. The basic reason they were soon attacked by illnesses, was that they were unable to breathe fresh air. Because there was no one available who could give them the necessary medications, these illnesses soon became chronic. In addition, those who already were living in reduction were plagued by venereal diseases, which they later transmitted to the robust and healthy Indians who arrived from outside the missions. Consequently, about one-third of the few children who were born would die, and another third would die before reaching puberty. The health of the remaining third was such that a good government would have placed them in hospitals as an act of charity.

Debilitated by such serious illness, it was common for them to succumb to any other minor illness which might attack them. Therefore, the annual burial and baptismal registries usually showed about two-thirds more burials than baptisms. Reverend Father Antonio Peyri also made this observation. When he was chosen to found Mission San Luis Rey, his knowledge of architecture helped him in many ways to design a structure most suitable for the church building the different workshops, and the other mission offices. He also added a room for a *curandero* and two long rooms to serve as a hospital, for the comfort of the sick. He even provided for their spiritual health by designing a chapel with doors which could be accessed from both sides and which were arranged so that the sick, both men and women, could hear mass from their beds. His insistence that his neophytes keep their bodies and their dwellings clean provided him with a great challenge. To meet it he had a trench dug from an adjacent bog toward the front of the main house. There he dug two large ditches, which drained into two well-constructed reservoirs of brick and mortar. One was designated the women's bath, and the other, the men's. Once the Indians became accustomed to bathing, one would find the baths occupied from four in the morning until eleven at night. He ordered the Indians' homes, a type of hut, to be constructed at a reasonably safe distance from each other, so that, once destroyed, they could be rebuilt. For example, if someone past the age of adolescence died in a hut, it would be set on fire. Immediately after the flames had consumed it, many men could build another hut for the family on the same spot. Under the threat of severe penalties, the *alcaldes* of the mission were entrusted with keeping a careful watch over the Indians to ascertain who was ill and who might have contracted a contagious disease. As soon as they detected such a case, they would take the person to the place designated for the sick, according to their sex. The Father would be notified so he could attend to the person's treatment With these efforts Reverend Father Peyri succeeded in making his mission the only one where the Indians made progress. Until

Painting by Ferdinand Deppe depicting Mission San Gabriel, 1832. Deppe (1794–1861) was a German naturalist, explorer and painter from Berlin who travelled to Mexico in 1824.

he left the territory for having sympathized with his friend Don Manuel Victoria, Father Peyri always cared for more than two thousand Indians at his mission, and they enjoyed better health than those at the other missions.

About the doings of Señor Figueroa, one can say that after this *jefe* arrived In Monterey and assumed the command of the territory, Captain Zamorano, the perpetual government secretary, briefed him extremely well on the state of affairs in the country and on all that had occurred since Lieutenant Colonel Don Manuel Victoria had arrived, Figueroa also learned the names of the most important members of the southern party. He was informed that people had been hopeful that he would arrive quickly and unify everyone under his command, so he began by circulating a decree of amnesty. It did not pertain to everyone, only to those who were or might have been insubordinate to the supreme government. At the same time Figueroa sent everyone very persuasive letters in which he offered himself and his services in exchange for their friendship, advice, and cooperation. He also expressed the hope that the territory would experience beneficial reforms

and improvements, given the good intentions he was bringing to such important tasks.

With great tact he managed to persuade them in his favor. From the beginning he easily was able to perceive the distinctiveness of the *californios*. They greatly appreciated the way he conducted himself and his effort to be respected rather than feared. They found in him the fine qualities they had hoped for and a good friend who was always ready to help in any manner which did not conflict with his decorum and duty. The disagreements caused by the spirit of party disappeared when he decided to assume the responsibility of being the principal agent of reconciliation. Making good use of the overall respect which people had for him, he obtained everything simply by stating that those were his desires and that everyone should work together for the good of the country.

It was recommended to him that he not allow the *diputación territorial* of Alta California to hinder his work and authority. Since elections for the *diputación* had not been held yet, he gave orders that they rake place. He then sent out the summons for them to meet in the capital. When the *junta* was installed, he concerned himself with the condition of the interior of the country. Later the missions' interests were the principal topic of discussion. This resulted in the divestment of the Reverend Fathers' temporal possessions and the placement at each mission of an Administrator who would receive a regular salary and whose hands would be tied only by the strength of his conscience.

During that time the change of climate began to affect Señor Figueroa's health, and he petitioned the general government to be kind enough to relieve him of the political command of the territory. He would retain only the military command. When this request became public, along with the fact that the temporal benefits of the missions had been taken away from the Fathers,

it was like news heralded by a horrible-sounding trumpet. It injured a few ears here, but when the echo was heard in Mexico, some people felt that it was very harmonious. At once two excellent schemers of considerable influence joined forces to obtain everything that they needed from the government for the success of their project. In order to maintain appearances, they proposed to take a colony of settlers from the capital to Alta California. They put into play all of their influence to get the government to approve their plan, give them sufficient money for their transportation, and appoint Don José Maria Híjar as director of the colony and *jefe politico* to relieve General Figueroa as he had asked.

4. The Cattle Drives of Early California

By Siegfried G. Demke

Secondary Source

On the Trail

The California drives from south to north traveled at a speed of ten to fifteen miles a day, and, depending on the total distance of the drive, *usually* would be from a month to a month and a half on the trail. The most manageable size of herd was from 700 to *1200* head. (The Texas herds usually were *2000* to 2500 head because a larger herd for the longer and less frequent drives was more profitable.) Larger herds stretched out too long on the drive and were more *difficult* to handle through mountainous parts of the drive. Also, the larger herds were more vulnerable to cattle thieves.

For the average sized herd the crew of drovers consisted of a *mayordomo,* or trail boss, and four to six vaqueros. Vaqueros were superior horsemen and cow handlers. Fewer of them were needed on the California drives—in relation to the number of cattle handled and the type of country travelled —than the number of American cowboys needed on the post-Civil War drives from Texas to the North. (The Texas drives to California also used mainly vaqueros as drovers.)

Food for the drovers on the drive consisted of hardtack, or hard bread, *carne seca* (dried beef), *pinole,* and tea. *Pinole* is corn that has been slightly roasted to dry out all moisture, then ground to a flour. In this condition the corn can be kept for

Mexican Rancheros by Carol Nebel, 1834. Nebel was a German engineer, architect and draftsman who was best known for his detailed paintings of the landscape and people of Mexico, especially of the battles of the Mexican-American War.

long periods of time without spoiling. Sugar, cinnamon, or other ingredients can be added for taste. When *pinole* is prepared for eating only water, or milk if available, needs to be added, and with cooking a palatable thick porridge is formed.

The supplies were transported on packhorses or pack-mules. There was no chuckwagon. The chuckwagon, with its cupboard and dropleaf table at the end of the wagon-bed was invented by Charles Goodnight in 1866 for use on his drives from Texas to Colorado. Because he was also in the freight hauling business and accustomed to its use, Pedro Lopez used a *carreta* pulled by two oxen on the 1841 drive to the Las Mariposas region. The problem with the use of the *carreta* was that unless it and the oxen were sold along with the cattle at the end of the drive it slowed down the return journey to the pace of the oxen.

The cattle lived off the land, with drives usually starting after the winter rains and after the first grass reached maturity. The drive's responsibility for damage done by the cattle to range land was negligible due to a special act of the California State Legislature. To continue the open range philosophy of the Spanish and Mexican rancho periods, on March 30, 1851, the first legislature of the State passed *Laws Concerning Rodeos and Defining the Duties of Judges of the Plains*. Nicknamed the "no fence law" and the "tresspass law," it established that farmers who wanted to protect their crops from cattle would have to fence in those crops. This law remained in effect until the early eighteen-seventies.

At first when the feasability of a drive from south to north became known, some northern buyers themselves, or their representatives, would travel south to the cow counties buy enough cattle from the rancheros to make up a herd, hire a crew of vaqueros and head north. With the first few drives it was established that the overall cost to drive a herd of cattle from the Los Angeles area to the northern market area averaged from two to four dollars a head. To the rancheros, who already had the cattle, this was a comparatively small expense to deduct from the gross income a drive produced. Most of the rancheros then decided to eliminate the middle-man, and increase their income from the cattle sale, by driving herds north with their own crews of vaqueros.

The Drive Routes

Just as for travelers of today, there were two routes north. One went through the Tehachapi Mountains and the San Joaquin Valley; the other was the coast route. The San Joaquin Valley route's beginning was an example of the longest way being the easiest if it is the most level in parts. When Los Angeles area herds reached what is now Newhall they turned northeast by Soledad Canyon. From today's Palmdale area the herd skirted the mountains on the south side of Antelope Valley in a northwest direction to what is now Gorman, then through the Tejon Pass, down the *Cañada de Las Uvas* (canyon of the grapes—now the "grapevine") and into the San Joaquin Valley. The coast route went beyond Newhall to what is now Castaic and turned west down the Santa Clara River Valley to Ventura. From there the drive travelled northward by Santa Barbara, through the Gaviota Pass, and along the Salinas River. On this route entry to the San Joaquin Valley was by the Pacheco Pass, for a shortcut to the mining region, or by the Livermore Valley. Using the Livermore Valley meant going through the San Jose area, where buyers were sometimes waiting to buy the herd for distribution to all the northern cities and the mining regions.

Although over-all it was shorter, the San Joaquin Valley route was not used as much as the coast route in the early years. It proved to be too dangerous. On October 5, 1850 Henry Dalton took action to try to profit from the high beef prices being paid in the North. He contracted with Pedro Lopez to drive 1000 head of cattle from Rancho Santa Anita and Rancho Azusa to Stockton. The contract called for Dalton to furnish supplies for the drive and Lopez to provide the vaqueros and

horses. Also, Lopez would be held responsible only for cattle lost through negligence on his part. The drive started too late in the year. Going over the Tejon Pass and Tehachapi route, storms and stampedes that tired the cattle and horses slowed the movement of the herd. By December the herd had only reached the Four Creeks area near present-day Visalia. Because there was, by then, plenty of winter grass in the area, Lopez decided to rest the cattle and take time to find fresh horses. Near-by was another northbound herd, with its owner, a Captain Dorsey of San Jose, as trail boss. This was the setting for hard-luck Dalton to experience one of his many calamities.

According to reports that reached Los Angeles January 4, 1851, an estimated three hundred Indians, armed with bows and arrows, first attacked the Lopez crew and then the Dorsey crew, killing all the men and driving off the cattle. As with most first accounts of disaster, the facts of this account were not accurate. Lopez was not killed, and having the facts to prove one man was not killed, it is possible to assume others escaped death also. Not only was Lopez not killed, but Dalton brought a breach of contract court action against him for the cost of the lost herd on the grounds Lopez had been negligent by hiring too few vaqueros to drive and guard the herd. Dalton won the case, and was awarded $2,000 damages. Whether or not the damages payment was made by Lopez is not known. Regardless of that, he lived on to be appointed a Judge of the Plains in 1856, and, according to San Fernando historian Jackson Meyers, records show that Lopez died in 1861.

Because of the Dalton and Dorsey herds disaster the San Joaquin Valley route was avoided for a number of years thereafter. When it was in use again, when the Indians had quieted down, its remaining problem was water—either not enough of it or too much of it. What was ideal was to have enough water for the herd's drinking needs but not so much that the herd had trouble crossing it.

Painting of a Vaquero in action roping cattle during 1830s Spanish California, artist unknown.

Some drives moved north through the San Joaquin Valley on the west side of the San Joaquin River in order to avoid having to cross its many tributaries on the east side. The prominent paradox in that arrangement was that, unless the goal was San Jose or San Francisco, the water crossing problem was compounded when the herd reached the end of its drive. With the herd on the west side, to get to Stockton, Sacramento, or the mining regions the San Joaquin River had to be crossed at its widest point. This was a time-consuming and hazardous undertaking. Cave Couts, bossing a drive for his brother-in-law Abel Stearns, wrote Stearns that the herd was delayed eight days waiting for the water level to drop so that the river could be crossed at Stockton; and this was in the later part of July of 1852. Couts also wrote his brother-in-law that when he reached the river (he had travelled the coast route) there were other herds, totaling in all 12,000 to 15,000 head, waiting to cross. It appears as though Couts never did cross the San Joaquin River with his herd, because later he wrote his brother-in-law that he sold the cattle on July 24 for $20 a head at San Joaquin City "opposite" the mouth of the Stanislaus River. This was up-river

from where coast route drives usually crossed. Also there is a peculiar bit of arithmetic resulting from a letter of August 14, 1852 that Couts wrote to Stearns. Couts started the drive with 800 head, yet he wrote Stearns he had sold 943 head. Couts did not explain the difference.

The other problems on the west side of the San Joaquin River were feed and drinking water. Grass on that side was sparse even in late winter and early spring. By late spring the sun was already burning it away. Also by late spring the few little streams coming out of the Coast Range began to dry up. The river could not be used very easily to water the cattle, as this was before levees restrained the river and many areas of its edge were marshland in which the cattle would bog down. Surveyor William Brewer, a really hardy traveller, described in his *Up And Down California*, his early and late summer travels through the San Joaquin Valley on the west side of the river as some of the worst he ever experienced due to too much heat and too little water.

For some drives the San Joaquin Valley route went up the east side of the river. Although there were more rivers to cross—the Kings, the upper

San Joaquin, the Merced, the Tuolumne, and the Stanislaus—these were smaller streams than the San Joaquin at its lower end and could be crossed easily. They, and the many smaller streams coming out of the west side of the Sierra Nevada, provided an easier means of watering the cattle. For feed the west side of the Sierra, with more rainfall, provided more grass. The main drawback of this route was the ultimate market for the cattle was limited to the mining regions and the comparatively smaller cities of Stockton and Sacramento. Beginning with the eighteen-sixties the cities around San Francisco Bay became the important beef market.

---

5. Spanish Colonial or Adobe Architecture of California

By Donald R. Hannaford and Revel Edwards

Secondary Source

During the years between 1830 and 1840, the country was very prosperous. Monterey, a sea port and the capitol of California at that time, was the center of life in the northern part of the State for the big ranches of the interior. Hides and tallow were plentiful and trading with the East coast was at its height. It was only natural, then as always, that wealth gave the time for social and cultural activities, and the inevitable building that followed is in itself a transcript of history, showing the virtues and defects in the lives of those producing it.

The larger houses, and even the cottages, were built for comfort and convenience and each suits its location, showing more than anything else that what is best adapted for its purpose is the most beautiful. They never pretended to be anything but what they were; there seems to have been no effort to complicate their construction or ornamentation, but merely a simple handing-on from generation to generation, from both the New England and Spanish settlers, of well worn and tried traditions worked with the materials of the locality. There is as a rule, nothing forced or fantastic in their outline nor frivolous in their detail-if there is picturesque confusion, it is the result of successive additions made with sympathetic materials and a directness of purpose, rather than of conscious effort.

The adobes of California possess many points in common-although those of the north, especially on the coast, were more influenced by workmen with New England traditions (many were ship carpenters)—and no attempt, therefore, is made to deal with them here from any novel standpoint or to trace at length their architectural or historical evolution but merely to draw attention to some of the typical features, both in their design and construction, that developed a distinctive type of architecture.

Except in the towns-where the established streets to a certain extent dictated the orientation —the houses, as a rule, were placed crosswise to the points of the compass so the sun, at some

Las Flores Estancia (station), also known as "San Pedro Chapel" as it appeared around 1850. The structure, along with its adjoining buildings, were constructed in 1823. Las Flores Estancia was situated approximately halfway between Mission San Luis Rey de Francia and Mission San Juan Capistrano. It is located today near Bell Canyon on the Camp Pendleton Marine Corps Base ten miles south of the City of San Clemente in northern San Diego County, California.

time of day, would shine into every room. The patio or courtyard was used as much for living as the house, usually facing south with the veranda on the north side (of patio) so it would get the warmth of the sun all day during the winter months. In many cases the veranda extended around three sides of the patio and was used as a corridor for rooms that would otherwise have been inter-communicating.

In brief, the typical plan of the early house was well adapted to the simple and hospitable life of the times. On the ground floor was the living room, dining room, ball room (if any), kitchen and storage rooms, and the veranda from which stairs led up to the balcony. All bed rooms were usually on the second floor and entered off the balcony; they were also inter-communicating. Of course some of the houses, particularly those built for the Yankees, had inside stairs. But these were

few. Later, however, practically all the outside stairs were removed and new ones built inside. It is now rare to find one on the exterior.

As the different types resembled each other in the relation of plan to elevation, so did they in their construction—which was simple in the extreme. Labor and dirt being plentiful, it was the natural thing to build, as the Mission builders had done, with sun dried adobe bricks. There was an abundance of redwood and pine in the forests but it was difficult to saw into lumber; then, too, the adobe walls kept the heat out in the summer and retained it in the winter. They also afforded better protection against stray bullets and Indian attacks, both of which there were many in the early days.

It is doubtful if there ever existed any formula, other than the recommendations of one's neighbor, for the making of adobe bricks. From some of the direct descendants of the old Spanish families, we have gathered the few facts that follow. A large basin about twenty feet in diameter and two feet deep was dug in the ground near the building site; into this was put loam, sand, clay, and straw, tile chips or other binder; then the materials mixed with water to a thick soupy consistency; the mixture then taken out, put into molds, and dried in the sun. This seems to have been the best method, for it is now clear to see that the well made bricks have stood the ravages of time far better than those of loosely packed coarse aggregate.

The walls were laid on light foundations, if any, of stone; which accounts for the ever present seeping of dampness, and the falling of walls during severe earth shocks. If a concrete foundation were used—one strong enough to sustain the heavy weight of the walls—adobe would still be a most satisfactory material to use in most parts of California.

On the ground floor, walls average about three feet in thickness and on the upper, about two feet. The offset, as a rule, being on the inside to add greater floor space to the rooms. Occasionally, it was on the outside with a few buttresses, the full width of the lower wall, extending up to the roof. Walls were laid with, approximately one inch wide, mud mortar joints. Chips of tile or small bits of broken pottery were often mixed with the mortar to give added strength.

The walls of the better houses were covered with mud plaster, which, by the way, was remarkably smooth and even in texture; after this, they were heavily whitewashed at least once a year to protect the surface from rain. "The whitewasher's brush is never still" is an old Spanish proverb that was very true in California, for on many of the old walls the whitewash is so thick it really forms a hard coat of lime plaster. Many of the walls that were either not plastered in the beginning or from which it had fallen, were later refinished with lime plaster, often marked off to imitate stone.

The use of boarding as a wall covering was usually a later addition or a protection for a crumbling adobe wall. Both V-joint and board and batten siding are found, but both were used sparingly.

There is an idea afoot, as is shown by some of the present day imitators in their "copies," that the walls were bulgy and bumpy. This is seldom so; however, many of the walls were not straight. The Olivos ranch house, for instance, has an outward curve of about eighteen inches in the front wall, but it is a graceful sweep and is barely perceptible in the wall which is about fifty feet in length.

Roof coverings varied in different localities. Where redwood was abundant, hand riven shingles or shakes were used; and tile, where good clay was found. Many of the houses originally having shake or shingle roofs were later covered with tile; many that were of tile are now covered with shingles—due in many cases to the low financial conditions of the owners who, in later years, sold their tiles; but far too often to the ruthless pilaging of some well meaning citizen of a nearby town.

The original tiles were hand made; some say over a shapely thigh, but this is highly improbable—it would have taken a small army of hardy legs to supply the thousands of human molds necessary to produce all the tiles used on these old buildings. An odd, but practical, custom was to use shakes on the balcony roof and tile on the rest of the roof. The reason, of course, was to relieve the cantilevered balcony from the additional weight of the tile.

Chimneys, simple in design and usually small in size—due to fireplaces built for heating rather than ornamentation, were invariably built in inside walls; hence came through the roof rather than being on the exterior of the building. There are exceptions, of course.

Gable vents were rarely used, because the space between eaves plate and top of rafters was usually open and gave ample ventilation for the attic.

Balconies were of three distinct types. The first, and most common, with supporting posts from the ground to the roof; second, the cantilevered balcony with posts supporting the roof; and third, of which only one example remains, the cantilevered balcony and cantilevered roof with no supporting posts. Practically all balconies and verandas had closed ends of wide vertical boarding or simple lattice work which gave more privacy and partial protection from the wind.

The massive walls seem to radiate a welcome; and to enter the venerable house is to know again the sincere hospitality that once prevailed in California. It is the satisfying proportions of the rooms, rather than studied detail, that gives to them this friendly feeling.

The wide hand hewn pine planks of the second floor and the hew joists that carry them usually form the ceilings of the lower floor rooms. The walls are, in most houses, of white plaster—sometimes papered. In one aged room we counted fourteen layers and found one of newspapers bearing the date 1849.

Much of the refinement is due to the exquisitely proportioned double hung windows–feminine in their daintiness. Panes, Colonial in scale, average eight by ten inches in size. Windows were usually set flush with the outside of the wall; the deep reveal, splayed about ten inches on each side and often paneled, was on the inside, forming a sort of bay or window seat.

Shutters were sometimes on the inside, folding back against the reveal; sometimes on the outside; and occasionally shutter blinds outside and paneled shutters inside. In the Larkin house, the reveal is so paneled that when the shutter is folded back, it becomes a part of the reveal paneling.

Exterior doors were often in pairs-each door being barely wide enough to pass through. On the inside, for protection in addition to the lock and bolts, a wooden bar-fitting into wrought iron brackets on each jamb—that could be placed

Adobe residence of Rancho Guajome, thirty miles north of San Diego, is representative of Spanish hacienda architecture dating from 1852, a time when much of California was divided into large land-estates controlled by a select minority of Mexican and American rancheros.

across both doors, was frequently used. Interior doors were of varied designs and sizes—often five feet nine inches in height and generally not over six feet. Wrought or cast iron butt hinges of various types and sizes and, often, surface hinges of simple design were used on interior doors. Of the many large surface locks so commonly used in the early days, only a few remain. Through the years they have disappeared or have been replaced with modern locks; however, on almost every door can be seen a few marks or holes where the original lock was fastened.

Upper floor rooms, as a rule, had ceilings of wide pine boards with beaded joints. As wooden lath was difficult to obtain, plaster ceilings, were they occur, are often the result of later remodeling.

In some of the early adobes the lower floors were of tile, but with the advent of the Americans, came dancing; so in due time a more suitable wooden floor, raised about six inches above the level of adjoining rooms, was built in many a home, and the "sale" or ball room was created. This, in part, explains the difference of floor levels found in some of the houses.

Exterior walls, eaves, rough woodwork, and under sides of balcony roofs, were commonly whitewashed—often a delicate pink, or a cream slightly off white. Balconies were frequently painted white, soft green, or warm gray, and sometimes whitewashed. Exterior doors, shutters, and trim were painted various tones of green, gray, or brown, and occasionally to match the walls.

Interior walls were invariably white. Ceilings sometimes painted light olive green, dull white, or warm gray; and not infrequently blue or whitewashed. Woodwork was white, deep cream, or gray green. Mantles were sometimes white, cream, or gray, but most often dull black; which after all was a very sensible color for them. In short: Color was the result of the dictates of fancy rather than of tradition.

Picket fences and adobe garden walls are prominent characteristic features. They are the ties between house and garden—the last elementary touch that completes and blends the two into a harmonious ensemble.

---

6. A Young Lady of the House in Mexican California

By Margaret Gilbert Mackey and Louise Pinkney Sooy

Secondary Source

Hair: Unmarried women drew the hair over the ears, parted it in the middle and either allowed it to fall unconfined down their backs or wore it in one or two braids that fell over the shoulders and down below the waist, sometimes braided or wound with colored ribbons. Married women wore their hair parted in the center; two braids crossed and wound around the head near the top and back, little black velvet bow on the top of the head where the ends met; or cut over forehead like bangs; lock on each side hung on the cheek; sometimes gathered in back in colored silk net. Often they protected the hair while in the house with a colored silk kerchief wound around like a cap.

Bodice: Cloth, printed cotton or calico, silk, satin, or velvet; black, blue, green, red, or other colors; hooked or buttoned up front to neck, or hooked or laced up back if the neck should be low; came a little below the waistline with a point in front; waist uncorseted, whalebones in the bodice supplying all the support; sleeves full length to wrists, with or without lace edging; sometimes three-quarter length with flaring cuffs, either plain or decorated with embroidery or lace; often short, being drawn tight around upper part of the arm by a draw string, but not puffed. Short or three-quarter length sleeves were worn with the round or V-shaped neck; long sleeves with the high-necked bodice, which was finished with a small roll collar fastened with a brooch.

Neckerchief Silk: flowered or plain colors; around neck and shoulders, points crossed over breast with ends fastened with pins on each side to belt.

Skirt: Of same or different material and color as bodice; very full, six to twelve petticoats with many ruffles being worn in place of hoops; long, corning to the instep; if made of lightweight material, carried two or three wide ruffles, flouncing,

Untitled portrait of a Mexican woman, c. 1856. This photograph is an ambrotype (a photograph that creates a positive image on a sheet of glass using the wet plate collodion process) of an anonymous Californio woman during the Gold Rush years. The Californios were a group of Spanish speaking people who had come from Mexico to settle in California after the establishment of the first Spanish mission in 1769.

or diagonal strips of another material, around the bottom; sometimes embroidered.

Sash: Silk, satin, or thread net; color blending with bodice and skirt; worn around waist over bodice; tied on side with ends finished in fringe and felling over skirt, and often reaching to the bottom of the hem.

Stockings: Cotton or silk; black or white.

Shoes: Calfskin or morocco leather; brown material made of hemp; heavy cloth, satin; often of same material as the dress; with moderate heels of light wood; sometimes without heels; thin-soled; low cut like a slipper; finished with buckles or embroidery around the edges.

Shawl: The shawls which became famous as "Spanish shawls" were in reality from China. They were brought into Spain and the Spanish colonies by the Manila Galleon and therefore were known as mantones de Manila (shawls of Manila). They were of the characteristic Chinese type, heavily embroidered in highly colored figures of one kind or another, and with long fringe around the edges. They were worn folded in a triangle and used as a wrap, that is, for warmth and protection both indoors and out, and never as a dancing costume.

Addenda:

a) It must be remembered that, although the period of this costume has been designated as between the years 1776 and 1825, this style of dress was seen throughout both the Spanish and Mexican periods. Styles of women's dresses did not change perceptibly any more often than did those of the men. The dates have been fixed only to indicate the advent of a different style and not to announce the disappearance of the old one. Dresses were worn until they were no longer serviceable, and, such was the durability of goods at this time, the service they rendered often continued through to the second and third generation. Consequently, during the last ten or fifteen years before the American conquest, every style and its variance was to be seen among rich and poor alike.

It must also be remembered that during the first thirty years along the California frontier, the feminine personnel of the colonies could not be exactly described as having *ton.* The common soldier was forced into the position of paterfamilias and was married as quickly as possible to an Indian woman in order to fulfill with the least delay the Royal Mandate to populate His Majesty's possessions. Those of the military who had any claim to aristocratic blood and were already married left their wives in New Spain, where the conveniences of life insured their comfort.

As already pointed out, the year 1782 saw the first nobly born woman enter California, and she finally had to flee from the hardships that confronted her in Monterey, the capital city, and return to New Spain in 1791.

Therefore, the first of the century rolled around before the crudities of life in California had become sufficiently eliminated to permit the development of a social life that also possessed taste.

b) A *señorita* who had refused the hand of a suitor often became the object of revenge. The jilted lover, when opportunity afforded it, would seize one of the young lady's long and glossy braids and with a quick stroke of his knife cut it off about six inches from her head. He would then dash away on horseback, waving the trophy flauntingly in the air. The young lady's vexation was only increased when, upon meeting her persecutor again, she found that he had braided her long tresses into an attractive watch fob which he wore conspicuously across his chest, or into a lash at the end of his reins which he was careful to whirl whenever he passed her window.

c) A young, unmarried girl was never seen away from home unattended by either her father, mother, or a *dueña,* and at night she was securely locked in her room. Courtships, therefore, were carried on furtively, a suitor having generally to voice his sentiment in song, posting himself under

the window of his *querida* and accompanying his words of passion on a guitar.

d) Marriages were arranged by the parents, honorable intentions of matrimony being announced personally to the girl's father by the father of the suitor. The sentiments of the young lady in question were then taken into consideration, and if they were favorably inclined all was serene. A week or so before the wedding, the suitor would call and take the measurement of his dear one's foot, and on the morning of the great event would deliver to the bride her wedding slippers which he had made with his own hands. He also brought with him at least six sets of wearing apparel, and woe to him if they did not fit!

On their way to church, the bride rode in the saddle before her godfather, her foot resting in a sash looped over the horn and her godfather riding on the apron behind her. The groom had before him the bride's godmother, whom he supported carefully with an arm about her shoulders. At the ceremony, it was a custom to wind a sash loosely about the necks of the bride and groom, thus binding them together as they knelt for the priest's blessing.

During the ride home, a different arrangement was observed. This time the groom held the bride before him in the saddle, while the godfather watched after the godmother. Upon arriving at the house, the bridegroom, before he could dismount, was surrounded by his friends and deprived of his spurs, which he had to buy back, generally with a drink all around, before he could take part in the festivities that followed.

e) One of the daily rites performed by the women of the family was that of combing and braiding the queues of their men folk.

f) Punishment of children was mental rather than physical, although both father and mother had the privilege of beating a son as long as he was unmarried. Even after marriage, and after the son passed middle age, a mother indignant at her son's conduct was known to lay a cat-o'-ninetails across his shoulders as he knelt humbly before her to receive the blows. An effective lesser punishment was to require the culprit to kneel before a stool set in the corner of the dining-room where, while the rest of the family ate at table, with a coarse earthen spoon, a wooden plate, and a tin cup he consumed the very little allowed him from the family board. His sisters, taking compassion on him, would usually seek an opportunity to put a *tamale* or a piece of beef on his plate.

7. Dances of Early California Days

By Lucile K. Czarnowski

Secondary Source

Fandangos, Bailes and Fiestas

The fandangos, bailes and fiestas which occupied such a prominent place in the social life of early California, warrant closer observation. The term fandango had a unique meaning at that time. It was not only the name of a Spanish dance which some performed, hut it was likewise the name given an informal dancing party; in fact, in the early days of the ranchos any entertainment in which dancing was a major event was called a fandango. With the growth of towns and as society became more stratified, fandangos referred to the dances of the lower classes. The bailes referred to dances of the upper classes and large affairs of social significance. For the latter, formal invitations were issued.

On the ranchos, the dancing took place in the sala, a long room with benches on either side with a special place reserved for the musicians and singers. Sometimes, dancing took place outside on the hard packed ground under the trees. This might be the setting upon returning from a huckleberry picnic or a mussel bake. If the party was large, a *ramada* was built. Coronel gave a graphic description of this type of structure. It was a large arbor constructed in a favorable location in front of the house. Three sides were enclosed, with the fourth open save for palings or posts which formed a barrier across it. It was the custom for men on horseback to view the dancing and occasionally dismount and take part. The open side was to accommodate these guests and the barrier was made to prevent the horses from encroaching on the dancing space. There was considerable movement among the riders to secure a front line view. On the inside walls of the closed area white cloth was stretched. These walls were gaily decorated with ribbons and artificial flowers. Seats for the women were placed around the three enclosed sides, the musicians and singers took their places on a slightly raised platform. The men remained entirely separate from the women, some standing in the opening in front of those on horseback.

A master of ceremonies at a fandango, called *El Tecolero,* directed the dancing. He conducted the ladies to the floor when a dance was played which they were to perform alone, and he introduced them in turn at the start of the dancing. This followed a definite pattern. Moving in time to the music, he went to the first lady seated on one side of the room and standing in front of her clapped his hands several times. This was the signal for her to stand and go to the center of the dancing space.

Trajes Mexicanos, un Fandango, **Mexican dresses. Artist C. Castro, 1869.**

Catching up the sides of her skirt and spreading it out in the shape of a fan, she began to keep time with her feet and after turning several times in place, she retired to her seat. Progressing around the edge of the room, all the while keeping time with his feet, El Tecolero continued to introduce each lady in turn. Those who did not know how to dance, or did not care to do so walked around the room as a complimentary gesture and then took their seats.

If the dance played was one that called for a partner, the young men on horseback who wished to dance, dismounted, removed their spurs which were hung on the pommel of the saddle and with sombrero in hand entered the dancing space. Each one then invited a lady to dance and conducted her out upon the floor. At the conclusion of the dance the ladies returned to their chaperons and the men remounted.

Cascarone balls were distinctly Californian and were very colorful social events. They might be given between November and Lent and were a part of the carnival week preceding Lent. Cascarones were beautiful colored eggs which had been emptied of their contents through a small hole at each end, dried and later filled with finely cut gold, silver, or colored paper, or cologne, and on special occasions with a limited amount of gold dust. The holes were sealed with wax or colored paper. The eggs were brought to the ball and carefully concealed until time to be used. The breaking of the cascarone was done in a formal manner, or in a carnival spirit depending upon the formality of the occasion and how well the participants were acquainted. After the ball had progressed well into the evening, a gentleman would approach a chosen lady to salute her in this fashion, whereupon she would shyly bow her head while he broke the eggshell in his hand, permitting the contents to scatter over her head and shoulders. She would return the compliment at the proper moment. Occasionally, the lady was the first to break the cascarone. She, unknown to the favored gentleman would break it over his head while his back was turned. She then slipped away to conceal her identity. The gentleman quickly sought out the lady to return the honor. She was usually not hard to find. Cascarones added to the gaiety of the occasion not only because of the spirit of fun which they engendered, but the glittering spangles in dark tresses lent beauty to the carnival scene.

The suggested programs are given to indicate the use of the dances in centennial celebrations, school programs, or any other occasions for which the historical setting is presented with the dances.

In planning a program of dances, the occasion largely determines the number of participants, the size and type of dance space, and the length of the program. The programs presented, therefore, are suggestive in nature, and allow for additions and changes to meet the situation.

A Fandango After a Wedding

Setting: A ramada
Time: Late afternoon
Order of Dances:

El Borrego	Danced by the children
El Coyote	Danced by younger guests

Introduction of dancers by El Tecolero.

La Yucca	Danced by younger guests
La Varsouvianna	Danced by younger guests
Los Camotes	Danced by younger guests

Older guests enter, dance La Contradanza and then leave.

El Sombrero Blanco from Los Angeles	Danced by married and younger guests
Las Empanadas	Danced by younger guests
La Cachucha	Demonstration given by two couples
El Jarabe	Demonstration given by two couples
California Vals Jota	Danced by married and younger guests
Spanish Waltz	Danced by married and younger guests

Cascarone Ball

Setting: A sala in one of the large ranch homes
Time: Evening
Order of Dances:

Introduction of the dancers by El Tecolero.

La Varsouvianna	Danced by married guests
La Contradanza from Los Angeles and Santa Barbara	Danced by the older guests
El Sombrero Blanco from Los Angeles	Danced by the younger guests, who have been given permission to dance by their parents

Breaking of some of the Cascarones

Waltz Contra	Danced by married couples
Los Camotes	Danced by young guests
La Paloma	Demonstration presented by three couples
El Jarabe	Demonstration by two couples
California Vals Jota	Danced by married couples
Spanish Waltz	Danced by married couples and young guests

A Ball in 1849[1]

Setting: A concert hall, or early opera house
Time: Evening
Order of Dances:

Grand March
Schottische from Sonoma
Heel and Toe Polka from Santa Barbara
The York
The Danish
The Lancers
Heel and Toe Polka in Jig Time
Rye Waltz
Supper
Mazurka from Santa Barbara
Waltz Contra

---

1 Illustrates multiculturalism in California in period following the war with Mexico.

8. Recipes of the Ranchos

By Mildred Yorba MacArthur

Secondary Source

Recipes of the Ranchos

This booklet is dedicated to the ladies and gentlemen of California, who during the golden era of the ranchos, from 1810 to 1860, elevated cooking to a fine art and a way of life, which formed the basis of our present day outdoor entertaining. These old recipes have been passed on from one generation to another. In preparing them for modern use I have retained the original and have only added a substitute where it simplified the process, but took nothing from the "gusto" or flavor of the recipe.

Carne Asada a la Parrilla—Open Grill Barbeque

Some of the tricks of the trade, followed by outdoor chefs, whether at home or on the range, past and present. The bare essentials are …

Wood
Water
Salt and pepper
Meat
Garlic, if used with a light rein
(The rest is window dressing.)

If you expect a group of punctual guests who will all sit down to eat at one time, use avocado wood for your coals. It burns fast, dies quickly, and gives a fine flavor to the meat. If you expect several calls to dinner and competition from the bar, by all means use orange or walnut wood. It burns slowly, and the coals will wait.

Parillada Carne Asada.

Have a bit of water handy in order to discourage the flames. Sprinkle it without fear, for it will not hurt the coals, and you'll never have a charred steak.

When steaks are first placed on the hot grill move them from side to side and they'll never stick.

Salt steaks generously on both sides and let them stand for an hour or more before barbecuing. This is also the time to rub a clove of garlic over them, for those that like garlic.

A dot of butter dropped on the meat just as it is taken from the grill is an added treat.

Samuel P. Kraemer, Jr.
Rancho San Juan Cajón de Santa Ana

Barbacoa Enterrada—Pit Barbecue

Time and talent are the prime requisites for this type of old California barbecue.

Orange or eucalyptus wood are best for heating the brick or stone-lined pit. This takes about six hours.

Grade A commercial beef is used. Usually top or bottom rounds or shoulder clods, which must be boned, trimmed, and rolled. Before rolling, season with salt, pepper, crushed Oregano and rosemary and a generous helping of chopped onions and a hint of finely mulled garlic.

Wrap each roll in foil paper and then in burlap sacks, tightly laced. Put them into the hot brick-lined pit and cover with earth and any stray hot rocks or bricks that might be handy.

The average cooking time for a large barbecue is 9 or 10 hours. This timing is the difference between a good and a bad barbecue and where experience is the only teacher.

Anselmo Ames
Rancho Santiago de Santa Ana

Sopa De Albóndiga—Meatball Soup

1 lb. ground beef
¼ lb. ground pork
¼ lb. ground veal
Mix the above and add
1 tablespoon salt
½ tablespoon coarse ground pepper
1 heaping tablespoon of crushed oregano
2 tablespoons of minced parsley
1 beaten egg

9. *Ramona*—A Novel of Mexican California

By Helen Hunt Jackson

Secondary Source

The Señora Moreno's house was one of the best specimens to be found in California of the representative house of the half barbaric, half elegant, wholly generous and free-handed life led there by Mexican men and women of degree in the early part of this century, under the rule of the Spanish and Mexican viceroys, when the laws of the Indies were still the law of the land, and its old name, "New Spain," was an ever-present link and stimulus to the warmest memories and deepest patriotisms of its people.

It was a picturesque life, with more of sentiment and gayety in it, more also that was truly dramatic, more romance, than will ever be seen again on those sunny shores. The aroma of it all lingers there still; industries and inventions have not yet slain it; it will last out its century,—in fact, it can never be quite lost, so long as there is left standing one such house as the Senora Moreno's.

When the house was built, General Moreno owned all the land within a radius of forty miles,—forty miles westward, down the valley to the sea; forty miles eastward, into the San Fernando Mountains; and good forty miles more or less along the coast. The boundaries were not very strictly defined; there was no occasion, in those happy days, to reckon land by inches. It might be asked, perhaps, just how General Moreno owned all this land, and the question might not be easy to answer. It was not and could not be answered to the satisfaction of the United States Land Commission, which, after the surrender of California, undertook to sift and adjust Mexican land titles; and that was the way it had come about that the Senora Moreno now called herself a poor woman. Tract after tract, her lands had been taken away from her; it looked for a time as if nothing would be left. Every one of the claims based on deeds of gift from Governor Pio Pico, her husband's most intimate friend, was disallowed. They all went by the board in one batch, and took away from the Senora in a day the greater part of her best pasture-lands. They were lands which had belonged to the Bonaventura Mission, and lay along the coast at the mouth of the valley down which the little stream which ran past her house went to the sea; and it had been a great pride and delight to the Senora, when she was young, to ride that forty miles by her husband's side, all the way on their own lands, straight from their house to their own strip of shore. No wonder she believed the Americans thieves, and spoke of them always as hounds. The people of the United States have never in the least realized that the taking possession of California was not only a conquering of Mexico, but a conquering of California as well; that the real bitterness of the surrender was not so much to the empire which gave up the country, as to the country itself which was given up. Provinces passed back and forth in that way, helpless in the hands of great powers, have all the ignominy and humiliation of defeat, with none of the dignities or compensations of the transaction.

Mexico saved much by her treaty, spite of having to acknowledge herself beaten; but California lost all. Words cannot tell the sting of such a transfer. It is a marvel that a Mexican remained in the country; probably none did, except those who were absolutely forced to it.

Luckily for the Senora Moreno, her title to the lands midway in the valley was better than to those lying to the east and the west, which had once belonged to the missions of San Fernando and Bonaventura; and after all the claims, counter-claims, petitions, appeals, and adjudications were ended, she still was left in undisputed possession of what would have been thought by any new-comer into the country to be a handsome estate, but which seemed to the despoiled and indignant Senora a pitiful fragment of one.

Moreover, she declared that she should never feel secure of a foot of even this. Any day, she said, the United States Government might send out a new Land Commission to examine the decrees of the first, and revoke such as they saw fit. Once a thief, always a thief. Nobody need feel himself safe under American rule. There was no knowing what might happen any day; and year by year the lines of sadness, resentment, anxiety, and antagonism deepened on the Senora's fast aging face.

It gave her unspeakable satisfaction, when the Commissioners, laying out a road down the valley, ran it at the back of her house instead of past the front. "It is well," she said. "Let their travel be where it belongs, behind our kitchens; and no one have sight of the front doors of our houses, except friends who have come to visit us." Her enjoyment of this never flagged. Whenever she saw, passing the place, wagons or carriages belonging to the hated Americans, it gave her a distinct thrill of pleasure to think that the house turned its back on them. She would like always to be able to do the same herself; but whatever she, by policy or in business, might be forced to do, the old house, at any rate, would always keep the attitude of contempt,—its face turned away.

One other pleasure she provided herself with, soon after this road was opened,—a pleasure in which religious devotion and race antagonism were so closely blended that it would have puzzled the subtlest of priests to decide whether her act were a sin or a virtue. She caused to be set up, upon every one of the soft rounded hills which made the beautiful rolling sides of that part of the valley, a large wooden cross; not a hill in sight of her house left without the sacred emblem of her faith. "That the heretics may know, when they go by, that they are on the estate of a good Catholic," she said, "and that the faithful may be reminded to pray. There have been miracles of conversion wrought on the most hardened by a sudden sight of the Blessed Cross."

There they stood, summer and winter, rain and shine, the silent, solemn, outstretched arms, and became landmarks to many a guideless traveller who had been told that his way would be by the first turn to the left or the right, after passing the last one of the Senora Moreno's crosses, which he couldn't miss seeing. And who shall say that it did not often happen that the crosses bore a sudden message to some idle heart journeying by, and thus justified the pious half of the Senora's impulse? Certain it is, that many a good Catholic halted and crossed himself when he first beheld them, in the lonely places, standing out in sudden relief against the blue sky; and if he said a swift short prayer at the sight, was he not so much the better?

The house was of adobe, low, with a wide veranda on the three sides of the inner court, and a still broader one across the entire front, which looked to the south. These verandas, especially those on the inner court, were supplementary rooms to the house. The greater part of the family life went on in them. Nobody stayed inside the walls, except when it was necessary. All the kitchen work, except the actual cooking, was done here, in front of the kitchen doors and windows. Babies slept, were washed, sat in the dirt, and played, on the veranda. The women said their prayers, took their naps, and wove their lace there. Old Juanita shelled her beans there, and threw the pods down on the tile floor, till towards night they were sometimes piled up high around her, like corn-husks at a husking. The herdsmen and shepherds smoked there, lounged there, trained their dogs there; there the young made love, and the old dozed; the benches, which ran the entire length of the walls, were worn into hollows, and shone like satin; the tiled floors also were broken and sunk in places, making little wells, which filled up in times of hard rains, and were then an invaluable addition to the children's resources for amusement, and also to the comfort of the dogs,

Helen Hunt Jackson, c. 1850s–1860s

cats, and fowls, who picked about among them, taking sips from each.

The arched veranda along the front was a delightsome place. It must have been eighty feet long, at least, for the doors of five large rooms opened on it. The two western-most rooms had been added on, and made four steps higher than the others; which gave to that end of the veranda the look of a balcony, or loggia. Here the Senora kept her flowers; great red water-jars, hand-made by the Indians of San Luis Obispo Mission, stood in close rows against the walls, and in them were always growing fine geraniums, carnations, and yellow-flowered musk.

Besides the geraniums and carnations and musk in the red jars, there were many sorts of climbing vines,—some coming from the ground, and twining around the pillars of the veranda; some growing in great bowls, swung by cords from the roof of the veranda, or set on shelves against the walls. These bowls were of gray stone, hollowed and polished, shining smooth inside and out. They also had been made by the Indians, nobody knew how many ages ago, scooped and polished by the patient creatures, with only stones for tools.

Among these vines, singing from morning till night, hung the Senora's canaries and finches, half a dozen of each, all of different generations, raised by the Senora. She was never without a young bird-family on hand; and all the way from Bonaventura to Monterey, it was thought a piece of good luck to come into possession of a canary or finch of Senora Moreno's raising.

Between the veranda and the river meadows, out on which it looked, all was garden, orange grove, and almond orchard; the orange grove always green, never without snowy bloom or golden fruit; the garden never without flowers, summer or winter; and the almond orchard, in early spring, a fluttering canopy of pink and white petals, which, seen from the hills on the opposite side of the river, looked as if rosy sunrise clouds had fallen, and become tangled in the tree-tops. On either hand stretched away other orchards,— peach, apricot, pear, apple pomegranate; and beyond these, vineyards. Nothing was to be seen but verdure or bloom or fruit, at whatever time of year you sat on the Senora's south veranda.

A wide straight walk shaded by a trellis so knotted and twisted with grapevines that little was to be seen of the trellis wood-work, led straight down from the veranda steps, through the middle of the garden, to a little brook at the foot of it. Across this brook, in the shade of a dozen gnarled old willow-trees, were set the broad flat stone washboards on which was done all the family washing. No long dawdling, and no running away from work on the part of the maids, thus close to the eye of the Senora at the upper end of the garden; and if they had known how picturesque they looked there, kneeling on the grass, lifting the dripping linen out of the water, rubbing it back and forth on the stones, sousing it, wringing it, splashing the clear water in each other's faces, they would have been content to stay at the washing day in and day out, for there was always somebody to look on from above. Hardly a day passed that the Senora had not visitors. She was still a person of note; her house the natural resting-place for all who journeyed through the valley; and whoever came, spent all of his time, when not eating, sleeping, or walking over the place, sitting with the Senora on the sunny veranda.

---

10. Colonial Russian America

Fort Ross, California, c. 1830s

By Kyrill T. Khlebnikov

Primary Source

The Farallon Artel

The Farallon Islands are located opposite the port of San Francisco, about fifteen miles southwest of Drake's Head. When our ships first stopped there, they found a good many fur seals and many other seals. When the settlement was built, our people felt that it was necessary to occupy these islands. They are treeless, and have only a bit of grass; the largest of them is no more than three miles in circumference. They were created by volcanic action, which is obvious from their

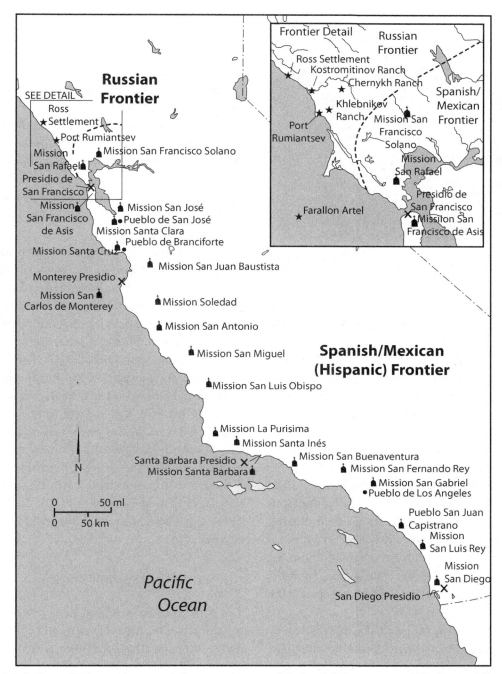

Kent G. Lightfoot, "Dimensions and Consequences of Colonial Encounters," *Indians, Missionaries, and Merchants: The Legacy of Colonial Encounters on the California Frontiers.*

characteristic barrenness, and the lack of minerals. Persons who live there say that during storms the islands shake, and one can hear a kind of moaning noise against the breaking waves. The islands have no fresh water or driftwood, and consequently persons who stay there have a very hard time sustaining themselves. The following advantages caused us to occupy them.

From the beginning of occupation, that is from 1812 to 1815, over the period of six years during Kuskov's administration, 8,427 fur seals were taken there, an average of 1,200 to 1,500 each year. Later

Modern-day reconstruction of the chapel at Fort Ross.

this gradually decreased, and in recent years not more than 200 to 300 pelts are taken there each year.

Some of the American captains said that prior to our occupation of those rocks, they had stopped there one fall and taken as many as 10,000 fur seals. These are smaller than those to be found on the Pribylov Islands; their fur is darker and coarser, and consequently they do not have the same value.

Every year up to 200 sea lions are killed for their hides, called lavtaks, their intestines and meat and fat. The lavtaks are used to make baidarkas in the settlement; the intestines are used for making kamleis, [waterproof garments] and as much as 100 or 150 puds of meat is salted; in addition, the Aleuts dry some 200 or 300 chunks of it. The fat is stored in small kegs and is used both as food for the Aleuts and for lighting purposes.

From 5,000 to 10,000 sea ducks are killed every year, but in 1828 50,000 were killed. They are dried and sent to the artel as food; some are also sent to the fort. In 1828 100 puds of meat was supplied from these. The skins of the birds are not used for any purpose, so once the feathers are plucked, the skins are discarded. In 1827 the artel supplied nine, and in 1828, eleven inflated bladders of feathers; each weighed 30 puds, at a value of twenty rubles per pud; they were sent to New Arkhangel. They collect a good many eggs from these ducks, which

they use for themselves and send to the fort. One can get some idea of the abundance of these birds from the number taken in 1828.

There is one Russian administrator for the artel, and generally from six to ten men, both Aleuts and Indians. They live in earthen dugouts; they bring in water and wood by baidarka; they try to collect rain water in winter; and in order to save wood, they cook by burning sea lion bones which have been soaked in oil.

A baidarka is sent there five or six times a year to supply the artel with water, wood, barrels for oil and meat; and to bring back prepared provisions and lavtaks. The island where the artel lives is very rocky and their is always a strong tide. There is only one place where boats can land, and even that is quite dangerous; thus boats dock and embark with great difficulty and peril. Small transhipments are made in baidarkas, and two baidarkas are always left with the artel. If there is a wind, it takes the baidarkas a week or two or more to make the trip. It is always difficult to sail around Drake's Head in the open sea, and nearly impossible to return if there is a strong northwest wind. Consequently they have to wait in Drake's Head. The frequent dense fogs also add to the difficulty of bringing in supplies.

Climate and Location

The climate of New Albion does not differ from the climate of the areas of northern California; it is quite temperate. There are two seasons of the year: winter and summer. Winter begins in November or December, and is marked by torrential rains and strong southeast and southwest winds which continue, with intermittent periods of clear skies, until march or April. Sometimes there is snow, which will remain several weeks on the mountains, but at lower elevations and in areas close to the sea, the snow melts as soon as it touches the ground. There are no frosts, but the cold in the morning can

A 19th century drawing of Fort Ross (circa 1843), located in Northern California—a former Russian colonial fort and fur trade outpost.

sometimes be quite penetrating. But the extreme low seldom if ever reaches below the freezing point. In summer the south winds stop and the wind comes from the northwest, when there are usually hard storms. If often happens that one cannot see the sun for two or three months, and the weather is quite cold. But these storms reach only as far as the mountains close to the sea and do not go beyond them. When one crosses the mountains, sometimes no more than one or two or three versts from the shore, entirely different weather will be encountered. The sun shines, the air is warm, the sky clear, and the climate is uniformly pleasant. Storms linger in the foothills of the mountains like waves at sea.

The ridge of mountains parallels the shore along the entire peninsula of California, and sometimes spreads appreciably inland. According to some observers, these mountains form an integral part of the Andes.

When traveling east of Fort Ross for three days, we did not find any flat land. In 1823 Schmidt and the prikashchik Dorofiev and some Aleuts took a baidarka along the Slavianka [Russian] River which empties into the sea halfway between Bodega Bay and the settlement; they went out about 100 versts

from the fort. Behind the mountains they found beautiful meadows covered with forests where many Indians lived. From Bodega Bay along the Avacha River the meadows begin near the sea, and the farther one goes the more fertile the soil is. North of the Ross settlement the coastal mountains are forested, but south of the settlement there are no forests; trees can be seen only on far off high mountains; the hills close to the sea are treeless. One river, the Slavianka, is of a good size and can take small rowing vessels. Its mouth is sometimes choked with sand, at other times open. Almost everywhere in the mountains the soil is chernozem; there are always springs of pure water. There is no water on the sand hills.

Natural Resources

Every Scientific observer knows that there are many new things in all parts of the New World, but what is of interest to a scientist is of little import to us, and consequently what we shall attempt to do is to comment here only on the highlights, on things that have been most noticed.

Wildlife. Among quadrupeds the most important are bears, lynx, ordinary wolves, and small ones which the Spaniards call coyotes, small skunks that exude a very vile odor, wildcats, elk, buffaloes, mountain goats, rams, rabbits, an abundance of moles, small mince and other rodents; and although it happens rarely, nonetheless one does sometimes see close to the American settlements American lions [puma] and amphibious animals such as river beavers and otters.

There are numerous snakes, lizards and frogs, and occasionally scorpions. There has been no incidence of snake bite. It seems that they are not poisonous, at least the Indian believe this to be true.

There are white eagles, all varieties of hawks, magpies, crows, woodpeckers, wild pigeons, condors and quite a few birds of the sparrow family. Some of these have beautiful feathers. There are huge flocks of blackbirds which the Spaniards call chanatas, which live near the grain fields and destroy the harvest. Ducks, numerous various kinds of woodcocks and geese come down from the north to spend the winter; there are also swans, cranes, herons, many grey and white pelican, sea gulls, sea ducks, urils, albatross and loons.

Close to shore there are many whales which the Aleuts hunt. Kushov said that they found a whale eighteen sazhens long, but they are usually smaller, from four to five sazhens. From this size one can obtain a pure oil, as much as twelve large barrels, that is, 30 to 36 vedros. Sea lions and sea elephants abound on the Farallons, and they also bask on various rocks along the coast. There are a few seals at present, and these are found only around the cape of Barro de Arena. Along the shore they angle for such fish as perch, mackerel; herring come in seasonally. They catch sturgeon in the Slavianka River when the channel is open.

Among shellfish there are blue crabs, other crabs, crawfish, and small turtles in the lakes beyond the mountains. In October, 1822, men sailing from the Farallons in baidarkas killed an unusually large sea turtle which had exceptionally delicious meat; but this does not happen often.

Vegetation. It has been noted that there is a forest near Fort Ross which is very dense as one goes north. There are such conifers as ordinary pine, fir, larch, silver fir, and bugbane, so called because it has a very sharp ordor, similar to the smell of the insect that has that name. This tree appears to belong to the cypress family, and is similar to the Alaska cypress in Sitka. The chaga, or redwood, is a red pine distinguished by its softeness; it is not very resinous but very moist, and it has a dark red color. The redwood is exceptionally tall and straight and unusually large in circumference. I measured one which was growing near the fort; the circumference was 33 feet, thus it was 11 feet in diameter.

Among deciduous trees, there are two kinds of oak, maple, elm, poplar, two kinds of alder, horse chestnuts, laurel, willow, purple willow, and some ten other varieties whose names are unknown. Our promyshlenniks call one of these a palm, but this is quite inaccurate. Many of these trees are heavy, hard and excellent for making furniture which will be varnished. The leaf of the laurel has a strong odor, much stronger than the East Indian variety.

Of the shrubs, there are currants, hazelnuts, raspberry, buckthorn and elderberry. The Indians sometimes collect a great many delicious nuts. There are sometimes blueberries and nagoonberries. There are many other varieties which are unknown to us, but which the Indians eat.

D.B. [probably Dr. Eduard Blaschke] records such medicinal plants as globularia and acnothera, and familiar herbs such as wormwood, wild mint, fern, scurvy grass, and sea onion. The onion-like root of one plant which grows on sand dunes near the sea can be used instead of soap; it gives a white foam, but it is injurious to white fabric and rapidly destroys it. But it is very good for cleaning decks and floors. Wild roses grow in many meadows. Horsetails grow more than a sazhen high in damp areas, and they are very firm and hard. There are also many kinds of reeds which grow.

Indians always eat wild rose haws, collecting them after the flower has finished blooming, and storing them. In fall they burn the grass and dig for edible roots. Acorns are a major food for both Indians and woodpeckers. These birds use their bills to peck holes in the bark of redwood trees; they put an acorn in each hole to save it for winter. One can see a whole tree studded with acorns. Often the Indians will gather in the cache of the birds after they have eaten their own supply.

Minerals. The mountains near the sea are almost all made up of granite and syenite; and there is much sandstone beneath the surface of the soil. The settlement uses some varieties of this for grindstones and whetstones. There is plenty of good soil in various places. At the mouth of the Slavianka River there are whole blocks of green rock with small bits of granite, and iron ore has been found in its upper reaches. On top of some of the mountains they have found obsidian, serpentine and hornstone. A pure iron-bearing sand is carried up on the sandy shores from the sea.

Suggestions for Improving the Settlement

If the settlement of Ross were to remain forever a possession of Russia, and were to be duly acknowledged by the other governments, then it could become a permanent settlement and attention could be given to more important considerations.

The government of California, in its dealings with the head of the Company, the late Kuskov, several times expressed dissatisfaction, and even insisted that he dismantle the settlement and leave. During the administration of the noted [Agustin de] Iturbide in Mexico, a special official came to the port of San Francisco and expressed a similar demand; however it was subsequently discovered he had no authority to do so. Several times the administration in Monterey resorted to hostile actions such as imprisoning our people. Finally in 1819 the Spanish Ambassador to our Court sent an official note to our minister concerning this problem. At the request of the Minister of Finance the Governing Board prepared an explanation, and the affair has remained unresolved from that time because of changing political circumstance. Meanwhile, the local California administration sees that the present developments give it a protective leverage by using her Russian neighbors. During a recent Indian uprising against the Spanish missions, the Company supplied weapons to the Spaniards, although we had a shortage of them ourselves, thus we demonstrated genuine assistance to them.

Considering the opposition of the California administration to our settlement in New Albion, which the Spanish Ambassador has reiterated, it should be noted that the Spanish had extended the right of Spain to control the entire coast of New Albion all the way to the straits of Juan de Fuca. That such a claim is unfounded is clearly evident, in the first place, by the testimony of the Indian tribes as to their independence, and moreover, that the authority of the Spanish never extended beyond the port of San Francisco; and secondly, that the government of the United States authorized itself to occupy the mouth of the Columbia River, a situation which we have just imitated for ourselves; and subsequently, the southern [sic] border of Louisiana was declared to lie at the 42nd parallel, that is, a full five degrees south of the straits of Juan de Fuca.

The Ross colony presently consists of a small wooden fortress with seventeen small caliber cannon. Within the fortress there are the administrator's home, an office, barracks, a two-story warehouse and several other buildings. Those who live in the fortress work at various jobs; all are in the Company service. There are 50 persons in addition to the Aleuts who are periodically sent out on sea otter hunts. Of the 38 promyshlenniks there, 12 are engaged in agricultural pursuits, most by their own volition rather than by obligation. They plant grain, about 200 puds of wheat and 40 puds of barley, although cultivation is carried on without any great improvement of the soil, in fact, without any systematic plowing; nonetheless the harvest is tenfold. The example of the neighboring Spanish missions, who have a fortyfold harvest, indicates that if agriculture were to be handled properly, we could expect this in Ross. The climate is such that vegetables can be planted twice a year, and every kind of vegetable and fruit can be grown there.

Ross [in the early 1830s] has the following number of livestock: 46 horses 213 bulls and cows, 81 pigs and 842 sheep. The abundance of wild livestock, and the oak forest, makes it easy to operate tanneries. Sheepherding alone, which is so easily increased, would provide the Company with countless advantages.

Generally speaking, on the basis of this first experience, one can easily believe that once agriculture in Ross is carried on properly, the Company could be fully supplied with grain in all of its American colonies.

11. The Arrival of a North American Wagon Train, 1841

By Mariano Guadalupe Vallejo

Primary Source

Most Excellent Sir: On the return of Captain Don José Castro to this Department, I had a number of conferences with him; and I had decided that he should return to that capital in company with Captain of Militia and Secretary of the Commandancy General Don Victor Prudón, to place in Your Excellency's hands an exact report of the state in which this country finds itself, a country that is so promising but which can accomplish nothing; for its happiness is conditional, and its misery positive. Its geographic location, the mildness of its climate, the fertility of its soil, the amenity of its fields, the safety of its ports, among which that of San Francisco deserves to rank among the principal ones of the world, its navigable rivers and inlets, etc. guarantee it a state of prosperity which it is not permitted to attain, due to its lack of population. From that lack of population results its lack of defense, and from this, its insecurity. Thus it is that daily, throughout the whole extent of the Department with the exception of this frontier, where I maintain a military force of forty men at my own expense, there are Indian raids which ravish the fields with impunity and destroy the only effective wealth of the country, the cattle and horses. The otter and beaver which abounded in California have been exterminated, the first by the Russians and the latter by the Columbians [trappers from the Columbia River], who still continue to trap them to the point of extinguishing the species, as the Russians have done with the otter. And we have to endure all those ills because we cannot prevent them, since we have not troops. All that we have suffered and shall endure, if we do not avert the tempest which is presaged for us by the thick clouds that darken our political horizon, is derived from one and the same source; it comes from one single cause: all of it we should attribute to the lack of troops.

This has been, Your Excellency, the motive which inspired me with the idea of addressing to you, by the aforementioned Commissioners, the

Photo of a wagon train, ca. 1850–1899.

various notes which they shall have the honor to place in Your Excellency's hands, all of them relative to the exigencies of the country, with the hope that Your Excellency's zeal and acknowledged patriotism will be exerted to contribute toward the salvation of this valuable portion of Mexican Territory. The Commissioners will be able to satisfy Your Excellency about all of which you may judge opportune to inform yourself.

On the ninth of November, last, while at Mission San José, during a conference with Don José Castro, I received word of the arrival at the town of San José of a party of thirty-three foreigners from Missouri. I had them appear before me to demand their passports, and I was told that they had none, because they did not deem them necessary, since they did not use them in their country. I took a list of their names and the object of their journey. I asked them to return to their country and to get the required documents, and I gave them provisional papers so that they might travel in safety to Monterey to see the Governor and get the necessary permission from him to travel in the country. I gave the Governor an account of everything but do not know the results. I took what seemed to me the only way to reconcile justice with the present circumstances, since we find ourselves forced to accept them, as we cannot prevent them from entering, and all because we lack troops. This party numbers thirty-three, but it is said that a larger one is on the way.

The total population of California does not exceed six thousand souls, and of these two-thirds must be counted as women and children, leaving scarcely two thousand men. But we cannot count on the fifteen thousand Indians in the towns and missions, because they inspire more fear than confidence. Thus we have this lamentable situation in a country worthy of a better fate. And if the invasion which is taking place from all sides is carried out, all I can guarantee is that the Californians will die; I cannot dare to assure you that California will be saved. This people, loyal to their flag, will follow the same course and fate. They will be replaced by or dominated by another race at least. Those others will probably conserve their great past, raising their flag to wave in the breeze. Thus also the noble people of California will preserve their noble attitude of free men while a drop of blood remains in their veins, and will bite the dust before kissing the enemy's hand.

Have the kindness to excuse this burst of feeling in a soldier who laments not having arms when he sees the treasure being stolen. I regret to bother Your Excellency's patriotic zeal, but I must be a truthful steward when speaking of the national interests. The danger seems closer than the help, and it is urgent, and it is with the hope of getting it that I have the honor of addressing Your Excellency.

12. Reminisces on Life and Customs of Mexican California

By Antonio Coronel

Primary Source

When the Híjar-Padrés colony arrived in California, the total population loosely called white (*gente de razón*) was no mere than five thousand, including the garrisons. The education of the inhabitants consisted generally of Catholic doctrine introduced by the fathers. The same Fathers taught one or two Californians to write, after a fashion. In the *presidios* there were a few Californians with a little more primary education: reading and writing, the rudiments of which formed the principal, or essential branch of instruction. Even this small advance was due to the military officers resident in the *presidios*, who had been educated elsewhere or learned from contact with the old Spanish officers and the merchants and others who came on ships. To this nucleus add the arrival of Mexican families, well-educated and soon scattered throughout the country.

In the interior settlements there were very few people who could be said to write and figure. Even after the arrival of intelligent and educated people, education remained at a low level. The women learned even less, because they had been convinced that book-learning was bad for girls; they could barely read, let alone write. But in spite of their lack of education, the ladies were highly moral, diligent, and clean, dedicated to their household duties; some even carried out duties that properly belonged to men. These women were charitable and hospitable; they did not care to sell food but shared among families, one supplying what another might lack.

A traveler could go up to any house in California, confident he could stay however many days he liked and pay nothing for roof, bed, food, and even horses to continue his journey. But the mothers took great care of their daughters, and the traveler often met only the men of the family.

The men busied themselves almost exclusively with livestock, which meant they only worked at certain times, such as the roundup and branding or slaughtering time. The hides and tallow were their income as well as all the coinage there was at that time. The Californians were not much given to farming, because they could buy grain at the missions. A few grew crops for their families only—but as the missions declined, agriculture of necessity became more widespread.

The men who were already full-grown in that epoch kept the character of their Spanish ancestors. They were upright and honorable men, imperious, and their word without documents or witnesses was good for any amount of money. This character also declined rapidly as what was termed "Enlightenment" arose. The most important family value was respect for the head of family—to the point where the parents still governed married sons and daughters, who had to submit humbly to punishment still.

Daughters had very little choice of husbands. The parents arranged marriages for young people before they even met each other. Young married couples lived with one or the other set of parents, just as if they were still minors. They helped with the work, and the parents provided for all. Just what relations were is impossible to calculate. The inhabitants of California were all related to each other, by law and by custom.

Religious education was observed in all homes. Before dawn each morning, a hymn of praise was sung in chorus; at noon, prayers; at about six p.m. and before going to bed, a Rosary and another hymn. I saw this on several occasions at balls or dances when the clock struck eight: the father of the family stopped the music and said the Rosary with all the guests, after which the party continued. I saw the same thing sometimes at roundups, when the old men stopped work to pray at the accustomed hours, joined by all present.

When young people met their godparents anywhere, they were obliged to take off their hats and ask a blessing. The godparents' obligation was to substitute for the parents if they should die, if necessary provide for the godchild's keep and education, and give good advice. The *compadrazgo* was a relationship between the parents and godparents of the child, ties recognized by the Church but not by civil law. At every baptism the priest explained the obligations entailed by the relationship. When two men were united in a friendship superior to the common run, they called each other *valedor*—this term was often used among the ranchers as a term of appreciation and trust.

Women's work was harder, longer, and more important than men's. They were in charge of the kitchen. They made all their clothes, which was a laborious task because the petticoats were edged with lace or embroidered with cutwork in the most exquisite fashion. They were also fond of fine bed linens, and the sheets and pillowcases had to be lace-edged or embroidered too. Since clothing was expensive, they turned and altered used clothing until it was almost new. Most of them ironed the clothes with their hands, patting and stretching the fabric until it was perfectly smooth. They also sewed exquisite clothes for

their husbands, fathers, and brothers: broadcloth jackets with worked buttonholes, embroidery on some of them, braid and trapunto [decorative quilting] on others. Vests were generally made of silk or wool, embroidered in colors; the short breeches also. The sleeves on riding jackets, made of wool or corduroy, were trimmed with velvet, corduroy or fringe. The women also had to comb the menfolks' hair every day and tie it up. Many women also baked bread, made candles and ordinary soap, and some I knew brought in the harvest and threshed the grain.

With regard to the clothing I described above, I was referring to families who enjoyed a good economic position. Poor people wore the same kinds of clothes, but made of cheaper material. The clothes worn by well-off ladies of 1834 and 1835 were a short, narrow tunic of silk or organdy, a high, tight bodice trimmed with silk ribbons or flowers according to the caprice of the lady, and red flannel (or another color) underneath according to taste. A shawl, similar to the Spanish *mantilla*, was also worn, and low cloth slippers.

The hair was pulled back smoothly and braided, tied with ribbon and a small ornament or silk flower very prettily. The final touch was a silk handkerchief at the neck, the ends crossed and tied in front. Some women used a *camorra*, which was a black silk handkerchief tied gracefully around the head.

We have already mentioned that men's work was exclusively on the ranches. Some grew crops, but there was no market except what they might sell to the *presidios*.

Men's clothing consisted of knee breeches slit six inches on the outer side and adorned with ribbon or braid and four to six silver buttons (or other metal, depending on the individual's relative prosperity); the fly front had another such button, almost the size of a *peso*. A long vest of wool, silk, velvet, or corduroy (according to economic circumstances), variously adorned, was worn under a longer jacket of the same material and adorned in the same style.

High-heeled boots were made of a whole tanned deerskin, dyed black or red and tooled or embroidered with silk according to the preference of the individual. The leather had a lace or drawstring to put the foot into; then it was rolled down to a little below the knee, covering the calf and half the instep, and tied with the lace. To go with the boot, shoes were made of what was called *berruchi*, four to six pieces of red and black calfskin or suede with an embroidered vamp. The sole was a single thickness of flexible calfskin to grip the stirrup securely. The toe had a point, turned upward, to keep the *tapaderos* of the stirrups from rubbing the shoe.

The hat was broad-brimmed with a round crown, stoutly made of wool. It was kept on with a chin strap two inches wide, formed into a big rosette under the chin. Almost all the men covered their heads with a black bandanna tied like an Andalusian peasant.

The saddle had a big, rough, wooden tree, strong enough to stand hard use. Underneath, it was padded with calfskin; cowhide thongs secured it to the horsehair cinch. A square of tooled calfskin went over the saddle, and over that a larger hide, more finely carved, embroidered with silk or even silver or gold, nearly covered the horse on both sides. These were called the *corazas*. There was also a matching crupper and saddlebags to carry necessities.

The most important item for any Californian was the lariat. This was made of four or six rawhide strips one-half inch wide, plaited and worked until the lariat was perfectly flexible. When it was not needed, it was tied to the back of the saddle with a special strap; when in use, it hung on the pommel.

The knife was also of first importance. It was carried in a sheath on the outside of the right boot, fastened to the bootlace. Every man had a

sword—though the civilians had not much use for it—carried on the left of the saddle under the leg. The *serape* was also indispensable, and much more useful. When not worn, it was rolled and tied behind the saddle with the lariat. In the hazards of ranch work, if it happened a man had to spend the night out, the saddle served for a pillow, the *corazas* and saddlebags for a bed, the *serape* for a blanket.

This same Californian, if he had to go on a campaign to fight Indians, or for military service, added a long, padded leather coat of seven layers, which covered him from neck to knee. This *cuera,* as it was called, provided protection from arrows. A small oval shield, concave on the inside, presenting the convex side to the enemy, could be slipped on the left arm. The usual weapon was an old flintlock shotgun, perhaps a lance, or a pair of pistols. This last was very unusual, and only the leaders carried pistols, but every man had a good Spanish blade from Toledo.

Officers wore the same dress, distinguished only by their insignia of rank. All these customs eventually changed, particularly after the arrival of the colonial families from Mexico. The Californians took up the long pants buttoned from hip to ankle on both sides, low boots, short jacket, and the low-crowned, wide-brimmed, white felt hat and Mexican saddle.

The ladies exchanged their fitted dresses for voluminous ones, took out their braids and piled their hair up elaborately, held with small combs instead of the large one they had used up until then. Women of modest means, and usually the older women of any economic level, wore petticoats of suitable material (instead of the tunic) from the waist down. The blouse had sleeves below the elbow, and the neck and chest were covered with a black silk or cotton kerchief folded diagonally and tied in back; the front was pinned to the waist of the petticoat.

The small-town women continued using the shawl, of linen or cotton, and homemade shoes called *berruchis* because they were pointed like the men's, only smaller, with a point at the heel too. All women usually wore stockings, leaving no part of themselves uncovered but face and hands—any more display was considered immodest.

Section V

Americanization of California:
The Gold Rush Era, 1840–1850

Section Five

Introduction to California's Gold Rush Era, 1840s–1850s

Sources

---

1. Journal of a Mormon Pioneer, c. 1850s
2. Proclamation of Independence for California as the Bear Flag Republic, 1846
3. Treaty of Guadalupe Hidalgo, 1848
4. Constitution of the State of California, 1849
5. California Land Act of 1851
6. A Pioneer at Sutter's Fort, 1850

7. *The Californian* Modestly Announces the Discovery of Gold, 1848
8. The Impact of the Gold Rush, 1849
9. California As I Saw It, 1848
10. Life in the Mines in 1849
11. The Dame Shirley Letters, 1851
12. Blacks in Gold Rush California
13. My Darling Clementine

Mexican-American War and U.S. Statehood

"Our claim is by the right of our manifest destiny," wrote the New York journalist John L. O'Sullivan in 1845, "to overspread and to possess the whole of the continent." This phrase propelled thousands of white American settlers to leave their eastern homes and set their vision on westward settlement. American mountain men had trapped beaver in California since the late 1820s, opening the way for other American entrepreneurs, such as ranchers, agriculturalists, vineyardists and merchants to establish businesses in California throughout the 1830s. With the first American settlers arriving via the California Trail in 1841, when California was still the property of the Mexican Republic, the pressures attendant to the growing presence of United States citizens up and down the California Coast only foreshadowed a population explosion that would have no match in the annals of United States History. It would be from among these American settlers that cries of independence from Mexican rule would ring out in the days preceding the Mexican-American War. This expansion of the United States into territories west of the Mississippi brought Americans into direct conflict with the Republic of Mexico. Even though the conflict was built around the U.S. annexation of Texas, U.S. expansionists had their eyes on the true prize of war—California—a province of Mexico that comprised areas we know today as California, Nevada, Utah, Arizona, New Mexico, and parts of Colorado and Wyoming.

1846 saw the beginning of the best organized mass migration in American history. The participants of this mass exodus to the West, the Mormons, established thriving communities throughout the western frontier in what was considered by many to be a worthless desert. From 1846 to 1869, more than 70,000 Mormons trekked across the plains on the Mormon Pioneer Trail. This was a movement of an entire people, an entire religion, and an entire culture driven by religious fervor and the determination to live their religious beliefs in spite of the persecutions they endured. As did all migrating peoples heading west at this time, the Mormon pioneers walked hundreds of miles through suffocating dust, violent thunderstorms, mud, temperature extremes, bad water, poor forage, sickness, and death. They recorded their experiences in journals, diaries, and letters that have become a part of our national heritage. The first selection, from **the journal of Mormon pioneer Daniel Duncan McArthur**, ties the 1846 Mormon expulsion directly to the impending war with Mexico. McArthur's journal recounts the enlistment of over 500 Mormon men in July 1846 into a regiment of the U.S. Army, called the Mormon Battalion, to join in the war with Mexico. Daniel's youngest brother Henry Morrow McArthur, a member of Company D of the Mormon Battalion, participated in the longest infantry march in U.S. Army history—over 2000 miles from Council Bluffs, Missouri, to San Diego, California, where they camped at the Mission of San Diego on January 29, 1847.

John C. Frémont, a U.S. Army officer, led his second scientific expedition to California a year earlier, when he encouraged the American ranchers in the North to revolt against Mexican rule. In May they seized Sonoma and proclaimed California an independent republic. The second selection in this section was written by **William B. Ide, the Commander of the short-lived California Bear Republic** and a prominent California pioneer, who participated in seizing the pueblo of Sonoma and capturing the Mexican Commandant of Northern California, Mariano Guadalupe Vallejo. In it, one can easily read the undertones of Manifest Destiny. On July 7, 1846, U.S. sailors under the command of Commodore John D. Sloat raised the American Flag at Monterey and claimed California to be a part of the United States, promising American citizenship to its inhabitants. The Bear Flag Republic had lasted as an independent nation for about six weeks. Meanwhile, the war with Mexico had started. The north was quickly taken and the south submitted to American forces in 1847. Mexico ceded California and other Mexican territories for the exchange sum of $15 million to the United States under the terms of **the Treaty of Guadalupe Hidalgo on February 2, 1848**, the next selection in this series, which ended the Mexican-American War. The United States era of colonization in California advanced rapidly following the 1848 treaty. By the war's end, Mexico had lost nearly half of its territory, the present American Southwest from Texas to California, and in the process the United States became a continental power. Only the virulent racism of certain American leaders prevented the complete annexation of the entirety of the defeated Mexican Republic. Few knew that gold had already been discovered at Sutter's Mill just days earlier. One has to wonder what the outcome of the peace negotiations would have been, had Mexico known it had turned over the richest ore deposits on the continent. The fourth selection is **the 1849 Constitution of the State of California**, which propelled California beyond the traditional territorial waiting period, positioning it to become the 31st state of the Union.

As the nation ended one war that seemed to move it imperceptibly to another, California struggled with conflicts between the Californios and the Americans. When California gained its statehood, most of its 14 million acres were held between 800 land grants that were owned by Mexican rancheros, whose right of ownership was guaranteed by the Treaty of Guadalupe Hidalgo. But the passage of **the 1851 California Land Act**, the next selection in this group, nullified their rights of ownership until legal proof of title could be produced so they could reclaim their lands. Ligation often lasted for years and in the meantime, the ranchos were declared "public lands" and American miners, ranchers, businessmen, and homesteaders took over the ranchos and exploited the land for themselves. By this time, gold had been discovered and California was booming.

The Gold Rush

After securing California for the United States in the Mexican-American War, discharged Mormon Battalion members went on to build the first courthouse in San Diego, Fort Moore in Los Angeles, and numerous buildings and structures throughout California. Men from Company A were responsible for opening the first wagon road over the southern route from California to Utah in 1848. Battalion members built the race at Sutter's Mill near Sacramento, assisting in the discovery of gold that fueled the California Gold Rush between 1849 and 1860. Their participation in the early development of California contributed significantly to the growth of the West. Aided by the arrival of persecuted Mormon settlers into San Francisco via the clipper ship Brooklyn in July 1846, along with the arrival of fellow religionists of the Mormon Battalion into San Diego in January 1847, California-bound immigrants would soon pour into the Bear Flag State from every continent of the world. Few people knew that when Mexico signed over its possession of California to the United States in February 1848,

gold had already been discovered at Sutter's Mill a week earlier.

"I have found it," exclaimed John W. Marshall to his Mormon workers as they gathered around him to feel the glowing dust and test the golden nuggets. In earlier years, Swiss pioneer John Sutter had owned a sawmill in partnership with James Marshall in a town called Coloma, an area where John Sutter had already established a mercantile enterprise in 1839 originally named New Helvetia (New Switzerland) and later called Sutter's Fort. Marshall had been a "Bear Flagger" serving under John C. Fremont prior to rejoining his business partner, John Sutter, in building the water-driven saw mill on the South Fork of the American River about 30 miles N.E. of Sutter's Fort, known today as Sacramento. Marshall had hired discharged Mormon Battalion carpenters and Native Americans as laborers to build the mill and form the mill-races that would carry fast flowing water to the hydro-powered saw mill—a saw mill that was never finished and never made operational. Marshall had discovered gold in the mill race on January 24, 1848, and the future of California, and indeed even of the United States and the world, changed forever.

Sources

Gold fever swept over the land immediately. Mormon workers searched for gold in their off hours and Sutter's employees at the Fort abandoned their jobs, purchased equipment and food, and headed for nearby streams and rivers to pan for gold. After the news had reached San Francisco, stories of gold discoveries spread widely and by late Spring of 1848, the Gold Rush was in full swing. In an astonishing two-year time, California would undergo a rapid "Americanization" process that would propel the Mexican province directly into U.S. Statehood. Selection 6, the first document in this series on the Gold Rush, **A Pioneer** at Sutter's Fort—October 1846, was written by a young immigrant who enlisted in the U.S. Army upon his arrival at Sutter's Fort in the Fall of 1846. His descriptions of the area, its fields of wheat and grazing cattle, may be one of the last literary witnesses to the area prior to its desecration by gold seekers. His description of Yerba Buena (San Francisco) at this time revealed a village of about fifty houses with less than 200 inhabitants. The next selection, *The Californian* **Modestly Announces the Discovery of Gold, 1848**, is a copy of a page from a San Francisco newspaper that printed a small article on March 15, 1848 announcing the discovery of gold in what seems to be a very understated fashion.

The unearthing of gold at the mill was first recorded in the journals of discharged Mormon Battalion members Azariah Smith and Henry Bigler. Once the discovery became public, the news spread like a raging virus and over the next decade nearly ½ million people from all over the American continents and beyond both oceans converged on California to seek their fortunes. Walter Colton, the co-founder of *The California* newspaper, came as a Chaplain for the U.S. Navy in 1846 and was appointed Alcalde of Monterey almost immediately. Colton spent 3 years as a regional governor of nearly all of Northern California, keeping a journal of his experiences during that time. Following his return to the East in 1849, he published his journal in 1850, *Three Years in California*, which is regarded as one of the best detailed accountings of pre-Gold Rush California and the transformation of California during the early Gold Rush era. This edition's extract from his book, **Walter Colton Describes the Effects of the Gold Rush, 1848**, recounts the get-rich-fever sweeping the inhabitants of the area as many of the early prospectors made fortunes.

The next selection, from J.E. Pleasants, **Life in the Mines in 1849**, recounts a mining town set up on the banks of the Feather River at a place called Bidwell Bar, where sixty or more miners lived together and worked their 25 sq. ft. claims together. Pleasants described the mining equipment in detail and other aspects of mining life. Selection 9, **California as I Saw It, 1849–1850**, is the first-hand account of William S. M'Collum, who first came to California in 1849 and then again later to work as a physician for the Panama Railroad Company. His 1850 book recounted his experiences prospecting on the Tuolumne River near Jacksonville, an historic California site now fully submerged under Don Pedro Reservoir. It was once one of the largest mining towns in California, accommodating thousands of miners. The town had several stores, a post office and three "luxury" hotels. This excerpt tells about the population boom in San Francisco, relating about housing shortages, ships in port, and the language diversity of the booming population, likening it to the "confusion of tongues" at the Tower of Babel.

The next two selections in this Gold Rush section represent two groups of non-traditional participants in the California Gold Rush, women and Black Americans. Louisa Amelia Knapp Smith Clappe, a well-educated and published writer from Massachusetts, arrived in San Francisco in 1849 at the age of 30 in the company of her husband, Dr. Sylvanus Clappe. For health reasons, they left for the Sierra Nevada Mountains in 1851, where they spent more than a year at two mining camps, Rich Bar, and Indian Bar, on the Feather River. Writing under the pen name of **Dame Shirley**, Clappe wrote 23 letters to her sister Molly, detailing the crude style of living in the mining camps—an interesting discourse from the view of a proper New England lady. The next selection, published in 1977, is actually **a secondary source written by Rudolph M. Lapp** after twenty years of extensive research scouring archives, historical societies, attics, etc., looking for primary sources from which he could form a history of Black Americans in California before, during and after the Gold Rush. In this excerpt from his book, *Blacks in Gold Rush California*, Lappe included several primary sources with information about slaves and free Blacks participating in the Gold Rush. Lappe informs his readers that by 1860, twelve years after gold had been discovered, more than 5,000 Black Americans had made the trek to California to seek their fortunes with the rest of the world. The last selection in this section, **Oh My Darling, Clementine**, is the best known of all the camp songs that came out of this period. Attributed to Percy Montrose, it was first published in 1887. The words tell of a lover pining for his sweetheart, the daughter of a miner in the California gold fields. She dies in a drowning accident, and he consoles himself towards the end of the song with Clementine's "little sister."

The questionable morality of the verse about the little sister was often left out of folk song books intended for children.

Most immigrants to California did not find the fulfillment of their dreams in the gold and silver mines, but rather in the support industries that sustained the burgeoning population of treasure hunters. In less than two years, California went from being a provincial Mexican outpost to becoming the 31st state of the union on September 9, 1850 as insignificant Mexican trading posts transformed into thriving American ports and cities. The small fishing village of Yerba Buena became the bustling port city of San Francisco, growing during this decade to a population of 50,000, and becoming a portal for population and cultural dispersion across the state.

Readings

1. Journal of a Mormon Pioneer, c. 1850s

By Daniel Duncan McArthur

Primary Source

In the Spring of 1842 My Father and Family mooved from Adames Co to Naughvoo where they could injoy the Society of those whome they loved.

On the 14th day of December 1845 I maried me a nother Wife by the name of Matilda Caroline Fuller who was Born in the town of Providence Saratoga Co State of New York on the first day of May 1820 Daughter of Edwin, M, and Hannah Fuller we were maried by the [36] Patriarch John Smith uncle to the Prophit Joseph Smith Father Fuller maid a good Supper for the Invited on the occation we had a fine Dance after the Supper was over all felt well

On the first of Febuary 1846 I and my Wife went into the Temple and Recieved our washings and anointings and on the Same day after we had got our Indowments we went into the Sealing Room and I hade Matilda Caroline Sealed to me for time and all Eternity By President Willard Richards over the Alter Prepared for that purpose. Also hade Cordelia Clark my first wife was dead

Purcecurtion continuing to rage against the Church at Naughvoo the Saints were compelled to leave their homes and flee to the Wilderness for Safety Concequently on the 26th of Febuary 1846 myself and Family in company with [37] my Father in-Law Fuller and his Family with a host of the Bretherin and Sisters left our homes and crossed the Misissippa River and took up our march for the west not knowing where we were going we pitched our Tents the first night on Sugar Creek a distance from the Misissippa eight Miles. This was a place of Rendisvouse for the Saints to geather at as they were fleeing from their Enemys My Father and Family hade left Naughvoo a day or two before I left Brother Brigham Young astablished this place for the Collection Of the Saints as he hade become the leader of the Church by a unanamus vote of the whole Church as well as the vois of God Brother Heber C Kimble was his first Counciler and Brother Willard Richards was his Second Counciler Brother Brigham Young hade led the [38] Church from September 1844 and the Lord was with him and his council all the time

U.S. Mormon Battalion March

Legend:
March Route
Return to Utah Route
Return to Iowa Route
Sick Detachments

0 300 mi
0 300 km

Map Created by Brian Cole

he hade the Revillations of god So resting upon him that he was able to tell the Saints the Cours for them to take under all the trials they were compelled to bair from their Enemys

The Saints continued to collect at Sugar Creek till a large Camp had got to gether and were properly arganised 3y the Prophet Brigham with Captains of hundreads of fifties and of teens and in the first of March the Camp took up the line of march for the west not knowing as yet where we were going onely that it was the mind of God for us to west- we continued our march Stoping by the way to get feed for our Stalk where ever we could the Cuntry through which we hade to travel was a perfect [39] Wilderness with now and then a Setler scatered here and there we hade all our roads and Bridges to make as we went. Our corse was through the State of Iowa or then the Territory of Iowa, this was a hard Journey on the old and infirm it caused meny a wone to lay down thier Bodys to moulder away to Dust, it was a weet and could Spring we hade to fall Trees so

that our Oxen and Cows could Brouce the tops for their food and whenever a chance would present its self for us to purches some Corn we would do it and by this prosses we were inabled to preserve our Stake till the Grass grew. The Camp stoped a distance of one hundred and fifty miles from Naughvoo and opened up a farme of five hundread achores. Built a good fence around it of Railes and put up fourteen good Logg houses here and Left a good meny [40] poor in this place who were not able to proseede any farther.

This place was opened up by the Prophet Brigham expressly for the Poor that were not able to go any further and for those who were yet behind that were Compelled to leave Naughvoo or be Slaughtered by their Enemys and this prooved to be a great help to the poor for meny a Family maid their fit out at this place so that they could proseede on thier Journey a distance of one Thousand and one hundred and fifty miles westward.

here I left my Fathers Family as they could not go iny further for the want of a teem as I was abliged to take my Team which I had furnished them thus far on their journey

In the Month of May Brother Brigham Started for the [41] west again with all those who were able to go. I was organised with my Father in law Fuller and Family in Bishop George Millers Company we continued our March westward making our Road through woods and Praries Bridging meny Streems till we came in Sight of the Missouria River and at this Moment we were met with a united States Officer by the name of Allen Demanding of us five hundread men to turnout and go and help the united States to fight in the Mexican war, which Demand the Prophet Brigham Complied readily as Soon as the Camp hade arived at the Banks of the Missouria River and hade got their Tents pitched Brother Brigham Young went to work and raised the five hundread Mormon Boys for the united States Army although we were then [42] at this time being driven from our homes and firesides and Spoiled of all our goods which we hade laboured hard to obtain in the Short Space of Seven years as it was onely Seven years from the time we were driven from the State of Missouria by a Hellish mob who were ortherised to do so by the athority of the State Save the small potion we were alble to take with us in our flight My Brother Henry was one of the number that composed the five hundred and twenty five as there was twenty five Boys went over and above the number cauld for by the goverment. these Boys Recieved their Blessings from under the hands of the Cirvants of God and and then Started on their long and tedious Journey acrss the Plains and Desets with their napsacks on their Backs to help fight the Battles for the Goverment in the Mexican war [43] although we as a people were fleeing for our lives from the Same power that cauld upon us to help them subdue the Mixicans to their power. our feelings on this occasion is onely felt or realised by those who were the paticipaters in these seens. Fathers were compelled to leave their Wives and Children in their Waggons in the midst of the Savages or Red men of the forest without food or a place to lay their heads also Fathers and Mothers had to part with their Sones not knowing as they would ever behold their faces again though all fild with good faith that they would and all would be right, for the Prophet Brigham hade told the Boys that if they would go and do right they Should all return again for all that the Enimy could do the Boys Started of with churful harts with the Blessings of God on their heads and done all that the Goverment wished them to do. the Mexicans were compelled to yeald the point and become Subject to the Goverment of the united States [44] this army of Mormon Boys was cauld the Mormon Battalion they taken to the Coast of the Pasiphick and there discharged by goverment left without means and to make their way back to their Famileys and friends the Best they could. Such an act is not known on the pages of Histry but the Boys took it all right and went and found work where they could to get means to help them selves home with and some of them hade hired to a man to Dig a mill Race and being busily ingaged diging at this Race one day a Brother by the name of Iry Willis Discovered Some Gold Dust and took it up and examind it and found it to be pure Gold and this of course caused the Boys to turn their attention to the Diging of Gold as they could make a fit out much quicker and from this time foth the news flew like wild fire till the whole wourld was put in commotion. this Discovry was maid in the Spring [45] of 1847 and Emence quantities of Gold was dug in a Short time by the Boys so that they were able to return to their Family and Friends.

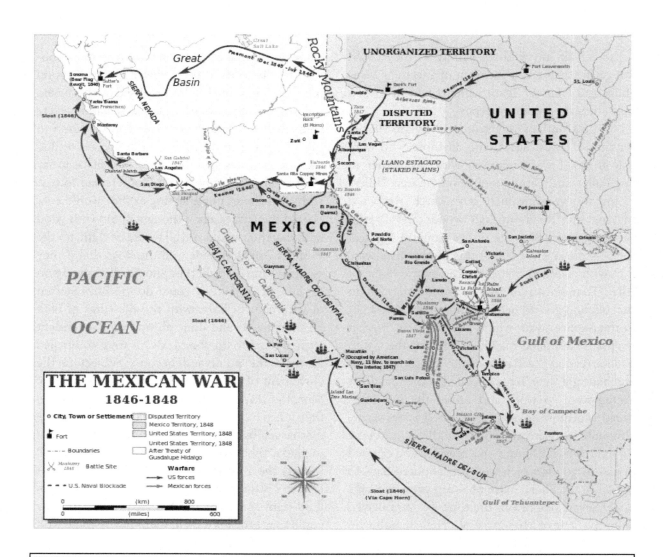

2. Proclamation of Independence for California as the Bear Flag Republic, 1846

By William B. Ide

Primary Source

To all persons, Citizens of Sonoma, requesting them to remain at peace, and to follow their rightful occupations without fear of Mollestation.

The Commander in Chief of the Troops assembled at the Fortress of Sonoma give his inviolable pledge to all persons in California not found under arms that they shall not be disturbed

A photo of the original Bear Flag, ca. 1890. The flag was later destroyed in 1906.

in their persons, their property or social relations one to another by men under his command.

He also solemnly declares his object to be First, to defend himself and companions in arms who were invited to this country by a promise of Lands on which to settle themselves and families who were also promised a "Republican Government," who, when having arrived in California were denied even the privilege of buying or renting Lands of their friends, who instead of being allowed to participate in or being protected by a "Republican Government" were oppressed by a "Military Despotism," who were even threatened, by "proclamation" from the Chief officer of the aforesaid Despotism, with extermination if they would not depart out of the Country; leaving all their property, their arms and beasts of burden, and thus deprived of the means of flight or defence. We were to be driven through deserts, inhabited by hostile Indians to certain destruction. To overthrow a "Government" which had seized upon the property of the Missions for its individual aggrandizement; which has ruined and shamefully oppressed the labouring people of California, by their enormous exactions on goods imported into this country; is the determined purpose of the brave men who are associated under his command.

He also solemnly declares his object in the Second place to be to invite all peaceable and good Citizens of California who are friendly to the maintenance of good order and equal rights (and I do hereby invite them to repair to my camp at Sonoma without delay) to assist us in establishing and perpetuating a "Republican Government" which shall secure to all; civil and religious liberty; which shall detect and punish crime; which shall encourage industry virtue and literature; which shall leave unshackled by Fetters, Commerce, Agriculture, and Mechanism.

He further declares that he relies upon the rectitude of our intentions; the favor of Heaven and the bravery of those who are bound to, and associated with him, by the principle of self preservation; by the love of truth: and by the hatred of tyranny—for his hopes of success.

He further declares that he believes that a Government to be prosperous and happifying in its tendency must originate with its people who are friendly to its existence. That its Citizens, are its Guardians, its officers are its Servants, and its Glory their reward.

Signed *William B. Ide*
Headquarters
Sonoma June 15th 1846

Treaty of peace, friendship, limits, and settlement between the United States of America and the United Mexican States concluded at Guadalupe Hidalgo, February 2, 1848; ratification advised by Senate, with amendments, March 10, 1848; ratified by President, March 16, 1848; ratifications exchanged at Queretaro, May 30, 1848; proclaimed, July 4, 1848.

In the name of Almighty God.

ARTICLE I

There shall be firm and universal peace between the United States of America and the Mexican Republic, and between their respective countries, territories, cities, towns, and people, without exception of places or persons.

ARTICLE IV

All prisoners of war taken on either side, on land or on sea, shall be restored as soon as practicable after the exchange of ratifications of this treaty. It is also agreed that if any Mexicans should now be held as captives by any savage tribe within the limits of the United States, as about to be established by the following article, the Government of the said United States will exact the release of such captives and cause them to be restored to their country.

ARTICLE V

The boundary line between the two Republics shall commence in the Gulf of Mexico, three leagues from land, opposite the mouth of the Rio Grande, otherwise called Rio Bravo del Norte, or Opposite the mouth of its deepest branch ...

In order to designate the boundary line with due precision, upon authoritative maps, and to establish upon the ground land-marks which shall show the limits of both republics, as described in the present article, the two Governments shall each appoint a commissioner and a surveyor, who, before the expiration of one year from the date of the exchange of ratifications of this treaty, shall meet at the port of San Diego, and proceed to run and mark the said boundary in its whole course to the mouth of the Rio Bravo del Norte. ...

The boundary line established by this article shall be religiously respected by each of the two republics, and no change shall ever be made therein, except by the express and free consent of both nations, lawfully given by the General Government of each, in conformity with its own constitution.

ARTICLE VI

The vessels and citizens of the United States shall, in all time, have a free and uninterrupted passage by the Gulf of California, and by the river Colorado below its confluence with the Gila, to and from their possessions situated north of the boundary line defined in the preceding article ...

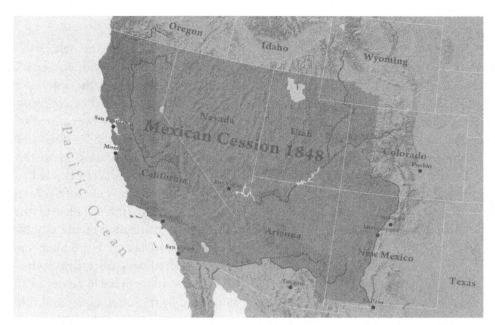

Map of the territories ceded by Mexico in 1848 under the Treaty of Guadalupe Hidalgo.

ARTICLE VII

The river Gila, and the part of the Rio Bravo del Norte lying below the southern boundary of New Mexico, being, agreeably to the fifth article, divided in the middle between the two republics, the navigation of the Gila and of the Bravo below said boundary shall be free and common to the vessels and citizens of both countries; and neither shall, without the consent of the other, construct any work that may impede or interrupt, in whole or in part, the exercise of this right; not even for the purpose of favoring new methods of navigation. Nor shall any tax or contribution, under any denomination or title, be levied upon vessels or persons navigating the same or upon merchandise or effects transported thereon, except in the case of landing upon one of their shores. If, for the purpose of making the said rivers navigable, or for maintaining them in such state, it should be necessary or advantageous to establish any tax or contribution, this shall not be done without the consent of both Governments.

The stipulations contained in the present article shall not impair the territorial rights of either republic within its established limits.

ARTICLE VIII

Mexicans now established in territories previously belonging to Mexico, and which remain for the future within the limits of the United States, as defined by the present treaty, shall be free to continue where they now reside, or to remove at any time to the Mexican Republic, retaining the property which they possess in the said territories, or disposing thereof, and removing the proceeds wherever they please, without their being subjected, on this account, to any contribution, tax, or charge whatever.

Those who shall prefer to remain in the said territories may either retain the title and rights of Mexican citizens, or acquire those of citizens of the United States. But they shall be under the obligation to make their election within one year from the date of the exchange of ratifications of this treaty; and those who shall remain in the said territories after the expiration of that year, without having declared their intention to retain the character of Mexicans, shall be considered to have elected to become citizens of the United States.

In the said territories, property of every kind, now belonging to Mexicans not established there, shall be inviolably respected. The present owners, the heirs of these, and all Mexicans who may hereafter acquire said property by contract, shall enjoy with respect to it guarantees equally ample as if the same belonged to citizens of the United States.

ARTICLE IX

The Mexicans who, in the territories aforesaid, shall not preserve the character of citizens of the Mexican Republic, conformably with what is stipulated in the preceding article, shall be incorporated into the Union of the United States, and be admitted at the proper time (to be judged of by the Congress of the United States) to the enjoyment of all the rights of citizens of the United States, according to the principles of the Constitution; and in the mean time, shall be maintained and protected in the free enjoyment of their liberty and property, and secured in the free exercise of their religion without restriction. …

ARTICLE XV

The United States, exonerating Mexico from all demands on account of the claims of their citizens mentioned in the preceding article, and considering them entirely and forever canceled, whatever their amount may be, undertake to make satisfaction for the same, to an amount not exceeding three and one-quarter millions of dollars. To ascertain the validity and amount of those claims, a board of commissioners shall be established by the Government of the United States, whose awards shall be final and conclusive; provided that, in deciding upon the validity of each claim, the boa shall be guided and governed by the principles and rules of decision prescribed by the first and fifth articles of the unratified convention, concluded at the city of Mexico on the twentieth day of November, one thousand eight hundred and forty-three; and in no case shall an award be made in favour of any claim not embraced by these principles and rules.

If, in the opinion of the said board of commissioners or of the claimants, any books, records, or documents, in the possession or power of the Government of the Mexican Republic, shall be deemed necessary to the just decision of any claim, the commissioners, or the claimants through them, shall, within such period as Congress may designate, make an application in writing for the same, addressed to the Mexican Minister of Foreign Affairs, to be transmitted by the Secretary of State of the United States; and the Mexican Government engages, at the earliest possible moment after the receipt of such demand …

ARTICLE XVI

Each of the contracting parties reserves to itself the entire right to fortify whatever point within its territory it may judge proper so to fortify for its security.

We, the people of California, grateful to Almighty God for our freedom, in order to secure its blessings, do establish this Constitution.

Article I.

Declaration of Rights.

Sec. 1. All men are by nature free and independent, and have certain inalienable rights, among which are those of enjoying and defending life and liberty, acquiring, possessing, and protecting property: and pursuing and obtaining safety and happiness.

Sec. 2. All political power is inherent in the people. Government is instituted for the protection, security, and benefit of the people; and they have the right to alter or reform the same, whenever the public good may require it.

Sec. 3. The right of trial by jury shall be secured to all, and remain inviolate forever; but a jury trial may be waved by the parties, in all civil cases, in the manner to be prescribed by law.

Sec. 4. The free exercise and enjoyment of religious profession and worship, without discrimination or preference, shall forever be allowed in this State: and no person shall be rendered incompetent to be a witness on account of his opinions on matters of religious belief; but the liberty of conscience, hereby secured, shall not be so construed as to excuse acts of licentiousness, or justify practices inconsistent with the peace or safety of this State.

Sec. 5. The privilege of the writ of habeas corpus shall not be suspended, unless when, in cases of rebellion or invasion, the public safety may require its suspension.

Sec. 6. Excessive bail shall not be required, nor excessive fines imposed, nor shall cruel or unusual punishments be inflicted, nor shall witnesses be unreasonably detained.

Sec. 7. All persons shall be bailable, by sufficient sureties: unless for capital offences, when the proof is evident or the presumption great.

Sec. 8. No person shall be held to answer for a capital or otherwise infamous crime, (except in cases of impeachment, and in cases of militia when in actual service, and the land naval forces in time of war, or which this State may keep with the consent of Congress in time of peace, and in cases of petit larceny under the regulation of the Legislature) unless on presentment or indictment of a grand jury; and in any trial in any court whatever, the party accused shall be allowed to appear and defend in person and with counsel, as in civil actions. No person shall be subject to be twice put jeopardy for the same offence; nor shall he be compelled, in any criminal case, to be a witness against himself, nor be deprived of life, liberty, or property, without due process of law; nor shall private property be taken for public use without just compensation.

Sec. 9. Every citizen may freely speak, write, and publish his sentiments on all subjects, being responsible for the abuse of that right; and no law shall be passed to restrain or abridge the liberty of speech or of the press. In all criminal prosecutions on indictments for libels, the truth may be given in evidence to the jury; and if it shall appear to the jury that the matter charged as libellous is true, and was published with good motives and for justifiable ends, the party shall be acquitted; and the jury shall have the right to determine the law and the fact.

Sec. 10. The people shall have the right freely to assemble together, to consult for the common good, to instruct their representatives, and to petition the legislature for redress of grievances.

Sec. 11. All laws of a general nature shall have a uniform operation.

Sec. 12. The military shall be subordinate to the civil power. No standing army shall be kept up by this State in time of peace; and in time of war no appropriation for a standing army shall be for a longer time than two years.

Sec. 13. No soldier shall, in time of peace, be quartered in any house, without the consent of the owner; nor in time of war, except in the manner to be prescribed by law.

Sec. 14. Representation shall be apportioned according to population.

Sec. 15. No person shall be imprisoned for debt, in any civil action on mesne or final process, unless in cases of fraud; and no person shall be imprisoned for a militia fine in time of peace.

Sec. 16. No bill of attainder, ex post facto law, or law impairing the obligation of contracts, shall ever be passed.

Sec. 17. Foreigners who are, of who hereafter become bona fide residents if this State, shall enjoy the same rights in respect to the possession, enjoyment, and inheritance of property, as native born citizens,

Sec. 18. Neither slavery, nor involuntary servitude, unless for the punishment of crimes, shall ever be tolerated in this State.

Sec. 19. The right of the people to be secure in their persons, houses, papers and effects, against unreasonable seizures and searches, shall not be violated; and no warrant shall issue but on probable cause, supported by oath or affirmation, particularly describing the place to be searched, and the persons and things to be seized.

Sec. 20. Treason against the State shall consist only in levying war against it, adhering to its enemies, or giving them aid and comfort. No person shall be convicted of treason, unless the evidence of two witnesses to the same overt act, or confession in open court.

Sec. 21. This enumeration of rights shall not be construed to impair or deny others retained by the people.

Article II.

Right of Suffrage.

Sec. 1. Every white male citizen of the United States, and every white male citizen of Mexico, who shall have elected to become a citizen of the United States, under the treaty of peace exchanged and ratified at Queretaro, on the 30th day of May, 1848 of the age of twenty–one years, who shall have been a resident of the State six months next preceding the election, and the county or district in which he claims his vote thirty days, shall be entitled to vote at all elections which are now or hereafter may authorized by law: Provided, nothing herein contained, shall be construed to prevent the Legislature, by a two–thirds concurrent vote, from admitting to the right of suffrage, Indians or the descendants of Indians, in such special cases as such proportion of the legislative body may deem just and proper.

Sec. 2. Electors shall, in all cases except treason, felony, or breach of the peace, be privileged from arrest on the days of the election, during their attendance at such election, going to and returning therefrom.

Sec. 3. No elector shall be obliged to perform militia duty on the day of election, except in time of war or public danger.

Sec. 4. For the purpose of voting, no person shall be deemed to have gained or lost a residence by reason of his presence or absence while employed in the service of the United States; nor while engaged in the navigation of the waters of this State, or of the United States, or of the high seas; nor while a student of any seminary of learning; nor while kept at any almshouse, or other asylum, at public expense; nor while confined in any public prison.

Sec. 5. No idiot or insane person, or person convicted of any infamous crime, shall be entitled to the privilege of an elector.

Sec. 6. All elections by the people shall be by ballot.

5. California Land Act of 1851

State of California

Primary Source

Act to Ascertain and Settle the Private Land Claims in the State of California

Be it enacted by the Senate and House of Representatives of the United States of America in Congress assembled, That for the purpose of ascertaining and settling private land claims in the State of California, a commission shall be, and is hereby, constituted, which shall consist of three commissioners, to be appointed by the President of the United States, by and with the advice and consent of the Senate, which commission shall continue for three years from the date of this act, unless sooner discontinued by the President of the United States.

Sec. 8. *And be it further enacted,* That each and every person claiming lands in California by virtue of any right or title derived from the Spanish or Mexican government, shall present the same to the said commissioners when sitting as a board, together with such documentary evidence and testimony of witnesses as the said claimant relies upon in support of such claims; and it shall be the duty of the commissioners, when the case is ready for hearing, to proceed promptly to examine the same upon such evidence, and upon the evidence produced in behalf of the United States, and to decide upon the validity of the said claim, and, within thirty days after such decision is rendered, to certify the same, with the reasons on which it is founded, to the district attorney of the United States in and for the district in which such decision shall be rendered.

Sec. 9. *And be it further enacted,* That in all cases of the rejection or confirmation of any claim by the board of commissioners, it shall and -may be lawful for the claimant or the district attorney, in behalf of the United States, to present a petition to the District Court of the district in which the land claimed is situated, praying the said court to review the decision of the said commissioners, and to decide on the validity of such claim; and such petition, if presented by the claimant, shall set forth fully the nature of the claim and the names of the original and present claimants, and shall contain a deraignment[1] of the claimant's title, together with a transcript of the report of the board of commissioners, and of the documentary evidence and testimony of the witnesses on which it was founded; and such petition, if presented by the district attorney in behalf of the United States, shall be accompanied by a transcript of the report of the board of commissioners, and of the papers and evidence on which it was founded, and shall fully and distinctly set forth the grounds on which the said claim is alleged to be invalid, a copy of which petition, if the same shall be presented by a claimant, shall be served on the district attorney of the United States, and, if presented in behalf of the United States, shall be served on the claimant or his attorney; and the party upon whom such service shall be made shall be bound to answer the same within a time to be prescribed by the judge of the District Court; and the answer of the claimant to such petition shall set forth fully the nature of the claim, and the names of the original and present claimants, and shall contain a deraignment of the claimant's tide; and the answer of the district attorney in behalf of the United States shall fully and distinctly set forth the grounds on which the said claim is alleged to be invalid, copies of which answers shall be served upon the adverse party thirty days before the meeting of the court, and thereupon, at the first term of the court thereafter, the said case shall stand for trial, unless, on cause shown, the same shall be continued by the court.

Sec. 10. *And be it further enacted,* That the District Court shall proceed to render judgment upon the pleadings and evidence in the case, and upon such further evidence as may be taken by order of the said court, and shall, on application of the party against whom judgment is rendered, grant an appeal to the Supreme Court of the United States, on such security for costs in the District and Supreme Court, in case the judgment of the District Court shall be affirmed, as the said court shall prescribe; and if the court shall be satisfied that the party desiring to appeal is unable to give such security, the appeal may be allowed without security.

6. A Pioneer at Sutter's Fort, c. 1850

By Marguerite Eyer Wilbur

Primary Source

Sutter's Fort

As we approached Sutter's Fort, my companion, Heinrich Thomen, and I, tossed our hats into the air and shouted for sheer joy, now that the long overland trip from St. Louis to California, a trip of more than four months' duration, was almost over. After weeks of plodding over hot dusty plains and scaling the rugged Sierras, it was an immense relief to know that our goal, the fort, was only a few miles away. My heart pounded with excitement.

It was not long before the road swung toward the left and curved past a clump of willows on the bank of the American Fork where I saw some blackberry vines. Hungry for fresh fruit, I stopped long enough to pick a handful of these luscious berries. Unfortunately they stained my best suit, which I was wearing in honor of the occasion; it took me a long time and a considerable amount of scrubbing with cold water dipped out of the river to get it clean again. But the fruit was unbelievably delicious; I never ate better berries while I was in California. The following year I tried to locate the same bushes, but in some mysterious way they had vanished.

As I rounded a sharp bend in the irregular road, I saw in the distance several cattle corrals; beyond them, not far from the trail, stood a plain, even primitive house where two attractive white women were leaning out of an open window, watching us approach. They spoke to us as we drew near, and said the property on which they were living belonged to a Mr. Sinclair, a Scotsman who was justice of the peace. One of the two women who talked to us was his wife. The building was delightfully situated near the bank of the American Fork at a point where the river was unusually smooth and broad.

There was no ferry across the American Fork, so Thomen and I had to wade the crystal-clear but shallow stream with our bare feet. We reached the opposite bank without difficulty, where the trail meandered first through marshlands which were often entirely under water when the river overflowed, and then up and across high ground, where a solitary Indian hut stood on a dry knoll near a deep waterhole.

As the road we were walking now curved again, suddenly a commodious adobe structure, whose walls contained large holes that held guns, loomed up near us; directly east of it stood two small corrals and a dry lake which was filled in the spring when the American Fork broke through its banks. This was where Sutter kept the flocks of sheep he hired me to take charge of two years later. Even a superficial glance showed that the soil on either side of the trail leading to the fort was too poor to raise crops on, but not far away was the lush, river-bottom land where the energetic Sutter had planted the grain that yielded such enormous harvests. His wonderful wheatfields were already famous all over California.

A mile or more beyond the river, the trail crossed a small hill; from its crest the massive walls of Sutter's Fort, which its owner called New Helvetia, were now visible. It was one of the happiest moments of my life, as I stood there and gazed at my actual, my final destination. After passing several more adobe corrals Thomen and I reached the main gate of the fort. There a gruesome sight met my eyes: the long, black hair and skull of an Indian dangling from one of the gateposts. Even more impressive were the large cannon that stood ominously on either side of the entrance and gave the fort a cold, inhospitable look. Fifty or sixty feet inside of the fort I saw a two-story adobe structure; its door was also guarded by guns, mounted on wheels, that pointed their cold muzzles at all visitors.

At that particular moment, however, I was much more interested in meat and bread than in guns. Food, I was told, was sold in a room directly east of the adobe house. As I was making some purchases in the fort store, I was accosted by several young men who had recently enlisted in the United States army, not so much from abstract patriotic motives as from the concrete fact that Uncle Sam supplied three square meals a day. As a result, these young fellows now spent their time urging every new emigrant in from the States to sign up for service. After considerable argument between us and explanations on their part, I finally enlisted. With the fresh meat we had bought, Thomen and I prepared supper over a campfire near the fort; each of us devoured an enormous beeksteak, a cut of meat for which California was then famous. Later we went to the nearby barracks.

This thing of being a member of the United States army was a new experience to me, as you can understand, so I meekly obeyed orders. After being assigned to one of the companies, I was told to remain at the fort until more volunteers enlisted. Meanwhile, Thomen left the military post to explore the surrounding countryside. When he returned, he told me he had met and talked with the famous Captain Sutter, who had regaled him with tales of his wonderful experiences of adventurous pioneering in California.

During their conversation, Thomen told him all about his own trip west, and of course he mentioned me. Sutter assured him that I was just the type of man he needed at the fort and added that he would like to make me his overseer in place of a drunken Englishman who was called Smith. Unfortunately, I was not free to accept this offer, having already signed at the request of my friend Rippstein, for military service. But it was an opportunity any young man would have welcomed, and I now regretted bitterly that I had decided to become a soldier.

I was eager to meet my distinguished countryman. For years all the newspapers in the United States had been full of stories about him; the amazing tales of his adventures were familiar to everyone. The noted Sutter, according to reports, had been a captain in the Swiss guards, and had fought under Napoleon. He had made the same favorable impression on Thomen that he did on every traveler who came to the fort, and my friend was so loud in his praises of his affable ways, fine appearance, and generosity, that he seemed almost superhuman. I had been brought up to believe that "all is not gold that glistens," and I began to wonder just what Sutter was actually like under his suave exterior.

No sooner had Thomen departed than I saw a man who resembled his description of the Swiss captain come out of the large house and walk over toward one of the small rooms that lined the inner walls of the fort. He looked around and saw me; I was somewhat bashful, but finally decided to go up and introduce myself. I was delighted to find that it was Sutter himself, who, when he heard that I was the young man Thomen had told him about, was extremely cordial, and seemed genuinely disappointed when I said I could not accept his offer of employment because I had joined the army. Sutter made me promise, however, that I would return and work for him when the war was over. I blamed myself bitterly now for the rash step I had taken just before this unusual opening appeared, and told my new friend that I would

A drawing of Sutter's Fort, ca. 1840s. Engraved by J. H. Richardson.

accept his offer the moment that I was discharged from military service.

After that we talked together for a long time. The captain reviewed the main events of his past life at considerable length; as I listened to his pithy conversation, to his tales so highly colored with romance and adventure, I was spellbound. He was an incredibly entertaining talker, and for the time being at least, believed it all, in spite of myself.

Upon reaching the Pacific Coast, young Sutter made friends with the crew of a ship from Sitka, a fur- trading post owned by a Russian company and when he told them he was an ex-captain of the Swiss guards, they were so favorably impressed that they invited him to accompany them when their ship left for the north.

The dreary, fog-bound town of Sitka was a disappointment to Sutter; he left on the first vessel sailing for the balmy land of Honolulu. After eight pleasant, leisurely months in the Hawaiian Islands, he crossed the Pacific in a small bark with a group of native men and women called Kanakas, and landed at the Mexican port of Mazatlan.

There he met Senor Juan Alvarado, who had just been appointed Mexican governor of Upper California and who was about to leave for his new post at Monterey. From him Sutter learned that the Sacramento and San Joaquin valleys, which were inhabited only by Indians, were among the most fertile regions in all California and that the policy of the Mexican government was to colonize this country as soon as possible. Alvarado made an agreement with him whereby the Swiss captain was to receive some light iron cannon and some old muskets, provided he would settle in the Sacramento Valley. The governor also promised him food, beads, and miscellaneous garments for the Indians and agreed that when he had induced ten white men and their families to settle along the Sacramento, Feather, and Yuba rivers, the American Fork, or Bear Creek, he would receive eleven square leagues of land, a small principality, from the Mexican government.

In colorful language Sutter described how he and his Kanakas placed what equipment and supplies they needed in several small boats, crossed the bay toward the entrance to the Sacramento, located its mouth, sailed up to its branch, the American Fork, and ascended it for a short distance. It was there on high open ground on the right bank that he decided to camp and found a settlement. He was the first white man to live in this Indian country.

7. *The Californian* Modestly Announces the Discovery of Gold, 1848

The Californian

Primary Source

WM. H. [...]
Wholesale and Retail Merchant.
San Francisco, Alta California.

KILBORN, LAWTON & CO.
General Commission Merchants,
AND DEALERS IN
OREGON PRODUCE.
Consignments respectfully solicited.—
Refer to
C. L. ROSS,
San Francisco.
S. H. WILLIAMS, & Co.,
Honolulu, S. I.
Oregon City, Nov. 1st, 1847,   23-tf

L. EVERHART,
FASHIONABE TAILOR.
Montgomery Street, San Francisco, U. C.

L. W. HASTINGS.
Attorney and Counsellor at Law, and
Solicitor in Chancery.
San Francisco, Upper California.   y-5

EVERETT & CO.,
General Commission Merchants,
E. P. EVERETT, }
J. JARVES.   } Honolulu, Oahu, H. I.
☞ Money advanced, on favorable terms,
for Bills of Exchange on the United States,
England and France.
Honolulu, 1847.   tf-33

S. H. WILLIAMS, & CO.
General Commission Merchants,
HONOLULU, OAHU.
S. H. WILLIAMS, }
J. F. B. MARSHALL, } HAWAIIAN ISLANDS.
WM. BAKER, JR. }
Exchange on the United States & Europe,
taken on the most favorable terms.   26-3m

JASPER O'FARRELL.
Civil Engineer and Land Surveyor,
By appointment of Col. R. B. MASON, Gov.
of California.
(Office Portsmouth Square, San Francisco.)

J. D. [...]LURG, y Co.
Los Angeles y 8 de Enero de 1848. 37-tf

KNOW ALL MEN BY THESE PRE-
SENTS, that I, RICHARD B. MASON, Col.
1st Regiment of Dragoons, United States
Army, and Governor of California, by virtue
of authority in me vested, do hereby appoint JACOB R. SNYDER, Land Surveyor, in
the Middle Department of Upper California.
Done at Monterey, the Capital of California, this the 22d day of July 1847, and the
72d of the Independence of the United
States.
R. B. MASON, Col. 1st Drag's.
12-tf   Gov. of California.

JUST LANDED.
1 case superior Ladies Hosiery, to be
sold low by the dozen, at the
40   BEE HIVE.

IRON POTS.
100 three-leg'd Iron Pots for sale, a bargain, at the
40   BEE HIVE.

TO INVALIDS & OTHERS.
Messrs DICKSON & HAY have just received, and now on hand 100,000 lbs. superior ARROW ROOT and 500 lbs. COCOA,
recommended by the faculty, well worthy the
attention of Invalids, &c.

GOLD MINE FOUND.—In the newly
made raceway of the Saw Mill recently
erected by Captain Sutter, on the American Fork, gold has been found in considerable quantities. One person brought thirty
dollars worth to New Helvetia, gathered
there in a short time. California, no doubt,
is rich in mineral wealth; great chances
here for scientific capitalists. Gold has
been found in almost every part of the
country.

8. The Impact of the Gold Rush, 1849

By Walter Colton

Primary Source

...

The excitement produced was intense; and many were soon busy in their hasty preparations for a departure to the mines. The family who had kept house for me caught the moving infection. Husband and wife were both packing up; the blacksmith dropped his hammer, the carpenter his plane, the mason his trowel, the farmer his sickle, the baker his loaf, and the tapster his bottle. All were off for the mines, some on horses, some on carts, and some on crutches, and one went in a litter. An American woman, who had recently established a boarding-house here, pulled up stakes, and was off before her lodgers had even time to pay their bills. Debtors ran, of course, I have only a community of women left and a gang of prisoners, with here and there a soldier, who will give his captain the slip at the first chance. I don't blame the fellow a whit: seven dollars a month, while others are making two or three hundred a day! that is too much for human nature to stand.

Saturday, July 15. The gold fever has reached every servant in Monterey; none are to he trusted in their engagement beyond a week, and as for compulsion, it is like attempting to drive fish into a net with the ocean before them. Gen. Mason, Lieut. Lanman, and myself, form a mess; we have a house, and all the table; furniture and culinary apparatus requisite; but our servants have run, one after another, till we are almost in despair: even Sambo, who we thought would stick by from laziness, if no other cause, ran last night; and this morning, for the fortieth time, we had to lake to the kitchen, and cook our own breakfast. A

general of the United States Army the commander of a man-of-war, and the Alcalde of Monterey, in a smoking kitchen, grinding coffee, toasting a herring, and pealing onions! These gold mines are going to upset all the domestic arrangements of society, turning the head to the tail, and the tail to the head. ...

Thursday, Aug. 16. Four citizens of Monterey are just in from the gold mines on Feather River, where they worked in company with three others. They employed about thirty wild Indians, who are attached to the rancho owned by one of the party. They worked precisely seven weeks and three days, and have divided seventy-six thousand eight hundred and forty-four dollars—nearly eleven thousand dollars to each. Make a dot there, and let me introduce a man, well known to me, who has worked on the Yuba river sixty-four days, and brought back, as the result of his Individual labor, five thousand three hundred and fifty-six dollars. Make a dot there, and let me introduce another townsman, who has worked on the North Fork fifty-seven days, and brought back four thousand five hundred and thirty-four dollars. Make a dot there, and let me introduce a boy, fourteen years of age, who has worked on the Mokelumne fifty-four days, and brought back three thousand four hundred and sixty-seven dollars. Make another dot there, and let me introduce a woman, of Sonoranian birth, who has worked in the dry diggings forty-six days, and brought back two thousand one hundred and twenty-five dollars. Is not this enough to make a man throw down his leger and shoulder a pick? But the deposits which yielded these harvests were now opened for the

Advertisement for ships to California, c. 1850s.

first time: they were the accumulation of ages; only the foot-prints of the elk and wild savage had passed over them. Their slumber was broken for the first time by the sturdy arms of the American emigrant.

Tuesday. Aug. 28. The gold mines have upset all social and domestic arrangements in Monterey; the master has become his own servant, and the servant his own lord. The millionaire is obliged to groom his own horse, and roll his wheel barrow.
…

9. California As I Saw It, 1848–1850

By William S. M'Collum

Primary Source

So much for the topographical description of San Francisco, and now it is presumed, some account of the city, "as I found it," will be looked for: and it is a difficult task, for it is unique—a thing without a parallel,—one that admits of no comparisons, for there is nothing like it in the histories of cities. We have prided ourselves in this country of knowing something of the sudden rise of towns and cities: we have had our Lowell, Syracuse, Rochester, Lockport, Buffalo, and farther Cleveland, Toledo, Detroit, Chicago, Milwaukee. But all these are eclipsed, by the enterprise of our own people, in a locality, far, far away, upon the western coast of the Pacific, in a region of which we knew nothing, but a few years ago, save that which we gleaned from an occasional book of travels; where it is less than two years since the "stars and stripes" were first thrown out to the breeze, to confirm our accession and jurisdiction! True has it been said that the world's history has no page so marvellous as the one that has been turned here!

Such an anomaly must be seen to be justly appreciated. No language will convey to the reader, a tithe of its singular features. I will speak of it here, as it was upon our arrival the 5th of July, and in another connection, as it was a few months after, when we passed through it on our return home. The Population of all kinds, permanent residents, gold diggers on their way to the mines, and miscellaneous adventurers, was between six and seven thousand. There was a show of frame and brick buildings on one or two streets, some of them tolerably respectable in size and architecture, but most of them exhibiting evidence that they were put up in a hurry. Canvass houses and tents completed the landscape of the embryo city, and they were scattered about in profusion, occupying vacant lots and squares, here and there stretching off in some favored locality, and forming detached colonies. It was a ragged, novel scene. There were at least four thousand "dwellers in tents" and canvass houses. It was a busy population, bustling, full of excitement, of bright and buoyant hopes. With the newly arrived adventurer, there was a foretaste of what his imagination could easily convert into a self-possessed reality; there were the glimmerings, the assurances, of the full fruition of his most ardent expectations. The returned gold-diggers were there with their "piles," exhibiting the glittering "lumps" and bags of "scales" and "dust"; elated with their acquisitions; in some instances, giddy with their suddenly acquired wealth- opening to the imagination of the new comers rich "placers" and a wide field bestrewed with the object of their long and tedious journey; weaving upon a warp of reality a glittering woof of fancy. "Light comes, light goes," is an old adage, and it was well illustrated at San Francisco. There were prudent men among the returned gold diggers, but the majority of them were as reckless of their gain, the

product of severe toil and privation, as if they had scooped it from the surface of the earth, instead of delving for it beneath. There was but little coin in circulation—no paper money of course—gold as it came from the mines was the principal medium of exchange and traffic. It was rated at sixteen dollars an ounce, and weighed in all manner of scales; many of them such as our apothecaries would not trust with their moderately high priced drugs. No body thought of disputing weights, or contending against "down weights," as some of our economical farmers would, when selling their coarse grains. There was not much difficult? growing out of infinitesimal, or homoeopathic fractions and divisions, for there were allopathic prices for everything- Liberality, profusion, was catching: those going to the mines, seeing how flush those were that had been and returned, depleted their consumptive purses as if they had been plethoric. The conclusion was, that when their money was gone, they had only to go out to the mines, stoop down, and pick up more. But ah! that *stooping* down, that creaking of joints under a new discipline—that forward leaning of the vertebra, till it described a half circle, and keeping it there until it would hesitate to go back to its place, like the bow which has been too long bent; that back-ache and head-ache; there was far less of fun in it, of play and poetry—it was, to tell the truth, more "like work" than had been taken into the account; as the reader shall be told, if his patience will continue with us in our adventures.

Most, of all we found in San Francisco, were from this country, though there was a sprinkling of Mexicans, Chileans, Peruvians, Chinese, Sandwich Islanders, and a very few from England and France. The Chinese were generally, carpenters, laborers, and keepers of rude shops and eating houses. They were not, I should judge, your real "celestials," but a kind of half way "outside barbarians," who acquired a little knowledge with the world, by dwelling in the commercial

A photograph of the San Francisco harbor (aka Yerba Buena Cove), ca. 1850–1851.

marts of China. The shop keepers were as keen as if they had taken lessons in our own Puritan, over-reaching, New England; and although the cooking in their eating houses, was generally of a strange hash medley, I saw no "chop sticks,"—no mourners of the canine species, for their martyred companions; no veritable rat tails in their soups. The Chileans were generally traders and keepers of eating houses; were mostly harmless and inoffensive. The "Kanakers [Kanakas]," or Sandwich Islanders, were common laborers and porters. There were a few native Californians, not to exceed two hundred. The city government consisted of an alcalde, and some kind of city council; the municipal affairs were crude and undigested, as a matter of course; and yet there was a tolerable government, a security of life and property which could hardly have been anticipated; its strength

and support being the character of a large majority of those suddenly thrown together, whose self-preservation depended upon the maintenance of law and order.

There were not less than one hundred vessels in port, mostly American; a few Chilean brigs. The number was rapidly accumulating. When a vessel reached there, it was soon deserted by its crew, and left with its officers; and in many instances officers and all, were off to the mines leaving the vessel to take care of itself. Sailors are proverbially fond of their pursuit—have usually a contempt for land service; but gold, its supposed easy acquisition—in this instance, prevailed over enlistments, engagement, and discipline.

Gold and gold digging absorbed everything. California was emphatically, a country of "one idea." It was there, the reign of Mammon,—all were his votaries, and they were as absorbed, as "set apart" for his service, as if bound by religious vows. There had been but little of systematic agricultural pursuits, since the breaking up of the mission establishments, many years previous, but, on the discovery of gold, this, as well as all other ordinary pursuits, was abandoned. In a semi-official letter, from Captain S. [*i.e.*, Joseph] L. Folsom of the U. S. Army, serving in California, of date, September 18th, 1848, a little over seven months from the first discovery of gold, the following graphic sentence occurs:—

"Villages and districts, where all had been bustle, industry and improvement, were soon left without a male population. Mechanics, merchants, lawyers, doctors, magistrates, were alike off to the mines, and all kinds of useful occupation, gold digging excepted, were apparently at an end. In most cases the crops were remarkably good; but they are generally lost for the want of laborers to secure them. In some parts of the country hundreds of acres of fine wheat will rot in the field from the improbability of getting white laborers. Vessels are left swinging idly at their anchors, while both captains and crews are at the mines."

And all this had been increasing, with a rapid influx of adventurers from abroad, in the time that had intervened between the date of Capt. Folsom's letter, and the period of our arrival. There were but two branches of business, that to any great extent diverted from gold digging, and those, arbitrarily, were principally consequent upon it. Building, in the principal marts of the mining districts, had to be done of course, to shelter persons and property;

and there was necessarily a carrying trade upon the waters of the bay and its tributaries. All this demanded the employment of labor, and the prices paid were enormous. They were regulated by the earnings in the mines;—no man would work for less than he supposed he could earn in gold digging, and many got much more than they would have got in the mines. There was a brisk commercial business going on upon the bay, the Rio Sacramento, the Rio San Joaquin, and their navigable tributaries, that flowed from the mining districts. Not less than one hundred steamboats, schooners, brigs, sloops, lighters and whale boats, were upon these waters, carrying forward miners, their tools and camp equipage. San Francisco was the focus, the temporary halting place of the great throng that came across the Isthmus, and arriving by sea, spread themselves over the extended gold region. It may well be imagined that in the mass so suddenly thrown together, there was bustle and excitement; parties were leaving the newly arrived vessels and pitching their tents for a few days of preparation, or stowing themselves away in the crowded and ill-provided hotels and boarding houses; others, who were allowed a few days' stay upon the vessels they came in, were trans-shipping, directly for Sacramento and Stockton. Squads of newly arrived adventurers, were gathering here and there, to listen to the stories of returned miners, and take their advice as to the most promising localities in the mining district, and the best mode of getting there. There was a "confusion of tongues" as in the building of the tower of Babel, for the greater portion of the world had their representatives there.

10. Life in the Mines in 1849

By J. E. Pleasants

Primary Source

In October in 1849 our train of about one hundred people arrived at Bidwell's Bar. This is on Feather river about sixty miles north of Sacramento. It is a beautiful spot, a swift mountain stream flowing between mountains covered with pine forests. The camp was named for General Bidwell who discovered gold there and was still working his claims with Indian labor. John Bidwell was a fine type of the western pioneer, a young man who had left home at an early age to make his own way in the world, and a prime mover in organizing the first emigrant train to cross the plains. As he was going in to Sacramento a few days after our arrival he took in letters for the whole train, the first they had been able to send home since leaving Ft. Laramie. The bar was about a quarter of a mile long and two to three hundred yards wide. The gold had been deposited in these bars where the water had thrown them up on the sides of the streams, leaving the channel clean. There were about thirty or forty miners on the bar ahead of our train, but there were still some claims to be staked. It was supposed to be rich diggings, so the claims were only twenty five feet square on the bar. Back in the ravines they were larger. Only twenty of our train stayed at Bidwell's, the rest scattered out to other camps. My father decided to stay. The first thing to be done was to make some provision for the stock. There was no feed for them in the mountains, so they were sent down to the Sacramento valley where grass was abundant. The Sacramento valley at that time was covered with wild oats. The miners made themselves comfortable for the winter in log or shake cabins made from the pines that grew on the hill sides along the river. Each cabin had its stone chimney, which served both for warmth and cooking. Some of our party who were in a great hurry to go to mining satisfied themselves with camping in their wagons and tents, but I think they must have regretted it before the winter was over, as 1849 was a wet winter, my father's claims turned out very well. On an average claim a man could make ten to twenty dollars a day. It was placer diggings and worked with a rocker and pan. The rocker was a box four or five feet long set on rockers like an old fashioned cradle, with riffles in it to hold the gold as it was washed. There was a hopper in the upper end with a screen. The pay dirt, was shovelled into this, water thrown in and the rocker kept in motion, throwing out the rocks and gravel occasionally, until there was nothing left but the gold and the black sand. There was considerable scale gold as large as cucumber seed, also finer dust, which was collected from the sand by using a magnet. The miners made laws among themselves, as it became necessary and saw that were enforced. This regulated the size of claims according to conditions. A claim must be worked at least one day in the week in order to be held. Out of these grew our present mining laws. California was a pioneer in this, as mining was a new thing in the United States.

Provisions were high, but there was little complaint as every one had money. Flour was a dollar a pound and other things in proportion.

The main staples were pickled pork, flour, beans, coffee brown sugar molasses and dried fruit, principally apples. Milk and butter were not

A 1849 photo of California Gold Rush miners.

on the bill of fare. Just before Christmas one of the miners went down to the Sacramento valley and brought up a fat ox, which he butchered and sold for a dollar a pound. The meat was very much appreciated by the miners and it netted the owner five hundred dollars. There was little for entertainment in the evenings. There were few books and no newspapers to be had.

This being the case every body played cards, but among the miners in the camps I never saw them play for money. In Sacramento there were luxurious gambling houses, brilliantly lighted, and entertained their guests with fine music. A good string band was usually supplied Minors were not allowed to play at any of the games in these houses. I have visited them with my father to see the sights and listen to the music, he never played. On two occasions I remember seeing the proprietor refuse to let boys play. We stayed through the winter at Bidwell's, then my father had worked out his claims and we went over to

the Honcut, where he had heard there were some good prospects. We stayed there about a year, returning to the bar for provisions as we needed them. We had to carry all our supplies from there on our backs. It was while on the Honcut that my brother and I found the heads and horns of some of our oxen that had brought us across the plains.

It was at a deserted Indian village in the foothills. And as we never saw any of our cattle again, my father concluded that the Indians had killed and eaten them. The Honcut was quite a thriving camp.

There was one old Frenchmen who had some good claims which he was working with Indians, The old chief's son robbed our camp one day when we were all away, and my father had to use strenuous measures to get the goods back. The miners were a very generous set of men. Money was plentiful, and they spent it freely. I will relate a case in point which well illustrates the temper of the day. A Missouri miner lost his eyesight in an

Map of California gold fields..

explosion. He had not yet taken out much gold, and this left him helpless. The Missourians called a meeting to see what could be done.

The chairman after calling the meeting to order, said we will not call on any except Missourians to help". Instantly there arose a New Yorker to protest against this. He said "That is not fair to the rest of us, we all want to help." The chairman had to explain that he did not wish to bar the others, but was only not asking them to contribute.

The chairman then asked one manto take the scales and another to take charge of the dust; and in less than half an hour there was collected five thousand dollars for the blind man. There was a miner from his county in Missouri, who had made his pile and was going home, that would take charge of the blind man and take him back to his family.

The early miners were not the rough set that we often hear them called. They were for a great part young men from the Eastern farming sections. There was also a fair sprinkling of professional men. In our camp at Bidwell's Bar there were several women, which was unusual that early. There was one man with his wife from our train, and I well remember a doctor and his wife and two little girls. I one day heard the doctor tell his wife who evidently took care of the drugs, to be careful of the Quinine, because he said its worth ounce for ounce.

My father only stayed in the mines about eighteen months, then took up land in the little valley that bears his name, about thirty miles from Sacramento. There we had for one of our nearest neighbor Mr. John Wolfskill, a brother of William Wolfskill of Los Angeles. Mr. Wolfskill had settled there in 1842. He had a fine ranch well stocked, and was a very kind and hospitable neighbor. There lived at his house at the time young George Donner and Solomon Hook his half brother, who were two children, survivors of the ill-fated Donner party. Edward Wolfskill his son and these boys and I were playmates. Edward is still living at the old home.

J. E. Pleasants.

11. The "Dame Shirley" Letters, 1851

By Louisa Amelia Knapp Smith Clappe

Primary/Secondary Source

RICH BAR, MIDDLE FORK OF FEATHER RIVER,
FROM A PAINTING MADE IN 1851, IN POSSESSION OF MR. F. B. WHITING, QUINCY.

Rich Bar, middle fork of Feather River, in gold fields of Northern California. From a painting made in 1851, artist unknown.

Letter Sixth

A Trip into the Mines

Rich Bar,
East Branch of the North Fork of Feather River,
September 30, 1851

I think that I have never spoken to you of the mournful extent to which profanity prevails in California. You know that at home it is considered vulgar for a gentleman to swear; but I am told that here, it is absolutely the fashion, and that people who never uttered an oath in their lives while in the "States," now "clothe themselves with curses as with a garment." Some try to excuse themselves by saying that it is a careless habit, into which they have glided imperceptibly, from having been compelled to associate so long with the vulgar and the profane; that it is a mere slip of the tongue, which means absolutely nothing, etc. I am willing to believe this, and to think as charitably as possible of many persons here, who have unconsciously adopted a custom which I know they abhor. Whether there is more profanity in the mines than elsewhere, I know not; but during the short time that I have been at Rich Bar, I have *heard* more of it than in all my life before. Of course, the most vulgar blackguard will abstain from swearing in the *presence* of a lady; but in this rag and card-board house, one is compelled to hear the most sacred of names constantly profaned by the drinkers and gamblers who haunt the bar-room at all hours. And this is a custom which the gentlemanly and quiet proprietor, much as he evidently dislikes it, cannot possibly prevent.

Some of these expressions, were they not so fearfully blasphemous, would be grotesquely sublime. For instance; not five minutes ago, I heard

Handbill from the California Gold Rush.

two men quarrelling in the street, and one said to the other, "only let me get hold of your beggarly carcase once, and I will use you up so small that God Almighty himself cannot see your *ghost!*"

To live thus in constant danger of being hushed to ones rosy rest by a ghastly lullaby of oaths, is revolting in the extreme. For that reason, and because it is infinitely more comfortable during the winter season, than a plank-house, F. has concluded to build a log-cabin, where, at least, I shall not be *obliged* to hear the solemn names of the Father and the dear Master so mockingly profaned.

But it is not the swearing alone which disturbs my slumber. There is a dreadful flume, the machinery of which, keeps up the most dismal moaning and shrieking all the livelong night—painfully suggestive of a suffering child. But, oh dear! you don't know what that is, do you? Now, if I was scientific, I would give you such a vivid description of it, that you would see a pen and ink flume staring at you from this very letter. But alas! my own ideas

on the subject, are in a state of melancholy vagueness. I will do my possible, however, in the way of explanation. A flume, then, is an immense trough, which takes up a portion of the river, and, with the aid of a dam, compels it to run in another channel, leaving the vacated bed of the stream ready for mining purposes.

There is a gigantic project now on the *tapis* of fluming the entire river for many miles, commencing a little above Rich Bar. Sometimes these fluming companies are eminently successful; at others, their operations are a dead failure.

But in truth, the whole mining system in California is one great gambling, or better, perhaps—lottery transaction. It is impossible to tell whether a "claim" will prove valuable or not. F. has invariably sunk money on every one that he has bought. Of course, a man who works a "claim" himself, is more likely—even should it turn out poor—"to get his money back," as they say—than one who, like F., hires it done.

A few weeks since, F. paid a thousand dollars for a "claim," which has proved utterly worthless. He might better have thrown his money into the river than to have bought it; and yet some of the most experienced miners on the Bar, thought that it would "pay."

But I began to tell you about the different noises which disturb my peace of mind by day, and my repose of body by night, and have gone instead, into a financial disquisition upon mining prospects. Pray forgive me, even though I confess that I intend some day, when I feel *statistically* inclined, to bore you with some profound remarks upon the claiming, drifting, sluicing, ditching, fluming and coyoting politics of the "diggins."

But to return to my sleep murderers. The rolling on the bowling alley never leaves off for ten consecutive minutes at any time during the entire twenty-four hours. It is a favorite amusement at the mines; and the only difference that Sunday makes, is, that then it never leaves off for *one* minute.

Besides the flume and the bowling alley, there is an inconsiderate dog, which will bark from starry eve till dewy morn. I fancy that he has a wager on the subject, as all the other *puppies* seem bitten by the betting mania.

A *propos* of dogs; I found dear old Dake—the noble New Foundland which H. gave us—looking as intensely black, and as grandly aristocratical as ever. He is the only high-bred dog on the river. There is another animal, by the plebeian name of John, (what a name for a *dog!*) really a handsome creature, which looks as if he might have a faint sprinkling of good blood in his veins. Indeed, I have thought it possible that his great-grandfather was a bull-dog. But he always barks at *me*—which I consider as proof positive that he is nothing but a low-born mongrel. To be sure, his master says, to excuse him, that he never saw a woman before; but a dog of any chivalry would have recognized the gentler sex, even if it *was* the first time that he had been blessed with the sight.

In the first part of my letter, I alluded to the swearing propensities of the Rich Barians. Those of course would shock you; but though you hate slang, I know that you could not help smiling at some of their *bizarre* cant phrases.

For instance, if you tell a Rich Barian anything which he doubts, instead of simply asking you if it is true, he will *invariably* cock his head interrogatively, and almost pathetically address you with the solemn adjuration, "Honest Indian?" Whether this phrase is a slur or a compliment to the aborigines of this country, I do not know.

Again; they will agree to a proposal, with the appropriate words, "Talk enough when horses fight!" which sentence they will sometimes slightly vary to "Talk enough between gentlemen."

If they wish to borrow anything of you, they will mildly inquire if you have it "about your clothes." As an illustration; a man asked F. the other day, "If he had a spare pick-axe about his clothes." And F. himself gravely inquired of me this evening at the dinner-table, if I had "a *pickle* about my clothes."

If they ask a man an embarrassing question, or in any way have placed him in an equivocal position, they will triumphantly declare that they have "got the dead-wood on him." And they are everlastingly "going narry cent" on those of whose credit they are doubtful. There are many others which may be common enough every where, but as I never happened to hear them before, they have for me all the freshness of originality. You know that it has always been one of my pet rages, to trace cant phrases to their origin; but most of those in vogue here, would, I verily believe, puzzle Horne Tooke himself.

12. Blacks in Gold Rush California

By Rudolph M. Lapp

Secondary Source

When the gold rush began in 1848, the black population in California was no more than a few dozen. They were a blend of the earlier, pre-American period, arrivals and those who came with the American conquerors of Mexican California. By the end of 1848, their numbers were augmented by the deserters from New England ships, mostly whalers from New Bedford, Massachusetts, and by the Afro-Latin Americans who came from Mexico, Chile, and Peru. By the end of 1849, the great wave of gold seekers brought blacks from every region of the United States and the West Indies. California played host to the broadest representation of Afro-Americans in the western hemisphere. Black New Englanders met slaves from Missouri, New York blacks met black Jamaicans, and free blacks from Ohio met free Spanish-speaking blacks from south of the border. American blacks were by far the largest group, and more of them were free than slave.

According to the census of 1850, there were 962 persons of color in California, including some Sandwich Islanders (often called *Kanakas*). The majority of those called black in the census, between 600 and 700 living in the gold rush counties, were of North American origin. The others, who included Latin-American blacks, were distributed throughout the state, with some concentrations in San Francisco and Sacramento. Many of the Latin-American blacks, however, soon left California to return to their homes, chiefly in Mexico and Chile.

Well over half of the Afro-Americans in the Mother Lode counties by the beginning of 1850 were free persons. The overwhelming majority, whether free or slave, were classified as miners. Blacks from the United States who were in the mines by 1850 came from three geographic regions: the free states, chiefly New York and Massachusetts (134); the slave states of the lower and Deep South (91); and the border states of the South, to which Virginia was the greatest contributor (374). More than half of this latter group may well have been free, because the border states had the largest free Negro populations. Also, many of these black men and women, born in border states of the South, had resided in the North prior to their departure for California.

The unceasing flow of people to California had, by 1852, more than doubled the black population of the state, although blacks remained about one percent of the population. There were more than 2,000 Negroes in California by then. While the black communities of San Francisco and Sacramento became somewhat larger, the black population increase was greater in the mining communities.

There were over 1,000 blacks in the Mother Lode country, while San Francisco and Sacramento had 444 and 338 black residents respectively. In Los Angeles County there were only 45 blacks. Most of these had come with Mississippi Mormons, their former masters, to found and build the town of San Bernardino.

Gold rush maps of the Mother Lode bear witness to the presence of the Afro-Americans in those frenzied years. One finds, for instance, the place names Negro Hill or Nigger Hill, Negro Bar, and Negro Flat. They represent sites where a black man made a lucky strike or where groups of black men lived and mined. Erwin G. Gudde, historian of California place names, found over thirty locations in the state that used the term *Nigger* or *Negro* and in some cases *Negros* where the Spanish recognized the presence or importance of some black man. In addition to the above, there were sites named Negro Butte, Negro Run, Nigger Bill Bend, Nigger Jack Slough, and Arroyo de los Negros. While the word *Negro* has evaporated from current maps of California, the story of the black gold miners has survived. From splinters of information scattered among obscure sources there emerge tales of good fortune, bad luck, courage, and despair.

Many black miners tried their luck in the gold fields, but only those whose luck was exceptional gained any notice. Perhaps the first of these fortunate gold hunters was a cook named Hector, who deserted the naval squadron ship *Southhampton* in Monterey in 1848. An on-the-spot observer was present when Hector returned to Monterey with $4,000 in gold. One of the richest strikes made by anyone was that of a black man known only as Dick, who mined $100,000 worth of gold in Tuolumne County in 1848, only to lose it by gambling in San Francisco.

The stories of the two Negro Hills tell much of the black experience in gold rush California. The first Negro Hill was located on the American River, not far from where gold was originally discovered on the south fork of the river. The hill was first mined by blacks in 1849. According to one source, these men were a Massachusetts black named Kelsey and a black Methodist minister. Digging in that area continued to prove rewarding, as new finds were being made into the following year. Early in 1850 the San Francisco *Daily Alta California* reported:

> About four miles below Mormon Island on the American River, there have been new diggings discovered which prove to yield exceedingly well. They are called "Nigger Diggings" from the fact that some colored gentlemen first discovered them.

Two years later another strike was made nearby. Its proximity to Negro Hill was felt by miners to insure that a long run of profit would follow.

The original success of the two black men resulted in the growth of a Negro mining community around the hill, as well as on a nearby hill that came to be called Little Negro Hill. In 1852 two Massachusetts blacks opened a store and boardinghouse, around which a concentration of black residences grew up. Since the diggings continued to be sufficiently rewarding, the Negro Hill community continued to survive and was even stable enough to deserve the attentions of a minister. By 1854, a white Methodist clergyman was offering Sunday evening services on a regular basis. A young white New Englander, who attended these services occasionally, commented that the majority of the congregation was black. He wrote to his sister that he would have attended more consistently if he did not have to fight his prejudices every time. By 1855 the Negro Hill community had grown to about 400. Other minority peoples, particularly Chinese and Portuguese miners, became residents of this village. In 1855 Negro Hill was still described as an area with "scores of hardy miners making good wages." However, trouble soon appeared because

many of the Negro Hill community were white and prejudiced. That year drunken whites looking for a fight attacked the Negro quarters and killed one black man. They were arrested, tried, and set free by a Coloma court.

The experience of blacks in nearby Massachusetts Flat stands in contrast to that of Negro Hill. This mining community, founded by New Englanders in 1854, was composed largely of Negroes and Portuguese by the following year. Here blacks were never harassed. In the presidential election of 1856, further evidence of the contrast between Negro Hill and Massachusetts Flat is found in the voting returns. The racist Negro Hill community gave Fremont only *22* percent of their vote, while Massachusetts Flat gave this antislavery candidate 75 percent of their vote. The second Negro Hill story took place in 1851, in the southern mines near Mokelumne Hill, not far from the Mokelumne River. Unlike the Negro Hill of the northern mines, this area had many white miners working there before a black man's lucky strike. The history of this strike is associated with legend that has the ring of truth to it. As the story goes, a black man wandering into the Mokelumne Hill area looking for a claim was told by white miners to keep moving, as every spot he started to prospect was claimed to be some white man's diggings. Finally, some jokester told the black prospector to go to a high point nearby where everyone "knew" there was no gold. It was here, by digging deep enough, that he made an incredibly rich strike. The news of this find spread far and wide. The lucky black (never named in the press) soon had a black partner. As the local paper put it:

> A couple of negroes who had been at work at the cayote diggings of Mokelumne Hill went home in one of the steamers … with eighty thousand dollars that they took out of one hole during the past four months.

Thus "Negro" or "Nigger Hill" got its name and immediately became the object of a rush of miners, both black and white.

Because the black miner who gave this Negro Hill its name returned a few years later to the Mokelumne Hill area, and because Andrew Hallidie of cable-car fame, who was prospecting there, happened to meet him, a bit more is known about this man. Hallidie tells us that his name was Livingston and that he

> … was a character … over six feet, erect and well proportioned, he would attract attention anywhere, had quite a dignified way of talking and used unusually good language. …

According to Hallidie, Livingston left for England after his strike, where he had a fine time spending his money, and then decided to return to the scene of his triumph to recoup his fortunes. Livingston asked Hallidie to go into a partnership with him. At first, Hallidie balked, but he soon realized he could not work his claim alone. So he agreed to sell his claim to Livingston and a black associate. The claim was worth eight dollars a day for Livingston and his partner.

From one end of the Mother Lode counties to the other the lucky finds of black men continued to be reported through the 1850s. Items like the following were noted:

From Stockton:

> An impression has got abroad among the miners that this famous old negro has struck upon extraordinary rich diggings about two and half miles from town. … Jenkins is known to have been fortunate in all his mining operations.

From Sonora:

> Moses Dinks, a Negro, … started from his cabin between Jackass Hill and Tuttletown, … he noticed a gleaming object poking its nose skyward. Not wishing to carry twenty-five pounds of gold nor desiring to turn back to his cabin, he buried the chunk of precious metal on the spot.

From Indian Gulch, Sonora:

> A Negro, a few days ago, panned out in a few hours twenty four ounces.

From Mariposa:
Last week a German boy named Fritz, and a colored man named Duff, … found a block of gold bearing quartz, weighing one hundred and ninety three pounds … value … from $5,000 to $10,000.

On the Feather River:

> Rich diggings were accidentally discovered by a negro on this same river above Ophir.

Again from Sonora:

> … a party of colored miners … at the southern end of Jamestown, … struck upon a very rich lead, prospecting as high as one hundred and twenty dollars to the pan.

And as late as 1859 from Mariposa:

> … two colored men named Perkins and Oscar made a rich strike in a small ravine a short distance from Mariposa. … they … struck a lead or vein of decomposed slate, out of which they took in two days the sum of $1,300.

13. My Darling Clementine, 1887

By Percy Montrose

Secondary Source

66 *My Darling Clementine," perhaps the best known of all the California gold rush songs, was written by Percy Montrose a number of years after the gold rush. The song was published in Henry R. Waite's College Songs by Oliver Ditson & Company in 1887.*

In a canyon, in a cavern, excavating for a mine,
Dwelt a miner, forty-niner, and his daughter Clementine.
Light she was and like a feather, and her shoes were number nine,

Herring boxes without topses, sandals were for Clementine,
CHORUS
Oh my darling, oh my darling, oh my darling Clementine,
You are lost and gone forever, dreadful sorry, Clementine.
Drove she ducklings to the water every morning just at nine,
Stubbed her toe upon a splinter, fell into the foaming brine.

Ruby lips above the water, blowing bubbles soft and fine,
But alas, I was no swimmer, so I lost my Clementine. CHORUS

In a church-yard, near the canyon, where the myrtle doth entwine,
There grow roses, and other posies, fertilized by Clementine.
Then the miner, forty-niner, soon began to peak and pine,
Thought he oughter jine his daughter, now he's with his Clementine, CHORUS

In my dreams she still doth haunt me, robed in garments soaked in brine,
Though in life I used to hug her, now she's dead, I'll draw the line, CHORUS

New verses to "Clementine" continue to appear:

How I missed her, how I missed her, how I missed my Clementine,
So I kissed her little sister, and forgot my Clementine.
Now you scouts should take a lesson from the story of this rhyme,
Mouth-to-mouth resuscitation would have saved my Clementine.

Section VI

California's Early State Expansion, 1850s–1860s

Section VI

Introduction to California's Early State Expansion, 1850s–1860s

Sources

Emigrants, "Undesirables" & Native Americans

In the first decade of California's statehood, between 1850 and 1860, California experienced a population increase in excess of 400%. While the Americanized version of El Dorado drew emigrants from all corners of the globe, the actual task of getting to California, whether by sea or by land, was an arduous process, taking anywhere from six months to a year to achieve. Over 700 individually published Gold Rush documents recorded experiences of getting to the gold fields in that decade. Works included fictionalized stories, plays, diaries, essays, letters, song lyrics, and satires, written in various languages by people from all over the world.

Sources

One such set of documents are **the diaries of an Italian nobleman, Count Leonetto Cipriani**, who came to California as Consul for Sardinia. Cipriani's diaries are most noted for his 1853 cattle drive from Missouri to California, in which he drove 500 cattle, 600 oxen, 60 horses, 40 mules and 11 wagons with the assistance of 24 hired hands. In his earlier diary's excerpt, included here, Cipriani tells about his plans for immigrating to California and of his voyage abroad the steamship

Georgia, in which he expounds upon the sailing experience from New York to San Francisco.

Another important set of literary documents from this era were guide books with directions on how to get to the golden state and what supplies would be needed in the process. The next two selections in this grouping come from this genre. **The Emigrants Guide to the Gold Mines**, published in 1848, may have been composed by a ghost writer, as it seems to be a blending of fact and fantasy. The purported author, Henry I. Simpson, alleges to be a member of the 1st Regiment of New York Volunteers, but no such person can be located in the historical records of the regiment. This excerpt, which dwells on the many ways in which one can journey to California, seems to have been written by someone familiar with the different routes. Another guide book written by a real historical person this time, Joseph E. Ware, was first printed in St. Louis in 1849, **The Emigrants Guide to California**. Ware wrote the book before making the trek himself—a journey he failed to complete as he died before he ever reached California. Nevertheless, his practical advice for preparations and needed supplies and equipment was often reprinted in other guides.

With so many foreign emigrants pouring into California during the gold rush years, interracial conflicts became inevitable. White Americans objected to the competition and price undercutting coming from people whom they considered racially inferior—the Chinese and the Mexicans. In response, the new state government of California enacted **the Foreign Miners' Tax in 1850**, our fourth selection in this section. This tax aimed at discouraging immigration by forcing disfavorable foreigners out of the mines. The law required all persons who were not American citizens, with exception of Native Americans, to pay $20 for monthly licenses allowing them to mine—equivalent to $500 in today's economy. Mexican and other Latino prospectors left, turning their

mines over to their tormentors. Thus the Chinese then became the largest nonwhite group of miners, resulting in a rise in anti-Chinese sentiment throughout the 1850s. Consequently, the next foreign miner tax enacted in 1852 targeted the Asians. Ultimately, the federal Chinese Exclusion Act of 1882 would bar entry of Chinese workers in the United States altogether.

Although exempt from these discriminatory taxes, the Native Americans fared no better in the face of the white population explosion, as another 1850 act aimed at California's native tribes allowed them to be kept as indentured servants in the numerous large mining operations. Selection 5 is **a letter written by William Swain on January 16, 1850**, which is just one of many pieces of correspondence he wrote as part of his Gold Rush diaries. Swain, 28 years old, left his wife and children in Youngstown, New York to seek his fortune in California's gold fields in April 1849. He hoped to mine at least $10,000 in gold before he returned home, but he only made about $500. He gave up gold-seeking in late 1850 and returned home to his family. This letter laments the treatment of the Indians at the hands of white miners, while at the same time demonstrating the generalized attitude that most white Americans shared about the "redskins." Others in the state resented the presence of Indians in the mines altogether and either called for their annihilation or, at the very least, their removal and segregation onto reservations. In an attempt to settle this growing "Indian problem," Washington D.C. negotiated eighteen separate peace treaties with 139 Native Californian "chiefs," in which seven million acres of Indian lands were ceded to the United States in exchange for "reserved portions" upon which the Indian tribes could live, i.e. reservations. Their hopes that they would be protected on portions of their own lands under the terms of the treaties vanished when senators from California lobbied against the treaties, which then were never ratified. The next document, **A Maidu Woman Recalls an Escape to Fort Wright, 1850s**, was written by a Maidu Indian who recounted the many injustices suffered by her people at the hands of white settlers and soldiers. These kinds of slaughters that Mota recounted occurred well into the 1850s. In 1854, the U.S. Military established seven reservations, but without negotiations and terms of habitation, they became little more than refugee camps for the persecuted. The last selection in this group, **an 1855 editorial written in the *Sacramento Union***, heralded a "war of extermination" against California Indian tribes in the North. California's native population dropped from about 150,000 in 1848 to just 30,000 over the next twelve years. Historian Hubert H. Bancroft once described these actions as "one of the last human hunts of civilization, and the basest and most brutal of them all." There was no possible way in which California's Native American tribes could have survived intact as their resources and habitats were destroyed or polluted in the wake of millions seeking their fortunes in the West. California's Americanization that rapidly took it from provincial insignificance to being the center of the world beset the Golden State with an inordinate amount of greed among some of its citizens, and all other vices and conditions that accompany such degrees of avarice.

Emigrants and Businesses

The rapidly growing urban economies that propelled California towns into bustling cities were not based on the mining of gold, but rather on commerce, business, and finance. Many who saw the potential for new business ventures in California during the Gold Rush, built support industries to service the population explosion and new firms and businesses sprang up nearly overnight, industries such as Levi Strauss & Company and Wells Fargo Company. One of the great needs

in linking California to the rest of the nation was in the transportation of mail, goods, and people. From as early as 1847, steamships had been carrying these cargos to California via the ocean routes around the southernmost tip of South America and through a pattern of river and land routes in the Isthmus of Panama. Sometimes mail delivery to the West Coast could take six months to reach its final destination. This trip from New York to San Francisco via the Panama route could take 30 to 45 days. Due to the poor service and the growing corruption in the oceanic mail businesses, the Overland Mail Bill that passed Congress in 1858 authorized mail delivery to the West by land.

Sources

Selection 10 is an excerpt from **The Butterfield Overland Mail, 1857–1869**, which is a larger work by Roscoe P. Conkling and Margaret B. Conkling that details the founding and operation of the Butterfield Overland Mail, the first great overland mail service running from the Mississippi River to the Pacific Coast. The Conklings, husband and wife, supposedly traveled over 65,000 miles searching out and interviewing anyone associated with The Butterfield Overland Mail, which included persons involved in its organization and operation under Wells Fargo and Company in 1869. Most of the founding associates for these companies came from New York. The ninth selection, **Waterman Ormsby tells of the First Through Stage to California, 1858**, is the personal account of the first passenger of the Butterfield Line, a reporter for the *New York Herald*, who made the complete and arduous journey from St. Louis to San Francisco by stage all alone. As more and more people traveled West via the stagecoach companies, various travel hints were published in newspapers to help the travelers prepare for their journeys, such as the eleventh document in this series, **Travel Suggestions for Stagecoach Passengers, 1860s**.

In the 1850s, more than 25% of all Californians were Black Americans, Native Americans, Asians, or Hispanic. Over the next decade, California's diversity swelled even more as migrants came from other lands across the Atlantic. By 1860, nearly 40% of California's residents were foreign born, and more than 50% had at least one foreign-born parent. The growing presence of the "foreigner" in California, those of varying languages and cultural backgrounds who came seeking a new life in California, had often fled horrific circumstances in their native lands to get here. One such people were the thousands of persecuted Jews who fled the antisemitic *pogroms* of Europe and their continued persecutions on the East Coast to settle in California, where greater toleration and less violent reactions were experienced. Networks of Jewish merchants had dominated sea-faring trade of the Atlantic since the 17th and 18th centuries. It was only good business for Jewish merchants to be among the first to establish import-export establishments on the West Coast in linkage with their East Coast markets, thus becoming the avatars of import-export houses in the West. The final selection in this section, **Jewish Business, 1861**, was an article contributed by Henry J. Labatt and published in the San Francisco Jewish weekly, *True Pacific Messenger*, on May 24, 1861. Labatt was a lawyer and a commissioner of deeds in Louisiana before he moved to San Francisco in the 1850s. In this article he discusses the many and varied businesses owned by Jewish merchants and their contributions to the larger commercial community. Some of the more famous Jewish businesses in California included Levi Strauss & Company, J. Seligman & Company, and agents from the Rothchilds of London. In San Francisco alone, over 60 Jewish owned firms assessing at over $10,000 existed in the 1860s that traded in such items as dry goods, clothing, cigars and tobacco, jewelry and watches, gentlemen furnishings, hats and caps, carpet and upholstery, boots and shoes, wholesale groceries, insurance, real-estate, leather and wools, and glassware, as well as firms of bankers and stockbrokers. Jewish settlers were just one of many varied cultural groups who built thriving communities in California, weaving themselves permanently into the fabric of the state.

Readings

1. Diary of a Voyage to California, 1853

By Count Leonetto Cipriani

Primary Source

I returned to Leghorn from Montecatini. The idea of emigrating had been flitting through my mind when I happened to read an article on California in the *Journal des Débats*. I was greatly impressed. The writer of the article, Monsieur Derbec, (I met him later and we became good friends) wrote that California was an earthly paradise with its temperate climate, its spectacular vegetation and its inexhaustible mineral wealth. Furthermore, he advised those willing to work, or with money to invest, to go to California, where work was remunerated some twenty to fifty times more than elsewhere and where investments brought five and six per cent interest a month. And it was just as safe as living in Paris.

The information that I obtained from Mr. Benda, American consul in Leghorn, and from my close friend in New York, Michele Pastacaldi, confirmed these three essential points: California's delightful climate, its inexhaustible wealth, and perfect personal security. ...

From New York to Chagres

Once in New York, I heard more marvelous news from Pastacaldi and others about California, both with regard to the fabulous business activity and the inexhaustible mineral wealth. But also informed of the frightful cost of living in California, I remained in New York longer than I had intended, in order to give "La Distruzione" time to reach San Francisco, for then I would have both lodging and personal belongings at my disposal. Finally, in January 1852, I left on the steamship "Georgia," which sailed by way of the Isthmus of Panama.

Although two years had passed since the discovery of gold in California, and two hundred thousand people from America alone had emigrated, a great number were still going there. Rare was the sea crossing in which there were not more than a thousand passengers aboard ship, two thirds of whom were first-class passengers.

The "Georgia" was a steamship of four thousand tons, but, large as it was, it could not easily transport one thousand five hundred passengers,

The *Illinois*, a steamship built in 1851 that would have been similar to the *Georgia*.

even packing them like sardines, together with the provisions necessary for a twenty-four day voyage to and from its destination. The moment of embarking was enough to make one turn and flee, if he was not determined to leave at all costs.

Regardless of many precautions taken to avoid confusion and encumbrance, embarkation was the height of unparalleled disorder. Four gangways were extended from the deck to the dock, one for each class and one for baggage. At each gangway, two husky sailors stood guard, letting aboard only those who were to be embarked, and shoving the others aside so vigorously as to make them reel. To avoid encumbering the ship, the passengers were allowed to take aboard only a small valise. Trunks, cases, and sacks were thrown down the hatch like bales of hay. If they were smashed, so much the worse for those who had not been forewarned of the rough handling—rough, but perhaps the only way of getting both passengers and luggage aboard. ...

The most dramatic sight of all was at the third-class gangway, where besides the two husky sailors, a dozen policemen stood ready to intervene. Throngs of men, women and children, ragged, ill-garbed, mostly drunk, pushed forward. If they had

their tickets in their hands, a shove, and on board they were! If they stopped to look for tickets in their pockets, a shove, and out of line they would be, to make way for the others. If someone asked to accompany a relative or a friend, a shove, and out he was! And while passengers, friends, relatives and mere passers-by all yelled and shouted like fiends, the sailors' mouths were sealed tight as drums. They never spoke, they just shoved. And as for excess baggage, they did not so much as tell the poor passengers "Leave it!" Saying even that much might lead to discussion. Instead, they would grab it and toss it aside.

Departure was at eleven o'clock in the morning. A quarter of an hour earlier, the whistle and ship bell sounded. It was a signal for non-passengers to go ashore. Moments like this, the confusion really mounts! Some rush down the gangway, while late-arriving passengers, fearful of not being in time, rush up the same gangway, thus forming two opposite currents that meet head on, pushing and shoving. And the women, even sometimes the beautiful and rich ones, their hair now undone, yell like hellish furies. A last blast and the ship's engine begins to churn. Gangways are withdrawn and the gigantic cetacean moves away slowly amid the general uproar, while those who do not get aboard in time are left behind, fuming in exasperation.

In the meantime, the stewards, less bestial than the sailors, take the passengers to their cells, imparting all the necessary information. Each passenger, after glancing at those catacombs, leaves his luggage and climbs back to the deck. The banks of the river gradually disappear as it widens at the mouth, and a certain movement indicates that the ship is leaving the reign of gentle waters to enter that of salt water. If the sea is calm, the difference is hardly perceptible. But when the sea is stirred, half the passengers disappear in a wink, and crowd into the lower decks, each one hurriedly seeking out his own berth to throw himself on his bed. …

Another curious incident occurred on that same voyage. There were on board three ladies, two of whom were of about middle age, and a young one, at the most fifteen years old, who had long hair coming down to her shoulders. They were beautiful, and appeared very refined, modest and retiring. A priest would have offered them communion without confession. No one was acquainted with them.

The evening after we left Havana, while I was enjoying a breath of fresh air on deck, I saw one of the three at my side. As she happened to drop her handkerchief, I recovered it for her.

"*Merci*," she said.

"*Vous parlez français?*" I asked.

"*Oui, Monsieur.* My father is French."

"And are you going to California?"

"*Oui, Monsieur.*"

"And the ladies with you, are they going, too?"

"*Oui, Monsieur.* Is Monsieur French?"

"No," I answered, "I am Italian. And I am going to California as Consul for Sardinia."

"How delightful. My husband, who is the Swiss consul, and my friend's husband, the Consul for Prussia, will be your colleagues."

Ship routes to California during the Gold Rush era.

The acquaintance was thus made. Wives of colleagues are colleagues. Within a few days, we were on close terms. But, reservedly so, with all conventional politeness and respect. Later on, during the course of the voyage, I learned what these ladies really were. …

In the heat of the afternoon, while I was taking my siesta, I heard shrill laughter coming from the adjoining room. Irritated, I arose and approaching the closed door that connected my room to the adjoining one, I recognized the voices of the consuls' wives and the niece. Their outbursts and expressions were hardly becoming to ladies of their station.

I peered through the keyhole and saw the three of them, disheveled and naked as fish, all in the same bed, chasing each other on all fours, laughing and swearing like drunken Hussars. I at once understood everything. These "consuls' wives" were actually two notorious New York courtesans on their way to California to supply the element that was most lacking out there.

Thanks to Mr. Porter's recommendation of me to the captain, who was one of those rare Americans who can be considered gentlemanly, the rest of the voyage on the "Golden Gate" was exceedingly delightful.

We arrived in San Francisco at sunset, and it was already dark when we went ashore. The captain had advised me to spend the night on board ship but, overcome with curiosity to see the city, I took a stroll ashore, accompanied by a guide. Passing by a restaurant that displayed, among other edibles, much game of the country including deer and bear, we were tempted to celebrate our happy landing by dining on bear ribs.

So we went in. It was a huge dining room with more than a hundred little tables, and the four of us, Magnani and I, our servant and the guide, took our places.

The bear filet prepared with Madeira wine was exquisite and the Oregon pheasants were delicious, to say nothing of the rare French wines and a fine bottle of champagne. The bill—sixty dollars!

I paid, and returned on board ship. Lord only knows all that went through my mind as I tossed in my hard bed that night, thinking about those sixty dollars and wondering how I could survive in that whirlpool without being financially ruined in short order.

2. Land and Sea Routes to California, 1848

By Henry I. Simpson

Primary Source

The Isthmus Route

There are several routes to California, only two of which, however, are feasible with any degree of comfort or economy, and, we may add, safety. The Chagres steamer leaves New York monthly, as also the British West India Mail Steamers, and they reach charges on the Atlantic side of the Isthmus in about ten days. Canoes are here employed, and passengers carried thirty miles up, when they are transferred to the backs of mules, and in this way reach Panama in two days, where they will take either a steamer or sailing vessel for San Francisco. The steamers belonging to Aspinwall's line leave Panama on the first of every month, when fairly organized; but for the present they are advertised to leave January 5, February 15, and the 1st of March. After this, they take their regular monthly departure. The distance by this conveyance from New York to San Francisco, is about 5,500 miles, thus set down:—From New York to Chagres, 2000 miles, Chagres to Panama 50, Panama 10 San Francisco, on the arc of a great circle, 3,440. The whole distance will occupy from 25 to 30 days. The cost of crossing in this way the isthmus from the best sources of information, will not exceed $20, being performed, as we have already stated, by canoes and mule carriage. The former will soon give way to the steamer Orus, which has been purchased to run on the Chagres river. Passengers are in the habit of crossing the isthmus, who take the British line of steamers down the west coast of South America, which seems to establish the feasibility of its being without difficulty crossed. Passengers should provide themselves with the means to guard against contingencies, as they may arrive, from the non-arrival of the steamers at Panama. The greatest difficulty in going by this route will consist in a large amount of baggage; nothing over 150 pounds weight can be carried with safety. The price of passage on our steamers from New York to California, by the above route, first class, is $420. There is a medium class of passengers taken for considerably less, or sailing vessels leaving here for Chagres will take passengers much less. And there is also a third class passage from New York, by way of Panama, in the Orus and Aspin-Wall's steamers, by which the whole cost is less than $200, viz: $65 to Chagres, $20 to Panama, $100 to San Francisco.

The Cape Horn Route

The safest route is, doubtless, via Cape Horn. Ships will take passengers, from New York city to their destination, at from $300 down to $100—the price, in fact, depends upon the circumstances and on the accommodations offered.

This distance form New York to California, via Cape Horn, is about 17,000 miles, not 19,000, as stated, and will occupy about 150 days, or five months. Vessels generally, bound to the northwest coast, touch in at Valparaiso, Callao, or Panama, The only chance to forward or carry goods to California, is by ships bound direct; and now that there are so many up, freights are not very expensive.

The following is a correct statement of the time, price, and distance, by the two routes above mentioned to California:—

	Price	Distance	Time occupied
By Panama	$300 to 420	5,000	30 to 35 days
By Cape Horn	100 to 300	17,000	130 to 150 days

The difference in the price is from first to second class. The Bermuda steamers, which leave New York on the 13th of each month, touch at Chagres. Their price to that point is ten dollars less than in our own steamers.

Another new route will he opened in a few weeks, through the Isthmus of Tehuantepec in Mexico. The connection is expected to be made by uniting the navigable waters of the Guasacualco to those of the Chimalapa, the former running in the Gulf of Mexico, the latter in the Pacific The dividing ridge to be cut through is in height 1,375 feet: but the greatest difficulty here will be in securing a conveyance on the Pacific. The terminus of this road is not known by vessels trading on the west coast. The communication with this new route on the Atlantic side will be with New Orleans, principally, and, when completed, opportunities from that city will be frequent.

The Rocky Mountain Route

The other route is that across the Rocky Mountains and the great desert—a route which we can by no means recommend. The usual starting point is Independence, on the frontiers of the State of Missouri. The distance is very great; there are deserts to be crossed, mountains to be scaled, and hostile Indians to be encountered. The following is a table of the distances:—

	Miles
From Independence, Mo., to Fort Laramie,	672
From Fort Laramie to "Pacific Springs," (South Pass,)	311
From the South Pass to Fort Bridger,	133
From Fort Bridger to Salt Lake,	106
From Salt Lake to Mary's River,	315
Down Mary's River to the "Sink,"	274
From the Sink to Truckee Lake,	134
From Truckee Lake to Johnson's,	111
From Johnson's to Sutter's Fort,	5
Total distance from Independence to Sutter's Fort,	2091

The distance from Sutter's Fort by land, to the town of San Francisco, (via the Puebla of San Jose,) near the mouth of the Bay of S.F. and five miles from the Pacific Ocean, is	200
Total,	2291

Since 1845, many emigrating parties have traversed this region, some of which, during the year 1846, were exposed to much danger and suffering, having been stopped in their progress through the mountains by terrible storms of snow and hail, imprisoned for months in these regions, and subjected to all the horrors of starvation and destitution. The accounts received from the unfortunate sufferers compose a chapter of human misery, for which few parallels can be found in fact or fiction. The following description of the sufferings of one party of unfortunate emigrants, which had been lost among the mountains and imprisoned in the snows, and the horrible and revolting extremities to which they were reduced, is from the "California Star" of April 10th, 1847:—

"A more shocking scene cannot be imagined, than that witnessed by the party of men who went to the relief of the unfortunate emigrants in the California mountains. The bones of those who had died and been devoured by the miserable ones that still survived, were lying around their tents and cabins. Bodies of men, women, and children, with half the flesh torn from them, lay on every side. A woman sat by the side of the body of her husband, who had just died, cutting out his tongue; the heart she had already taken out; broiled, and ate! The daughter was seen eating the flesh of the father—the mother that of her children—children that of father and mother. The emaciated, wild, and ghastly appearance of the survivors added to the horror of the scene. Language cannot describe the awful change that a few weeks of dire suffering, had wrought in the mind of these wretched and pitiable beings. Those

who but one month before would have shuddered and sickened at the thought of eating human flesh, or of killing their companions and relatives to preserve their own lives, now looked upon the opportunities afforded them of escaping the most dreadful of deaths, as a providential interference in their behalf. Calculations were coldly made, as they sat around their gloomy camp-fires, for the next and succeeding meals. Various expedients were devised to prevent the dreadful crime of murder, but they finally resolved to kill those who had the least claims to longer existence. Just at this moment, however, as if by Divine interposition, some of them died, which afforded the rest temporary relief. Some sunk into the arms of death cursing god for their miserable fate, while the last whisperings of others were prayers and songs of praise to the almighty.

"After the first few deaths, but the one all-absorbing thought of individual self-preservation prevailed. The fountains of natural affection were dried up. The cords that once vibrated with connubial, parental, and filial affection, were rent asunder, and each one seemed resolved, without regard to the fate of other, to escape from the impending calamity. Even the wild, hostile mountain Indians, who once visited their camps, pitied them; and instead of pursuing the natural impulse of their hostile feelings to the whites, and destroying them, as they could easily have done, divided their own scanty supply of food with them.

"So changed had the emigrants become, that when the party sent out arrived with food, some of them cast it aside, and seemed to prefer to putrid human flesh than still remained. The day before the party arrived, one of the emigrants took a child of about four years of age in bed with him, and devoured the whole before morning; and the next day ate another about the same age before noon."

The town of Independence is situated about six miles from the Missouri river, on the southern or left hand side as you ascent it. The surrounding country is undulating, picturesque, and highly fertile. Its population is about one thousand; and in the spring of the year, when emigrating parties usually assemble there, every man seems to be actively and profitably employed. It has been for some years the principal outfitting point for the Santa Fe traders, and will probably so continue. Many of the houses around the public square are constructed of brick, but the majority of the buildings are frames. In the spring, among the busy multitude moving to and fro through the streets, may be seen large numbers of New Mexicans, and half breed Indians. With their dusky complexions and dragged and dirty costumes. They are generally mounted on miserably poor mules or, houses, and present a most shabby appearance. Long trains of oxen, sometimes as many as ten or fifteen yokes strung together, and pulling huge tended wagons, designed for some Santa Fe expedition, move about the streets under the directions of numerous drivers cracking their whips and making a great noise. Ox teams seem to be esteemed as preferable in these journeys to either mules or horses. The average price paid per yoke is 822, which may be considered very cheap. The streets are filled with oxen offered for sale by the neighboring farmers, but few, of them are filled with oxen offered for sale by the neighboring farmers, but few of them are in good condition or well trained; they are mostly young cattle, however, and easily improvable. Young and medium sized cattle should be selected for a journey over the plains and mountains, in preference to the heavy bodied and old; the latter almost invariably become foot-sore, and give out after traveling a few hundred miles.

The Nicaragua Route

In addition to the various routes we have already mentioned, is one which offers to travelers bound to California, or to any of the ports on the Pacific, as many inducements as any now known. The we allude to, is the isthmus of Nicaragua, The distance from St. Juan, on the Atlantic side, to Raelejo, on the Pacific, is about 156 miles. St. Juan is a town, upon the river of that name, with which we have an extended commerce. This river debouches into lake Nicaragua, which, connected with the river St. Juan, makes the distance traveled by water 120 miles to the two of Leon; from thence to Raelejo, 36 miles, by a good carriage road, over a level country free as is our own from fevers or epidemics. The traveling on the river St. Juan and on the lake is done by canoes, of all sizes, in which merchandise to almost any extent can be carried. The lake is dotted with small, islands, many of which are inhabited by a straggling set of half breed Indians, who trade with the boats and travelers bound across the lake.

A Leon there is a population of more than twenty thousand inhabitants, and provisions of every description can be obtained in abundance. When this place is reached, the distance, as we have said, is thirty-six miles to Raelejo, which is on the Pacific coast, and is celebrated among whalers and merchantmen for the facilities it affords in its splendid harbor and in the excellent provisions, with which it abounds. Vessels trading on the Pacific with the ports on the coast, and the Sandwich Islands, make this town their principal stopping place to recruit and provision, and this is why we recommend persons now going to California to take this route, as the chances of obtaining a passage from Raelejo to San Francisco here are much greater than from Panama or any of the isthmus ports on the Pacific. The probable cost of proceeding to California by this route will not exceed the present prices asked for a passage across the Isthmus of Panama, as the influx at this latter point must render all conveniences of living and travel very scarce, and consequently expensive.

The greatest advantage we see in the Nicaragua route is the ease with which it may be travelled, and the certainty of proceeding with comfort and safety. The country over which you travel by this route, is at all seasons passable; so thickly inhabited that labor is cheap, rendering the conveyance of baggage easier than by any other mode, except by the long and tedious navigation around Cape Horn. Moreover, the country, being fertile, provisions are abundant; and if by any chance the traveller should be detained at Raelejo his expenses would be very moderate, with the certainty of always having a sufficiency.

The Acapulco Route

Another route to the Gold Region is *via* Vera Cruz, city of Mexico and Acapulco on the Pacific. The passage to Vera Crux is $80, made in about eighteen days. From Vera Cruz *via* Mexico the transit occupies about ten days, at a cost of $75. The portion of the journey between the city of Mexico and Acapulco is performed on horseback. From Acapulco, where the American Mail Steamers are to stop, excepting the first one, the passage is $125, and the distance about 2,000 miles The cost, therefore, by this route would be $280, and the time occupied about forty days. If the passage from New York to Vera Cruz was made in a steamer the time would be reduced to thirty or thirty-two days.

The Guadalaxara Route

Another route still, and one which presents some advantages, is to go from the city of Mexico to Mazatlan on the Pacific *via* Guadalaxara. The journey from the last-named place would be made on horseback, and the whole journey from Vera Cruz to Mazatlan performed in about twenty days, at a cost of about $125. When at Mazatlan the traveller is 2,000 miles north of Panama. The cost of passage by the Mail Steamers from Mazatlan to San Francisco is $75. Mazatlan is a place of large business, and there are almost always vessels there by which passage could be obtained up the coast. The cost by this route to San Francisco would be $275, and the time occupied about forty-five days. In companies of ten or twelve Americans there would be no danger of robbery in traveling either of the above named routes.

3. Provisions for Overland Travel to California, 1849

By Joseph E. Ware

Primary Source

The question is not: how quickly can I get to California; there are other things to be regarded, the most serious enquries are, as to the best, surest, and safest routes to be taken—what supplies you need to take along with you, and what provision you need to make for your future necessities. There is information to be had on all these points, and no sensible man will set off on so important an expedition, leaving anything to uncertainty or chance. From the best observations made we are satisfied that no person should attempt to leave the frontier with more than lbs

2,500 weight, or with a team of less than four yoke of cattle, or six mules. Let your waggons be strong, but light, with good lock chains, and the tire well riveted through the fellowes—if not thus fastened, you will have to wet your wheels every day, to prevent them from coming off. You want your waggon covers well coated with paint, and a few pounds to spare. You want good stout ropes, 60 feet long, with stakes about 30 inches long, having the heads shod with an iron band, with an eye for fastening your mules to, and probably your cattle. You cannot be too careful of your teams, to prevent their straying. Have also a spare chain or two,—if you intend to farm, you want the iron work of a plough, a set of harrow teeth, axes, hoes, cradle, scythes, &c., including a small cast iron hand Corn Mill—be sure to have a good draw knife and frow together with a few other carpenter's tools; If you mean to "dig for gold," you want a short pick axe, strong in the eye, a spade, several tin and copper pans, a meal seive (have a gold washing machine if you can afford it) of brass or copper wire; iron wire will rust—take spare wire webb along with you—see yourself that everything you want is procured; do not trust to others. Be sure to have a well bound cask 20 gallons in size, for supplying yourself with water, across dry plans. For provisions for each person: you want a barrel of flow, or 180 lbs ship biscuit that is kiln dried, 150 to 180 lbs bacon, 25 lbs coffee, 240 lbs sugar, 25 lbs rice, 60 lbs beans or peas, a keg of clear cooked beef suet, as a substitute for butter, (butter will become rancid in a few days on the plains) a keg of lard, 30 or 40 lbs of dried peaches, or apples; also some molasses and vinegar. For arms, you want a good rifle, and a pair of long pistols, (some companies foolishly talk of taking small cannon along,) or a revolver, 5 lbs of powder, "Laftin's" best, with 10 lbs of lead, and a few pounds of shot. If you have room to spare fill up with additional provisions, as they will be scarce after you get through; four persons are enough for one team. The first subject of importance in the mind of the enquirer, is, as to the cost of the outfit, & c. From careful estimate we arrive at the following result, and think it about correct. We base the calculation upon the supposition that four persons club together to travel with the same wagon. And below we subjoin a second estimate for three persons using oxen only, as a team—this is compiled by another individual and for one year's provisions.

Estimate 1.

For 4 persons, with Mule teams. Wagon, harness, and 6 good Mules.

Wagon, ----	$85 00
3 sett of harness, $8 each, $24; Mules, $75	
each, $450; wagon cover painted with two coats, $8. Total for team, -----	$567,00
Flour for 4 persons,—824 lbs. at $2 per 100 lbs.	16,48
Bacon, do. do. 725 " 5 " " "	36,25
Coffee, do. do. 75 " 7c " lb.	5,25
Sugar, do. do. 160 " 5c " "	8,00
Lard and suet, do. do. 200 " 6c " "	1200
Beans, do. do. 200 " 40c " bu.	1,60
Peaches and apples, 135 " 80c " "	3,20
Salt, pepper, saleratus,&c. 25 lbs.	1,00
	$650,78
Cooking utensils, including tin plates, spoons, coffee pot, camp kettle, knives, and extras,	20,00
	$670,78
Making the cost to each one of the party,	167 69

From which deduct value of wagon, teams, &c., at journeys end, - - -	450,00	
Leaving cost of travel, - - -	220,78	
Cost to each individual, - - -	55,19	

Estimate 2.

For one year for 3 persons, with Ox teams:

Four yoke of oxen,	at $50,	$200,00
One wagon cover, & c.,		100,00
Three rifles,	at $20,	60,00
Three pair pistols,	at $15,	45,00
Five barrels flour,	1080 lbs.,	20,00
Bacon,	600 "	30,00
Coffee,	100 "	8,00
Tea,	5 "	2,75
Sugar,	150 "	7,00
Rice,	75 "	3,75
Fruit, dried,	50 "	3,00
Salt, pepper, & c.,	50 "	3,00
Salaratus,	10 "	1,00
Lead,	30 "	1,20
Powder,	25 "	5.50
Tools, & c.,	25 "	7.50
Mining tools,	36 "	12,00
Teat,	30 "	5,00
Bedding,	45 "	22,50
Cooking utensils,	30 "	4,00
Lard,	50 "	2,50
Private baggage,	150 "	
Matches,		1,00
One mule,		50,00
Candles and soap,	50 "	5,30
	2,583	$600,00

Cost to one man, $200,00.

Persons having families, with children, will find it necessary to make nearly as large an estimate for each child, as for an adult Men, women and children, eat twice the quantity on the road that they would otherwise require at home. Make no calculation upon any thing in the shape of game—you will need that too. Do not encumber yourselves with any thing not absolutely essential to your comfort; take blankets, sheets, quilts, coverlets and pillows, (omit beds,) with oil cloth, or India rubber spread, to lay on the ground under you. Take no horses unless of the Indian breed; the common horse cannot stand the road. Do not start with the intention of changing your wagons, for mules and Indian horses at Fort Laramie, as recommended by one through the press—it cannot be done—they are not to be had in any number. Cattle are best, except for packing over steeps. Oxen upon the whole, are the best; they need no shoeing, as the hot sand of the plain renders their hoofs so hard as to supersede the use of shoes. Some recommend cows, do not take them as a team.

Extra axle-trees are useful. Every mechanic should have his tools within his reach for emergencies on the road. Fish-hooks and lines are useful; seeds of most kinds are needed; all kinds of garden seeds, particularly peach, cherry, and plum stones—tobacco, cotton, rice, and other useful seeds.

For clothing, you want plenty of strong cheap goods, for hard service—as well as boots, hats, caps, &c. When rightly equipped, the undertaking is not so serious as may be supposed. One thing we would enjoin, particularly *get up early* when on the route; start your cattle up to feed as early as 3 o'clock—start on your journey at 4—travel till the sun gets high—camp till the heat is over. Then start again and travel till dark—do most of your heavy cooking at the noon camp. *Never travel on the Sabbath*; we will guarantee that if you lay by on the sabbath, and rest yourselves and teams, that you will get to California 20 days sooner than those who travel seven days in the week.

An act <u>for the better regulation of the Mines, and the government of Foreign Miners</u>.[1]

Passed April 13, 1850

<u>The People of the State of California</u>, <u>represented in Senate and Assembly</u>, <u>do enact as follows</u>;

1. No person who is not a native or natural born citizen of the United States, or who may not have become a citizen under the treaty of Guadalupe Hidalgo (all native California Indians excepted), shall be permitted to mine in any part of this State, without having first obtained a license so to do according to the provisions of this Act.

2. The Governor shall appoint a Collector of Licenses to foreign miners for each of the mining counties, and for the county of San Francisco, who, before entering upon the duties of his office, shall take the oath required by the Constitution, and shall give his bond to the Senate with at least two good and sufficient sureties, conditioned for the faithful performance of his official duties, which bond shall be approved by the Governor, and filed in the office of the Secretary of State.

3. Each Collector of Licenses to foreign miners shall be commissioned by the Governor.

4. It shall be the duty of the Comptroller to cause to be printed or engraved a sufficient number of licenses, which shall be numbered consecutively, and shall be in form following, to wit:

"Number_____. Date.) A.B., a citizen of _____, age _____ years, complexion _____, is hereby licensed to work in the mines of California for the period of thirty days."

The Comptroller shall countersign each of such licenses, and shall transfer them to the Treasurer, keeping an account of the number so transferred.

5. The Treasurer shall sign and deliver to each Collector of Licenses to foreign miners so many of the licenses mentioned in the preceding section as he shall deem proper, and shall take his receipt for the same and charge him therewith. Such collector and his sureties shall be liable upon his bond for the number so furnished him, either for their return or the amount for which they may be sold; and the moneys collected, as herein provided, shall be paid into the treasury as prescribed in this Act.

6. Every person required by the first section of this Act to obtain a license to mine, shall apply to the Collector of Licenses to foreign miners, and take out a license to mine, for which he shall pay the sum of twenty dollars per month; and such foreigners may from time to time take out a new license at the same rate per month, until the Governor shall issue his proclamation announcing' the passage of a law by Congress, regulating the mines of precious metals in this State.

7. If any such foreigner or foreigners shall refuse or neglect to take out such license by the second Monday of May next, it shall be the duty of the Collector of Licenses to foreign miners of the county in which such foreigner or foreigners shall be, to furnish his or their names to the Sheriff of the county, or to any Deputy Sheriff, whose duty it shall be to summon a posse of American citizens,

---

1 *Cal. Stats.* (1850), 221.

Charles Nahl's "On the Way to the Mines," depicting Indian and Chinese miners, circa. 1850. Charles Nahl, was a German-born painter who is considered by many to be California's first significant artist. Born in Kassel , Germany, he was one of thousands who came for gold, ultimately moving to San Francisco in 185, where he lived until his death in 1878..

and, if necessary, forcibly prevent him or them from continuing such mining operations.

8. Should such foreigner or foreigners, after having been stopped by a Sheriff or Deputy Sheriff from mining in one place seek a new location and continue such mining operations, it shall be deemed a misdemeanor, for which such offender or offenders shall be arrested as for a misdemeanor, and he or they shall *be* imprisoned for a term not exceeding three months, and fined not more than one thousand dollars.

9. Any foreigner who may obtain a license in conformity with the provisions of this Act, shall be allowed to work the mines anywhere in this State, under the same regulations as citizens of the United States.

10. It shall be the duty of each Collector of Licenses to foreign miners to keep full and complete register of the names and description of all foreigners taking out licenses, and a synopsis of all such licenses to be returned to the Treasurer.

11. Each license, when sold, shall be endorsed by the Collector selling or issuing the same, and shall be in no case transferable; and the Collector may retain, out of the money received for each license, the sum of three dollars, which shall be the full amount of his compensation.

12. Each Collector of Licenses to foreign miners shall, once in every two months, and oftener, if called upon by the Treasurer, proceed to the seat of government, settle with the Treasurer, pay over to that officer all moneys collected from foreigners not before paid over, and account with him for the unsold licenses remaining in his hands.

13. If any Collector shall neglect or refuse to perform his duty as herein provided, it shall be the duty of the Comptroller, upon receiving a notice thereof from the Treasurer, to give information thereof to the District Attorney in whose district said officer may have been appointed, who shall bring an action against such Collector and his sureties upon his bond, before any court of competent Jurisdiction; and upon recovery bad thereon, the said District Attorney shall receive for his services ten per cent, upon the, amount collected, the balance to be paid by him into the

Treasury in the manner provided by law for like payments.

14. It shall be the duty of the Governor, so soon as he shall have been officially informed of the passage of a law by the United States Congress, assuming the control of the mines of the State, to issue his proclamation, requiring all Collectors of Licenses to foreign miners to stop the issuing of licenses.

15. It shall be the duty of the Secretary of. State, immediately after the passage of this Act, to have two thousand copies each, in English and Spanish, printed and sent to the mining districts for circulation among the miners, and also to have the same published for thirty days in the Pacific News at San Francisco, and in some newspaper at Sacramento City and at Stockton.

An engraving of Chinese gold-mining in California. Artist unknown.

5. A Miner Remembers Crimes Against California's Natives, 1850

By William Swain

Primary Source

January 12

We have had heavy rains and high water, but the weather has now cleared off fine, like Spring. And spring is here, for the mountain oaks are putting out their leaves and all things are assuming a green hue. We are in hopes of having dry weather soon—then, "you see!"

["Many of the miners here are moving up the river to find locations for their summer's- work, and we hear of thousands at Sacramento City who are all ready to come up as soon as the rainy season is over, which will probably be in the month of February. We see by the papers that there is a tremendous number of emigrants intending to come out to California this season from the States. Thousands will be disappointed."] It is just for me to say that if my health is good and I do not have extraordinary good luck, I may not be home till next Fall. Mr. Bailey is well and sends his love to his family.

January 16

The rapidity with which this country is settling is only equaled by the change being made by Yankee enterprise. Three weeks ago but one steamboat plowed its way across San Francisco Bay and but one traversed the Sacramento River. Now four steamers may be seen making their regular trips from San Francisco to Yuba City, and flour which was then selling at 75 cents is now worth 40 cents per pound, as I have just heard '' m Mr. Hutchinson, who has come home from Long's Trading Post.

When we first located on this stream, no more than six houses were built on it. Now, within a distance of ten miles, 150 dwellings are built. [Some of the cabins "have cloth roofs, but others have quite decent clapboard roofs. Some are covered on the outside with green cowhides. Other miners have dug holes in the ground and covered them with pine brush and dirt." The largest camp or settlement "is called Stringtown, which is some forty buildings strung a l o n g … a sand or gravel bar on one side of the river. …" "Trading posts or stores are very numerous, and the traders appear to be doing a flourishing business. A large part of the trading is done on credit . . . with the expectation that the miners will pay as soon as they get to work in the bed of the river." "A miner can go into a store and get trusted for $1,000 in provisions."]

The "redskin" who four months ago roamed in his nakedness, the undisputed lord of these mountains and valleys, may now be seen on the hilltops gazing with surprise upon the scenes below—the habitations, the deep-dug channels and the dams built. The sound of the laborer's ax, shovel, pick and pan are sounds new to his ear, and the sight one to which his eye had never been accustomed.

The natives of these mountains are wild, live in small huts made of brush and go naked as when they are born. They subsist on acorns and what game they kill with their bows and arrows. They are small in stature, and their character is timid and imbecile. When they visit the camps of the miners, they evince the most timid and friendly nature. They are charged with killing miners occasionally when they find one alone, away among the hills hunting. The miners, especially the Oregon men, are sometimes guilty of the most brutal acts with the Indians, such as killing the squaws and papooses. Such incidents have fallen under my notice that would make humanity weep and men disown their race. [The men from Oregon "say they will kill or drive off every Indian in the country, and they will do it, for they had rather shoot an Indian than a deer any time."

["Indians are now frequently employed in the mines for a mere trifle. They generally contrive to get a shirt and a few get rich enough to buy a coat and pantaloons. But since the rains have set in . . . hundreds are seen wading the streams for fish or traveling on the plains, naked and paying no more regard to the wet, chilly storm than dumb beasts. In the valley they are now inoffensive, as the numbers of whites overawe them; but in the mountains they sometimes give miners trouble and some collisions have taken place."]

I send this by a man who is going to Sacramento City and to San Francisco on purpose for mails. He leaves here Saturday and will return in two weeks, when I shall probably get my letters by him, paying $2 apiece for bringing them up.

I shall write often as I can and shall fill my engagements to different persons to whom I promised to write as soon as I have gained sufficient knowledge of the country to do so understandingly. Say to Mr. Burge that this climate in the mines requires a constitution like iron. Often for weeks during the rainy season it is damp, cold, and sunless, and the labor of getting gold is of the most laborious kind. Exposure causes sickness to a great extent, for in most of the mines tents are all the habitation miners have. But with care I think health can be preserved.

Give my love to Sabrina and kiss little Cub for me.

Goodbye George,

William

6. A Maidu Woman Recalls an Escape to Fort Wright, 1850s

By Evelene Mota

Primary Source

This [Sacramento Valley] was a place where the People lived. There was water, good hunting, plenty of wild fruit and berries. It was the home of the Concow, a small branch of the Maidu.

For many years they lived here in relative peace and harmony with nature and other tribes. There were always rumors about the strange white men that were seen about, but no one thought they would ever see one.

But then the rumors became fact. They were there, and they were not very good people. They stole food, they ran off the game, and worst of all they stole the young girls. Some they sent back to the tribes—after they were through with them—but others were sold to other people. This created bad feelings for the whites, and there were killings. Many young men were killed—the warriors.

The land was good, and white families wanted to build homes and start farms. The Indian was in the way. A problem had to be solved.

One day the soldiers came. Everyone was rounded up: men, women, old people, children. In these times all the People had learned to live with the knowledge that they would have to leave their homes, sometimes in the middle of the night. So they were always packed, their food baskets and blanket roll ready. The women and children would have on all the clothes they owned—ready!

They came in the early morning, many soldiers. Everyone was rounded up in the middle of the village and told they were going to a better place. So they started walking. Along the way many old ones and many babies died. When someone tried to run away, they were killed.

Somewhere between the mountains and the Pacific Ocean they came upon some Indians who told them that to the south was a valley where there were soldiers and white people, but also many Indians of all tribes—some taken there by soldiers, some there on their own.

A young girl listened to all this and wondered if this was where they were going. She discussed it with her friend and decided they could make it there somehow.

But, instead, they finally got to the ocean and they were all amazed at the amount of water, so much more than any of them could even imagine. Then the soldiers started running them, hitting and shooting anyone who didn't run, right up to and over the edge of a high cliff, down into the water.

The two young girls swam for a long time. When the smaller one got tired, the bigger one put her on her back and swam with her. In time they made it to the other side, for, you see, it was a bay—Humboldt Bay. Many people died that day.

After they got out of the water, they started walking south to what the people called the Valley. They ate berries and wild vegetables, and sometimes the bigger girl would again have to carry the smaller one. But eventually they arrived in the Valley. It was beautiful. A prison, yes, but with more freedom than they had otherwise.

They spoke only the Concow language, but they went to the fort and asked for work. They

Photograph of Maidu headmen standing behind treaty commissioners, ca. 1851.

were strong and growing and were soon maids at Fort Wright. The older one worked for a major and his wife.

And that's how Mary Major came to Round Valley.

7. A *Sacramento Union* Editorial Ponders the Indians' Fate, 1855

Sacramento Union

Primary Source

The accounts from the North indicate the commencement of a war of extermination against the Indians. The latter commenced the attack on the Klamath; but who can determine their provocation or the amount of destitution suffered before the hostile blow was struck.

The intrusion of the white man upon the Indians' hunting grounds has driven off the game and destroyed their fisheries. The consequence is, the Indians suffer every winter for sustenance. Hunger and starvation follows [*sic*] them wherever they go. Is it, then, a matter of wonder that they become desperate and resort to stealing and killing? They are driven to steal or starve, and the Indian mode is to kill and then plunder.

The policy of our Government towards the Indians in this State is most miserable. Had reasonable care been exercised to see that they were provided with something to eat and wear in this State, no necessity would have presented itself for an indiscriminate slaughter of the race.

Council of Indians before their relocation, Warner's Ranch in San Diego, March 1902.

The fate of the Indian is fixed. He must be annihilated by the advance of the white man; by the diseases, and, to them, the evils of civilization. But the work should not have been commenced at so early a day by the deadly rifle.

To show how the matter is viewed on the Klamath, we copy the following from the Crescent City *Herald.* The people look upon it there as a war of extermination, and are killing all grown up males. A writer from Trinidad, under date of January 22d, says:

> I shall start the two Indians that came down with me to-night, and hope they may reach Crescent City in safety, although I think it exceedingly doubtful, as the whites are shooting them whenever an opportunity offers; for this reason I start them in the night, hoping they may be out of danger ere morning. On the Klamath the Indians have killed six white men, and I understand some stock. From the Salmon down the whites are in arms, with determination, I believe, if possible, to destroy all the grown up males, notwithstanding this meets with the opposition of some few who have favorite Indians amongst them. I doubt whether this discrimination should be made, as some who have been considered good have proved the most treacherous. I understand that the ferry of Mr. Boyce, as also that of Mr. Simms, has been cut away. Messrs. Norton and Beard have moved their families from Elk Camp to Trinidad; they were the only white females in that section that were exposed to the savages. I have no doubt there will be warm times on the Klamath for some weeks, as the Indians are numerous, well armed and determined to fight.

8. The Cattle on a Thousand Hills

Southern California, 1850–1880

By Robert Glass Cleland

Secondary Source

Despite the uncertainty and confusion caused by the Land Act of 1851 and the ultimate absorption of most of the great ranch holdings by Americans, southern California remained a typical cattle frontier for almost twenty years after the Gold Rush, and all the activities of its people took form and color from the traditions of the open range.

"Large quantities of arable and grazing land are held under Mexican or Spanish titles, and occupied by rancheros of the ancient order of shepherds and herdsmen" wrote the assessor of San Diego in 1855, in describing the characteristics of the county and the adherence of its inhabitants to old forms and customs. "Many of them are averse to the changes and innovations brought about by the advent of American rule, and cleave manfully to the time-honored institutions of rawhide ropes, wooden ploughs, and stumpy wheeled ox-carts. ... Several thousand cattle of a fierce and savage breed infest the valleys of this whole county."

The assessor added that the presence of the cattle made "the Surveyor's duty of running lines through their range a matter of some personal risk and uncomfortable foreboding," and that he had "had an unsuspecting flag man prostrated once by a charge in the rear from an infuriated bull." In the same report the assessor of San Bernardino County pointed out that in his county there were no "bridge companies, toll bridges, canals, turnpikes, railroads, electro-magnetic telegraphs, Artesian wells, etc."

The dominant influence of the old order was further shown by the survival of Spanish as the common language of the country and by the unconscious incorporation into the American settler's vocabulary of such Spanish words as *vaquero, rodeo, reata, fierro, caballada, paisano, zanja, cañon, arroyo,* and the like. His adoption of a score of simple, commonplace practices employed by the Californians in everyday life showed still further the intermingling of the old culture with the new. This was illustrated by such a simple thing as the use of raw hide as a general "repair all" for farm and household purposes. ...

On the great ranchos themselves life flowed on in its familiar, long-established channels. Bearing the picturesque name of family, saint, or Indian rancheria, each huge, manorial-like estate supported a population of several hundred people, maintained a variety of household manufactures, produced its own grain, vegetables, and other foodstuffs, grazed thousands of head of cattle, sheep, and "beasts of burden," and constituted an economically independent, self-sustaining community. ...

In 1851 the state legislature passed an act, dealing with almost every phase of the cattle industry, entitled *Laws Concerning Rodeos, and Defining the Duties of Judges of the Plains.* For the most part the law merely recognized the practices already in effect among California rancheros and gave legal sanction to those ancient customs which had been introduced into New Spain from the cattle ranges of Andalusia at least three centuries before.

The act required each ranchero to brand his cattle with three separate brands and to register these in the County Recorder's "Book of Marks and Brands." The brands were called, respectively, the *fierro,* or range brand; the *señal,* or earmark; and the *venta,* or sale brand. The *fierro* was branded on the hip; the *serial* was a slit, notch, or hole cut in the ear; and the *venta,* often called in English the counterbrand, was burned on the shoulder when the animal was sold. …

Early Cattle Brands of Los Angeles County

1. Brand of the Mission San Gabriel
2. Brand of José Maria Verdugo (Rancho San Rafael, 1787)
3. *Venta,* or counterbrand, of Abel Stearns
4. Brand of José and Francisco Sepúlveda
5. 5a and 5b Brands of Juan Bandini
6. Brand of Vicente Lugo
7. Brand of the Compañía Agricultura (Rancho Los Alamitos; Abel Stearns)

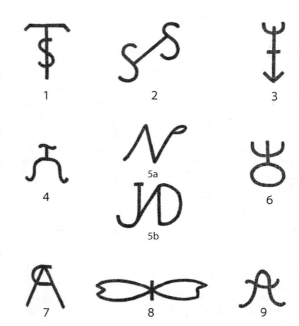

8. *Señal,* or earmark of Abel Stearns
9. Brand of Vicente Domínguez

9. Recollections of the First Through Stage to California, 1858

By Waterman Ormsby

Primary Source

Overland to California

Special Correspondence of the New York Herald
San Francisco, Oct. 10, 1858

Safe and sound from all the threatened dangers of Indians, tropic suns, rattlesnakes, grizzly bears, stubborn mules, mustang horses, jerked beef, terrific mountain passes, fording rivers, and all the concomitants which envy, pedantry, and ignorance had predicted for all passengers by the overland mail route over which I have just passed, here am I in San Francisco, having made the passage from the St. Louis post office to the

Concord stage coach in the American West, ca. 1869.

San Francisco post office in twenty-three days, twenty-three hours and a half, just one day and half an hour less than the time required by the Overland Mail Company's contract with the Post Office Department. The journey has been by no means as fatiguing to me as might be expected by a continuous ride of such duration, for I feel almost fresh enough to undertake it again.

The route is prolific in interest to the naturalist, the mineralogist, and all who love to contemplate nature in her wildest varieties, and throughout the whole 2,700 miles the interest in new objects is not allowed to flag. I have found the deserts teeming with curious plants and animal life, the mountain passes prolific in the grandest scenery, and the fruitful valleys suggestive of an earthly paradise; while, if this trip may be considered a criterion, the alleged danger from Indians is all a bugbear. ...

The road winds over some of the steepest and stoniest hills I had yet seen, studded with inextricable rocks, each one of which seems ready to jolt the wagon into the abyss below. It is enough to make one shudder to look at the perpendicular side of the canon and think what havoc one mischievous man could make with an emigrant train passing through the canon.

The great peak towers as if ready any moment to fall, while huge boulders hang as if ready, with the weight of a rain drop, to be loosened from their fastenings and descend with lumbering swiftness to the bottom, carrying destruction in their paths. The water appears to have washed away the soil of the peak and its minor hills, revealing the strata like so many regularly built walls of a fortress, and the whole mass presents a scene of stupendous grandeur. Just before the bottom of the canon is reached there stands by the roadside the grave of a Mexican guide, who had ventured in advance of his party and was murdered by the Indians—a thrilling reminder of another of the dangers of this dreadful pass.

We got through about sunset, and I never shall forget the gorgeous appearance of the clouds: tinged by the setting sun above those jagged peaks, changing like a rapid panorama, they assumed all sorts of fantastic shapes, from frantic maidens with dishevelled hair to huge monsters of fierce demeanor, chasing one another through the realms of space. We had hardly passed through before the sound of voices and the gleaming of light denoted that there was a party ahead of us. The awe inspiring scenery and the impressive sunset had almost set me dreaming as I lay listlessly in the wagon; but the possibility of meeting foes, perhaps a band of murderous Indians, in this wild and lonely spot filled me for a time with fears; but I had great faith in the captain's prowess, and felt somewhat easier when he declared it to be his opinion that the party was an American one.

In a moment we were upon them, and, to our astonishment, found that it was the overland mail which left San Francisco on the 15th [of] September, with five through passengers, and which was now eight hours ahead of time. After exchanging congratulations and telling bits of news, both parties passed on, I availing myself of the opportunity to send to the *Herald* a despatch which I had nearly written for the occasion.

10. The Butterfield Overland Mail, 1857–1869

By Roscoe P. Conkling and Martha B. Conkling

Secondary Source

Photographs of Roscoe P. and Martha B. Conkling, circa 1860–1865.

Butterfield was among the first to recognize the value of a good road, and his success was largely due to his efforts in improving and maintaining his road. [...]

From the most reliable sources it is estimated that the Company employed at the height of its career on the Southern route, a total of two thousand men in various capacities, exclusive of superintendents. ...

"The horses," Agent Rumfield observes, "are of the most powerful description to be found, and when once thoroughly trained to the service perform the laborious run with apparent pleasure and delight." Four, five, and six-horse teams were employed depending on the character of the stage and the load carried. Mules replaced the horses through the dangerous Indian country from Fort Belknap, Texas, to Fort Yuma, California. A fresh relay team was held in readiness at each station.

The coaches used on the route were the product of three of the leading firms of coach builders of the time J. S. Abbot & Sons of Concord, New Hampshire; James Goold of Albany, N.Y., and Eaton, Gilbert and Company of Troy, N.Y. The harness sets were all of the finest quality and workmanship from the shops of James B. Hill & Sons of Concord, N.H.

Two types of thoroughbrace suspension coaches were used, the regular or "Southern style" as it was later known, and a specially built stage-wagon called a "celerity" wagon, similar to what was later known as a mud-wagon. The regular type full-bodied coach had a capacity of about 4,000 pounds, and could accommodate nine passengers inside, and an unlimited number outside. The Troy coaches had a seat located directly back and above the driver's seat, and some of the coaches were also provided with a sort of a dickey seat for the conductor located above the rear boot. The interiors of the coach bodies were lined with russet leather, and the cushions and side curtains were of the same material. Damask and fringe of the same was used for additional finish inside. Wire pattern candle lamps provided the interior illumination. The leather straps or thorough-braces on which the bodies were hung over the carriages, were stitched three and a half inches wide. Some of the coach bodies were painted and varnished red, while others were a dark bottle green. The carriages were all painted straw yellow and striped in black or brown. Many of the coach bodies were further ornamented with an original hand painting on the lower panel of each door. Besides the Company's serial number the title, "Overland Mail Company," was lettered across the top paneling of each coach. The axles were specified to be two and a half inches ill diameter, and the tires of the wheels, one and seven-eights inches Wide by three-quarters of an inch thick. The gauge or track of the wheels was five feet two inches, center to center. Each of the regular coaches weighed about 3,000 pounds. The price of the coaches varied with the type, size,

extra ironing, finish and equipment, but the average cost was $1,400, at the factory.

The "celerity" wagon was an innovation on the part of Butterfield to provide a lighter and faster type of vehicle for use on the rougher sections of the route, and also to furnish something like an overland mail coach sleeper. The carriage of this vehicle was built on the same lines as that of the regular coach, but had smaller wheels. The lower part of the body was fashioned much the same as the regular coach body also, but the top was a frame structure covered with heavy duck, the doors and sides provided with curtains of the same material. This vehicle had a capacity for nine inside passengers only. The three inside seats were so constructed that they could be adjusted and made into a bed. With its low center of gravity this wagon was less liable to an overset than the regular coach. The first consignment of one hundred of these were built by Goold (plate 14).

The regular coach was used over the First division from Tipton, and Syracuse, and on to Springfield, during the early operations, and later on as far as Fort Smith. At this point a change was made to the "celerity" wagons which were used all the way to Los Angeles where a change was again made to the regular coaches for the continuation of the journey to San Francisco.

Referring to this practice, Ormsby states: "Our stay [at Springfield] was just long enough to change from the coach to one of the wagons which are used from this point to San Francisco. They are made much like the express wagons in our city which are used for transshipment, only are heavier built, have tops of canvas, and are set on leather straps ... Each one has three seats, the backs of which can be let down to form one bed capable of accommodating from four to ten people, according to their size and how they lie ... When the stage is full, passengers must take turns sleeping. Perhaps the jolting will be found disagreeable at first but a few nights without sleeping will soon obviate that difficulty, and soon the jolting will be as little of a disturbance as the rocking cradle to a sucking babe. For my part I found no difficulty in sleeping over the roughest roads, and I have no doubt that anyone else will learn quite as quickly. A bounce of the wagon which makes one's head strike the top, bottom or sides will be equally disregarded, and 'Nature's sweet restorer' found as welcome on the hard bottom of the wagons as in the downy beds of the St. Nicholas." He adds: "White pants and kid gloves had better be discarded by most passengers," and "that the wagons and coaches can hardly be expected to equal the Fourth Avenue horse cars for comfortable riding."

At the beginning of the operations in September, 1858, there were one hundred forty-one stations reported. Early in the ensuing year the number was increased to nearly two hundred.

The stations averaged about twenty miles apart. Some at a minimum distance of nine miles, and others at a maximum distance of sixty miles. Through Missouri, Arkansas, and Indian Territory the buildings were all log houses. Through Texas, New Mexico, Arizona and Southern California they were either stone or adobe structures. Four of the stations were located on Mexican territory in Lower California just south of the international boundary line (plate 15).

"Each is tenanted," Tallack writes, "by several well armed men whose duty it is to look after the mules and their provender and have relays punctually ready on arrival of the stages … Passengers and luggage are shifted into a fresh coach about every three hundred miles."

From two to four employees were boarded and lodged at the home-owned stations. At most of the company-owned stations, from four to six men were employed besides the station-keeper; and at the larger stations and those located in the Indian country, the number of men was increased to eight or ten.

The price of meals at the stations varied from forty cents to one dollar. With reference to the meals served along the route, Ormsby observed somewhat sarcastically, "that the fare could hardly be compared to that of the Astor House in New York." Tallack who

appears less critical than some,. States: "Meals are provided for passengers twice a day. The fare though rough, is better than could be expected from civilized districts, and consists of bread, tea, and fried steaks of bacon, venison, antelope, or mule flesh—the latter tough enough. Milk, butter, and vegetables can only be met with towards the two ends of the route—that is, in California and at the 'stations' in the settled parts of the western Mississippi valley."

Other travelers evidently not favorably impressed with the culinary departments of the stations, reported a fixed menu of jerked beef, mesquite beans, corn cake baked in hot ashes, black coffee, and a strange and mysterious concoction known as "slumgullion" (plates 16 and 17).

To keep the stations provided with forage for the stock, supplies and provisions for the help and passengers, was no easy task, especially in the remote and isolated regions. Each station had to be provided with from fifty to one hundred tons of hay each year. Hay, in California, cost forty-three dollars a ton, and barley, six cents a pound, to which had to be added the cost of the long freight haul. …

Probably the fastest time ever made over the route was made by Mr. Pardee, a company express rider, who carried a copy of the president's message and reports of the secretaries to California. He left Saint Louis on December 6, 1858, and made the trip in the remarkable time of nineteen days and fifteen hours, arriving in San Francisco December 26th, two days ahead of the steamship mail which also brought a copy of the message.

The operating time over the route was regulated in accordance to a time-table schedule, the first issue of which was prepared by Daniel Butterfield, to which the Mails adhered with a remarkable degree of accuracy. It is doubtful if a coach mail time-schedule, so accurately and carefully prepared as this had ever been published before (plates 18 and 19). The passenger fare first in effect from Saint Louis to Memphis to San Francisco was two hundred dollars, and from San Francisco' to Memphis or Saint Louis, one hundred dollars. Severe criticism of this arbitrary rate which favored east-bound traffic, resulted in fixing the fare at two hundred dollars each way in the early part of 1859. Shortly afterwards, however, the through fare was reduced and maintained at one hundred fifty dollars each way. The "way" fare was ten cents a mile. Passengers were each allowed forty pounds of baggage free. It was strictly against the rules and practice of the company to allow any large amounts of money or valuables to be transported over the line. This rule was made to discourage hold-ups of the mails, and also because shipments of money and other valuable matter were handled through the agency of Wells, Fargo and Company which was affiliated with the Overland Mail Company, and operated over the steamship lines.

The through tickets were made out in hand writing, merely bearing, in addition to the date and signature of the agent, "Good for the passage of the bearer by the Overland Stage from San Francisco to the terminus of the Pacific Railroad," or "From the terminus of the Pacific Railroad or Memphis to San Francisco."

All through places were usually taken far in advance, and the "way" passenger traffic was always heavy and much complained of by the through fares, because of the overcrowding of the coaches. In this connection Tallack states on leaving San Francisco: "At starting, our conveyance was not a mere waggon as afterwards, but a regular coach, holding nine inside (three behind three in front, and three on a movable seat, with a leather strap for a back), by dint of close sitting and tightly dovetailed knees. Outside the driver the conductor, and an indefinite number of passengers, as, by popular permission, an American vehicle is never 'full' there being always room for 'one more.' With these their luggage, and a heavy mail in strong sacks stowed, away under and between our feet, or overhead and elsewhere, we started from the Plaza or Grand Square of an Francisco."

So great was the rush for seats," [at Saint Louis] said the New York *Herald* "that applicants adopted the course of deciding by lot who should adopted the course of deciding by lot who should take passage.

Upward of one hundred applications were made this trip and as high as one hundred dollars premium was offered for seats." ...

A conductor accompanied the mail on each coach, and he was responsible for its safety over his division which on some portions of the route was over a distance of five hundred miles. The pouches were never to be left unguarded or out of the conductor's or driver's sight. The driver's "runs" were limited to the stage or stages with which he was most familiar.

Each conductor was provided with a small brass bugle on which he sounded a call on approaching the stations (plate 20). "Throughout our Overland journey," says Tallack, "our approach to a station, whether previous to a relay or a meal, was announced at a distance by a long blast of the conductor's horn, often heard far away in the silence of the wilds, and serving to economize time by enabling the station-keepers to prepare the requirements both of hungry passengers and jaded mules."

The Indian threat was always a serious problem, and although military protection for the line had been promised, such protection with a sufficient show of force to insure it, was never forthcoming, in spite of Butterfield's repeated appeals to the administration for an increase in the military strength along the frontier and the establishment of additional bases of operation. Small detachments of foot soldiers were detailed for guard duty at some of the stations in the Indian country' but only in the face of an emergency would a mounted escort of soldiers be furnished to accompany the Mails over some of the more dangerous stages.

Company employees were duly warned to have nothing to do with the Indians and avoid trouble with them but at the same time to be always prepared for any emergency.

A conciliatory policy followed at first by the Company, failed, and it was found necessary for the protection of the lives of the men and the Company property, to provide arms and ammunition for all the stations in the dangerous Indian country.

During the first year of the Company's operations, the postal receipts amounted to $27,229.94. The amount of letter mail carried over the route continued to Increase until by the year 1860, the number of letters transported exceeded the number sent by the ocean route. During this year the postal receipts increased to $119,766.76. The postal rate was ten cents for each letter.

The Overland Mail gained an international reputation as a transcontinental carrier. Great Britain inaugurated a regular schedule for the transportation of her letter mail to the Pacific coast and British Columbia, by way of the Butterfield route. The letter rate from the British Isles was twenty-four cents for each letter.

Pliny Miles, the leading British authority on international commerce and transportation, projected the Butterfield route on a map prepared by him to accompany his exhaustive report on postal communication between Europe and America. He added in his description of the Butterfield route, "There is no route of land travel on the eastern continent that so nearly resembles on the California Overland Mail as the from Moscow and. St. Petersburg to Pekin, through Tartary and Siberia, by way of Irkoutsk and Kiachta."

The following appeared in a London newspaper on October 30 1858: "The opening of the Overland Mail route to California through the United States, is a matter of the greatest importance to Europe, inasmuch as it will open up a vast country to European emigration, will be the precursor of the railway and land telegraphic communication from New York to San Francisco, and will greatly facilitate English intercourse with British Columbia."

WELLS, FARGO & CO.,

General Express Forwarders, and Carriers of the Overland Mail.

Daily Stages to and from the Terminus of the **Union Pacific Railroad, of Omaha, and the Central Pacific Railroad, of California.** Passengers ticketed from Omaha to Denver, Salt Lake City, Austin, Virginia, Nevada, Sacramento, California, and intermediate points.

Stages leave SALT LAKE CITY daily to the above points, and on alternate days for Virginia City and Helena, Montana, Boise City, Idaho, and other points in those Territories.

THE COMPANY RUN AN

OVERLAND EXPRESS

In connection with their Stage line, and are prepared to carry PARCELS, BANK NOTES, BULLION, GOLD and SILVER COIN, and EXPRESS FREIGHT to all parts of the world at greatly reduced rates. **Collections and Commissions** promptly attended to. Particular attention paid to the delivery of EXPRESS LETTERS at all points on our routes.

For particulars apply at the office, on East Temple Street, Salt Lake City.

THEO. F. TRACY, Agent.

Oct. 1, 1868.   76-1yr

A 1868 display advertisement for Wells, Fargo & Co.'s express and stagecoach services.

---

11. Travel Suggestions for Stagecoach Passengers, 1860s

By Anonymous

Primary Source

The best seat inside a stage is the one next to the driver. Even if you have a tendency to seasickness when riding backwards, you'll get over it and will get less jolts and jostling. Don't let any sly elph trade you his midseat.

In cold weather don't ride with tight fitting boots, shoes or gloves. When the driver asks you to get off and walk, do so without grumbling. He won't request it unless absolutely necessary. If the team runs away—sit still and take your chances. If you jump; nine out of ten times you will get hurt.

In very cold weather abstain entirely from liquor when on the road; because you will freeze twice as quickly when under the influence.

Don't growl at the food received at the station; stage companies generally provide the best they can get. Don't keep the stage waiting. Don't smoke a strong pipe inside the coach—spit on the leeward side. If you have anything to drink in a bottle pass it around. Procure your stimulants before starting as "ranch" (stage depot) whiskey is not "nectar."

Don't swear or lop over neighbors when sleeping. Take small change to pay expenses. Never shoot on the road as the noise might frighten the horses. Don't discuss politics or religion. Don't point out where murders have been committed if there are women passengers.

Don't lag at the wash basin. Don't grease your hair because travel is dusty. Don't imagine for a moment that you are going on a picnic. Expect annoyances, discomfort, and some hardship.

---

12. Jewish Business

From the *True Pacific Messenger*, San Francisco, May 24, 1861

By Henry J. Labatt

Primary Source

On a first arrival in our city, it becomes a matter of astonishment to all who see the large number of mercantile houses conducted by Israelites, being much greater, in proportion to the commerce, than in any other city in America. Every line of business is engaged in by them, with credit to themselves and honor to the community.

Among the largest importers, rank foremost many Jewish firms, the prosperity of whose engagements is evident in the large returns which are made on every steamer day.

The influence they command upon the trade in the State, the weight of their transactions, and the generality of their mercantile callings, may well class them among the most useful, beneficial, and respectable merchants.

Each mining town and city has a large representation, and everywhere you hear of their success and prosperity, which in turn they devote to the improvement of the place, by erecting substantial buildings and warehouses for the increase of their business, caused by industry, economy, and attention.

In all the great fires which have devastated the settlements of California, they have been great sufferers. Year after year, have they seen the hard earnings of their labor swept away by the ruthless conflagration, and yet, with the indomitable energy of their race, have they toiled on to regain what they thus were deprived of by misfortune. Often, indeed, would they not only lose what they had accumulated, but become reduced by being brought into debt by the destruction of their stock. Even this would not deter them.—The previous character which prudence and honesty had stamped upon them, created unmistakable confidence and sympathy, and they soon rose above these accidents.

Every where they seemed anxious to guard against this great affliction of our country and, by erecting substantial tenements, avoid another calamity.

In all commercial enterprises they keep pace with the marked improvements of the day, and, as merchants, are courted, admired—nay, even sometimes envied.

The almost universal success of the Jews, as merchants, in California, must be attributed to some peculiar reasons; for while many of all nations have succeeded in this State, yet, as a general thing, no class of people who began with so small a capital, have accumulated the same amount of fortune. Any close observer will find that their individual industry dispenses with the necessity for extra clerks, who, at the exorbitant rates necessary for their support, soon make sad inroads upon the monthly profit. They seldom pay unwarrantable rents, being willing to submit to many inconveniences rather than indulge in extravagance. They eschew all display of brilliant fixtures, or other unnecessary expenses, but study economy in every department of their business. Yet, after years of success, when they are conscious of their ability to display their wares and merchandise, then you may find a few who indulge in such outlays.

Their method of conducting business is also worthy of consideration. They seem anxious to dispose of their stock in a short time, and at little profit, and you will generally find throughout the country, that their stores are known as the "cheap stores." This is a great secret of trade; and when once that reputation is acquired, the custom will seek that store. For the most part, they first seek this enviable notoriety for their establishment, and then, by courtesy and a determination to give

Levi Strauss was a German-born Jew who founded the first company to manufacture blue jeans. His firm, Levi Strauss & Co. depicted in this label, began in 1853 in San Francisco, California.

satisfaction, success seems inevitable; and what is thereby gained, economy secures.

Their quick perception gives them an insight into the requirements of every branch of trade, and when they once embark in it they are determined to call to their assistance every available faculty; and the natural sympathy of, and connection with, the other members of their faith, incite them to an emulation, the result of which is a high commercial position in the community.

Merchandise, from the time it is freighted on the clipper ships until it is consumed, passes principally through the hands of the Jewish merchants. As importers, jobbers, and retailers, they seem to monopolize most of the trade, and our business streets are thickly studded with their warehouses, shops, and stores. Their commercial position is high indeed, and without them now, trade would almost become stagnated in the State. The Express Companies of the interior depend mainly upon them for support, and the freight and package lists continually abound with their names. This position they have not acquired without great attention, honesty, industry, and personal sacrifice, and by unremitted prudence and civility; and they seem determined to add to it dignity and wealth.

This has had much influence in banishing the shameful prejudices otherwise existing against the Israelites, as a sordid and cunning race.[5] Practice and experience in California have taught our neighbors the falsity of these opinions. Nowhere in America is the Jew so well understood, and so readily appreciated, as in this State; and nowhere does he more deserve the respect and esteem of his fellow citizens. May it always be so. May this abandonment of those prejudices be as lasting as it is just; and the Jew, as he is just and honest, ever merit that esteem and regard which has been so long withheld from his nation, and which always the liberty of America, and the honesty of California, is willing to accord to his enterprise, civility, forbearance, and capability.

Section VII

Connecting California to the Nation:
War, Railroads, and Agribusiness, 1860s–1870s

Section VII

Introduction to Connecting California to the Nation, 1860s–1870s

Sources

1. An Appeal for Free Soil, 1847
2. Compromise of 1850
3. Speech Before Senate on the Admission of California into the Union, 1860
4. Letter to Abraham Lincoln on Secession Crisis, 1861
5. California's Newspapers Debate the War, 1861–1863
6. To the Voters of the State of California: The 15th Amendment, 1869
7. Impressions Concerning the Chinese Railroad Workers, 1865"
8. The Great Theme—The Pacific Railroad, 1865
9. Recollections on the Completion of the Pacific Railroad, 1869
10. What the Railroad Has Done for California, 1875
11. California Vineyards and Agriculture, 1865
12. Orange Culture in California, 1880
13. The Patrons of Husbandry on the Pacific Coast: A Summary of California, 1875

Civil War

California's entrance into the Union in 1850 after nine months of Congressional debates, during which the nation moved ever closer toward Civil War, threatened to upset the tenuous balance of power maintained between Free States and Slaves States by equal representation in the U.S. Senate. In spite of a multitude of political compromises federally instituted to mollify the South into accepting the entire State of California as a Free State into the Union, Californians struggled for the next decade to keep their state intact against the designs of many to politically severe southern California from its northern counter-part. Ironically, it was the impending threat of secession of Southern States from the Union that actually halted the separation of southern California into becoming part of the Colorado territory. When America started moving west of the Mississippi River, conflicting sentiments from advocates of Free Soil Labor versus Slave Labor heightened when the acquisition of Mexican Territories drew near—Congressional expansionists from both camps vied for the new territories. In August 1846, just days after the start of the Mexican-American War, Northern Democratic Congressman David Wilmot proposed an amendment to an appropriations bill that prohibited the extension of slavery into any new territories acquired by the United States as a result of its war with Mexico. This Wilmot Proviso meant to thwart the extension of the 1820 Missouri Compromise territorial line of demarcation at the 36°30′ parallel that divided the Kansas-Nebraska Territories between Slave Labor States to its south and Free Labor States to its north. Had this boundary line been extended all the way to the West Coast, California and New Mexico Territories would have been divided into northern and southern regions with the institution of slavery extended into the southern holdings.

Sources

Congressional battles over the **Wilmot Proviso**, the first selection in this section, went on for years as Congress endeavored to maintain their fragile equilibrium through just enough legislative ambiguity to stall any decisive actions on the subject of slavery and expansion to another day. That day came in 1850.

America's victory over Mexico, once likened by American writer Ralph Waldo Emerson to a celebratory man drinking arsenic, brought Congressional conflict over California to a new feverish pitch. Once again, Congressional conciliation tried to appease both sides of the free soil-slavery issue for just a little while longer with the provisions of the **Compromise of 1850**, the second selection in this section. The Compromise of 1850 linked the Statehood of California to other politically charged issues of the time, namely: the concept of popular sovereignty that allowed territories to choose their own labor status, free or slave; the abolition of slave trading in Washington

DC; and the enforcement of the Fugitive Slave Act of 1793. In securing the entirety of the State of California as a free state, Congress agreed through this legislation to allow popular sovereignty in the territories of Utah and New Mexico, while abolishing slave trade in the nation's capital but forming a new harsher Fugitive Slave Law that permitted southerners to hunt for runaway slaves into northern territories. Reactions to the provisions drove the heated enmity between the North and the South to new heights, resulting in regional conflicts during the next decade leading up to the Civil War.

Although designated a Free State, California experienced sectional conflicts and racial issues throughout the 1850s and 1860s. Southern Californians, some who were dispossessed Californios and others who were ardent advocates for slavery, attempted three times in the 1850s to achieve a separate statehood for Southern California, or at least territorial status separate from Northern California. The Pico Act of 1859, which passed the California State Legislature and was signed and approved by the Governor and the voters, proposed Southern California become the Territory of Colorado. It was sent to Washington D. C. and awaited Congressional review with a strong advocate in Senator Milton Latham. However the national secession crisis in 1860 led to the Pico Act never coming to a vote. Southern Californian's divisive behavior was due to the presence of one-time slave owners who had brought their human property into the state in the previous decade. By the late 1850s there were only 2,500 African Americans in California. But Southern sympathizers were greatly outnumbered by pro-Unionists throughout the state. The next document, **Speech Before Senate on the Admission of California to the Union, 1860**, confirms California's loyalty to the Union. But this did not dissuade some in Washington to lobby for another compromise with the South in order to stave off secession from the southern states. Selection 4, **Letter to Abraham Lincoln on Secession Crisis, 1861** by John D. Defrees, discusses the secession crisis as it related to California. Defrees was a newspaperman and a politician, who along with others, controlled Republican party politics in Indiana. When Lincoln became President, he named Defrees Public Printer. This document reveals that attitudes still prevailed in Washington that wanted to see California split by the Missouri Compromise border at the 36 parallel, making Southern California a slave state. This they believed would appease the South and prevent their schism from the Union.

When the Civil War commenced in early 1861, politicians and citizens throughout the state contested the war, as evidenced in the selection **California's Newspapers Debate the War**. Always maintaining their state to be pro-Union and anti-slavery, about 16,000 Californians enlisted for military duty during the Civil War. Since transportation to the battle fields in the East was long and expensive, most volunteers remained in California, guarding local garrisons, overland mail routes, and protecting setters against Indians in the northwest. A battalion of 500 joined the 2nd Massachusetts Cavalry, at their expense, and fought mostly in Virginia campaigns. In 1862, another 2,350 men, in what was known as the California Column, marched across Arizona to expel the Confederates from Arizona and New Mexico. But pro-Union sentiment in California did not necessarily translate into social and political tolerance for the status of the Freedmen once the Civil War ended and Reconstruction began. When the U.S. Congress approved the Reconstruction legislation known as the Fifteenth Amendment on February 25 and 26, 1869, it was sent immediately to the states for ratification or rejection. A three-quarters majority of states (28 of 37) was needed for its adoption. The last selection in this group, **To the Voters of the State of California: The 15th Amendment, 1869**, issued by the Democratic State Central Committee, demonstrates an unwillingness of many Californians to accept the freed Blackman as an equal whose rights white men should uphold. Pundits of the time tied the ratification of the 15th Amendment to the probable enfranchisement of "Chinamen" in California as well—an assured rhetoric that they felt would squelched the ratification of the amendment in California—which it did. California did not ratify the amendment for nearly another century, in 1962.

The Railroads and the Chinese

The end of the Civil War allowed the attention of the nation to turn again to the West. As already seen, transportation industries expanded as ships, wagon trains, stagecoaches, and eventually railroads brought fortune seeking immigrants from every continent to the Golden State in ever increasing numbers, making California the most racially diverse population in the entire country.

Sources

The transcontinental railroad connecting Sacramento, California to Council Bluffs, Iowa that was constructed between 1863 and 1869 had brought tens of thousands of Chinese families into California as cheap laborers on the railway lines. Samuel Bowles gave just one of many first-hand accounts of the role of the Chinese working for the Central Pacific Railroad line. Bowles was an American journalist, as well as the publisher and editor of *The Republican*, a newspaper out of Springfield, Massachusetts. In 1865, he accompanied a rather large touring party in the company of Schuyler Colfax, the Speaker of the United States House of Representatives. Bowles's published monograph on that summer's tour across the United States to the Pacific Coast by stagecoach recounted his impressions about the labor of the Chinese workers and the significance of the railroad that they were building in these two letters from Samuel Bowles: **Impressions Concerning the Chinese Railroad Workers, 1865** and **The Great Theme—The Pacific Railroad, 1865**.

Another eyewitness to the construction of rails by the Central Pacific Railroad was Sidney Dillon, a railroad executive and one the nation's most successful railroad builders. Because of his role as one of the principal contractors for the Union Pacific, he helped lay some of the last rails at Promontory Summit for the First Transcontinental Railroad in 1869, for which he received one of the ceremonial silver spikes used to complete the project. We can read his account of that day in the next selection, **Recollections on the Completion of the Pacific Railroad, 1869**. That connection of the Central Pacific Railroad with the Union Pacific at Promontory Summit of May 10, 1869 formed the first transcontinental rail-line that could carry passengers from New York to California in a week. The world had become instantly smaller.

One of the thousands of travelers who then journeyed West via the transcontinental route was D. L. Phillips, who took his tubercular son to California in 1876 hoping that the climate change from the East Coast to the West Coast would help relieve his son's respiratory ailment. Phillips posted return letters from California, which were then published in the Illinois State Journal. Among other things, the letters described their travel experiences on the rails as they went West. They also recounted their impressions upon their arrival at San Francisco, along with voyages down the West Coast to San Diego and excursions into the interior valleys. Phillips gave his assessment of the contributions of the Trancontinental Railroad to the development of California in this next selection, **What the Railroad has Done for California, 1875**." The ever-increasing number of railway lines that kept being added across the nation and from region to region fueled the rapid growth of California's true goldmine—its agricultural bonanza.

Agribusiness in California

The worth of all the gold mined from California's soil between 1849 and 1862, an estimated $10 billion in today's currency, pales when compared to the agricultural output from California's soil, which today is nearly $20 billion annually. After years of droughts in the early 1860s that literally wiped out California's cattle industry, generous rainfall in the late 1860s and into the 1870s gave rise to new agricultural ventures. The cattle industry was then overtaken by the sheep industry for a brief time as California's major agricultural enterprise. The first census in 1850 identified 17,514 head of sheep—by 1860 it was a million head, and the industry finally peaked in 1876 at nearly 6.5 million. But, even before the sheep industry peaked, vast acreages of golden fields of wheat were rapidly springing up on large, expansive ranches, some approaching one million acres in size. It was California's most profitable crop for the next 30 years. Barley was added to California's crops and their combined acreage exceeded one million acres in 1867 and peaking at nearly four million acres in the late 1880s. Also at the end of the drought years Hungarian-born farmers introduced 1400 European varieties of grapes to Sonoma Valley and by the 1870s, California's 40,000 acres of vineyards were producing two million gallons of wine annually.

Sources

The selection in this section recounting the vineyards of California and other agricultural pursuits is taken from the travel diary of Samuel Bowles that was mentioned earlier: **Vineyards** and Agriculture, 1865. California's wine industry would go on to produce 19 million gallons of wine in 1900, producing over 80% of the nation's wine output.

California's agricultural revolution of the 1860s and 1870s that capitalized on advances in irrigation and transportation technologies set the stage for the blossoming of the deserts in Southern California with some of the greatest agricultural accomplishments the state has ever known. Marketed to combat scurvy in California's mining towns, the sour and less desirable Spanish "mission" orange that ripened in the summer was augmented by the large sweet winter-ripening Bahia naval orange from Brazil in the 1870s. These dual citrus crops, in conjunction with the already hearty lemons brought over by the Spanish, established Southern California as the citrus growing capital of the nation, producing ⅔ of its orange output and over 90% of its lemons. The next selection, **Orange Culture in California, 1880**, written by Thomas A. Garey, a 30-year resident of California, reveals the attitudes of this citrus-growing agribusinessman for the potential of the industry in California.

This volume's final document is a fitting summary of agricultural production in California since its Spanish days, highlighting the agribusiness developments of wheat, wool, and wines—**The Patrons of Husbandry on the Pacific Coast: A Summary of California Agriculture, 1875."** The author Ezra Slocum Carr was a physician, an educator, a university professor, and an agriculturalist. He taught at several medical colleges on the East Coast before moving to Wisconsin in 1856, where he taught chemistry and natural history at the university and served as commissioner of the state geological survey. In 1867, when his contract was not renewed, Carr moved to California where he taught agriculture at the University of California for six years and was later appointed California state superintendent of public instruction. His larger work published in San Francisco in 1875, which embodies the extract about California we included here, offers a complete history of the origin, condition and progress of agriculture throughout the world as context for his distinctive description of California having the grandest fields of agriculture "to be found on the surface of our planet."

Readings

1. An Appeal for Free Soil, 1847

By David Wilmot

Primary Source

But, sir, the issue now presented is not whether slavery shall exist unmolested where it now is, but whether it shall be carried to new and distant regions, now free, where the footprint of a slave cannot be found. This sir, is the issue. Upon it I take my stand, and from it I cannot be frightened or driven by idle charges of abolitionism.

I ask not that slavery be abolished. I demand that this government preserve the integrity of free territory against the aggressions of slavery—against its wrongful usurpations.

Sir, I was in favor of the annexation of Texas. … The Democracy [Democratic party] of the North, almost to a man, went for annexation. Yes sir, here was an empire larger than France given up to slavery shall further concessions be made by the North? Shall we give up free territory, the inheritance of free labor? Must we yield this also? Never, sir, never, until we ourselves are fit to be slaves. …

But, sir, we are told that the joint blood and treasure of the whole country [are] being

David Wilmot, January 20, 1814–March 16, 1868, was a U.S. politican who sought to ban slavery in all territories acquired from Mexico in the Mexican–American War of 1846–1848.

expended in this acquisition, therefore it should be divided, and slavery allowed to take its share Sir, the South has her share already; the installment for slavery was paid in advance. We are fighting this war for Texas and for the South. I affirm it—every intelligent man knows it—Texas is the primary cause of this war. For this, sir, Northern treasure is being exhausted, and Northern blood poured upon the plains of Mexico. We are fighting this war cheerfully not reluctantly—cheerfully fighting this war for Texas; and yet we seek not to change the character of her institutions. Slavery is there; there let it remain. ...

Now, sir, we are told that California is ours, that New Mexico is ours—won by the valor of our arms. They are free. Shall they remain free? Shall these fair provinces be the inheritance and homes of the white labor of freemen or the black labor of slaves? This, sir, is the issue—this the question. The North has the right, and her representatives here have the power. ...

But the South contend that, in their emigration to this free territory, they have the right to take and hold slaves, the same as other property.

Unless the amendment I have offered be adopted, or other early legislation is had upon this subject, they will do so. Indeed, they unitedly, as one man, have declared their right and purpose so to do, and the work has already begun.

Slavery follows in the rear of our armies. Shall the war power of our government be exerted to produce such a result? Shall this government depart from its neutrality on this question, and lend its power and influence to plant slavery in these territories?

There is no question of abolition here, sir. Shall the South be permitted, by aggression, by invasion of the right, by subduing free territory and planting slavery upon it, to wrest these provinces from Northern freemen, and turn them to the accomplishment of their own sectional purposes and schemes?

This is the question. Men of the North, answer. Shall it be so? Shall we of the North submit to it? If we do, we are coward slaves, and deserve to have the manacles fastened upon our own limbs.

2. Compromise of 1850

By Senator Henry Clay

Primary Source

It being desirable, for the peace, concord, and harmony of the Union of these States, to settle and adjust amicably all existing questions of controversy between them arising out of the institution of slavery upon a fair, equitable and just basis: therefore,

1. Resolved, That California, with suitable boundaries, ought, upon her application to be admitted as one of the States of this Union, without the imposition by Congress of any restriction in respect to the exclusion or introduction of slavery within those boundaries.

2. Resolved, That as slavery does not exist by law, and is not likely to be introduced into any of the territory acquired by the United States from the republic of Mexico, it is inexpedient for Congress to provide by law either for its introduction into, or exclusion from, any part of the said

States and Territories of the United States of America
September 9 1850 to March 2 1853

territory; and that appropriate territorial governments ought to be established by Congress in all of the said territory, not assigned as the boundaries of the proposed State of California, without the adoption of any restriction or condition on the subject of slavery.

3. Resolved, That the western boundary of the State of Texas ought to be fixed on the Rio del Norte, commencing one marine league from its mouth, and running up that river to the southern line of New Mexico; thence with that line eastwardly, and so continuing in the same direction to the line as established between the United States and Spain, excluding any portion of New Mexico, whether lying on the east or west of that river.

4. Resolved, That it be proposed to the State of Texas, that the United States will provide for the payment of all that portion of the legitimate and bona fide public debt of that State contracted prior to its annexation to the United States, and for which the duties on foreign imports were pledged by the said State to its creditors, not exceeding the sum of dollars, in consideration of the said duties so pledged having been no longer

applicable to that object after the said annexation, but having thenceforward become payable to the United States; and upon the condition, also, that the said State of Texas shall, by some solemn and authentic act of her legislature or of a convention, relinquish to the United States any claim which it has to any part of New Mexico.

5. Resolved, That it is inexpedient to abolish slavery in the District of Columbia whilst that institution continues to exist in the State of Maryland, without the consent of that State, without the consent of the people of the District, and without just compensation to the owners of slaves within the District.

6. But, resolved, That it is expedient to prohibit, within the District, the slave trade in slaves brought into it from States or places beyond the limits of the District, either to be sold therein as merchandise, or to be transported to other markets without the District of Columbia.

7. Resolved, That more effectual provision ought to be made by law, according to the requirement of the constitution, for the restitution and delivery of persons bound to service or labor in

any State, who may escape into any other State or Territory in the Union. And,

8. Resolved, That Congress has no power to promote or obstruct the trade in slaves between the slaveholding States; but that the admission or exclusion of slaves brought from one into another of them, depends exclusively upon their own particular laws. ...

An Act for the admission of the State of California into the Union.

Whereas the people of California have presented a constitution and asked admission into the Union, which constitution was submitted to Congress by the President of the United States, by message dated February thirteenth, eighteen hundred and fifty, and which, on due examination, is found to be republican in its form of government ...

An Act to amend, and supplementary to, the Act entitled "An Act respecting Fugitives from Justice, and Persons escaping from the Service of their Masters," approved February twelfth, one thousand seven hundred and ninety-three. ...

SEC. 6. And be it further enacted, That when a person held to service or labor in any State or Territory of the United States, has heretofore or shall hereafter escape into another State or Territory of the United States, the person or persons to whom such service or labor may be due, or his, her, or their agent or attorney, duly authorized, by power of attorney, in writing, acknowledged and certified under the seal of some legal officer or court of the State or Territory in which the same may be executed, may pursue and reclaim such fugitive person, either by procuring a warrant from some one of the courts, judges, or commissioners aforesaid, of the proper circuit, district, or county, for the apprehension of such fugitive from service or labor, or by seizing and arresting such fugitive, where the same can be done without process, and by taking, or causing such person to be taken, forthwith before such

court, judge, or commissioner, whose duty it shall be to hear and determine the case of such claimant in a summary manner; and upon satisfactory proof being made ...

SEC. 7. And be it further enacted, That any person who shall knowingly and willingly obstruct, hinder, or prevent such claimant, his agent or attorney, or any person or persons lawfully assisting him, her, or them, from arresting such a fugitive from service or labor, either with or without process as aforesaid, or shall rescue, or attempt to rescue such fugitive from service or labor, from the custody of such claimant ... when so arrested ... that such person was a fugitive from service or labor as aforesaid, shall, for either of said offences, be subject to a fine not exceeding one thousand dollars, and imprisonment not exceeding six months, by indictment and conviction before the District Court of the United States. ...

SEC. 9. And be it further enacted, That, upon affidavit made by the claimant of such fugitive, his agent or attorney, after such certificate has been issued, that he has reason to apprehend that such fugitive will be rescued by force from his or their possession before he can be taken beyond the limits of the State in which the arrest is made, it shall be the duty of the officer making the arrest to retain such fugitive in his custody, and to remove him to the State whence he fled, and there to deliver him to said claimant, his agent, or attorney. And to this end, the officer aforesaid is hereby authorized and required to employ so many persons as he may deem necessary to overcome such force, and to retain them in his service so long as circumstances may require. The said officer and his assistants, while so employed, to receive the same compensation, and to be allowed the same expenses, as are now allowed by law for transportation of criminals, to be certified by the judge of the district within which the arrest is made, and paid out of the treasury of the United States. ...

An Act to suppress the Slave Trade in the District of Columbia.

Be it enacted by the Senate and House of Representatives of the United States of America in Congress assembled, That from and after the first day of January, eighteen hundred and fifty-one, it shall not be lawful to bring into the District of Columbia any slave whatever, for the purpose of being sold, or for the purpose of being placed in depot, to be subsequently transferred to any other State or place to be sold as merchandize. And if any slave shall be brought into the said District by its owner, or by the authority or consent of its owner, contrary to the provisions of this act, such slave shall thereupon become liberated and free. …

3. Speech Before Senate on the Admission of California into the Union, 1860

By William H. Seward

Primary Source

Speech of the Hon. WM. H. Seward, in the Senate of the United States, on the Admission of California. [Delivered March 8, 1860.]

Mr. Seward arose and said—*Mr. President*: Four years ago, California, scarcely inhabited and quite unexplored, was unknown even to our usually immoderate desires, except, by a harbor, capacious and tranquil, which only Statesmen then foresaw would be useful in the Oriental Commerce, of a far distant, if not merely chimerical future.

A year ago, California was a mere military dependency of our own, and we were celebrating, with enthusiasm and unanimity, its acquisition, with its newly discovered, but yet untold and untouched mineral wealth, as the most auspicious of many and unparalleled achievements.

Today Calfornia is a State, more populous than the least, and richer than several of the greatest of our thirty States. This same California, thus rich and populous, is here asking admission into the Union and finds us debating the dissolution of the Union itself.

No wonder if we were perplexed in the changing embarrassment, no wonder if we are appalled by ever increasing responsibilities! No wonder if we are bewildered by the ever augmenting magnitude and rapidity of national vicissitudes]

Shall California be Received? For myself, upon my individual judgment and conscience, I answer Yes! For myself, as an instructed Representative of one of the States, of *that* one even, of the States, which is soonest and longest to be pressed in commercial and political rivalry by the new Commonwealth, I answer, Yes! Let California come in. Every new State, whether she come from the East or from the West, coming from whatever part of the Continent she may, she is welcome. But California, that comes from the clime where the West dies away into the rising East—California which bounds at once the Empire and the Continent,—California the youthful Queen of the Pacific, her robes of Freedom, gorgeously inlaid with gold, is doubly welcome.

And now I enquire, first, why should California be rejected? All the objections are founded only in the circumstances of her coming, and in the organic law which she presents for our confirmation.

First. California comes unceremoniously, without a preliminary consent of Congress, and therefore by usurpation. This allegation, I think, is not quite true,—at least not quite true in spirit. California is not here of her own pure volition. We tore California violently from her place in the confederation of Mexican States, and stipulated by the treaty of Guadalupe Hidalgo, that the territory should be admitted, by States, into the American Union as speedily as possible.

The second objection is that California has assigned her own boundaries,without the pre- vious authority of Congress. But she was left to organize herself, without any boundaries fixed by previous law, or by prescription. She was obliged, therefore, to assume boundaries, since without boundries she must have remained unorganized.

A third objection is, that California is too large. I answer; first, there is no common standard of States. California, though greater than many, is less than one of the States. Second, California if too large, may be divided with her own consent, which is all the security we have for reducing the magnitude: and averting the preponderance of Texas. Thirdly, the boundaries of California seem not at all unnatural. The territory circumscribed is altogether contiguous and compact. Fourth, the boundaries, are convenient. They embrace only inhabited portions of the country, commercially connected with the port of San Francisco.

No one has pretended to offer boundaries more in harmony, with the physical outlines of the region concerned, or more convenient for civil administration.

But to draw closer to the question, *what* shall be the boundaries of a new State concerns, first, the State herself, (and California, of course, is content;) secondly, adjacent communities—Oregon does not complain of encroachment, and there is no other adjacent community to complain;—thirdly, the other States of the Union. The larger the Pacific States, the smaller will be their relative power in the Senate. All the States now here are Atlantic States and inland States, and surely they may well indulge California in the largest liberty of boundaries.

The fourth objection to the admission of California is that no previous census has been taken and no laws prescribing the qualifications of suffrage and apportionment of Representatives in Convention existed.

I answer, California was left to act *ab initio*. She must begin somewhere without a census and without such laws. The Pilgrim Fathers began in the same way on board the *Mayflower*; and since it is objected that some of the electors in California may have been aliens, I add that the Pilgrim Fathers were aliens and strangers to the Commonwealth of Plymouth.

The fifth objection is, that California comes under Executive influence, first in her coming as a *free* State, and second in her coming at all. The first charge rests on suspicion only, and is peremptorily denied, and the denial is not controverted by proofs. I discard it altogether. The second is true to the extent that both the late President and the present President advised the people of California, that having been left without any civil government, under the military supervision of the Executive, without any authority of law whatever, the adoption of a constitution, subject to the approval of Congress, would be regarded favorably by the President.

I have now reviewed all the objections raised against the admission of Caliiornia. It is seen that they have no foundation in the law of nature and of nations. Nor are they found in the Constitution; for the Constitution prescribes no form or manner of proceeding in the admission of new States, but leaves the whole to the discretion of Congress. "Congress may admit new States." The objections are all merely formal and technical. They rest on precedents which have not always, nor even generally, been observed.

I proceed to state my reasons for the opinion that California ought to be admitted. The population of the United States consists of natives of Caucasian origin, and exotics of the same derivation. The native mass rapidly assimilates to itself and absorbs the exotic: and these, therefore, constitute one homogenous people. The African race, bond and free, and the aborigines, savage and civilized, being incapable of such assimilation and absorption, remain distinct, and owing to their peculiar condition constitute inferior masses, and may be regarded as accidental if not disturbing political forces.

Allowing due consideration to the increasing density of our population, we are safe in assuming that long before this mass shall have attained the maximum of numbers indicated, the entire width of our possessions from the Atlantic to the Pacific ocean, will be covered by it, and be brought into social maturity and complete political organization.

The question now arises, shall this great People, having a common origin, a common language, a common religion, common sentiments, interests, sympathies, and hopes, remain one political State, one Nation, one Republic, or it shall be broken into two conflicting and probably hostile Nations

State flag of California.

or Republics? There cannot ultimately be more than two, for the habit of association already formed, as the interests of mutual intercourse are forming, and the central portions if they cannot all command access to both oceans, will not be obstructed in their approaches to that one which offers the greatest facilities to their commerce.

And now it seems to me that the perpetual unity of our empire hangs on the decision of this day, and of this hour. California is already a State—a complete and fully appointed State. She never again can be less than that. She can never again be a Province or a colony. Nor can she be made to shrink and shrivel into the proportions of a federal, dependent Territory. California then henceforth and forever must be what, she is now—a State. The question whether she shall be one of the United States of America has depended on her and on us. Her election has been made. Our consent alone remains suspended, and that consent must be pronounced now or never. I say now or never! Nothing prevents it now but want of agreement among ourselves. Our harmony cannot increase while this question remains open. We shall never agree to admit California unless we agree now.

Washington, Jany 8 1861.

M y dear Sir,

Insanity is sweeping over the whole South like a dreadful epidemic, and is still on the increase. The bad passions of the poor, ignorant American people have been so aroused by the infernal demagogues who have been so long uttering their falsehoods of us that it is now impossible to control them. The mob may yet take vengeance on those who have mislead them, as during the French revolution.

The Republicans here have no amount of action, except a determination to enforce all the laws and to maintain the Union at all hazzards. Many think that something, having at least the semblance of a compromise, ought to be made, while others say, "Stand firm—yield not an inch to the unreasonable demands of the traitors!—"

Those in favor of some kind of compromise say, that, they would do it, not to satisfy the extremists of the South—but the real Union men of that part of the country—that, by doing so, all except the Cotton States can be kept in the Union. The proposition most favored is what is called the border state plan, which is the extension of 36–30 to California, the prohibition of Slavery North, and non-interference South of it.

Many Southern men say, that, if they can have something from you with which they can go before their people and tell them that the Republicans have been <u>misunderstood</u> (they ought to say misrepresented) they can yet prevent the formation of a Southern Confederacy. They urge, that, if you would only take occasion to write a letter to some one for publication, covering the following points, it would avail all they desire.

1. Recommend the repeal of all laws intended to obstruct the enforcement of the fugitive Slave law.

2. The maintenance of all the laws enacted by Congress.

3. Oppose the abolition of Slavery in the District of Columbia, except in accordance with the wishes of the people, and then only when remuneration is made owners.

4. Oppose interference with slavery in the States, arsenals and dock yards where it exists by sanction of state laws.

5. Not oppose the admission of new States because of the recognition of Slavery in Constitutions which have been submitted to a vote of the people.

6. Whatever may be your views of the expediency of any Congressional legislation in relation to the Territories it will meet official approval unless in conflict with the Constitution. [This is an old Whig doctrine and is right.]

Altho' at first agreeing with you that no letter from you ought to be expected, I am beginning to believe that the most extraordinary condition of the public mind requires a departure from the usual course. At any rate, it is worthy the most serious consideration. Patriotism demands every possible effort to prevent a resort to violent means.

Hamilton wrote in the Federalist, "When the sword is once drawn, the passions of men observe no bounds of moderation. The suggestions of wounded pride, the instigations of irritated resentment would be apt to carry the State against which the arms of the Union were exerted, to any extremes necessary to avenge the supposed affront, or avoid the disgrace of submission." We might be able to overcome the South—but, what then?

As to Southern members of your Cabinet I suppose E. Etheridge and Winter Davis are the only men having courage, character, ability and position enough to accept places if tendered. They are true men.

Gen. Scott is here and making arrangements to have a strong police force for the 4 of March.

I do not believe the madmen of the South dare attempt to carry out their threats of preventing an inaugeration.

The threat to prevent counting the votes cannot be carried.—Senator Bright told me, a few days ago in the most emphatic manner, that you shall be inaugurated and that no northern Senator will lend himself to any ~~revolution~~ revolutionary scheme to prevent it.

Praying for the best, I am
Truly Yours,

Jno. D. Defrees.

---

5. California's Newspapers Debate the War, 1861–1863

Primary Source

Pro-Confederates

Sonora Democrat, January, 1861, upon the formation of the Confederacy;

> We are for a Pacific Republic. … We believe it to be the true policy of California … to cut loose from both sections, and not involve herself in the general ruin. … We shall never consent to pay taxes for the coercion of a sovereign state; neither do we desire to see California linked on to fragment of this Union.

San Joaquin (Stockton) Republican, September 10, 1861:

> … [T]he war is waged for the defence of Southern homes and firesides, so southern nationality.

San Jose Tribune, December 19, 1861 on Lincoln:

> … [A]n illiterate backwoodsman who is not only destitute of the first requirements of a statesman, but who can

COL. E. D. BAKER'S
CALIFORNIA REGIMENT.

A RENDEZVOUS

For the enrollment of a

COMPANY OF PICKED MEN

WILL BE OPENED ON

Monday, August 12, 1861,

AT THE HOUSE OF HENRY REDDING,

PASSYUNK ROAD

OPPOSITE QUEEN STREET.

This Company will leave for the Seat of War in two weeks, or sooner, if full.

JOSEPH C. TITTERMARY, Captain.

Philadelphia, August 12, 1861.

California Regiment recruiting poster.

scarcely write a sentence of the English language correctly!

Mariposa Free Press, March 21, 1863:

What cares Abraham Lincoln for the

good of the hands dripping with the blood of his countrymen.

Pro-Unionists

Stockton Argus, May, 1861:

We are for unconditional support of the Government of the United States in its efforts to suppress rebellion and treason, and agree with Seward that "party must be forgotten in our effort, to save the Union."

San Francisco Bulletin, June 29, 1861:

—If the government is so much in need of ready-made cavalry, let it send to California. We can raise, equip, and march across the plains, in six months, ten regiments of the best horsemen in the world. We just ask to let our vaqueros have a chance.

Los Angeles Southern News, March 19. 1862:

We hope every leader of this iniquitous rebellion will be hung, if they fall into the hands of the Government.—Traitors who have plunged the country into a bloody and devastating civil war to subserve their own selfish ambition, should meet with no mercy.

San Francisco Alta California, January 5, 1863, on the Proclamation of Emancipation:

—The universal sentiment is that if slavery must die that the Republic may live, let its death-knell be sounded, no matter what the consequences.

6. To the Voters of the State of California

The 15th Amendment, 1869

By the Democratic State Central Committee

Primary Source

Impressed by a sense of the importance of the approaching election for members of the Legislature, we take this method of addressing you.

The Legislature to be elected on the first of September will be called upon to ratify or reject the proposed Fifteenth Amendment to the Constitution of the United States.

We do not propose to discuss the merits of the Amendment, but to declare to you in this definite form certain facts as to the objects and what will be the results of the Amendment if it should be adopted, and what we now declare to you no candid man of any party will deny, and no one who attempts to evade the facts thus stated in worthy of the slightest belief or respect.

First.—The objects of the Amendment are to abolish all distinctions in this Government between men on account of color, and immediately to confer the right to vote upon the negroes *in all the States of the Union.*

Second.—If the Amendment should be adopted, the direct result will be that the negroes will vote in the State of California at the next election after its adoption.

No further legislation or action of any kind will be necessary to confer upon negroes the right to vote and to hold office in this state.

By the adoption of the Amendment, negroes will be invested with the right to vote and hold office in California. Because by virtue of the Fourteenth Amendment to the Constitution, which is adopted, negroes born in the United States are *citizens,* and do not require to be naturalized in order to become voters. The Fifteenth Amendment, if ratified, prevents the States of the Union from depriving them of the right to vote, and no act of the State which does not exclude white men from the right to vote can exclude any negro, AND NO ACT OF THE STATE CAN EXCLUDE ALL NEGROES FROM THE RIGHT TO VOTE.

Another effect, or result of the adoption of the Amendment will be to confer upon Congress the power to make voters of Chinamen *in spite of any regulation existing in this State to prevent it.*

We know that three-fourths of the people of this State are opposed to negroes being allowed to vote in California, and that four-fifths of the people are opposed to Chinese being allowed to vote. The law as it now is excludes both from voting in this State. The Amendment at once gives the right to negroes to vote, and takes from you the power to prevent the Chinese from becoming voters.

The election of the republican legislative tickets, or a majority of them in this State, will insure the ratification of the Amendment in this State. The election of the Democratic tickets insures its rejection.

An individual Republican candidate in some places may pledge himself in opposition to the Amendment to gain your votes and secure his election, but once elected his opposition will be silenced by a caucus of Republicans, and the Amendment will receive his support under the pressure of party discipline.

It is urged by the Republican speakers and journals that the Amendment will be ratified by a sufficient number of States without California and therefore that we should accept the situation and consent to the ratification.

To this we reply: First that if the assertion were true in fact it would not justify the people of this State in acting contrary to the dictates of their judgment. Just men never yield to wrong while they have power to combat it.

Second. It is not true that the ratification is assured without the vote of California.

To be ratified the Amendment *must* receive the approval of some one of the States of Ohio, California or Oregon, unless some one of the States which has refused to ratify, should reconsider its action, and this is hardly to be expected. If Legislatures elected upon a distinct issue have once refused to ratify, it is scarcely possible that any subsequent Legislature will change the action of the State upon so grave a question.

With all the lights before us we announce to you our distinct belief that Ohio and Oregon will vote as they did at the last election in each of those States, upon the questions of negro suffrage, and that the Amendment will be defeated in each of those States. If we are correct in our opinion the vote of California will decide the question. If California should be seduced from her integrity, the Amendment will probably be ratified, and negroes will be voters. If California rejects the Amendment we believe that it never will be ratified.

Our opponents will endeavor to mislead you as to the certainty of the ratification, but the honest and honorable portion of them will not deny our statement as to the purpose or effect of the Amendment. Those who claim that the Amendment will certainly be ratified, anyhow, may be mislead by zeal and hope, any by the unauthorized statements of unscrupulous newspapers;

but we assure you that any array of the names of States which have ratified, or will ratify the Amendment, is not authorized, and we assure you the wrong *is not yet accomplished.* You may be, and probably will be able to prevent it. The issue is with you. Shall negroes vote in California? Shall Congress have power without your consent to make voters of Chinamen in California?

The man who tells you that negroes will not be allowed to vote under the laws as they already exists, if the Amendment should be adopted, is neither honest nor honorable. The man who tells you that Congress will not have power to make voters of Chinamen in this State, in defiance of any existing law of the State, if the Amendment should be adopted, is a knave or a madman.

We appeal to the honest masses to save the honor of the State. Politicians may evade and shirk the issue, but the issue before you, we repeat, is: Shall negroes vote and hold office in this State? The election of a Democratic Legislature will answer NO! The election of a Republican Legislature will answer YES!

White men of California, vote understandingly. Do not remain away from the polls, but do your duty as free men. Give one day to your race and country, and by the united voice of your own race, save your ballot-box from the pollution of negro and Chinese votes.

JOSEPH P. HOGE,
Chairman of State Central Committee.

THOMAS N. CAZNEAU,
Secretary State Central Committee.

FRANKLIN LAWTON,
Assistant Secretary.

7. Impressions Concerning the Chinese Railroad Workers, 1865

By Samuel Bowles

Primary Source

LETTER XXIII.

THE CHINESE: GRAND DINNER WITH THEM.

San Francisco, August 18.

I have been waiting before writing of the Chinese in these Pacific States, till my experience of them had culminated in the long-promised grand dinner with their leaders and aristocrats. This came last night, and while I am full of the subject,—shark's fins and resurrected fungus digest slowly,—let me write of this unique and important element in the population and civilization of this region. There are 110 fewer than sixty to eighty thousand Chinamen here. They arc scattered all over the States and Territories of the Coast, and number from one-eighth to one-sixth of the entire population. We began to see them at Austin, in Nevada, and have found them everywhere since, in country and city, in the woods, among the mines, north in the British dominions, on the Coast, in the mountains,—everywhere that work is to be done, and money gained by patient, plodding industry. They have been coming over from home since 1852, when was the largest emigration, (twenty thousand.) A hundred thousand in all have come, but thirty thousand to forty thousand have gone back. None come really to stay; they do not identify themselves with the country; but to get work, to make money, and go back. They never, or very rarely, bring their wives. The Chinese women here are prostitutes, imported as such by those who make a business of satisfying the lust of men. Nor are their customers altogether Chinese; base white men patronize their wares as well. Some of these women are taken as "secondary" wives by the Chinese residents, and a sort of family life established; but, as a general rule, there are no families among them, and few children.

The occupations of these people are various. There is hardly anything that they cannot turn their hands to,—the work of women as well as men. They do the washing and ironing for the whole population; and sprinkle the clothes as they iron them, by squirting water over them in a fine spray from their mouths. Everywhere, in village and town, you see rude signs, informing you that See Hop or Ah Thing or Sam Sing or Wee Lung or Cum Sing wash and iron. How Tie is a doctor, and Hop Chang and Chi Lung keep stores. They arc good house servants; cooks, table-waiters, and nurses; better, on the whole, than Irish girls, and as cheap,—fifteen to twenty-five dollars a month and board. One element of their usefulness as cooks is their genius for imitation; show them once how to do a thing, and their education is perfected; no repetition of the lesson is needed. But they seem to be more in use as house servants in the country than the city; they do not share the passion of the Irish girls for herding together, and appear to be content to be alone in a house, in a neighborhood, or a town-

Many are vegetable gardeners, too. In this even climate and with this productive soil, their painstaking culture, much hoeing and constant watering, makes little ground very fruitful, and they gather in three, four and five crops a year. Their garden patches, in the neighborhood of cities and villages, are always distinguishable from the rougher and more carelessly cultured grounds of their Saxon rivals. The Pacific Railroad is being built by Chinese labor. Several thousand Chinamen are now rapidly grading the track through the rocks and sands of the Sierra Nevadas,—without them, indeed, this great work would have to wait for years, or move on with slow, hesitating steps. They can, by their steady industry, do nearly as much in a day, even in this rough labor, as the average of white men, and they cast only about half as much, say thirty dollars a month against fifty dollars. Besides, white labor is not to be had in the quantities necessary for such a great job as this. Good farm hands are the Chinese, also; and in the simpler and routine mechanic arts they have proven adepts;—there is hardly any branch of labor in which, under proper tuition, they do not or cannot succeed most admirably. The great success of the woolen manufacture here is due to the admirable adaptation and comparative cheapness of Chinese labor for the details. They are quick to learn, quiet, cleanly and faithful, and have no "off days," no sprees to get over. As factory operatives they receive twenty and twenty-five dollars a month, and board themselves, though quarters are provided for them on the mill grounds. Fish, vegetables, rice and pork are the main food, which is prepared and eaten with such economy that they live for about one-third what Yankee laborers can.

Thousands of the Chinese are gleaners in the gold fields. They follow in crowds after the white miners, working and washing over their deserted or neglected sands, and thriving on results that their predecessors would despise. A Chinese gold washer is content with one to two dollars a day; while the white man starves or moves on disgusted with twice that. A very considerable portion of the present gold production of California must now be the work of Chinese painstaking and moderate ambition. The traveler meets these Chinese miners everywhere on his road through the State; at work in the deserted ditches, or moving from one to another, on foot with their packs, or often in the stage, sharing the seats and paying the price of their aristocratic Saxon rivals.

Labor, cheap labor, being the one great palpable need of the Pacific States,—far more indeed than capital the want and necessity of their prosperity,—we should all say that these Chinese would be welcomed on every hand, their emigration encouraged, and themselves protected by law. Instead of which, we see them the victims of all sorts of prejudice and injustice. Ever since they began to come here, even now, it is a disputed question with the public, whether they should not be forbidden our shores. They do not ask or wish for citizenship; they have no ambition to become voters; but they are even denied protection in persons and property by the law. Their testimony is inadmissible against the white man: and, as miners, they are subject to a tax of four dollars a month, or nearly fifty dollars a year, each, for the benefit of the County and State treasuries. Thus ostracized and burdened by the State, they, of course, have been the victims of much meanness and cruelty from individuals. To abuse and cheat a Chinaman; to rob him; to kick and cuff him; even to kill him, have been things not only done with impunity by mean and wicked men, but even with vain glory. Terrible are some of the cases of robbery and wanton maiming and murder reported from the mining districts. Had "John,"—here and in China alike the English and Americans nickname every Chinaman "John"—a good claim, original or improved, he was ordered to "move on,"—it belonged to somebody else. Had he hoarded a pile, he was ordered to disgorge; and, if he resisted, he was killed. Worse crimes even are known against them; they have been wantonly assaulted and shot down or stabbed by bad men, as sportsmen would surprise and shoot their game in the woods. There was no risk in such barbarity; if "John" survived to tell the tale, the law would not hear him or believe him. Nobody was so low, so miserable, that he did not despise the Chinaman, and could not outrage him. Ross Browne has an illustration of the status of poor "John," that is quite to the point. A vagabond Indian comes upon a solitary Chinaman, working over the sands of a deserted gulch for gold. "Dish is my land,"—says he,—"you pay me fifty dollar." The poor celestial turns, deprecatingly, saying: "Melican man (American) been here, and took all,—no bit left." Indian, irate and fierce,—"D— Melican man,—you pay me fifty dollar, or I killee you."

Through a growing elevation of public opinion, and a reactionary experience towards depression, that calls for study of the future, the Californians are beginning to have a better appreciation of their Chinese immigrants. The demand for them is increasing. The new State, to be built upon manufactures and agriculture, is seen to need their cheap and reliable labor; and more pains will be taken to attract them to the country. But even now, a man who aspires to be a political leader, till lately a possible United States Senator, and the most widely circulated daily paper of this city, pronounce against the Chinese, and would drive them home. Their opposition is based upon the prejudices and jealousy of ignorant white laborers,—the Irish particularly,—who regard the Chinese as rivals in their field, and clothes itself in that cheap talk, so common among the bogus democracy of the East, about this being a "white man's country," and no place for Africans or Asiatics. But our national democratic principle, of welcoming hither the people of every country and

clime, aside, the white man needs the negro and the Chinaman more than they him; the pocket appeal will override the prejudices of his soul,— and we shall do a sort of rough justice to both classes, because it will pay. The political questions involved in the negro's presence, and pressing so earnestly for solution, do not yet arise with regard to the Chinese,—perhaps will never be presented. As I have said, the Chinese are ambitious of no political rights, no citizenship,—it is only as our merchants go to China that they come here. Their great care, indeed, is to be buried at home; they stipulate with anxiety for that; and the great bulk of all who die on these shores arc carried back for final interment.

There is no ready assimilation of the Chinese with our habits and modes of thought and action. Their simple, narrow though not dull minds have run too long in the old grooves to be easily turned off. They look down even with contempt upon our newer and rougher civilization, regarding us barbaric in fact, and calling us in their hearts, if not in speech, "the foreign devils." And our conduct towards them has inevitably intensified these feelings,—it has driven them back upon their naturally self-contained natures and habits. So they bring here and retain all their home ways of living and dressing, their old associations and religion. Their streets and quarters in town and city arc China reproduced, unalleviated. Christian missionaries make small inroads among them. There is an intelligent and faithful one here (Rev. Mr. Loomis,) who has an attractive chapel and school, but his followers are few, and not rapidly increasing. But he and his predecessors and assistants have been and are doing a good work in teaching the two diverse races to better understand each other and in showing them how they can be of value to one another. They have been the constant and urgent advocates of the personal rights of the Chinese. ...

Photograph of Chinese workers building the railroad where it passes through the Sierra Nevada Mountains, ca. 1860s.

But as laborers in our manufactories and as servants in our houses, beside their constant contact with our life and industry otherwise, these emigrants from the East cannot fail to get enlargement of ideas, freedom and novelty of action, and familiarity with and then preference for our higher civilization. Slowly and hardly but still surely this work must go on; and their constant going back and forth between here and China must also transplant new elements of thought and action into the home circles. Thus it is that we may hope and expect to reach this great people with the influences of our better and higher life. It is through modification and revolution in materialities, in manner of living, in manner of doing, that we shall pave the way for our thought and our religion. Our missionaries to the Five Points have learned to attack first with soap and water and clean clothes. The Chinese that come here are unconsciously besieged at first with better food and more of it than they have at home. The bath-house and the restaurant are the avant couriers of the Christian civilization.

The Chinese that come to these States arc among the best of the peasantry from the country

about Canton and Hong Kong. None of them are the miserable coolies that have been imported by the English to their Indian colonies as farm laborers. They associate themselves here into companies, based upon the village or neighborhood from which they come at home. These companies have headquarters in San Francisco; their presidents are men of high intelligence and character; and their office is to afford a temporary refuge for all who belong to their bodies, to assist them to work, to protect them against wrong, and send the dead back to their kindred at home. Beside these organizations, there are guilds or trade associations among the Chinese engaged in different occupations. Thus the laundry-men and the cigar-makers have organizations, with heavy fees from the members, power over the common interests of the business, and an occasional festivity.

The impressions these people make upon the American mind, after close observation of their habits, are very mixed and contradictory. They unite to many of the attainments and knowledge of the highest civilization, in some of which they are models for ourselves, many of the incidents and most of the ignorance of a simple barbarism. It may yet prove that we have as much to learn from them as they from us. Certainly here in this great field, this western half of our continental Nation, their diversified labor is a blessing and a necessity. It is all, perhaps more even, than the Irish and the Africans have been and are to our eastern wealth and progress. At the first, at least, they have greater adaptability and perfection than either of these classes of laborers, to whom we are so intimately and sometimes painfully accustomed.

---

8. The Great Theme—The Pacific Railroad, 1865

By Samuel Bowles

Primary Source

LETTER XXIV.

San Francisco, August 20.

To feel the importance of the Pacific Railroad, in measure the urgency of its early completion, to become impatient with government and contractor at every delay in the work, you must come across the Plains and the Mountains to the Pacific Coast. Then you will see half a Continent waiting for its vivifying influences. You will witness a boundless agriculture, fickle and hesitating for lack of the regular markets this would give. You will find mineral wealth, immeasurable, locked up, wastefully worked, or gambled away, until this shall open to it abundant labor, cheap capital, wood, water, science, ready oversight, steadiness of production,—everything that shall make mining a certainty and not a chance. You will find the world's commerce with India and China eagerly awaiting its opportunities. You will see an illimitable field for manufactures unimproved for want of its stimulus and its advantages. You will feel hearts breaking, see morals struggling slowly upward against odds, know that all the sweetest and finest influences and elements of society and Christian civilization hunger and suffer for the lack of this quick contact with the Parent and Fountain of all our national life.

It is touching to remember that between Plains and Pacific, in country and on coast, on the Columbia, on the Colorado, through all our long journey, the first question asked of us by every man and woman we have met,—whether rich or poor, high or humble,—has been, "When do you think the Pacific Railroad will be done?" or, "Why don't or won't the government, now the war is over, put the soldiers to building this road?"—and their parting appeal and injunction, as well, "Do build this Pacific Road for us as soon as possible,—we wait, everything waits for that." Tender-eyed women, hard-fisted men,—pioneers, or missionaries, the martyrs and the successful,—all alike feel and speak this sentiment. It is the hunger, the prayer, the hope of all these people. Hunger and prayer and hope for "Home," and what home can bring them, in cheap and ready passage to and from, of reunion with parent and brother and sister and friend, of sight of old valley and mountain and wood, of social influence, of esthetic elevation, of worldly stimulus and prosperity. "Home," they all here call the East. It is a touching and pathetic, though almost unconscious, tribute. Such an one "is going home next spring;" "I hope to go home another year;" "When I was home last;" "I have never been home since I came out;" "I am afraid I shall never go home again;"—these and kindred phrases are the current forms of speech. Home is not here, but there. The thought of home is ever rolled, like a sweet morsel, under the tongues of their souls.

Here is large appeal both to the sympathy and foresight of the eastern States. Here is present bond of union and means for perpetuating it. To build the railroad, and freshen recollection and renew association of the original emigrants, and to bind by travel and contact the children here with the homes and lives and loves of their parents there: this is the cheapest, surest and sweetest way to preserve our nationality, and continue the Republic a . unit from ocean to ocean. A sad and severe trial will ensue to the Union if a generation grows up here that "knows not Joseph." The centrifugal forces will ever be in hot action between the far-separated eastern and western sections of the Nation. First among the centripetal powers is the Pacific Railroad, and every year of its delay increases tenfold its burden; every year's postponement weakens in equal degree the influences here by which it shall operate.

What is doing to supply this great want of Pacific progress and civilization and national unity? What are the possibilities and probabilities of the great continental railway? are what you will wish to know from me. Our journey has lain along its most natural commercial route; we started from its eastern terminus on the Missouri border; we kept in the main line of population and travel, which it is desirable for it to follow; we finished our ride upon its beginnings at this end; and we have everywhere had the subject forced upon our thought, and made it constant study. Many of the obstacles to the great work grew feeble in travel over its line. Want of timber, of water, of coal for fuel; the steep grades and high ascents of the

two great continental ranges of mountains to be crossed, the Rocky and the Sierras; and the snows they will accumulate upon the track in the winter months,—these are the suggested and apparent difficulties to the building and operating of the Pacific Railroad. There is plenty of good timber in the mountains; and the soft cotton-wood of the Plains can be kyanized (hardened by a chemical process), so as to make sound sleepers and ties. There are sections of many miles, even perhaps of two hundred, which the timber will have to be hauled; but the road itself can do this as it progresses,—taking along over the track built to-day the timber and rails for that to be built to-morrow. As to water artesian wells are sure to find it in the vacant desert stretches, which are neither so long nor so barren of possible water as has been supposed.

The fuel question is perhaps more difficult to solve as yet. The Sierras will furnish wood in abundance, and cheaply, for all the western end; we know there is coal in the Rocky Mountains; and we were told almost everywhere over the entire line that it had been, or could undoubtedly be found,—in Kansas, on the Plains, among the hills of the deserts. But suppose the supplies of food for steam have to be carried over a few hundred miles of the road, east and west from the Sierras and the Rocky Mountains; that is not so hard a matter,—certainly nothing to daunt or hesitate the enterprise. We shall soon learn, too, to make steam from petroleum; and that is easily transported for long distances; besides which, prospectors are finding it everywhere from Missouri to Pacific. Build the road, and the intermediate country will speedily find the means for running it.

Now as to difficulties of construction, heavy grades and high mountains, and the winter snows as obstacles to continuous use.

The first third of the line, from the Missouri River to the Rocky Mountains, is mere baby-work.

Three hundred men will grade it as fast as the iron can be laid. It is a level, natural roadway, with very little bridging, and no want of water. It is a shame all this section is not finished and running already. The first of January, 1867, ought now to , be the limit for its completion. From here to Salt Lake, over the Rocky Mountains, there are apparently no greater obstacles to be overcome than your Western Road from Springfield to Albany, the Erie and the Pennsylvania Central have triumphantly and profitably surmounted. There are various contesting routes; northerly by the North Platte and the South Pass; by the South Platte and Bridger's Pass, which is the route we traveled in the stage;—or more direct still, from Denver through the present gold mining region of Colorado by Clear Creek and over the Berthoud Pass; or again by a kindred route to the last, up Boulder Creek and over Boulder Pass, both these last two entering the "Middle Park" of the Mountains, and through that to the head waters of the Salt Lake Basin. The Berthoud and Boulder Pass routes would probably involve higher grades and more rock cutting, and in winter deeper snows; but they would pass through a richer country, avoid the deserts of the north, and save at least one hundred miles of distance. A new road for the overland stages is this very season being cut through the Berthoud Pass route by the help of United States soldiers from Utah; and the stage line is expected to be transferred to it next spring. But by the Bridger or South Pass routes, the railroad can surmount the eastern slope of the Rocky Mountains with the greatest case. Our stage teams trotted up the hardly perceptible grades by the Bridger route without any effort. Coming down into Salt Lake Valley, there would be rougher work; but there are several considerable streams along whose banks the track could be brought, I am sure, with no greater labor or expense than has been incurred in a dozen eases by our eastern railroads.

From Salt Lake to the Sierra Nevadas are two routes; southerly through the center of Nevada, and striking Austin and Virginia City, the centers of the silver mining region,—which is the present stage and telegraph route,—and northerly by the Humboldt River. The former would pass more directly through the chief present and prospective populations; but it would encounter a dozen or fifteen ranges of hills to be crossed, and find little wood and scant water. The Humboldt route would be more cheaply built, and goes through a naturally better country as to wood, water and fertility of soil. It is generally conceded to be the true natural roadway across the Continent. The emigration has always taken it. If the railroad is built through it, Virginia City and Austin will be reached by branches dropping down to them through their neighboring valleys.

Now we reach the California border, and the toughest part of the work of the railroad,—the high-reaching, far-spreading, rock-fastened, and snow-covered Sierra Nevadas. But the difficulties here are mitigated by plenty of water and timber, and by the near presence of an energetic population, and are already being practically overcome by the energy and perseverance of the California Pacific Railroad organization. I only wish the East would get to Salt Lake with their rail so soon as the West can and will with theirs. It is not gratifying to eastern pride, indeed, to see how much more California, with its scant capital, its scarce labor, and its depressed industry and interests, is doing to solve this great practical problem of the continental railway, than your abounding wealth and teeming populations of the East, with a great network of railroads from the Atlantic, all needing and professing to seek an outlet west to the Pacific Coast.

Let me state the condition of the work on each end of the line.

Congress has given princely bounties to the enterprise, all that could be expected, everything that was asked. Government bonds are loaned to it to the amount of sixteen thousand dollars a mile through the plains and forty-eight thousand dollars a mile in the mountains; besides which half of all the land each side of the road for twenty miles deep is donated outright to the companies doing the work. The Union Pacific Railroad company is recognized at the East, and the Central Pacific Railroad company here, as entitled to this bounty, and are respectively authorized to construct the road from their starting points until they meet. The companies are further authorized to issue their own bonds to an equal amount to those granted by the government, and secure them by a first mortgage; the government loan taking the second place in security.

The business of supplying the populations of Colorado, Utah and Montana,—at least one hundred and fifty thousand persons,—invites the speedy construction of the road from the East. This business for 1864 is estimated at forty million pounds, and for 1865 at two hundred millions, and employed last year nine thousand wagons, fifty thousand cattle, sixteen thousand horses and mules and ten thousand men as drivers, laborers and guards; and the sum paid for freight in the former year is estimated by one authority at enough to build the railroad the entire distance at a cost of forty-eight thousand dollars the mile! And during the months of May and June, this year, counting both the emigration and the freight trains, there passed west over the Plains full ten thousand teams and fifty thousand to sixty thousand head of stock, according to data furnished from Fort Laramie and the junction of the overland routes on the Platte River. The shipment of supplies for the United States troops on the Plains and in the Mountains this season is alone over eleven million pounds.

All these statistics may not be perfectly accurate; but they have a substantial basis of fact, and with such generous gifts as the government

makes, and with such large railway interests behind to be benefited by farther extension of railway lines to the west, they would seem to justify and to demand a rapid construction of the road out from the Missouri River, especially when for the first five hundred to six hundred miles of that road, there is scarcely more required than to scrape a place in the soft soil for sleepers and ties and iron. And yet, though three to four years have passed since the company accepted the bargain of the government and assumed its responsibilities, not a mile of the main road is running from the Missouri west. The lower branch from Kansas City is open to Lawrence, forty miles, and graded to Topeka, sixty miles; but from Atchison and Omaha there is no iron down, and only small sections graded or half graded.

Is it said that by the government flooding the markets with better classes of its securities, there was no sale for the bonds allotted for this work, and so no means for its construction? The reply is that no set of men should step forward to accept this largess and undertake this enterprise, holding such sure profits in its future, that have not at least a million or two of their own to make a beginning with. Has the war absorbed all labor and capital during these years? Other railroads have been built meantime, and labor was cheaper on the Plains than in California. Beside, here are six months since the war ended, and the end witnesses no marked progress, no larger activity, than the beginning.

I know nothing of the men who form the Pacific Railroad Company of the East; I suspect their names are more familiar to Wall street than to the West or the railroad world; but I do know that all I could see or hear of them and their work, along the route of the continental railway, did not indicate either the earnestness or the power that should accompany their position, their responsibilities and their opportunities. After leaving the Missouri River, indeed, they offered no sign of

Photograph of the ceremony in which the golden spike was finally driven into the transcontinental railroad. Promontory Point, Utah, May 10, 1869.

life except in a single small party of engineers in Salt Lake City, who were on a straggling hunt for the best route through the Rocky Mountains, but who seemed to have no proper leadership, and no clear purpose, and in fact confessed that the company had no chief engineer worthy the name or position.

Here in California, however, there is more life and progress. Energy and capital are not perhaps the best directed possible; there has been and still is somewhat of controversy and waste of power as to the true route; but there is earnestness and movement of the right sort, and the track is fast ascending the Sierras on its progress eastward. It has no immediate way business to tempt it but the trade of Nevada with thirty thousand population,—much less, therefore, than that which invites the laying of the rails across the prairies to the Rocky Mountains,—but this business has constructed and amply paid for two fine toll-roads over the Sierras, and was, until a few days ago, building two railroads in their tracks. There being free water carriage from San Francisco

to Sacramento, these rival roads (both carriage and rail), have their base at the latter point, and branch off right and left into the mountains, and cross the summit of the latter some thirty or forty miles apart, coming together again at a common point in Nevada on the other side, namely, Virginia City. The distance between Sacramento and Virginia City is about the same, one hundred and sixty miles, by each road; and their rivalry has given excellent accommodations for travel and traffic, and helped to push forward the railroad tracks on both lines.

The original and heretofore most popular wagon road was that by Placerville and Lake Tahoe, over which we came into the State, as already described. The railway track on its line is now laid about forty miles from Sacramento or nearly to Placerville, which is among the foot-hills of the mountains. During the "flush" times of Nevada, 1862 and 1863, the business done over this line was immense; in the latter year about twelve millions dollars were paid for freights alone,—the cost of transportation being from five to ten cents a pound,—and the tolls on teams, received by the constructors of the wagon road, amounted to six hundred thousand dollars. The charge for a single team is about thirty dollars; and in 1864, when the business was much less than before, no less than seven thousand teams passed over this Placerville route; carrying all kinds of food and merchandise and machinery over into Nevada, but coming back nearly empty.

As showing how great and wasteful was and still is the cost of doing business in Nevada under such circumstances, it has been carefully estimated that the famous Gould & Curry silver mine at Virginia City would have saved two millions dollars in expenses in a single year, had a railroad been built and running over the mountains. The production of the mine that year was four millions and a half of dollars, but its expenses absorbed three millions and a half, leaving only one million profit to stockholders, against three millions, probably, had there been ready and cheap communication with the San Francisco markets.

The staging and freighting over these mountain toll roads are performed in the most perfect style, however. The freight wagons are bigger and stronger than anything ever seen in the East; generally a smaller one is attached as a tender to the main wagon; ten to twelve large and strong mules or horses, in fine condition, constitute the usual team; and the load ranges from five to ten tons. To each mule in the best teams a large bell is attached, and they are trained to keep step to their music, and so pull and move uniformly. Frequently the road will be filled with these teams for a quarter and a half mile, and the turning out for them is the only interruption to the steady trot or the grand gallop of the six-horse stage teams that, attached to the best of Concord coaches, usually loaded with passengers, go half-flying over these well-graded mountain roads, three to four each way daily. The stage horses are sleek and fat, gay as larks, changed every ten miles, and do their work as if they really loved it. The Placerville road is watered throughout nearly its whole line by sprinkling carts, in the same way as the streets of a city are wet in the dry summer season; and luxurious as this seems and is,—for the dust is otherwise most fearful,—it is found to be the cheapest way of keeping the road itself in good repair. When dry, the heavy teams cut up the track most terribly.

---

9. Recollections on the Completion of the Pacific Railroad, 1869

By Sidney Dillon

Primary Source

It was not a large crowd. In brass bands, fireworks, procession, and oratory, the demonstration, when ground was broken at Omaha, less than five years before, was much more imposing. A small excursion party, headed by Governor Stanford, had come from San Francisco; while on our side, besides our own men, there were only two or three persons present, among whom was the Rev. Dr. Todd, of Pittsfield. Not more than five or six hundred, all told, comprised the whole gathering, nearly all of whom were officials of the two companies—contractors, surveyors, and employees.

The point of junction was in a level circular valley, about three miles in diameter, surrounded by mountains. During all the morning hours the hurry and bustle of preparation went on. Two lengths of rails lay on the ground near the opening in the road-bed. At a little before eleven the Chinese laborers began levelling up the road-bed preparatory to placing the last ties in position. About a quarter past eleven the train from San Francisco, bringing Governor Stanford and party arrived and was greeted with cheers. In the enthusiasm of the occasion there were cheers for everybody, from the President of the United States to the day-laborers on the road.

The two engines moved nearer each other, and the crowd gathered round the open space. Then all fell back a little so that the view should be unobstructed. Brief remarks were made by Governor Stanford on one side, and General Dodge on the other. It was now about twelve o'clock noon, local time, or about 2 p.m. in New York. The two superintendents of construction—S. B. Reed of the Union Pacific, and S. W. Strawbridge of the Central—placed under the rails the last tie. It was of California laurel, highly polished, with a silver plate in the centre bearing the following inscription: "The last tie laid on the completion of the Pacific Railroad, May 10, 1869," with the names of the officers and directors of both companies.

Everything being then in readiness the word was given, and "Hats off" went clicking over the wires to the waiting crowds at New York, Philadelphia, San Francisco, and all the principal cities. Prayer was offered by the venerable Rev. Dr. Todd, at the conclusion of which our operator tapped out: "We have got done praying. The spike is about to be presented," to which the response came back: "We understand. All are ready in the East." The gentlemen who had been commissioned to present the four spikes, two of gold, and two of silver, from

A display poster advertising the Transcontinental Railroad, 1869.

Montana, Idaho, California, and Nevada, stepped forward, and with brief appropriate remarks discharged the duty assigned them.

Governor Stanford, standing on the north, and Dr. Durant on the south side of the track, received the spikes and put them in place. Our operator tapped out: "All ready now; the spike will soon be driven. The signal will be three dots for the commencement of the blows." An instant later the silver hammers came down, and at each stroke in all the offices from San Francisco to New York, and throughout the land, the hammer of the magnet struck the bell.

The signal "Done" was received at Washington at 2:47 p.m., which was about a quarter of one at Promontory. There was not much formality in the demonstration that followed, but the enthusiasm was genuine and unmistakable. The two engines moved up until they touched each other, and a bottle of champagne was poured on the last rail, after the manner of christening a ship at the launching.

10. What the Railroad Has Done for California, 1875

By D. L. Phillips

Primary Source

Letter No. VI.

The State of California has 150,000 square miles of territory, almost three times the number of Illinois; but it is, in a large measure, a State of vast mountains and very high hills. It has not, perhaps, one-half, and possibly not one-third, the number of square miles of arable land to be found in Illinois, and much of that is far less productive than that of our own great State. The mountains are grand, poetic, sublime. They may mix and mingle with the fervid, spread-eagle oratory of the 4th of July, and harmonize with the flights of the bird of freedom, when he fixes his gleaming eye on the sun, and pierces the heavens, to guard the eyrie of his mate as she feeds her eaglets on the dizzy heights; but these are about their immediate uses. You can not farm them; they are too elevated for that. They do not "pan out" to any extent in mining, or yield much to feed either man or brute. The truth is, they are very unhandy and very much in the way, and especially so when you attempt to travel over them or to build railroads among them. This has been found to be true everywhere, and it is now one of the embarrassing impediments besetting those attempting to construct roads so needed by the people of California to get what they raise to market. ...

At the breaking out of the rebellion in 1861, California had no well digested scheme of railroad improvements. For years the question had been discussed, re-discussed and laid aside. San Francisco controlled most of the wealth of the State. It was intensely Democratic, with its chief city in political control. The Gwinns, Terrys, Benhams and their co-laborers in the interests of Democratic ascendency on this coast, had no time to build railroads. They were only intent on holding the State in the orthodox faith of the defenders of the "peculiar institution" [slavery]. San Francisco had not a single dollar to invest in railways across the continent. Its citizens owned the steamboats that ran between here and Sacramento, and this city was the great commercial entrepot on the Pacific slope. What more was wanted? A few men, however, about Sacramento, were not content. They felt that if the State ever amounted to anything, it must have railroads, and especially one which should forever link them to the land of their fathers and the flag of their

country. …The Secessionists, who swarmed in California from 1855 to 1861, did not want a railroad that should connect them by bands of iron to the States of the Mississippi Valley, the Northwest and the Federal Union.

In Sacramento there was a firm doing business in hardware, the members of which were shrewd New England merchants. They had reached middle life, and had realized, in a carefully conducted business, competent fortunes. Over the door of that firm, still doing business at 54 K street, in their old two-story frame building, is the sign, *Huntington & Hopkins,*—two genuine, old-fashioned Yankees, the first from Connecticut, and the latter from Massachusetts. They were Republicans, of course—started out as such at the organization of the party, and are so yet. An upper room over the store was headquarters for Republicans. It was here they discussed politics, and organized to fight the Democratic party in the State; and when they tired of that, they talked railroad. …

To build a road through the Sierra Nevadas was deemed to be simply impossible, and to assert to the contrary, lunacy. Such was the general conclusion. But Huntington and Hopkins were not satisfied with this summary disposition of the matter. They continued to talk about it. They were joined by Leland Stanford and two brothers, the Crockers, natives of Indiana, from South Bend. Stanford is a native of New York, also a merchant, and afterward the first Republican Governor of the State. One of the Crockers was a judge, and both very able men. These five earnest men, busy in politics in 1856, 1859 and 1861—Stanford being elected Governor after a furious contest in 1861—sat down to scheme the building of a railroad, which then had no parallel in the world, a project which was denounced as too absurd and crazy to be listened to for a moment. But they did not give it up. They kept an engineer—the late Mr. Judah—who died before he realized the fruits of his labors—for years exploring the Sierras for a passage for a railroad. … Ten thousand dollars would be required to make the survey and location. Could such a sum be raised? Huntington, Hopkins, Stanford and the Crockers raised the sum, and Judah went into the mountains, and it was finally demonstrated that his explorations and observations were correct, and a good and entirely practicable location could be secured. But San Francisco had nothing whatever to put in so wild a scheme, and the five men named, with two others whose names I have not at hand, organized, at Sacramento, a corporation to build the Central Pacific Railroad themselves.

Central Pacific Railroad

They elected Leland Stanford President, C. P. Huntington Vice President, and Mark Hopkins Treasurer. That was fourteen years ago, and all these men remain in office to-day. There never has been any change. The hardware business began to look as if it was going to be lost sight of, and that it might suffer; but such has not been the case. The old, dingy Sacramento house, in Sacramento, stands yet, and has a good stock of hardware; and another and more pretentious house, with the sign of "Huntington & Hopkins" over the doorway, may be seen in San Francisco, just a few steps off Market street, by any one curious to look at it, where a very large stock of hardware may be found.

Huntington was sent to Washington to secure a land grant and subsidy from Congress, and succeeded, so that, in 1862, this little Sacramento company found itself in full possession of an elephant of unusual proportions, and started out to raise money, in the midst of a great civil war, to build a railway through plains, hills and mountains, a distance of almost 900 miles—and not one of them knew anything about practical railroad building at all. …

Huntington went to reside in New York, and manage financial matters. He set out with the grim determination that he would not pay a dollar of commissions for anything. He sold his bonds for cash, and paid cash for what he purchased. Iron, spikes, fish-bars, bolts, locomotives—everything used, came by way of the Isthmus of Panama and Cape Horn. The bonds of the United States went down to forty cents (gold) on the dollar; freights more than doubled, and everything used in constructing the road rose vastly in value. Still, these indomitable merchants pressed the work. At one time they kept 500 men at work for a whole year, paying them out of their own private pockets. But they never went in debt. They kept men at work, but paid them all at the end of the month. So they never had a floating debt. They determined to have a first-class road, and they got it. There is no more durable and substantial road in America than the Central Pacific. In places they literally hewed out of the Sierra Nevada Mountains a track for their iron. At Cape Horn, a point near Colfax, about 200 miles from San Francisco, the track of the road in the side of the mountain is said to be about 1,300 feet above the bed of the American river. It is cut out of the mountain side, almost perpendicular at this point; and it is stated, that to enable the Chinamen to drill and blast out a foothold, they were suspended from the summit of the mountain with ropes around their bodies, and so held until they accomplished their work. I do not think an Irishman, brave and ready as he is in railroad work, could have been hired with money to perform so awful a task. Just think of it: these Chinamen dangling by ropes 1,300 feet up the sides of a mountain cliff, cutting away a place, out of the solid rock, for a railroad track! The very thought makes one dizzy. Yet it was done, and with almost superhuman energy the work was pressed over mountains, through yawning cañons, over arid wastes, water being hauled sometimes for forty miles, until it was accomplished. The last ten miles of the 833, between San Francisco and Ogden, were completed in a single day—a feat in railroad building never equaled before or since.

A Treaty with the Indians

Charles Crocker, Esq., tells an amusing story of diplomacy with the Indians. Somewhere in Nevada, a tribe got involved in difficulty with the Chinese, and fired into a house belonging to the company, and threatened general war on the employees. Crocker says that Durant and his people had employed United States troops all the time, even to guard the engineers of the Union Pacific Railroad Company, while the Central people took their chances and gave the Government no trouble. In the instance above alluded to, they consulted and came to the conclusion that while no *State* could enter into any treaty with a foreign nation, there was no law to prevent a *corporation* from doing so; and, thereupon, they empowered their embassador—an old chap with a woolen shirt on and who could talk Indian—to go out and make a treaty with the exasperated red-skins. He was armed with a large sheet of flat cap, decorated with bright red ribbons on each side, to be written on as he and the Indians might agree. The terms of the treaty were, that the Indians should not attack the company's houses any more, or molest any of its property, or shoot the Chinamen. The company, on its part, was to give *free rides* to the Indians, their squaws and papooses, whenever they desired. The treaty was formally ratified by the high contracting parties, and duly signed and witnessed in duplicate, and thereafter all was peace. Crocker says, the Indians would come in, light their pipes, gravely mount the construction train, look solemn, ride off thirty or forty miles, wait for the train to load up, then get on, ride back, and march off like lords, never saying a word; and they have not had any trouble in the execution of the treaty. Huntington objected on the score of a sound financial policy.

He said it was an Indian war, and the Federal troops ought to have been called out; and that then the railroad would have been the recipient of the income from the transportation of troops, munitions of war, and the hungry host of traders, sutlers and camp-followers that are so numerous when an Indian war breaks out.

Crocker tells another story, of how a Shoshone Indian brave came from a long distance to see the trains. He waited patiently, sitting flat on the ground near the track, until the train came in sight. He then rose erect, and firmly planted himself to meet the coming monster. The train consisted of two engines and thirty car-loads of iron. As it swept past, the Indian stood firm, with his eyes looking as if they would start from their sockets. When the (to him) hideous thing had passed, he started up and exclaimed: "Ugh! heap wagon, no hoss!"

A locomotive pushes two flatcars on the First Transcontinental Line, May 9, 1869.

What California Railroads Have Done

But, turning away from the plunderings and rascally rogueries of the "corral of wild cattle" that gathers biennially at Sacramento, what have Leland Stanford and his associates done for this State of California? Let us see: In 1862, the people here had no railroads. Plundering mail contractors and stage companies held the carrying trade and passenger business of California, and, as between the Pacific Coast and the Middle and Atlantic States, communications were had overland once in about two months, and by the Pacific Mail Steamship Company, *via* Panama, in about the same time. The cost of transit from New York to San Francisco was about $300, and the same by stage-coach overland. California was, agriculturally, and in all else except the mines, as poor as poverty. To-day, the cost by sea or overland from New York to San Francisco, excluding board, is

$140—time, overland, six days; and, as a result, almost all the trade between China, Japan and the islands of the Pacific Ocean, is now gathering at the docks of San Francisco, and will, in a great measure, pass overland to Chicago and New York, and at reduced rates of freight as well as time. I saw, myself, as I came over, train-loads of tea, from China and Japan, on the way to Chicago and New York. For these vast benefits, San Francisco, its merchants and people are indebted to the energetic railroad men of Sacramento. …

Lying along this line of railway which has not cost the State one dollar, there is on each side a body of land 9 miles wide, which would be equal to 9,000 square miles, or 5,760,000 acres. This land, before the road was built, was worth, on the average, $1.25 per acre, but no man will hesitate now to tell you that its average value is $8 per acre. The net increased value, therefore, contributed directly to the wealth of the State, by the railroad company, is $6.75 per acre, or a sum equal to $48,888,000. To this sum may be fairly added the products, either present or prospective, of one-half the 5,760,000 acres of land thus directly affected. Suppose they should be in wheat, what would be the increase of wealth to the State each year? The one-half of 5,760,000 would be 2,880,000. Assume that the yield would be 20 bushels to the acre, the increased production of the State, in wheat, would be 57,000,000 bushels per annum, which, at $1.25 per bushel, would amount, in gold, to $69,500,000, or a sum equal to the yield of all the gold and silver mines of the Pacific Coast. The increased value of the land has been realized already, if not exceeded, and the productive capabilities of the country opened up are fully equal to the figures given. I do not think an intelligent man in California will dispute them. Nor is this all. The railroad company has opened other lines, equal to 600 miles more, and have, in doing so, added tens of millions to the permanent wealth of the State, and infinitely to the comfort of the people. Nor does it stop here. It will continue to build roads until it shall have penetrated every accessible portion of the State, thus opening up highways for the products of the people to markets, in all directions.

The question comes up, what are the crimes of this corporation, about which there is so much noise? I answer, they are two: First, the men who have poured untold millions of dollars into the various lines of these roads want reasonable passenger and freight rates for persons and property transported, of which they claim to be the judges--or, in other words, while they are conferring benefits they want some profits. Second, that Stanford and his associates have grown rich. As to the first, the rates charged for passengers is about four cents per mile, on the average. For freights, the local charges are a shade higher than in Illinois, but not in disproportion to the general charges for other things in California. As to the second,

I don't think that any decent, reasonable man in the United States will say that Stanford and his associates have made any more than they should. No one charges them with being dishonest. They are only charged with exacting exorbitant freight and passenger rates from the patrons of the road. People in California pay Wells, Fargo & Co. and the Coast Line Stage Company never less than ten, and often twenty cents per mile, for passage in their stages, and I hear no complaints. They pay those rates cheerfully. But when the Central Pacific Railroad Company charges four or five cents a mile on their cars, there is a general outery among demagogues, politicians and rapacious members of the General Assembly. In my judgment, Gov. Stanford and his associates have added in fifteen years $300,000,000 to the permanent wealth of California, and have done already, and will do in the future, more for its permanent wealth and prosperity than all the pseudo-reformers who have been or ever will be in the State. These old fellows have been honest, hard workers. They are not stock-gamblers--never have been. They are genuine railroad builders, and each of them deserves a monument and a statue after he is dead. They ought to be rich, every one of them. They will go down to posterity as benefactors to the people of this State and the nation. So far as I am concerned, I say, "may they live long and prosper." I wish Illinois had hundreds of Leland Stanfords and such men as his associates. They are a different breed of men, entirely, from the Sharons, the Mitchells, the Floods, O'Briens and the remainder of stock operators in California. They "make two blades of grass grow where one grew before." They add to the wealth, comfort and happiness of the farmer, the laboring classes—indeed, they are of them. Success, say I, to the wonderful Central Pacific Railroad Company in its schemes of improvement in the State of California.

San Francisco, Cal., Nov. 1, 1875.

11. California Vineyards and Agriculture, 1865

By Samuel Bowles

Primary Source

Back on the route of our morning ride, we then turned off into the neighboring valley of Napa, celebrated for its agricultural beauty and productiveness, and also for its Calistoga and Warm Springs, charmingly located, the one in the plains and the other close among mountains, and constituting the fashionable summer resorts for San Franciscans. The water is sulphurous; the bathing delicious, softening the skin to the texture of a babe's; the country charming: but we found both establishments, though with capacious head-quarters and numerous family cottages, almost deserted of people.

Past farms and orchards, through parks of evergreen oak that looked as perfect as if the work of art, we stopped at the village of Napa, twin and rival to Petaluma, and from here, crossing another spur of the Coast range, we entered still another beautiful and fertile valley, that of Sonoma.

Here are some of the largest vineyards of northern California, and we visited that of the Buena Vista Vinicultural society, under the management of Colonel Haraszthy, a Hungarian. This estate embraces about five thousand acres of land, a princely-looking house, large wine manufactory and cellars, and about a million vines, foreign and native. The whole value of its property is half a million dollars, including one hundred thousand dollars' worth of wine and brandies ready and in preparation for market. We tasted the liquors, we shared the generous hospitality of the estate, and its superintendent; but we failed to obtain, here or elsewhere, any satisfactory information as to the boasted success of wine-making, yet, in California. The business is still very much in its infancy, indeed; and this one enterprise does not seem well-managed. Nor do we find the wines very inviting; they partake of the general character of the Rhine wines, and the Ohio Catawba; but are rougher, harsh and heady,—needing apparently both some improvement in culture and manufacture, and time for softening. I have drank, indeed, much better California wine in Springfield than out here.

The vine and wine interest is already a great one, and is rapidly growing. Nearly all parts of the State are favorable to it: the deserted and exhausted gold fields of the Sierra Nevada valleys and hillsides, as well as the valleys of the Coast range and the southern mountains. Down in Los Angelos County, this season, though the grapes are twice as abundant as last year, the price is treble, because of the increased preparations for their manufacture, and the profit that is sure to be realized from the business when well-conducted. The Buena Vista vineyards have been making part of their wine into champagne the last year, and gratifying results are confidently predicted.

But as doctors never take their own medicine, the true Californian is slow to drink his own wine. He prefers to import from France, and to export to the East; and probably both kinds are improved by the voyages. More French wines are drank in California, twice over, than by the same population in any part of the eastern States. Champagne is mother's milk, indeed, to all these people; they start the day with "a champagne cock-tail," and go to bed with a full bottle of it under their ribs. At all the bar-rooms, it is sold by the glass, the same as any other liquor, and it answers to the general name of "wine" with both drinker and landlord.

From Sonoma, over another hill, to our steamboat of three days ago, and by that back in a few hours to the city. These three days seem long, they have been so rich in novelty and knowledge, in beauty of landscape, in acquaintanceship with the best riches of California. These valleys are, indeed, agricultural jewels, and should be held as prouder possessions by the State than her gold mines. The small grains, fruits and vegetables are their common, chief productions; and the yields are enormous, while the culture and care are comparatively light.

In California, from December till April and May is seed-time; from June till September is harvest. No barns are needed for housing stock; they can roam safely in pasture for the whole year. Neither are they needed for the harvests; threshing and winnowing are done as well in the open field,—sometimes, indeed, by the very machine that reaps, and at the same time,—and the grain is put in bags, and thus transported to the market; all at leisure, for there is no rain nor dew to spoil the crop; it lies safely in any shape in the open field. There is no hot, hurrying work with planting and harvesting, as in the East; no dodging of showers; no lost days during the long summer. Fifty bushels of wheat to the acre is more common here than twenty-five in the best wheat fields of the States, and seventy-five and eighty bushels are often obtained. Barley, which is another leading crop, yields still greater return; an authentic instance of one hundred and twenty bushels to the acre is before me; and crops that would astound an Eastern farmer are often gathered from the droppings of a last year's harvest. A single farmer in the neighborhood of San Jose, with a twelve hundred acre farm, has this year gathered in over fifty thousand bushels of wheat; and the county of Santa Clara, in which this farm is located, lying south fifty miles from San Francisco, and in between two sections of the Coast range of mountains, presents the following aggregates of agriculture: acres fenced in, two hundred and ten thousand; cultivated, one hundred and thirty thousand; grape vines, eight hundred and seventy-nine thousand nine hundred; apple trees, one hundred and twenty thousand; crops this year,—thirty-five thousand tons of hay, one hundred and thirty-five thousand bushels of wheat, one hundred thousand of barley, sixty thousand each of oats and potatoes, and four thousand of corn.

Nothing is wanting to the agriculture of California but a steady and extensive market: she sends north to Washington and the British Provinces; east to Nevada and Idaho; south to Mexico; is even trying China on the west, and with steam navigation hopes for large market for wheat there;—but most of her soil is still unbroken,—her productive power is but suggested, not proven, undeveloped. And still she buys half her butter in the East! Visit ranches in the interior, that boast their cattle by the tens of thousands, and the chances are two to one that neither milk nor butter can be had for love or money!

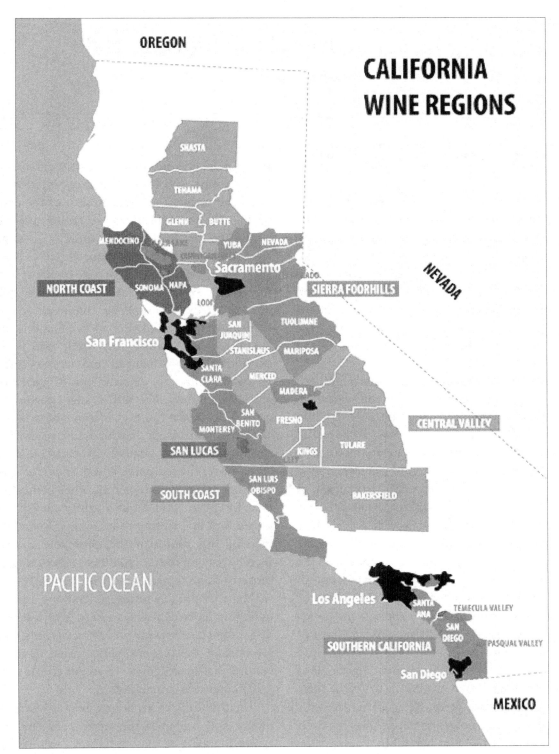

Map of wine regions in California.

Introductory Remarks on Orange Raising

That the culture of the citrus family of fruits is destined to become one of the leading industries of the great State of California is no longer disputed by the intelligent, reflective, progressive mind. That it is now, and will continue to be, one of the principal incentives to immigration into this State, is an acknowledged fact, which is amply proven by the testimony of all that have taken the trouble to inform themselves on the subject.

We may write and talk to our Eastern brethren about our great resources, and our ability to compete with any part of the world in the production of wheat, barley, corn, vegetables, fruits of all kinds, wool, wine and other productions; but, under the most favorable circumstances, only a partial attention can be secured, till the culture of the orange is mentioned, and the beauties of our orange groves portrayed and described in all their luxuriance and magnificence, and their profits set forth; then the ear and the attention of the investigator are fully gained. An individual or an audience never tires of listening to the history of our peerless groves of golden apples—the handsome, symmetrical, electrifying Golden Glory of the Pacific slope.

How grand, how beautiful is an orange orchard in full bearing! When planted artistically, their ever, enduring dark-green foliage, studded with beautiful gems of golden spheres, give renewed life and health to all that behold the orchards or partake of the fruit. Those who are so fortunate as to tread the soil in the shade of the majestic trees, and breathe their fragrant exhalations, look upward, and from their most interior selfhood they thank the Great Author of the grand, useful and beautiful in nature for so sublime a manifestation of His works, and His good gifts to mortals. There is inspiration, as well as beauty and princely profits, in an orange orchard. When tourists are examining our prolific fields of grain, our orchards of superior temperate-climate fruits, and our varied general productions, they are filled with wonder and admiration by our extraordinary possibilities, and our success in all the multifarious departments of agriculture and horticulture. But our orange groves only can call forth the full exclamations of wondrous excitement from our brothers and sisters from the frozen regions beyond the mountains, and these groves dilated upon, and their praises sung, are long remembered after all other scenes have been forgotten. Then let us magnify our great opportunities by planting more orange trees; let us increase this soul-inspiring, profitable industry, thereby leaving to our children a legacy that will cause us to be remembered with honor, and that will be a blessing to future generations. In order to do this, let us endeavor to start right, lest we be disappointed. I now purpose, as a warning voice, to consider the responsibilities usual in orange culture, that success may crown our efforts with a golden and substantial reward.

The founding of an orange orchard is not all poetry and romance; the stern, cold facts and responsibilities of the industry soon become apparent. The investment of money, time, labor, patience and perseverance required to plant an orange orchard and conduct it to a bearing and self-sustaining condition, is of more magnitude, notwithstanding all our advantages, than beginners generally imagine it to be. Many who are not apprised the start of what they have to contend with, get into debt and become discouraged, and the only apparent avenue of escape is a mortgage on their orchard. This is generally the first step to ruin, and it often results in the loss of the entire Investment. Few succeed in redeeming their property from an encumbrance of this kind. The orchard begins to fruit in a few years, but, alas! too late for the over-sanguine owner, and the end is usually reached in a summary manner through the courts assisted by the sheriff.

It is well to know at the threshold of the enterprise, that to plant, cultivate and bring an orange orchard to a remunerative condition requires money, determination and close application, and years of time and labor, to carry us safely through all the vicissitudes and disappointments continually encountered in orange raising. I do not make these statements for the purpose of discouraging the extension of our citrus interests but in all kindness, as a warning to the uninitiated, and, perhaps, to the over-zealous of our people. We are prone to be in too much of a hurry, and to go too fast for our ultimate good.

However strong may be my belief and faith in the grand profits destined to be realized from this industry my advice is be careful in your estimates, and do not go beyond your means: Be not too hasty to get rich in this branch of horticulture; be sure of your ability to carry to a successful termination the load you start with. It will be better to add a little from time to time, during your progress, than to break down by overloading, and never arrive at the promised land. Numbers among us have been wrecked on the hopeless beach of despair in their efforts to rush, without probation, to the realization of their golden dreams. Then, beware of quick sands, and

ford the river at a safe place. Let all, then, proceed patiently to peruse the following pages, and put in practice the information gained—information that has cost the author years of time—and if they then engage in this business they may reasonably hope for a golden reward.

I neither profess perfection nor aspire to it in the department of horticulture. As time rolls on, and orange culture shall have become more systematized, I sincerely believe that much knowledge superior to mine, and more practical than what may be found in these pages, will be garnered and assimilated; but I believe that this (perhaps the latest attainable at present) will be endured.

On this foundation let us work to build a grand superstructure. Those who profit from the hints in the preceding will surely be benefited, and will certainly succeed.

Exposure of a Vineyard

In this land of perpetual sunshine a level piece of land is preferable; and if a hillside, a northern exposure is preferable to a southern. A level piece of land will absorb nearly all the water that falls as rain, while a slope will shed it. Where irrigation is practiced, water will wash all the finer particles of soil—the valuable portions—away, whereas, the nearer a level, the more easily it will be flooded. Nearly all beginners in planting in this are almost sure to make a mistake, for they have learned that the finest vineyards of Europe and the East are grown on hillsides and southern exposures, but they do not remember that in this are almost sure to make a mistake, for they have learned that the finest vineyards of Europe and the East are grown on hillsides and southern exposures, but they do not remember that in this country the conditions of rain and sunshine are entirely changed. Here we have a lack of water, but an abundant supply of warmth. There a good season consists in a dry

View of Arlington Heights Citrus Groves in Riverside, CA, ca. 1903.

and warm summer; here in a wet season A hill-side is a necessity there, for it sheds the rains and sooner drains its water, which is taken up by the soil during the rain and every favorable condition to get all the warmth the sunshine can furnish has to be taken advantage of; whilst here, if grapes are not ripe in September they can hang on the vine until December.

What Kind of Soil is the Most Suitable

Life has as yet been too short to speak about this subject with certainty, and in a century from now opinions will still have to be modified. My experience is confined to my immediate neighborhood, and even in this limited space there have been trials only to a limited extent, for a soil that will suit one grape may be entirely unfit for another. There are, however, some general facts that are safe to accept. A finely divided sandy soil will absorb water readily and is easily worked. It will,

too, retain water in summer much better than adobe or clay, or a coarse, porous soil. Adobe and clay soils are good for the raising of such crops as grow in the winter, like grasses, wheat, barley and oats; sandy soils, on the other hand, are adapted for summer-growing products, like corn, melons, pumpkins, fruit trees, grape vines, and not suited to grasses. The first, in summer, with heat shrinks and cracks. It is in a favorable condition to evaporate its water easily, for a solid, hard earth will sooner lose its water than a soft, mellow surface, as can be seen by our roads, which always dry up sooner than the land on either side. The condition of its soil being close together, are favorable for drawing the water in warm weather out of its soil; where as a sandy soil, by its porosity, has less capillary power to draw the water to the surface and more capacity to take up air in daytime, which, by the cold at night is condensed into water, when more air is again taken up to go through the same changes. Man can do much to assist in retaining water in a soil by cultivation—stirring the soil. Even a very light soil will, by rains, dew, gravitation and other forces of nature, continually form a crust on top, harden, presenting favorable conditions for shedding rain and also for evaporation. By plowing, this is counteracted, and the oftener this is done the more moisture will be retained and added by giving free ingress to the air and cutting off evaporation; for a loose soil, if only a few inches on top, acts as a mulch. It cuts off communication with the lower strata of soil; it acts like a lamp that has its wick severed above the oil; it stops capillary connection with that below. Such a soil can be easily kept in such condition by cultivating, say once a month, with a minimum of labor; but an adobe or clay soil is very difficult to work; it breaks up in clods, giving more surface for wind and sun to act upon and dry; and, if broken up by beating the clods, makes an almost endless task, for the first rain to pack together again. Cultivation should be continued during the entire summer. The ground may be entirely without moisture on the surface; it may be dry to such a depth that weeds do not sprout any more, and every object apparently wanting for stirring the ground, yet you will find that your grape vines will show by their renewed vigor and growth after cultivation that it has not been labor lost. Of course this continued cultivation is only possible in vineyards the first and second years of their growth. When older, they early in the season cover the ground so that no horse can get through them, and by shading the ground, they prevent much of the evaporation and stop weed growth;

but, even with old vines, cultivation should be kept up as long as possible.

Cultivation should, too, be thorough and continued as long as any weeds make their appearance, for all growth is at the expense of water. Grass or weeds, while making an earlier growth, take up the water in your soil by their roots and evaporate it by their leaves more rapidly than your vines, for they run through to their maturity earlier, and many of them evaporate and use more water. At any rate, whatever you allow them to appropriate from your soil is lost to the grape.

The method of cultivation consists in plowing with a single horse, beginning in the center between two rows of cuttings with a back-furrow, and going backwards and forwards until all the land is plowed up to the cuttings. This requires a careful hand, or else many of the cutting will be destroyed. If your land is sandy and works easily, and free from clods, this will be all the plowing that will be necessary, and all after-stirring of the soil can be done with a cultivator, each time going the cross way from the time previous. This will level your ground, and by following it up once a month until July, and again, say in the middle of August, will keep cuttings growing vigorously, keep your ground free of weeds and looking like a garden. The kind of cultivation is of but little importance; the most simple, durable and cheapest will be the best, for your ground will be in easy condition for working. Stirring the soil in this way, breaking the crust which forms (a condition favorable for evaporation), destroying the weeds while they are small, and keeping the land level are the things you wish to accomplish.

To the Catholic missionaries, who, from the spacious harbor of San Diego to Mendocino Bay, prospected the grandest field for a successful agriculture to be found on the surface of our planet, belongs the credit of being the pioneer agriculturists of the Pacific Coast. It must also be confessed that they were the first labor monopolists; the whole race of aborigines were compelled to work without recompense, for the benefit of the Church, though the Fathers exacted no more than they cheerfully rendered in their own persons. All the improvements, the vineyards and orchards, the countless herds and flocks added nothing to the wealth of the ignorant natives who produced them. The missions were the centers of a stock-raising experiment on a vast scale without which the subsequent history of California would have been impossible; the trade in hides and tallow having brought in the settlers by whom the gold discovery was made.

The accumulation of wealth by the fathers was enormous. According to Rev. Walter Colton, chaplain of the U. S. chip *Congress*, the first Protestant clergyman that resided in California, in 1825, the Mission of San Francisco owned 76,000 head of cattle; 950 tame horses; 2,000 breeding mares; 84 stud of choice breed; 820 mules; 79,000 sheep; 2,000 hogs, and 456 yoke of working oxen.

The Santa Clara Mission had 74,280 cattle; 407 voice of working oxen; 82,540 sheep; 1,890 horses, broken to saddle; 4,235 breeding mares; 725 mules, and 1,000 hogs. This mission, in the year 1823, branded 22,400 calves, as the increase of that year.

The Mission of San José had 62,000 cattle; 840 broken horses; 1,500 mares; 420 mules; 310 yoke of working oxen, and 62,000 sheep.

The Mission of San Juan Bautista, as early as 1820, owned 43,870 cattle; 1,360 tame horses; 4,870 mares and colts, and 96,500 sheep.

The San Carlos Mission, in 1825, had 84,600 cattle; 1,800 horses and mares; 365 yoke of working oxen, and 7,500 sheep.

The Soledad Mission, in 1826, owned 36,000 head of cattle; a larger number of horses and mares than any other mission; 70,000 sheep, and 300 yoke of oxen.

The Mission of San Antonio, in 1822, had 52,800 head of cattle; 1,800 tame horses; 3,000 mares; 500 yoke of oxen; 600 mules; 48,000 sheep, and 1,000 hogs.

The San Miguel Mission, in 1821, had 91,000 cattle; 1,100 tame horses; 3,000 mares; 2,000 mules; 170 yoke of oxen, and 74,000 sheep.

The Mission of San Luis Obispo had 84,000 cattle; 2,000 tame horses; 3,500 mares; 3,700 mules; and 72,000 sheep. One of the fathers of this mission took one hundred thousand dollars with him when he left for Spain, in 1828.

All the other missions were equally rich in stock; while the specie in the coffers of the fathers, and the value of the gold and silver ornaments of the churches, exceeded half a million of dollars.

When John Gilroy, the first permanent homemaker settled in the Santa Clara valley, (1814), his nearest neighbors on the North were the Russians, at Bodega. Eight large ranches covered the land lying between San Jose and Los Angeles. There was not a flour mill or a wheeled vehicle on the coast. The people lived on wheat, cracked in mortars, maize, beef, fish and game. One thousand bushels of wheat, the first cargo I have seen mentioned, was shipped from Monterey to South America, prior to 1820. The product of 1874 reached twenty-eight millions seven hundred and eighty-four thousand five hundred and seventy-one bushels.

California, as we see, is not alone in this wonderful development of her resources. Oregon has some advantages over her for wheat and stock raising, and has improved them well. Both these young States are the reservoirs and sources of a river of breadstuffs which is flowing to the markets of the world in a stream of unequaled magnitude, commensurate with the scale of operations which have produced them. As we need to see the mammoth trees, not once, but many times, before the mind takes in the grandeur of their dimensions, so one must grow into a realization of the proportions of our agricultural industry and its requirements. From 1848 to 1862 California obtained her flour from Chili and the East. In 1856 and 1857 she imported one hundred and twenty thousand barrels from Oregon, and thirty thousand from the Atlantic States. These importations did not cease entirely, though they were diminished for two or three years, when the two years drought again raised them to seventy-two thousand nine hundred and thirty-six barrels from Eastern ports, forty-three thousand three hundred and forty-seven from Chili, and nineteen thousand five hundred and twenty-nine from Oregon. From that time the tide began to set in the other direction.

Some remarkable facts stand out prominently in connection with the Pacific slope States and Territories. First of all, it appears that the population increased, between 1850 and 1870, no less than three hundred and eighty-seven percent, or nearly quintupled. The increase during the latter ten years was not at as high a rate as during the former, but still it mounts to the very respectable figure of fifty-seven per cent. Between 1850 and 1860 the number of improved acres increased more than nine-fold; between 1860 and 1870 the increase was equal to almost one hundred and fifteen percent; and the number in 1870, as compared with 1850, was nearly twenty times as large. In the cash value of farms the increase shown is in a nearly similar ratio, the figures being almost thirteen times as large for 1870 as for 1860. The increase in the extent of wheat cultivation is yet more striking. There was over fourteen times as much wheat raised in 1860 as in 1850; nearly three times as much in 1870 as in 1860, and more than thirty-eight times as much in 1870 as in 1850. As to all kinds of cereals, there was over fifteen times as much produced in 1860 as in 1850, nearly two and one half times as much in 1870 as 1860, and nearly thirty-six times as much in 1870 as in 1850. The amount of cereals produced per head increased nearly seven-fold in the twenty years ending in 1870. The increase in the value of manufactured products during the same period was considerably more than five-fold. It is hardly necessary to say that no other group of States in the Union makes such an exhibit as this in reference to its agriculture.

In California we have the *largest wheat field in the world*. On one side of the San Joaquin river it extends for thirty miles, on the other about fifty, with an average width of eighty miles; six hundred and seventy-two square miles, or four hundred and thirty thousand and eighty acres. With the average yield, in good years, of sixteen bushels to the acre, this field will produce one hundred and six thousand four hundred and thirty-eight tons, and would require a train of cars nearly two hundred miles long to move it away. It is owned and worked by different parties, but is only broken by the river which flows through it.

The Livermore and San Joaquin valleys raised over twelve million bushels in the year 1872. Three wheat farms in the San Joaquin, with areas respectively of thirty-six thousand, twenty-three thousand, and seventeen thousand acres, averaged nearly forty bushels to the acre, some portions running up to sixty bushels.

The years 1870 and 1871 had been dry years, and nature had thus provided the wheat lands with a partial Sabbath. In 1872 an unusual breadth of land was seeded, but as the season advanced the estimates rose to ten, twelve, and finally to twenty millions of centals.

How could such a crop be disposed of? A prominent grain firm in San Francisco had already some sixteen warehouses in different part of the State, which would contain from five hundred to ten thousand tons each. Once in the warehouse, the farmer who is out of debt can afford to bide his time, and the advance in prices. If he is in debt, warehouse expenses only sink him deeper. One large commission house, that of Isaac Friedlander, was at this time buying three fourths of the grain exported, having agents scattered throughout the State, making estimates of the crop and the supply of tonnage required to move it, the rates at which it could be bought, etc., etc. All the wheat sent to England is purchased prior to arrival. Houses dealing in wheat here make known to the grain brokers in Liverpool all these facts, who, on behalf of the grain merchant there, contract with our merchants for the purchase and delivery of grain in that city; which, from the year 1869 to 1872, had taken twenty-four million centals. During this period, the Eastern States had taken of us about two million five hundred thousand centals. Australia, two thirds as much; China, about seven hundred thousand; Peru, two hundred thousand; the balance went to various points of the southern coast and islands. The flour export was also considerable; taken together, up to July, 1872, it had been thirty-seven million five hundred and fifty-nine thousand six hundred and twenty-seven centals, of a value of upwards of seventy-one million dollars. *How much of this went to the farmer?*

Few were prepared to answer this question. Many could say, that, practicing all reasonable economy, they could not make days' wages by raising wheat on their own lands, while the parties handling the wheat were becoming rich. Knowing these facts, they began to look into the reasons. The first thing they learned was, that the whole business of marketing had been taken out of their hands; that they were ignorant of a great many questions that affect legitimate trade; while to cope with speculative trade, they were utterly incompetent. The agents of production, commerce, and transportation, had got the upper hand, and were likely to hold it, unless they could free themselves by cooperation.

Finding that England was likely to be their principal market for many years, the wheat growers set themselves to learn something about ocean transportation. They found that in 1866, one hundred and twelve vessels carried off the crop; fifty-two were bound for Liverpool; twenty-four for Australia; twenty for eastern ports, and sixteen for China. The next year almost doubled the number; two hundred and twenty-three ships left the port of San Francisco laden with wheat. The crop of 1872 required three hundred and eighty-three vessels; the freight of which would go far to provide a mercantile marine for this coast. In July of that year, the rate of tonnage to Liverpool was £4 15s. per ton, or $1.14 per cental; the average for twelve years was about £2 11s. per ton, or a little more than sixty-one cents per cental.

The highest prices ever reached were in the years 1858, when it brought $6.75 per cental, and 1865, when it brought $5.30 per cental. The lowest price was in November, 1860, when distilling wheat was sold in San Francisco for $1.00 per cental. The farmers found that inland transportation was effected by rail, steamboat, and barge. The crop of 1872 was sufficient to load sixty-five thousand railroad cars; or about one thousand three hundred and forty average sized barges. The railroad freight rate from Merced, one of the great centers, was thirteen cents per cental; from Butte, by barge, $6.00 per ton; from Chico, $6.00; from Merced county, $4.20, and from Monterey, by steamer, $5.00. The handling, re-loading, etc., of this great crop would require the labor of several hundred persons.

Not only the cereal crops, but the other great staples of wine and wool were concerned in this question of transportation.

The wool interest has yielded the highest average profit. Indeed, California is the banner State in the quantity of the staple produced, the size of her flocks and the average weight of her fleeces. The climate is very favorable; and when wool-growing becomes essentially an agricultural business, from the necessary restrictions of the pasturage system, alfalfa promises to take the place occupied by grass and clover crops in the east, and to keep the proportionate advantages in our favor. But it is to the fruit and vine cultures that we may look for the most distinguishing features of our husbandry. As our wines grow in the world's esteem; as our raisins find their way into the world's markets; as our choice and luscious fruits, without loss of flavor, variously prepared for export, become indispensable luxuries, and bring remunerative prices, small farms will exceed in profit the large ranches of the present day; and California will more and more resemble the belt of fruit-growing States on the Atlantic Coast.

The following table shows the shipment of wine and wool to New York, *via* Panama, from January 1, 1874, to October 31, 1874:

Month	Wine		Wool, Raw	
	Gallons	Value	Pounds	Value
January				
February	113,088	$75,626	434,339	$78,248
March				
April				
May	172,629	109,702	286,679	70,407
June				
July				
August	150,813	92,212	338,985	69,598
September				
October	64,837	44,224	800,194	136,753
Totals:	501,367	$321,764	1,860,197	$355,066

San Francisco

The receipts and shipments by sea of flour and wheat for seventeen harvest-years, each closing June 30, were-as follows:

The receipts and shipments of the first six months of the harvest-year, closing December 31, 1873, were as follows: Flour, receipts, 202,068 barrels; shipments, 328,031; wheat, receipts, 9,614,186 bushels; shipments, 7,814,801 bushels; total wheat and flour reduced to wheat-bushels, receipts, 10,244,526 bushels; shipments, 9,485,016 bushels.

Years	Flour		Wheat		Total Wheat*	
	Receipts	Shipments	Receipts	Shipments	Receipts	Shipments
	Barrels	*Barrels*	*Bushels*	*Bushels*	*Bushels*	*Bushels*
1857	38,127	36,541	566,716	37,095	757,351	219,800
1858	35,456	5,387	405,086	6,335	582,366	33,270
1859	68,500	20,577	721,670	205	1,063,170	103,080
1860	91,400	58,926	1,641,710	636,880	2,138,710	931,510
1861	122,809	197,181	3,607,200	2,519,873	4,221,245	3,535,778
1862	111,269	101,652	2,419,110	1,419,740	2,975,455	1,928,000
1863	149,825	144,883	3,151,293	1,789,420	3,000,420	2,461,835
1864	99,298	152,633	3,073,366	1,785,486	3,509,556	1,548,651
1865	61,670	91,479	818,605	42,281	1,156,955	500,676
1867	300,397	465,337	8,697,560	6,060,306	10,199,145	8,386,891
1868	206,176	423,189	8,401,990	6,339,630	11,599,851	8,515,625
1869	207,980	453,920	10,558,971	7,230,878	11,603,871	9,560,473
1870	171,108	352,962	10,941,776	8,106,485	11,797,316	9,871,295
1871	120,913	196,219	7,697,096	5,953,073	8,571,055	6,984,108
1872	146,749	270,079	3,908,350	2,310,636	6,462,095	3,691,031
1873	328,990	263,645	18,580,830	16,371,146	19,725,780	17,488,371
* Including four reduced to wheat bushels.						

Connecting California

Conclusion

In 1769 California was an incredibly diverse region, economically and culturally, with an indigenous population of perhaps 300,000. At that point, when Father Serra arrived in San Diego, few people of European descent had even seen California. In the century that followed, the area would see changes so dramatic that few, if any, individuals could possibly comprehend what was happening.

By 1869, when the railroad reached from the east coast to the west coast of the United States, California was well on its way to becoming the modern state we know today. The state would see amazing population growth and dramatic changes in the coming decades, and these changes would follow patterns laid out in the mid to late 1800s.

To see how the California of the 1870s is connected to today, it would help to look at particular areas, such as higher education. In the 1870s, the University of California had only one campus. It had started in Oakland in 1869 and moved to Berkeley in 1873. In 1873, the university had about 200 students. Twelve men graduated that year. The following year, the graduating class would include women.

What we now call the California State University had its origins as a system of "normal schools" for training teachers. The City of San Francisco had set up the first one in 1857. The state legislature established the first state-funded teachers college in San Jose in 1862. Today that college is known as San Jose State University. The second state teachers college was established in Los Angeles in 1882.

Our state's political system is also connected to the 1870s. The Constitution adopted in 1850 would be replaced by a new Constitution at a convention in 1879. The 1879 Constitution is still with us today, though it has been amended about 500 times by the voters.

California's progress in agriculture also follows patterns laid out in the 1800s. The state has become one of the most productive agricultural regions in the world. While the economic base of the state has become much more diverse, with information technologies and manufacturing of many kinds, agriculture continues to be one of the leading industries.

Today California is considered a model of ethnic and cultural diversity, and it is worth remembering that this area was actually the most diverse part of

North America about two centuries ago, with over one hundred languages spoken. California is also considered an economic powerhouse today. Two hundred years ago California supported one of the highest population densities in North America, with a vibrant trading network.

The changes of the past two centuries have been immense, to be sure, and much of what we consider to be California society today has been brought over from somewhere else. The people and ideas that have arrived have always had to relate, in varying degrees, to what or who was already there. Many would argue our state has been best served when people with new ideas have been eager to work with the existing patterns. A dynamic of continuity as well as change has undoubtedly helped make California the exciting and creative place that it is.

Credits

Section I

Malcolm Margolin, "The Creation," *The Way We Lived: California Indian Stories, Songs & Reminiscences*, pp. 125–126. Copyright © 1993 by Heyday Books. Reprinted with permission.

California Maidu Map. Copyright in the Public Domain.

Malcolm Margolin, "Learning to Hunt," *The Way We Lived: California Indian Stories, Songs & Reminiscence*, pp. 17–18. Copyright © 1993 by Heyday Books. Reprinted with permission.

Malcolm Margolin, "A Man Without Family," *The Way We Lived: California Indian Stories, Songs & Reminiscence,* pp. 19. Copyright © 1993 by Heyday Books. Reprinted with permission.

Map 1. California Tribal Territories and Culture Areas. Based on maps in Robert F. Heizer, ed., California, vol. 8 of William C. Sturtevant, ed., *Handbook of North American Indians*, and Robert F. Heizer and Albert B. Elsasser, *The Natural World of the California Indians.* James Rawls, "Native American Cultures Map," *Indians of California— Changing Image*, pp. 7. Copyright © 1984 by University of Oklahoma Press. Reprinted with permission.

Randall Milliken, "Native American Societies in the San Francisco Bay Region," *Time of Little Choice*, pp. 21–24. Copyright © 1995 by Malki Museum Press. Reprinted with permission.

More than 250,000 pre-historic rock art petroglyph drawings can be found at the Coso Rock Art National Historic Landmark in the Mojave Desert, located on 36,000 acres at Naval Air Weapons Station China Lake, California. Copyright in the Public Domain.

Gerald Smith and Wilson Turner, "Native American Rock Art of Southern California," *Indian Rock Art of Southern California with Selected Petroglyph Catalog*, pp. 9–11, 13, 15. Copyright © by San Bernardino County Museum Association. Reprinted with permission.

"Painted Cave Art CA" © Jw4nvc (CC BY 3.0) at http://commons.wikimedia.org/wiki/File:PaintedCaveArtCA.jpg

Coso rock art of bighorn sheep near China Lake, California. Copyright in the Public Domain.

"Maze Stone" © David Scriven (CC BY-SA 2.5) at http://commons.wikimedia.org/wiki/File:MazeStone.jpg

William Hildebrandt and Michael Darcangelo, "The Culture of Wintu," *Life on the River: The Archaeology of an Ancient Native American Culture*, pp. 38, 40–41, 78–79. Copyright © 2008 by Heyday Books. Reprinted with permission.

Image of a Wintu woman pounding acorns, c. 1850, near Lassin's Rancheria, which neighbored Johnson's ranch, 50 miles from Sacramento City, west side of the Sacramento River going up the valley. Copyright in the Public Domain.

Anonymous early 17th century engraving of a Spanish galleon. Copyright in the Public Domain.

Decorative copper line engraving by Pieter van der Aa, charting Thomas Cavendish's circumnavigation of the world, published 1707, still showing California as an island. Cavendish was an English navigator who began the third circumnavigator of the globe in July 1585 after Ferdinand Magellan (1519–22) and fellow English navigator, Sir Francis Drake (1577–79). Copyright in the Public Domain.

Relation of the Voyage of Juan Rodríquez Cabrillo, 1542–1543 Copyright in the Public Domain.

Oil painting of Juan Rodríguez Cabrillo, artist and date unknown. Copyright in the Public Domain.

Locations visited by Cabrillo on his journey. Copyright in the Public Domain.

Sir Francis Drake Off the California Coast, 1579. Copyright in the Public Domain.

The Indians of California Greet Sir Francis Drake, engraving by Theodore de Bry, 1579. De Bry was an engraver, goldsmith and editor who created a large number of engraved illustrations for his books. Although most of his books were based on first-hand accounts by explorers, De Bry himself, acting as a redactor of the information, never visited the Americas. Copyright in the Public Domain.

Sebastián Vizcaíno, "Diary of an Expedition to the Port of Monterrey, 1602," *Lands of Promise & Despair: Chronicles of Early California, 1535–1846*, ed. Rose Marie Beebe and Robert M. Senkewicz, pp. 42–43. Copyright © 2001 by Heyday Books. Reprinted with permission.

Sebastián Vizcaíno, a 16th century Spanish explorer of the Americas, Pacific Ocean, and East Asia, portrayed in this facsimile of a 17th century engraving. Artist unknown. Copyright in the Public Domain.

Sebastián Vizcaíno, "A Letter From Vizcaíno to King Felipe III of Spain," *Lands of Promise & Despair: Chronicles of Early California, 1535–1846*, ed. Rose Marie Beebe and Robert M. Senkewicz, pp. 44–45. Copyright © 2001 by Heyday Books. Reprinted with permission.

Map L'Amerique, created by cartographer Nicolas de Fer in 1717. Copyright in the Public Domain.

"The Diary of Captain Luis Antonio Arguello—The Last Spanish Expedition in California, 1821," *The Diary of Captain Luis Antonion Arguello, October 17–November 17, 1821*, trans. Vivian C. Fisher, pp. 18–23. Copyright © 1992 by Bancroft Library. Reprinted with permission.

Section III

Kent G. Lightfoot, "MAP from 'Dimensions and Consequences of Colonial Encounters'," *Indians, Missionaries, and Merchants: The Legacy of Colonial Encounters on the California Frontiers*, pp. 4. Copyright © 2005 by University of California Press. Reprinted with permission.

Antonio de Ascensión, "First Plan for Missions in California—From a Report by Antonio de Ascensión," *Lands of Promise & Despair: Chronicles of Early California, 1535–1846*, ed. Rose Marie Beebe and Robert M. Senkewicz, pp. 48–53. Copyright © 2001 by Heyday Books. Reprinted with permission.

The first recorded baptisms in Alta California were performed in "The Canyon of the Little Christians" in what is now San Diego county, just south of Mission San Juan Capistrano. This is a 1922 sketch by Zephyrin Engelhard for the historical monograph, San Juan Capistrano Mission. Copyright in the Public Domain.

Plan for the Erection of Government, c. 1768. Copyright in the Public Domain.

Iris H. W. Engstrand, "Pedro Fages Writes a Letter to Jose de Galvez Reporting on Alta California, 1769," *Document Sets for California and West in U.S. History*, pp. 17. Copyright © 1993 by Houghton Mifflin Harcourt Publishing Company. Reprinted with permission.

Father Luis Jayme, "Reflections on Abuses of Soldiers on Indians, 1772," *Letter of Luis Jayme, OFM: San Diego, October 17, 1772*, ed. Maynard Geiger, pp. 31–35, 38–42. Copyright © 1970 by San Diego Public Library. Reprinted with permission.

Death of Father Jayme. Copyright in the Public Domain.

Antonio de Ascensión, "The Presidio at Monterey—From a Report by Pedro Fages, 1773," *Lands of Promise & Despair: Chronicles of Early California, 1535–1846*, ed. Rose Marie Beebe and Robert M. Senkewicz, pp. 162–168. Copyright © 2001 by Heyday Books. Reprinted with permission.

Antonio de Ascensión, "Rules for Towns and Missions by Felipe De Neve," *Lands of Promise & Despair: Chronicles of Early California, 1535–1846*, ed. Rose Marie Beebe and Robert M. Senkewicz, pp. 211–216. Copyright © 2001 by Heyday Books. Reprinted with permission.

Junipero Serra, "A Letter of Junipero Serra to the Reverend Father Preacher, Fray Fermin Francisco de Lasuen," *Life and Times of Fray Junipero Serra*, trans. Francis J. Weber. Copyright © 1987.

Portrait of Father Junipero Serra, circa 1750, artist unknown. Copyright in the Public Domain.

Jean Francois de La Perouse, "From: The Journals of La Perouse—Life in a California Mission, 1786," *Life in a California Mission: Monterey in 1786*, pp. 76–88. Copyright © 1989 by Heyday Books. Reprinted with permission.

A drawing of Mission San Carlos Borromeo de Carmelo (near Monterey) as prepared by Captain George Vancouver depicts the grounds as they appeared in November, 1792. From A Voyage of Discovery to the North Pacific Ocean and Round the World, U.S. National Oceanic and Atmospheric Administration collection. Copyright in the Public Domain.

Iris H. W. Engstrand, "The Los Angeles Census of 1781 Shows a Diverse Ethnic Mix," *Document Sets for California and West in U.S. History*, pp. 22–23. Copyright © 1993 by Houghton Mifflin Harcourt Publishing Company. Reprinted with permission.

Giorgio S. A. Perissinotto, "Everyday Life in Early Spanish California—Lists of Requisitions ," *Documenting Everyday Life in Early Spanish California: The Santa Barbara Presidio Memorias Y Facturas, 1779–1810*, trans. Catherine Rudolph and Elaine Miller, pp. 319, 353, 363. Copyright © 1998 by Santa Barbara Trust for Historic Preservation. Reprinted with permission.

Antonio de Ascensión, "Indian Life at San Luis Rey—from the Reminiscences of Pablo Tac," *Lands of Promise & Despair: Chronicles of Early California, 1535–1846*, ed. Rose Marie Beebe and Robert M. Senkewicz, pp. 330–333, 335–336. Copyright © 2001 by Heyday Books. Reprinted with permission.

Pablo Tac penned this drawing from his recollections of life at Mission San Luis Rey in the 1820s and 1830s. The drawing depicts two young men wearing skirts of twine and feathers with feather decorations on their heads, rattles in their hands, and painted decorations on their bodies. Copyright in the Public Domain.

Mission San Luis Rey, circa 1890. Copyright in the Public Domain.

Eulalia Pérez, "An Old Woman and her Recollections, 1877," *Testimonios—Early California through the Eyes of Women, 1815–1848*, ed. Rose Marie Beebe and Robert M. Senkewics, pp. 97, 99–106. Copyright © 2006 by Heyday Books. Reprinted with permission.

Antonio de Ascensión, "A Report on Alta California, 1827," *Lands of Promise & Despair: Chronicles of Early California, 1535–1846*, ed. Rose Marie Beebe and Robert M. Senkewicz, pp. 350–354. Copyright © 2001 by Heyday Books. Reprinted with permission.

Section IV

Juan Machada, "Juana Machada Wrightington Discusses the Changeover from Spanish to Mexican Rule, 1822," *Document Sets for California and West in U.S. History*, pp. 30–31. Copyright © 1993 by Houghton Mifflin Harcourt Publishing Company. Reprinted with permission.

Mexico's Flag from 1821–1823. Copyright in the Public Domain.

Angustias de la Guerra, "Occurrences in California as told to Thomas Savage in Santa Barbara, 1878," Testimonios – *Early California through the Eyes of Women, 1815–1848*, ed. Rose Marie Beebe and Robert M. Senkewicz, pp. 285–290. Copyright © 2006 by Heyday Books. Reprinted with permission.

Antonio M. Osio, "A Memoir of Mexican California, 1851," *The History of Alta California: A Memoir of Mexican California*, trans. Rose Marie Beebe and Robert M. Senkewicz, pp. 118–126. Copyright © 1996 by University of Wisconsin Press. Reprinted with permission.

Painting by Ferdinand Deppe depicting Mission San Gabriel, 1832. Deppe (1794–1861) was a German naturalist, explorer and painter from Berlin who travelled to Mexico in 1824. Copyright in the Public Domain.

Siegfried G. Demke, "'On the Trail' and 'The Drive Roust'," *The Cattle Drives of Early California*, pp. 16–22. Copyright © 1985 by Prosperity Press.

Mexican Rancheros by Carol Nebel, 1834. Nebel was a German engineer, architect and draftsman who was best known for his detailed paintings of the landscape and people of Mexico, especially of the battles of the Mexican–American War. Copyright in the Public Domain.

Painting of a Vaquero in action roping cattle during 1830s Spanish California, artist unknown. Copyright in the Public Domain.

Donald Hannaford and Revel Edwards, "Introduction," *Spanish Colonial or Adobe Architecture of California, 1800–1850*. Copyright © 1990 by Rowman & Littlefield Publishers, Inc. Reprinted with permission.

Las Flores Estancia (station), also known as "San Pedro Chapel" as it appeared around 1850. Copyright in the Public Domain.

"Hacienda Spanish Arch" at http://www.sandiegohistory.org/journal/74winter/index.htm. Copyright © by E. Alan Comstock.

Margaret Mackey and Louise P. Sooy, "A Young Lady of the House," *Early California Costumes, 1769–1847: And Historic Flags of California*, pp. 71–76. Copyright © 1932 by Stanford University Press. Reprinted with permission.

Untitled portrait of a Mexican woman, c. 1856. Copyright in the Public Domain.

Lucile Katheryn Czarnowski, "Fandangos, Bailes and Fiestas—Dances of Early California," *Dances of Early California Days*, pp. 22–23, 155. Copyright © 1950 by Pacific Books.

Trajes Mexicanos, un Fandango, Mexican dresses. Artist C. Castro, 1869. Copyright in the Public Domain.

Section VI

Robert Glass Cleland, "Early Cattle Brands of Los Angeles County," *The Cattle on a Thousand Hills: Southern California, 1850–1880*, pp. 51–54, 73. Copyright © 1951 by Huntington Library Publications. Reprinted with permission.

Recollections of the First Through Stage to California, 1858. Copyright in the Public Domain.

Concord Stagecoach 1869. Copyright in the Public Domain.

Roscoe P. Conkling and Margaret B. Conkling, "The Butterfield Overland mail 1857–1869," *The Butterfield Overland Mail 1857–1869, Volume I*, pp. 100, 130–136, 138–143, 145. Copyright © 1947 by University of Oklahoma Press. Reprinted with permission.

Wells, Fargo, & Co. Display Ad. Copyright in the Public Domain.

Travel Suggestions for Stagecoach Passengers. Copyright in the Public Domain.

Samuel Brannan. Copyright in the Public Domain.

Henry J. Labatt, "Jewish Business Interests in California," *True Pacific Messenger*, San Francisco, May 24, 1861. Copyright in the Public Domain.

Levi Strauss was a German-born Jew who founded the first company to manufacture blue jeans. His firm, Levi Strauss & Co. depicted in this label, began in 1853 in San Francisco, California. Copyright in the Public Domain.

Section VII

David Wilmot Appeals for Free Soil. Copyright in the Public Domain.

David Wilmot. Copyright in the Public Domain.

Compromise of 1850. Copyright in the Public Domain.

"United States 1850–1853–03" © Golbez (CC BY-SA 3.0) at http://en.wikipedia.org/wiki/File:United_States_1850-1853-03.png

Speech Before Senate on the Admission of California into the Union, 1860. Copyright in the Public Domain.

John D. Defrees to Abraham. Copyright in the Public Domain.

California's Newspapers Debate the War. Copyright in the Public Domain.

California Regiment Recruiting. Copyright in the Public Domain.

Joseph P. Hoge, Thomas N. Cazneau, Franklin Lawton, James H. Hardy, Joseph Naphtaly & Henry F. Willams, "Shall Negroes and Chinamen Vote in California?" *San Francisco Daily Examiner*, August 1869, pp. 2–4. Copyright in the Public Domain.

Impressions Concerning the Chinese Railroad Workers, 1865. Copyright in the Public Domain.

Photograph of Chinese workers building the railroad where it passes through the Sierra Nevada Mountains, ca. 1860s.. Copyright in the Public Domain.

The Great Theme—The Pacific Railroad. Copyright in the Public Domain.

Golden Spike Ceremony. Copyright in the Public Domain.

Recollections on the Completion of the Pacific Railroad. Copyright in the Public Domain.

Transcontinental Poster. Copyright in the Public Domain.

Letters from California. Copyright in the Public Domain.